Interpersonal Reconstructive Therapy
for Anger, Anxiety, and Depression

Interpersonal Reconstructive Therapy
for Anger, Anxiety, and Depression

It's About Broken Hearts, Not Broken Brains

LORNA SMITH BENJAMIN

AMERICAN PSYCHOLOGICAL ASSOCIATION
Washington, DC

Copyright © 2018 by the American Psychological Association. All rights reserved. Except as permitted under the United States Copyright Act of 1976, no part of this publication may be reproduced or distributed in any form or by any means, including, but not limited to, the process of scanning and digitization, or stored in a database or retrieval system, without the prior written permission of the publisher.

The opinions and statements published are the responsibility of the authors, and such opinions and statements do not necessarily represent the policies of the American Psychological Association.

Published by
American Psychological Association
750 First Street, NE
Washington, DC 20002
www.apa.org

APA Order Department
P.O. Box 92984
Washington, DC 20090-2984
Phone: (800) 374-2721; Direct: (202) 336-5510
Fax: (202) 336-5502; TDD/TTY: (202) 336-6123
Online: http://www.apa.org/pubs/books
E-mail: order@apa.org

In the U.K., Europe, Africa, and the Middle East, copies may be ordered from
Eurospan Group
c/o Turpin Distribution
Pegasus Drive
Stratton Business Park
Biggleswade Bedfordshire
SG18 8TQ United Kingdom
Phone: +44 (0) 1767 604972
Fax: +44 (0) 1767 601640
Online: https://www.eurospanbookstore.com/apa
E-mail: eurospan@turpin-distribution.com

Typeset in Goudy by Circle Graphics, Inc., Columbia, MD

Printer: Sheridan Books, Chelsea, MI
Cover Designer: Mercury Publishing Services, Inc., Rockville, MD

Library of Congress Cataloging-in-Publication Data

Names: Benjamin, Lorna Smith, author. | American Psychological Association, issuing body.
Title: Interpersonal reconstructive therapy for anger, anxiety, and depression: it's about broken hearts, not broken brains / Lorna Smith Benjamin.
Description: Washington, DC : American Psychological Association, [2018] | Includes bibliographical references and index.
Identifiers: LCCN 2017045507 | ISBN 9781433828904 | ISBN 1433828901
Subjects: | MESH: Mental Disorders–therapy | Psychotherapy—methods | Object Attachment
Classification: LCC RC480 | NLM WM 420 | DDC 616.89/14—dc23 LC record available at https://lccn.loc.gov/2017045507

British Library Cataloguing-in-Publication Data
A CIP record is available from the British Library.

Printed in the United States of America
First Edition

http://dx.doi.org/10.1037/0000090-000

10 9 8 7 6 5 4 3 2 1

This book is dedicated to Thomas Woolf, visionary administrator
and remarkable man with multiple talents, deep wisdom,
and great generosity of spirit.

CONTENTS

Preface ix

Chapter 1.   Introduction and Overview 3

I. Foundational Concepts 13

Chapter 2.   Natural Biology: Mechanisms of Psychopathology and Change 15

Chapter 3.   Structural Analysis of Social Behavior: The Rosetta Stone for Interpersonal Reconstructive Therapy Case Formulation and Treatment Models 53

II. The Case Formulation and Treatment Models 83

Chapter 4.   The Interpersonal Reconstructive Therapy Case Formulation Model 85

Chapter 5.   The Interpersonal Reconstructive Therapy Treatment Model 103

Chapter 6.   Phases of the Action Stage of Change 133

III. Applications to Affects Precipitated by Threat 151

Chapter 7.   Anger 153

Chapter 8.   Anxiety 175

Chapter 9.   Depression 203

IV. Empirical Support 243

Chapter 10.   Validity of the Interpersonal Reconstructive
                Therapy Models and Effectiveness of Treatment 245

Glossary 273

References 279

Index 301

About the Author 315

PREFACE

This book represents the fourth step in a series of efforts to contribute to a science of psychotherapy that combines the clinical wisdom in psychoanalysis with the objectivity of behaviorism as defined in its early years (Skinner, 1987). The first step was to develop a reliable method of describing what patients talk mostly about: relationships with themselves and others. In other words, assess the perceived, subjective world in behavioral terms. That is Structural Analysis of Social Behavior (SASB; e.g., Benjamin, 1974; Benjamin et al., 2006). The second step was to explore the clinical implications of SASB assessments by using them to describe personality disorders in ways that enhance understanding of the developmental roots of each disorder and that facilitate identification of differences among them (Benjamin, 1996a [2nd ed., 2003a]). The third step was to provide a psychotherapy treatment model that would offer a set of principles and models that can, on a case-by-case basis, guide the clinician's choice of interventions from any therapy approach to address a variety of common challenges. That book is the treatment manual for Interpersonal Reconstructive Therapy (IRT; Benjamin, 2003b [paperback ed., 2006]). The fourth step, described in this book, is to describe a version of natural biology that was foundational to the SASB and

IRT models and also can help ground the clinician at various stages of therapy. It is most useful when faced with difficult clinical choices.

Use of principles of natural biology suggests that threat affects such as anger, anxiety, and depression become symptoms if they are miscued by maladaptive lessons from attachment figures regarding what to fear and how to be safe. In Chapter 2, evidence and theory for this perspective is developed and this interpretation of anger, anxiety, and depression is applied in Chapters 3 to 9. A report on tests of effectiveness of the approach appears in Chapter 10.

There are several relatively unique features in IRT that result from appeal to the rules of evolution. For example, according to natural biology, negative affective symptoms (e.g., anger, anxiety, depression) are not decontextualized "bad" internal energies that must be suppressed, expressed, controlled, or redirected. Viewed as attempts to adapt, they are understood to be embedded in a sequence: perceived threat (C1), elicited affect (A), and predisposed behavior (B). An individual's C1AB sequences reflect modeling by early caregivers of what to fear and how to be safe. Such copying of behavioral information quintessentially relevant to survival is generally comparable to RNA copying DNA to pass along information about how to build bodily structures that have worked for the previous generations. The relatively new science of epigenetics explains how such copied information can be stored in ways that are heritable. It adds to descriptions of expression and silencing, yet another way of understanding how information about the environment can be recorded by genes in order to support life in this and following generations.

Treatment in IRT centers on the idea that loyalties to and love for attachment figures who modeled maladaptive rules for affect management sustain maladaptive patterns and therefore need to be altered. That is monumentally difficult for adaptive reasons including the fact that the primitive brain "wisely" resists change in rules for threat and safety. The complex process of change in IRT is discussed at length in Chapters 5 and 6 and illustrated in Chapters 7, 8, and 9. Effectiveness is tested by relating activation of mechanisms of change to outcome.

Learning to practice IRT is comparable to learning to play a musical instrument at the professional level. For music, the process of building competence includes lessons in theory, frequent modeling by experts, and in vivo review of trainee performance with feedback by experts. All that requires practice, practice, practice. For therapists, the principles in this book provide a road map, a guide for practice. Hopefully, therapist readers will use the principles to guide the training of their primitive brains to come up with creative but well-informed choices of interventions that resonate well with and are maximally helpful to individual patients with unique symptom "profiles."

Hearty thanks are due the many people who have been so helpful as I struggled with many rewrites of this book. At the top is Tom Woolf, director of clinical services at the University of Utah Neuropsychiatric Institute and to whom this book is dedicated; and Ross VanVranken, this hospital's executive director. Those two men made the IRT clinic possible, and much good work was accomplished there with the vital help of Ken Critchfield, my close colleague. Others who in different ways have offered very important support include Pio Scilligo, Harry Harlow, Carl Rogers, Ted Millon, Kathleen Levenick, Susan Grant, Dona Wong, Tim Smith, Tim Anderson, Elizabeth Skowron, Aaron Pincus, Tia Korogolis, Luigi Cancrini, Francesco Colacicco, Paola Ciapanna, Susanna Bianchini, Carla Denitto, and Dimetra Doumpioti. Special gratitude is due the patients who have shared their thoughts and feelings and stories and given me permission to write about them. And I thank my younger daughter, Linda B. Kidd, DVM, PhD, DACVIM, who was essential in the development of natural biology but is not responsible for any errors. My clever graduate students named at the end of Chapter 3 also deserve hearty thanks for their work and all the fun we had. Susan Reynolds has offered wise, consistent encouragement and suggestions. Last, but certainly not least, I am grateful to my dearest friend Sally Barlow, who deserves an award for sharing so lovingly in all the ups and downs of this process of trying to say so much briefly and in everyday terms.

Interpersonal Reconstructive Therapy for Anger, Anxiety, and Depression

1

INTRODUCTION AND OVERVIEW

The stories for two long-term patients, Amy and Jason, appear here to introduce and illustrate Interpersonal Reconstructive Therapy (IRT) in action.

AMY

While responding to her service satisfaction survey after many years of treatment in IRT, 45-year-old Amy answered the question, "What was the most beneficial part of your IRT therapy?" by writing, "I learned to stand up for myself. Putting myself first is not a selfish act. It has really helped me be a stronger person and love myself." In response to the question, "Was there any part of your IRT therapy that seemed not to help?" she reported, "It has always helped me." And finally, in response to "Other comments?" Amy

---

http://dx.doi.org/10.1037/0000090-001
Interpersonal Reconstructive Therapy for Anger, Anxiety, and Depression: It's About Broken Hearts, Not Broken Brains, by L. S. Benjamin
Copyright © 2018 by the American Psychological Association. All rights reserved.

wrote, "I really appreciate everything that all the people in the IRT clinic have done for me. For the first time in my life, I want to live and experience my life."

Amy's subjective responses mean as much to IRT practitioners as the standard measures of outcome, such as reduced symptoms, numbers of rehospitalizations and suicide attempts, that are discussed in Chapter 10. The science that supports IRT theory and practice is emphasized in Chapters 2, 3 and 10, but Amy's service satisfaction survey illustrates the fact that linking the subjective perspective of patients to the objective data also is central to IRT theory and practice.[1]

Amy's first of two treatments with IRT was supportive, lasted 2 years, and ended when her trainee therapist left for an internship. Amy was referred to a community psychiatrist for continued support and did well. By the time she returned to it several years later, IRT had grown from being a treatment model used for a psychology practicum to become the sole treatment model used at a university-affiliated clinic, the IRT Clinic at the University of Utah Neuropsychiatric Institute, alternately directed by Ken Critchfield and myself. This second treatment began with 9 months of electroconvulsive therapy (ECT) with supportive IRT plus a variety of medications to contain the critical voices that sponsored suicide and her crippling anxiety and depression. Following ECT, large doses of major medication continued for approximately 3 more years. She was not rehospitalized, and the medical interventions, plus supportive IRT, likely prevented suicide. During that time, Amy was very subdued and "absent" in how she looked and acted and, with rare exceptions, was socially isolated in her bedroom in the family home.

Amy had an extraordinarily traumatic history in childhood that continued into early adulthood. Nonetheless, before this breakdown, she had been functional at work and uncommonly generous with her earnings and time to partners, family, and friends. For years, she had carried a large debt for an ex-lover, she would clean a friend's house for no compensation, and she

---

[1]These remarks about context and subjectivity are inspired by recent experience in my private practice with two patients who were severely demoralized by psychological testing results required in child custody disputes. In each case, it appeared that the assessors, both of good repute, were relying too completely on statistical norms ("people who score [this result] tend to . . .") for their attributions. The reports were contradicted by clinical reality. For example, one person, who was extremely generous and helpful to people in trouble, was said to be "unaware of his impact on others." The fact that he ran a very successful large business and clearly was a good problem solver did not preclude calling him "disorganized" and suggesting he could work on this problem with practice organizing his personal effects. Another case report by a different clinician seemed disdainful, even mocking. That centered on the patient's optimism and determination in relation to severe long-term stresses that, along with a Minnesota Multiphasic Personality Inventory profile that was completely within normal limits, was taken as evidence of faking good. One has to wonder what training programs could do to cultivate more empathy, wisdom, and appropriate humility with less certainty about the prevailing versions of psychosocial science.

would buy whatever her children demanded even though that sometimes was difficult. Her work on active reengagement with life (e.g., dropping suicidal plans, allowing interests to arise, sharing her creative activities with the IRT team, making contact with less exploitative friends) began in earnest after Amy was assigned, in succession, two very skilled and highly adherent IRT trainee therapists, each of whom worked with her for 2 more years. During that time, Amy became progressively less symptomatic. Eventually, she chose to become medication free and had maintained well for several months prior to terminating IRT. About a year before termination time, following extensive and fearful deliberation, Amy married a very kind, considerate, respectful, and competent man. With him, she began to enjoy her life with ever more certainty.

Amy is a rare example of someone who has gone from a well-documented condition of severe illness all the way to "within normal limits." One can read about such recoveries in autobiographies such as *I Never Promised You a Rose Garden* (Green, 1964), a story about a multiyear inpatient treatment that permitted daily inpatient sessions of psychoanalytic therapy with Frieda Fromm-Reichmann. It is unusual to have had a person who hears a voice respond, as did Amy, to an outpatient therapy with once-a-week therapy sessions with trainees (meeting more often during emergencies, as prescribed by the IRT manual; Benjamin, 2003b [paperback ed., 2006]) while participating in an ongoing clinical research study. Amy was in the category "more severely disordered" in our research database (discussed in Chapter 10), but nonetheless, we believe that she should not need to enter a lengthy treatment again. She might well need a brief course of "reminder" sessions plus medications if she encounters specific stresses that reactivate old wounds and maladaptive responses. But most of the time, she is expected to remain within normal limits. Four years have lapsed since she left treatment, and so far as we know, she is well.

IRT AND AMY

IRT is an integrative, interpersonal, and intrapsychic psychotherapy that is organized by the IRT case formulation model that assesses each of a patient's presenting symptoms (one or more disorders) in relation to interactions between inherited proclivities (e.g., startle responses) and early lessons from caregivers about what to be afraid of (threat) and how to be safe (safety). Very briefly, the argument is that affective psychiatric symptoms represent miscued and maladaptive attempts to adapt to perceived stress. The miscuing part is programmed by maladaptive lessons about threat and safety from early caregivers. The method is copying automatically (be like him or her [identification], act as you did with him or her [recapitulation], and/or treat yourself as you were treated [introjection]). Such copying of messages about safety and threat is sustained by love for and loyalty to the copied loved ones. In IRT, the focus is on these environmental contributions to what develops within the "envelope of potential" determined by the genome.

For example, Amy's childhood was dominated by her very demanding and abusive cousin, the son taken into the family following the death of her mother's beloved older sister. The cousin would attack Amy both verbally and physically at any sign she might be his equal or better. If she locked her door for protection, he would break it down and punch her, and her mother would blame her for provoking him. Amy had learned she was safest if she hid her abilities and devoted herself to doing whatever he wanted whenever he wanted it.

Amy learned that extreme violence against her was "normal," and so she recapitulated her relationship with her cousin as she paired with abusers as an adult while being quite competent in serving them. Nobody protected her as a child, and so as an adult, she introjected abandonment and neglected her own interests as she continued to serve others. She also introjected her cousin's views of her and denigrated herself. The same happened in relation to her abusive adult partners.

As she repeated these self-sabotaging behaviors, Amy was following the rules and values of her cousin and her mother regarding what to fear (doing well) and how to be safe (criticize self and serve others, no matter what the cost to self). Such self-sacrificing copied behaviors provided testimony and demonstrated psychic loyalty to and love for the sponsoring attachment figures—Amy's mother and cousin. Implementing the self-sabotaging behaviors brought a subjective sense of calm and safety, even when the behaviors were maladaptive. Such automatically copied behaviors related to safety and threat are called Gifts of Love (GOLs; Benjamin, 1994, 2015b). Because they support copied behaviors, GOLs that subjectively "reward" maladaptive copy processes are the ultimate treatment target. But changing GOLs is frustratingly difficult. It is possible, though, and this book is about how to do it, even for people with a record of treatment resistance.

IRT AND JASON

Although the research on IRT reviewed in Chapter 10 was on a difficult dysfunctional population with a long record of treatment resistance, IRT also is appropriate for highly functioning "standard" outpatients who may or may not have been treatment resistant. For example, Jason, age 50, functioned, albeit irregularly, at high levels as an adult. He was very good at his work but found it hard to engage in it. He was an attractive and popular bachelor, but having been rejected once by a person whom he dearly loved, he was not inclined toward a long-term relationship. By his account, Jason had had dozens of psychotherapies since childhood and had engaged in savage acts of self-attack just short of suicidal. He also was vulnerable to angry outbursts, but he was most distressed by the mysterious impairment in his ability to complete important work products.

Here is Jason's story: He had been traumatized by his father's frequent, violent, degrading attacks, some of which came in the evening as he tried to do his homework and some in the middle of the night when his father came home drunk. His mother's hatred was explicit, and all family members joined her in excluding him. In the beginning of his IRT treatment, Jason's fear of intrusion and attack at bedtime was managed by preparations for immediate escape (as he would have done if he could, when his father burst into his bedroom at night and beat him), but he felt he had to remain alert, and so he did not sleep well. His inability to complete projects at work even though he clearly had the requisite technical skills was related to his father's rages that sometimes included punching him as he tried to do his homework.

As an adult, Jason also had bursts of anger, usually when people who were supposed to be smart were not doing smart things. He responded with verbal attacks to try to get them to change (just as his father did with him while he did his homework). His outbursts of anger temporarily made him feel in control, which was more comfortable than being the victim. In addition, by behaving like his father, he felt closer to him. His social alienation had mirrored his position in the family, leaving him feeling safest when alone, but lonely and anxious. Jason, like Amy and most IRT patients in an adherent therapy, agreed with their case formulations.

Jason and I managed to get him "unstuck" as he had fewer fights and began to have more work products. Two years into therapy, he had a significant victory in relation to an exploitative sibling. Shortly after that, he became angry with me and chose to travel the rest of the road to recovery on his own. Occasionally he "checked in" by email and in the main, the correspondence was collaborative. His notes revealed that he was making huge efforts to change himself in ways he wanted to.

Several years after termination, without any further treatment sessions with anyone, he wrote,

> Years ago, when I was in therapy, I asked you, "what would it be like if treatment were successful." And you said, "I think, that I might be writing you letters from time to time telling you how much fun I was having."

He enclosed a photo taken by a friend and said that it "shows, I think, that I can be happy." It did. Then he wrote,

> A lot is better than it was. I am no longer sleeping in the middle of the living room floor, wearing my street clothes and with the room lights on as I was not so very long ago. I have found ways of controlling my mood better than in the past. . . . I am still learning. And I have hopes of continued progress.

His note, like Amy's, marks the quintessence of reconstruction: lasting and marked reduction in symptoms and a much friendlier, more secure, functional stance in relation to self and others. He continues to this day occasionally to write, usually about his increasing, well-acknowledged productivity in work.

Jason demonstrated more clearly than usual that major behavioral change can, perhaps must, happen outside of the therapy office. After patients become ready and able to challenge and relinquish their GOLs to internalized representations of symptom-relevant attachment figures, called "*Family in the Head*," there can be, as Amy reported, progressively greater engagement in "living and experiencing" life. As the patient breaks free of old hopes and loyalties and moves forward on his/her own, the therapist increasingly functions as a Secure Base (defined in Chapter 2) and eventually fades into the background. Success in this follow-up activity depends mostly on acquiring the tools to address the GOLs and then pure grit and willingness by the patient to keep working at developing new patterns despite the terror and despair that come when trying to change internalized rules for safety and threat.

OUTLINE OF THIS BOOK

There are four sections to this book on how to offer IRT. Part I is about foundational concepts and includes presentations of Natural Biology in Chapter 2 and Structural Analysis of Social Behavior (SASB) in Chapter 3.

Natural Biology grounds IRT case formulation and treatment models in principles of evolution, suggesting that affective symptoms of mental disorder are embedded in social interactions and are evidence of attempts to adapt rather than of breakdown. It provides a description of normal developmental sequences and naturally evolved mechanisms that, under "average expectable conditions," appropriately link the affects of anger, anxiety, and depression to adaptive versions of what to be afraid of and how to be safe.

When developmental conditions do not provide adaptive information about threat and safety, the sympathetic and parasympathetic nervous systems are miscued, and affective symptoms (e.g., diagnosed problems with anger, anxiety, and depression) are the result. Medications can mitigate this damage, and psychotherapy can repair it if there is transformative work with the natural affect regulators, the internalized representations of attachment figures or "Family in the Head." The goal is to replace maladaptive rules about threat and safety with adaptive versions that support what Bowlby (1969, pp. 342–347) called Secure Base. The process requires that the patient engage in inner exploration, experiencing and changing as well as repairing old and building new benign relationships in reality.

In Chapter 3, a reliable and accurate method of pattern recognition is presented in the discussion of Structural Analysis of Social Behavior (SASB): (Benjamin, 1974, 1979a, 1996b). The SASB model and technology provide rigorous measurements of internalized representations of attachment figures (Family in the Head) as well as a method for recording objective observer ratings and analysis of content of the therapy narrative, all in the same metric. SASB-based self- and observer ratings can be applied in nearly any context that provides information about interactions that is specific enough to permit location of an event on the three dimensions that define the SASB model (Benjamin, 1987, 1979a; Benjamin, Rothweiler, & Critchfield, 2006). Those dimensions are attentional focus, attachment (hate to love), and interdependence (control/submit to emancipate/separate). IRT research on reliability, specificity, and sensitivity of the IRT case formulation model and on the effectiveness of the IRT treatment model relies often on SASB-based measurements. Although SASB typically is viewed as a research tool, adherent use of it also can elevate clinicians' skills in pattern recognition to high levels of speed and accuracy.

Part II is about the IRT case formulation and treatment models and begins with Chapter 4, on IRT case formulation. It provides detail and illustrates the mechanisms that connect a patient's presenting symptoms to perceived current stresses (persistent threat and failure to find safety) and also links those stresses and responses to earlier patterns shaped by lessons in safety and threat. The main mechanism for learning to recognize threat and find safety is copy processes in relation to attachment figures (be like him or her, act as you did with him or her, treat yourself as you were treated). Such copy processes are supported, whether they are adaptive or not, by fantasy Gifts of Love (GOLs). The GOL concept is elusive at first glance but refers to the subjective state that accompanies copying the caregiver under conditions of perceived threat. The mechanism is the primitive brain signaling "safety" (parasympathetic activity) while copying an attachment figure: Do what he/she did or what he/she said, and all will be well. For example, Jason reported that he felt clearest and most certain and centered when he was following the implicit rules and values he acquired from his father and his mother, who once tried to murder him. Failing to unleash his talent at work was his main strategy to avoid the wrath and somehow please his internalized parents and, as such, was a Gift of Love, a testimony of his loyalty to and love for his father.

Chapter 4 includes descriptions of evidence about the reliability, specificity, and sensitivity of the IRT case formulations (Critchfield, Benjamin, & Levenick, 2015) in a sample of highly comorbid hospitalized patients. IRT case formulations are designed to manage comorbidity because the challenge was to help the population referred for assessment and treatment of suspected personality disorder. They turned out to be treatment resistant and highly comorbid. One does not often see borderline personality disorder (BPD), for example, without disturbance in perceptions of threat (e.g., abandonment sensitivity), intense affect (e.g., desperate anger for control of attachment figure), and problematic behavior (e.g., BPD's vexing transitive focus on the therapist). To further compound the diagnostic challenge, consider that the name *borderline* originally referred to a permeable boundary between normal cognitive process and psychosis (Benjamin, 1996a [2nd ed., 2003a]).

In Chapter 5, there is a review of the IRT treatment model that was described in detail in Benjamin (2003b [paperback ed., 2006]). The five steps of the model are (a) collaborate; (b) learn about patterns, where they are from, and what they are for; (c) block problem patterns; (d) engage the will to change; and (e) learn new patterns. IRT is integrative in that any and all known therapist techniques or approaches may be used if they are used in ways that are consistent with the case formulation and treatment models. Treatment interventions that address GOLs and Family in the Head are likely to be psychodynamic. But any and all approaches can be used according to the clinician's best judgment about what will most likely address the challenge a given patient faces at a given stage of therapy on a given day. For example, there is quite a bit of "social homework" in IRT that helps with differentiation from destructive aspects of Family in the Head while simultaneously nurturing healthy current attachments and self-concepts. For more internal work, change in affect regulators can be facilitated by using behavioral "techniques" such as dialectical behavior therapy (DBT) self-help exercises (http://www.dbtselfhelp.com) and/or mindfulness meditation (https://www.mindfulnesscds.com).

The fourth step, engaging the will, is subdivided according to the stages of change model proposed by Prochaska, DiClemente, and Norcross (1992) for treatment of addictions. This is reasonable because loyalty to symptom-relevant Family in the Head is very much like an addiction. But not much is known about exactly how one masters the action part of Prochaska et al.'s series of stages. During IRT, the transition from talking about changing problem behavior to action, to actually changing, is where "the rubber hits the road." This is because the old method for finding relief (e.g., using substances, fantasizing about GOLs) is very hard to relinquish, and many skid marks are to be had when trying to give up those ways.

The problem with taking action is that overtly to defy internal rules for handling threat and safety necessarily increases anxiety because nature provides that old rules for safety never should be broken. And then, if the patient can tolerate the anxiety and actually behave differently (e.g., Jason completes a big task and tells people about it, Amy shows a project she completed in her IT class to the IRT team), the next challenge is deep depression and grief over all the losses that have flowed from life in the pathological state as well as loss of the fantasy that key loved ones (father for Jason, mother for Amy) ever will relent and become loving. With hard work and much patience, that all is followed by acceptance and realistic reconciliation of some sort, and the task of rebirthing and taking charge of one's own life on one's own terms can proceed on to reconstruction.

Part III is about applications of the IRT case formulation and treatment models to anger, anxiety, and depression in Chapters 7, 8, and 9, respectively.

Part IV, Chapter 10, provides data on the validity and effectiveness of the IRT case formulation and treatment models. This effort to apply stricter standards of precision and testability to a description of psychopathology and psychotherapy that nonetheless centers on subjective experience has been "in development" for almost 50 years. Progress is modest, but there is some, and that is promising.

I
FOUNDATIONAL CONCEPTS

2
NATURAL BIOLOGY: MECHANISMS OF PSYCHOPATHOLOGY AND CHANGE

> Of the various social influences that mammals experience, caregivers are by far the most powerful source of stress and the most effective defense against harmful stressors.
> —Gunnar & Quevedo, 2007, p. 164

The Natural Biology described in this chapter represents an effort to help bring clinical psychological science closer to using more of the knowledge base and methods of classical sciences such as physics, chemistry, and mainstream biology. That should yield a more accurate understanding of mechanisms that sponsor affective symptoms (e.g., anger, anxiety, depression) and related problem behaviors. The effort to define mechanisms begins with hypotheses (models, theory) that link purported cause to symptoms. If confirmed by evidence, such theory can help psychotherapists choose more effective interventions, even for patients who have long records of treatment resistance. Confirmation involves showing that activation of mechanisms of change during treatment relates directly to symptom change. The effectiveness of this perspective has been tested in the IRT clinic,[1] and results are reviewed briefly in Chapter 10.

From assessment to treatment, the IRT clinician considers current affective symptoms as they appear in specific interactions in specific contexts and relates them to adaptation. This approach is consistent with theoretical approaches in the basic sciences such as physics, chemistry, and astronomy, which are based on descriptions of interactions. In this book evolutionary theory is the basis of a view of affective symptoms in terms of their adaptive function rather than as evidence of broken brain mechanisms triggered by stress. The approach draws heavily on the Darwinian argument that the structure of living organisms is directly related to its adaptive functions during interactions. A special edition about the theory of evolution, titled "Darwin turns 200," includes several informative articles about this monumental work (Science News, January 31, 2009, pp. 1–36). For behavioral scientists, one of the most helpful analyses of the connection between structure and adaptive function is Tinbergen's (1951) *The Study of Instinct*.

This chapter is about the science, that is, the evidence that supports the uses of evolutionary theory in the IRT case formulation and treatment models. Briefly, the IRT case formulation method contextualizes affective symptoms as maladaptive attempts to adapt to threat that have been shaped by misguided interactions with attachment figures. The IRT treatment model uses that information to focus the clinician's attention on mechanisms that help realign attachment gone awry in ways that facilitate the patient's adaptation to reality.

UPDATING VIEWS OF THEORY

"Theory" related to psychopathology and psychotherapy has acquired a bad name, as if theory today is what philosophers offered when William James (1911/1947) wrote, "Too many philosophers have aimed at closed systems, established a priori, claiming infallibility, and to be accepted or rejected only as total" (p. 697). James contrasted that kind of theory (hypothesizing) with science, "On the other hand, using hypotheses only . . . seeking to verify them by experiment and observation, opens a way for infinite self-correction and increase" (p. 697).

Introductory psychology texts continue to repeat that description of science, but it is difficult to find psychotherapy treatment models that conform

---

[1]The IRT clinic existed for 10 years at the University of Utah Neuropsychiatric Institute, thanks to the vision and generosity of Thomas Woolf, Director of Clinical Services, and Ross VanVranken, Executive Director of the hospital.

closely to the standards—that is, psychotherapy treatment models that are explicit about assumptions and describe hypotheses or theory that (a) logically connect to the assumptions and (b) make specific predictions that can be confirmed or contradicted by data. Statistical tests that confirm pre–post symptom reduction or differences among treatment groups are important but do not qualify as tests of mechanisms of change. The present discussion of the science base for IRT does not mean that IRT is or ever could be 100% science based. Rather, as in medicine, the idea is that the practitioner draws on valid underlying science related to the structure and function of the body and mind, artfully attends to context, and combining it all, carefully makes choices of helpful interventions. The patient's subjective view of self and others is of primary concern because how the person sees the world determines how he/she interacts with it.

WHY BOTHER?

Some readers may be reluctant to engage with the present task of examining various types of evidence related to construct validity of the theory on which IRT case formulation and treatment models are based. They can skip this chapter and still use the IRT models to good effect. However, familiarity with the science base of IRT principles can support better treatment choices, especially in the many instances in which IRT models do not support common practices and in fact suggest unfamiliar alternatives.

An especially clear example of departure from conventional wisdom is the rejection of the popular cathartic treatment of anger ("get it out" and release the pressure, also known as the *hydraulic model*). Unrestrained expression of anger can be helpful, but it is possible to interpret that effect with alternative hypotheses based on the proposed functional analysis[2] in IRT. There, the hydraulic model is replaced by a functional analysis of anger that recommends addressing the patient's perceived adaptive reasons for rage in specific situations and addressing those directly.

In IRT, it is very important for therapists to let patients know why they make a difficult intervention because such disclosure helps enhance collaboration that is vital to success in therapy. As a part of collaboration, early in treatment, the therapist describes the case formulation to patients and includes relevant Natural Biological principles illustrated with their own words. This not only checks the accuracy of the therapist's view, but also

---

[2]For example, a child who goes into the "rage room" does feel better afterward. Perhaps it is because anger is forbidden at home and now credible adults do not condemn him for it. Or maybe he rages just like his father rages, and the identification is reassuring as a GOL, defined later in this book.

helps normalize patients' views of self. These features can strengthen willingness to engage in the very difficult and upsetting work of making personal changes that are radical enough to count as "reconstruction." An example of how to explain the case formulation to patients follows and will be called up later in this chapter when discussing Natural Biology.

EXPLAINING NATURAL BIOLOGY TO A PATIENT

Joseph was a 35-year-old man referred for an IRT consultation because of a long history of debilitating depression that had not responded to usually effective treatments. There was no evidence he had been sexually abused or suffered other obvious forms of trauma or familial economic stresses. Joseph said he was homosexual but had never acted on his wishes, and he had not suffered bullying or shaming. He recently had lost his job as an accountant and moved in with female friends, whose place was somewhat noisy. It was his fourth hospitalization. His diagnosis was major depression, severe, recurrent. He also qualified for the label avoidant personality disorder. He had had many treatments for depression, including Prozac, Wellbutrin, and Effexor and several series of electroconvulsive therapy treatments, including biweekly administrations recently. He had had psychotherapy, and the record noted, "applies DBT [dialectical behavior therapy] skills, but the effect is not lasting."

Joseph did well in high school but not so well in college because "it was less clear what I was supposed to do." He explained his suicidal reasoning simply, "The world would be better off without me." His father was a successful lawyer, a quiet, very devout man and a self-described people pleaser. His father embraced perfectionism and required that others follow his directions exactly. Joseph's mother resisted her husband's control and was defiant, sometimes going out to party with friends against his wishes. Joseph, by contrast, worked especially hard to avoid displeasing and disappointing his father and others. Joseph tried to provide what people wanted and needed "before they knew they wanted it." Joseph and his several siblings did not have specifically assigned duties at home as children but were expected to figure out what needed doing and do it without being asked. And if the dishes were not done "spontaneously," his father and mother would argue with each other until they chose the child who was to do them. Eventually his parents divorced, and Joseph worried he might have prevented those arguments and saved the family if he had been more perfect in making sure they were not displeased.

The substance of Joseph's case formulation was explained to him at the end of his in-hospital IRT consultation interview. Outpatients in IRT also get such an explanation. The procedure is emotionally intense and, if not performed in hospital under safe conditions, may need to go slowly over the first few outpatient sessions. Again, the explanation is given in a collaborative manner using concrete terms rather than abstractions and making specific reference to the patient's own words. In effect, the patient provides his/her own evidence base, and the discussion of the case formulation organizes it for his/her consideration.

Here is the case formulation delivered at the end of Joseph's consultation:

This Natural Biological explanation for your symptoms assumes the theory of evolution is correct, and if that is offensive to you, this perspective may not be useful for you. [Joseph gave permission to proceed.] Everything makes sense, including your depression. The story begins with the fact that we have two brains: the familiar, logical brain, based in the cortex, and the primitive, not necessarily logical or conscious, subcortical brain that monitors, among other things, whether there is a threat, something to be afraid of, and if so, how to be safe. Negative feelings like depression, anger, and anxiety originate there to help us respond to threat with behaviors that make us safe. Anger, for example, can support behaviors that control a threat or get rid of it; anxiety can mobilize us to work hard to respond to the threat. And depression is natural when nothing else works: One feels overwhelmed, defeated, and gives up, often condemning and disallowing one's own perspective.

I think we know already that your challenge is to please other people, to make sure they have what they want and need, or else bad things will happen, just as Mom and Dad would fight if somebody did not make sure the house was in order. In fact, the family ultimately fell apart because of their fights, and that hurt deeply. Now, outside of the family, you keep the internal rule that your job is to figure out what people want and make sure they get it. You have had this rule a long time. You did well in grade school and high school when expectations were clear, but in college, expectations were not so detailed, and you did less well. Work posed the same problem, and not doing well in work probably does not please your father. So now here you are, unable to please anybody, including yourself. That failure to please leads you to condemn yourself and conclude, "The world would be better off without me."

According to this Natural Biological perspective, your depression makes sense because you have been doing what you are supposed to do ("please others before they know what they want"), and that is completely impossible. So naturally you are defeated, helpless, without recourse. [Joseph agrees with this.] Sometimes it helps to understand how this all came to be. We learn from our caregivers about how to recognize threat and be safe. That learning is by copying, not by using logic or even by considering what works. Young primates cannot engage in such complex processes. Instead, we just copy rules for safety and threat, just as we learn language early in life. We feel safe if we perceive, feel, and do what the attachment figures feel, do, and say to do in situations involving safety and threat. For example, if the mother monkey is afraid to drink from the pond when crocodile eyes are showing, the baby monkey copies her: notes the crocodile, feels afraid, and runs away. The general idea is, identify threat, feel afraid, do what the parent does, feel safe.

There are three ways to copy attachment figures: We imitate (or *identify* with) them, as you copy Father as a quiet, devout, people pleaser. And we relate to others as we did with them (or *recapitulate*), as you do when you take with you the old rule of anticipate and satisfy others' needs from family to college and the workplace. And finally, we treat ourselves as we were treated (or *introject*). You show that process as you tell yourself you are a disappointment, reflecting your father's words. This primitive brain learning lasts forever, as it should, because threats in the jungle are always threats. Defying rules for safety is terrifying. Following them is satisfying, comfortable. So, as you give yourself this impossible assignment of pleasing people before they even know what they want, you show your loyalty to and love for your parents, who basically expected that. It is called a "Gift of Love" because we have representations of loved ones in our brain, and they are called "Family in the Head," and "they" are pleased when we do what they say.

What you need to do now is discover and nurture your Birthright Self, the self that would have evolved in a normal developmental sequence. That begins with attachment—which you did have. But you missed the next step: to explore the world and discover who you are separate from your attachment figures. That was not encouraged, and so you had little opportunity for peer play, in which one learns give and take and develops social skills needed to become a member of the adult community.

So let's start now, asking you to be curious about yourself. Here is an assignment: Please think about play; about doing some things that are simple, relaxing, and fun to do. No fair picking something that demands perfection! Go ahead and try to identify what you like and do not like. Pay attention to how that feels. Remind yourself it is OK to have a self and take care of yourself. Start small, and later, work on discovering what you might like in a larger picture for your life. This must include developing a better balance between concern about your own needs and those of others. And it will require working out a new understanding with your "Family in the Head." This is not easy, but updating to adult reality is good for everyone.

Joseph liked the interview and according to staff was making a list of "play" activities, and his mood lifted in the days that followed. After discharge, he was going to ask his outpatient therapist to help him continue this work of developing his self, of differentiating. Unfortunately, this is difficult and can take a long time for severely disordered patients, as Amy (Chapter 1) demonstrated. Change begins in earnest when patients grasp the implications of their case formulation and decide to reclaim their Birthright Self. They face the daunting task of challenging ancient ways of being safe and daring to cultivate more adaptive patterns. Most patients wonder, "But *how* do I change?" The generic answer is,

> Identify your patterns (list them), and understand where they came from (sketch early roots) and what they are for (touch on adaptive principles). Then decide if you want to engage in the difficult process of change. It won't be easy, but this a way to release and nurture your Birthright Self.

For the clinician, the answers to how to facilitate change are summarized in the figures, tables, and lists that follow in this book. They are not rigid algorithms. When making interventions, a skilled clinician selects judiciously for optimal relevance at the time. Almost always that means thinking about the sustaining force at the moment—that is, the Gifts of Love, the acts of self-sabotage that bring feelings of safety as they demonstrate loyalty and obedience to specific members of Family in the Head. But finding words and ways to address that (or not) is an art or craft as well as a science of psychotherapy (Benjamin, 2015a). An IRT therapist can be compared to the professional musician who expresses the music from the heart, even as he/she understands the underlying physics regarding pitch (overtones), harmony, rhythm, structure, and more.

PATHOLOGY AND NORMALCY IN THE NERVOUS SYSTEM

Nature has provided powerful mechanisms to assist survival, and IRT clinicians work directly with them to address affective symptoms. The present sharp focus on safety and threat was based on the following thought experiment: What is the primary requirement a life form must address? As any life force comes into existence, its main challenge is to survive, to continue to exist. At a bare-bones minimum, that requires acquiring and processing energy to support the living organism. What else is vital to staying alive? Obviously, it is to stay alive, and to do that one must first of all recognize threats to life and find safety. In sum, here are the essentials for survival: (a) acquire and process energy for life processes, (b) recognize what threatens existence, and (c) find safety from such threats. This is a maximally parsimonious yet inclusive list of essential requirements for survival.[3]

---

[3] Other suggested needs can be interpreted in terms of how they help cope with safety, threat, and/or energy. For example, we need social contact, and that counts as a safety mechanism for all primates because we depend on group behavior for survival. Sexuality also enhances social bonding and has a unique role in supporting survival of the species. We find pain to be very aversive; it requires turning attention to the threat (source of pain) and finding safety.

Sympathetic (Threat) and Parasympathetic (Safety) Nervous Systems

A common version of the autonomic nervous system (ANS) addressed all three of those essential requirements. Figure 2.1 sketches the present version, which includes the sympathetic (SNS) and parasympathetic nervous systems (PNS). The enteric nervous system, central to finding and processing food and water for basic maintenance, is not shown here and presently is listed as a separate part of the nervous system. An authoritative review of the ANS by P. Low (updated 2017) is available at https://www.merckmanuals.com/professional/neurologic-disorders/autonomic-nervous-system/overview-of-the-autonomic-nervous-system. The left-hand side of the figure represents the Sympathetic nervous system (SNS) and it can define and respond to threat. The right-hand side represents the Parasympathetic nervous system (PNS), which is important to defining and achieving safety. Traditionally, these two systems are described as the "fight or flight" and the "resting and relaxing" systems, respectively.[4] Among other things, they can, if not activated normally, sponsor symptoms of affective disorder such as anger, anxiety, and depression (left) and positive affectivity (right) such as mania, eating disorders, and substance abuses. Maladaptive versions of the biologically useful affects anger, anxiety, and depression are the focus of this book.

Notice in Figure 2.1 that the sympathetic (threat) and parasympathetic (safety) functions often work in opposition. If one activates, the other inhibits; one accelerates, the other slows; one relaxes, the other constricts. But they do not have equal "power." The threat system is faster because it has more direct connections to the spinal cord and therefore has more rapid access to the central nervous system, the overall manager. Moreover, there are threat system functions that are not countered by the safety system. For example, the sympathetic system connects directly to the liver and the adrenal glands, but the parasympathetic does not. In consequence, the safety system is not a good activator. Nor should it be! The threat system is faster and dominates function because threat poses the most immediate danger to life and demands mobilization, whereas feelings of safety vitiate feeling threatened and allow relaxation and play, which is very important to the bonding that is so critical to survival, but less urgent.

Nerves activate or inhibit the function of the organs to which they are connected. For example, the heart and the lungs have connections to each of these systems (SNS, PNS). When stressed by threat, the sympathetic nervous system increases the heart rate and respirations to help provide more energy to address the threat. When safety is perceived, the safety system

---

[4]The history of Figure 2.1 began in the 1500s. According to Ackerknecht (1974), Langley proposed the current version in the early 1900s, and he suggested the name *autonomic nervous system* to represent the enteric, sympathetic, and parasympathetic nervous systems.

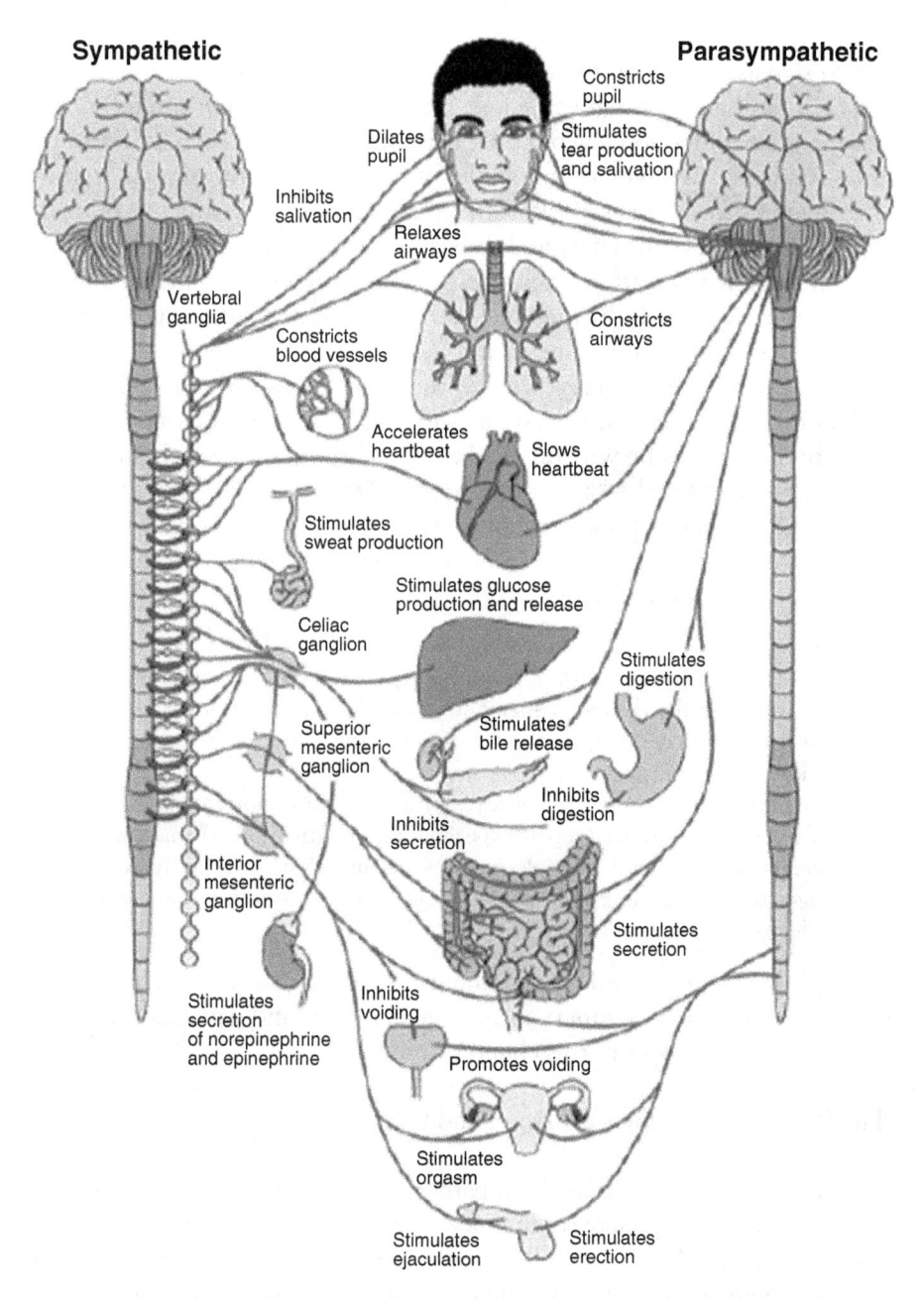

Figure 2.1. The sympathetic and parasympathetic nervous system, parts of the autonomic nervous system. The two parts of this familiar figure represent the threat (sympathetic) and safety (parasympathetic) systems. They are an important part of the primitive brain that regulates the threat affects that become symptoms if they do not correctly identify and address threat and safety in an adaptive way. The figure provides detail that explains how humans manage the fundamental task of recognizing threat and finding safety, the first order of business for a living organism. From the *Merck Manual Professional Version* (known as the *Merck Manual* in the United States and Canada and the *MSD Manual* in the rest of the world), edited by Robert Porter. Copyright 2017 by Merck Sharp & Dohme Corp., a subsidiary of Merck & Co., Inc., Kenilworth, NJ. Available at http://www.merckmanuals.com/professional. Accessed July 18, 2017. Reprinted with permission.

(PNS) signals slow down the respirations and heart rate to conserve energy and facilitate safety system behaviors. This is an oversimplification because nervous system function, even if only between two organs such as heart and lungs, typically involves very complex circuits with inhibiting as well as exciting messages. Porges (1995) offered a more complete analysis of heart and lungs in relation to safety and threat. Among other things, his work has made it possible to create credible sophisticated physiological measurements to assess whether an individual feels safe or is threatened, as in Skowron, Cipriano-Essel, Benjamin, Pincus, and Van Ryzin (2013).

It is important to acknowledge that this analysis of the ANS that includes equating the "threat system" with the SNS and the "safety system" with the PNS relies heavily on the "classical" tradition that characterized them respectively as the "fight or flight" and "rest and relax" systems. They and the ANS have additional functions. The complexity is illustrated by considering the role of the ANS in expression of emotions. Kreibig (2010) summarized this role as follows:

> Autonomic nervous system (ANS) activity is viewed as a major component of the emotion response in many recent theories of emotion. Positions on the degree of specificity of ANS activation in emotion, however, greatly diverge, ranging from undifferentiated arousal, over acknowledgment of strong response idiosyncrasies, to highly specific predictions of autonomic response patterns for certain emotions. A review of 134 publications that report experimental investigations of emotional effects on peripheral physiological responding in healthy individuals *suggests considerable ANS response specificity in emotion when considering subtypes of distinct emotions* [emphasis added]. (p. 394)

The italicized text in Kreibig's statement is consistent with the focus in IRT on the specific adaptive functions of anger, anxiety, and depression that are described in detail later in this chapter.

The Primitive (Subcortical) Brain and C1AB Links

The parasympathetic and sympathetic systems are important, but they are not the only components of the subcortical, primitive brain. They connect directly or indirectly to other subcortical structures such as the hypothalamic–pituitary–adrenal (HPA) axis,[5] the cerebellum, and more. The threat and safety systems also connect to the cortical "higher brain," the locus for full

---

[5]The hypothalamus is the

> region of the brain lying below the thalamus and making up the floor of the third cerebral ventricle. The hypothalamus is an integral part of the brain. It is a small cone-shaped structure that projects downward from the brain, ending in the pituitary

awareness, logic, and choice. Awareness in the primitive brain often is "subconscious" and is called the *primitive brain perception* in IRT. Porges (1995) suggested that primitive brain apprehension be called *neuroception*.

Whatever the name, IRT theory holds that primitive brain awareness (C1[6]) of conditions related to threat and safety releases affects (A) related to threat and safety. The affects then predispose[7] adaptive behaviors (B). In IRT, this sequence is symbolized as C1AB. In other words, if there is a primitive perception of threat (C1), a threat-related affect (A) such as anger, anxiety, or depression is released, and that predisposes an adaptive behavior (B) such as such as fighting, fleeing, hiding, feigning death, and more.

These primitive brain C1AB links,[8] whether about threat or safety, are vital to survival. Their meaning to the clinician is that affects such as anger, anxiety, or depression (A) should be explored in relation to perceived threat (C1) at the moment with mostly acquired beliefs about how best to respond (B) to that threat. For example, if the patient is angry, rather than begin with concern about anger management, the IRT clinician asks about the perceived "cause" of the anger in a specific episode of rage: "What made you so angry?" and "Can you say how that threatened you?" What happens from there is discussed at length in Chapters 4 and 5 on the IRT models.

Normal Development Through Secure Attachment

Initial reflexes preprogrammed at birth are all about attachment: grasping, Babinski sign, crying, startle, calming on ventral contact, rooting, placing, and sucking. The infant's preference for specific individuals evolves with experience, as does a lot else, including the ability to recognize patterned light (Singer & Rauschecker, 1982). Attachment reflexes are more obvious in monkeys than in humans. For example, both human and monkey babies clasp, but monkey babies support their own weight as they cling to the mother (fur helps), whereas human neonates have to be held. Both species love clutching a soft cloth in the absence of an attachment figure. Harlow (1958) related that to what he called "contact comfort." Mothers in both species also are actively

---

(infundibular) stalk, a tubular connection to the pituitary gland. The hypothalamus contains a control center for many functions of the autonomic nervous system, and it has effects on the endocrine system because of its complex interaction with the pituitary gland. (Utiger, 2017)

[6] I chose the term *primitive brain awareness* to represent a form of cognition that evolved first, and then I discovered in the literature that several others had used the same language. Clearly C1 is a viable concept even though its referents, "preconscious" and "unconscious," are not often used outside of Psychoanalysis.
[7] The word *predispose* is from classical biological descriptions of the sympathetic and parasympathetic nervous systems.
[8] I mentioned that affects, behaviors, and cognitions should be linked in Benjamin (1974) and credited others who also had done so. The present restriction of the linkage to subcortical processes specifically related to threat and safety is not common.

attached to their young; they are drawn to hold infants, especially when they cry, even if the baby is not their own. For example, a new baby monkey has value as a commodity. Other females will groom the mother to earn a chance to hold the baby (Milius, 2010).

Secure Base in Humans

Optimal patterns of attachment were called *Secure Base* by Bowlby (1969, 1977). In agreement with psychoanalysts such as Mahler (1968), Bowlby described the first two development stages in terms of (a) attachment or connection to the parent, defined by the SASB items listed in Table 2.1, followed by (b) differentiation, defined by the SASB items listed in Table 2.4, that begins later in the first year. This second stage is highly conflicted as the caregiver alternates between necessary episodes of control for socialization versus episodes of letting go to support self-definition.[9] At this time, the child matches the parent with a conflict between compliance (response to control) and going his/her own separate way (response to emancipation).

Although he understood the importance of control for socialization during this second stage, Bowlby chose to emphasize differentiation when describing secure attachment. Differentiation is very difficult for parents and children. In settings that do not offer a Secure Base, it is even more difficult. In the Appendix to this chapter, there is a poem by a gifted psychiatrist that conveys the terror a child can feel when forced to differentiate from his/her "transition object," the last point of contact comfort. In almost every one of the 282 IRT inpatient case consultations with the author while working at the University of Utah Neuropsychiatric Institute, differentiation failure was a central problem. Psychologically, patients loyally clung to the maladaptive rules and values of Family in the Head. Skowron, Stanley, and Shapiro (2009) completed a study that more formally showed a strong connection between differentiation failure and psychopathology.

Differentiation is the name of Stage 2 in IRT, and developing a friendly version of it almost always is a main treatment goal. During this stage, the parent who offers Secure Base conditions allows, even encourages, autonomy while remaining in control to ensure that social norms are honored as the child safely explores the world. That means the child is taught realistic ways to identify threat (e.g., "don't try to unlock the cabinet to play with Daddy's gun") and safety (e.g., "play with friends from families we know"). In a child with Secure Base, genuine threat will elicit fear or anxiety or anger, whereas safety will elicit relaxation, curiosity, and pleasure. Research based

---

[9]Freud (1959b) named the second stage "anal" as reflected in toilet training and suggested that it is about conflict between control by others and control of self. That makes sense, too. SASB coding (Chapter 3) helps distinguish between control of self and autonomy taking.

on Bowlby's definition of Secure Base repeatedly has shown that it is associated with physical and mental health (Cassidy & Shaver, 2008).

In Tables 2.1, 2.2, 2.3, 2.4, and 2.5, psychologically important interpersonal patterns such as Secure Base and differentiation are described in terms of items from the Structural Analysis of Social Behavior (SASB) Intrex questionnaires (Benjamin, 2000; defined fully in Chapter 3). As Secure Base and differentiation and other important patterns are discussed in various contexts throughout this book, the reader will be referred back to these tables for specific behavioral definitions of sometimes elusive clinical concepts.

Secure Base behaviors are described in Tables 2.1 and 2.2. The suggestion that SASB items describe Secure Base is backed by a study using SASB ratings of videos of mother–toddler pairs classified as secure or insecure according to Bowlby's definitions (Teti, Heaton, Benjamin, & Gelfand, 1995). The left-hand sides show one person's transitive behaviors in relation to another person's intransitive behaviors, which are shown on the right. For example, if a parent shows transitive focuses on a child with moderate degrees of friendliness and moderate degrees of control, the child is likely to match that in interpersonal space (as defined by SASB in Chapter 3) with moderate degrees of friendliness and submission. In this example, the names

TABLE 2.1
Moderate Degrees of Friendly Enmeshment as Defined by SASB Intrex Items

\multicolumn{2}{c}{Prototypical parent[a]}	\multicolumn{2}{c}{Prototypical child[b]}
Code	Item	Code	Item
141	I warmly, cheerfully invite her/him to be in touch with me as often as she/he wants.	241	I warmly, happily keep in contact with her/him.
142	I provide for, nurture, take care of her/him.	242	I warmly, comfortably accept help, caregiving when she/he offers it.
143	I look after her/his interests, take steps to protect her/him, back her/him up.	243	I am trusting. I ask for what I want and count on her/him to come through when needed.
144	I constructively, sensibly, persuasively analyze situations involving her/him.	244	I willingly accept, yield to her/his reasonable suggestions, ideas.
145	I stimulate and teach her/him, show her/him how to understand, do.	245	I learn from her/him, take advice from her/him.

Note. SASB = Structural Analysis of Social Behavior. Items for the region of friendly enmeshment describe secure base Gifts of Love, which support normative interdependent behaviors under safe conditions. Items with codes having the same last digit are complementary. Details for the SASB model appear in Chapter 3. SASB Intrex long form items are copyright © 1995 by University of Utah. Reprinted with permission.
[a]Prototypical parent = transitive action focused on another person. [b]Prototypical child = intransitive reaction focused on self.

TABLE 2.2
Moderate Degrees of Friendly Differentiation as Defined
by SASB Intrex Items

\multicolumn{2}{c	}{Prototypical parent[a]}	\multicolumn{2}{c}{Prototypical child[b]}
Code	Item	Code	Item
115	I actively listen, accept, and affirm her/him as a person even if our views disagree.	215	I freely and openly disclose my innermost self so she/he can truly know "who I am."
114	I understand her/him well, show empathy and warmth even if he/she doesn't see things as I do.	214	I express my thoughts in a clear and friendly manner so she/he has every opportunity to understand me well.
113	I warmly show how much I like and appreciate her/him exactly as she/he is.	213	I enthusiastically show, share myself or "thing" with her/him.
112	I gently stroke her/him verbally and/or physically; I lovingly give her/him pleasure.	212	I relax, enjoy, really let go with her/him. I feel wonderful about being with her/him.
111	I enthusiastically, very lovingly show her/him how glad I am to see her/him just as she/he is.	211	I am joyful and exuberant with her/him. I always expect to have wonderful fun with her/him.
110	Out of great love for her/him, I tenderly, lovingly touch her/him sexually if she/he seems receptive.	210	I ecstatically, joyfully, exuberantly, lovingly respond to her/him sexually.

Note. SASB = Structural Analysis of Social Behavior. Items for the region of friendly differentiation describe normative interpersonal behaviors for adults under safe conditions. Except for items 110 and 210, items in this table also describe secure base patterns between parent and child. Items with codes having the same last digit are complementary. Details for the SASB model appear in Chapter 3. SASB Intrex long form items are copyright © 1995 by University of Utah. Reprinted with permission.
[a]Prototypical parent = transitive action focused on another person. [b]Prototypical child = intransitive reaction focused on self.

for their respective positions are Protect (transitive action is more parent-like) and Trust (intransitive state is more childlike). That combination is a major part of descriptions of Secure Base conditions. In general, such transitive–intransitive matches are called *complementary* (Chapter 3), and they describe interpersonal attractions that may be like attraction between objects in physical space with a force equal to 1 divided by the square of the distance between them.[10]

---

[10]This is Newton's inverse square law: The moon circles Earth instead of shooting off into space under perpetual motion because its attraction to Earth, by the inverse square law, pulls it in a "fall" toward Earth. The force of Earth's gravity equals the force of perpetual motion, and so the moon has an orbit around Earth that is basically circular except at the more distant points, where gravity is weaker; that is why the orbit is elliptical. If the moon were closer and more attracted to Earth, it would fall to Earth. If it were farther away, it would fly off into outer space in perpetual motion. Newton's classical law about mass applies to light (electromagnetism) as well. If complementarity is the result of an inverse square law, it likely is on the basis of electromagnetism rather than mass.

TABLE 2.3
Extremes of Differentiation as Defined by SASB Intrex Items

Prototypical parent[a]		Prototypical child[b]	
Code	Item	Code	Item
116	I let her/him speak freely and can be trusted to negotiate fairly even if we disagree.	216	I am straightforward. I clearly express my positions so she/he can give them due consideration.
117	I leave her/him to do things on her/his own because I believe she/he is competent.	217	I assert, hold my own without needing external support.
118	I give her/him my "blessing" and leave her/him free to develop her/his own separate identity.	218	I have my own separate identity, internal standards.
120	I leave her/him free to do and be whatever she/he wants.	220	I freely come and go as I please.
128	I uncaringly let her/him go, do what she/he wants.	228	I go my own separate way.
127	I forget her/him, just don't remember our agreements and plans.	227	I do my own thing by doing the exact opposite of what she/he wants.
126	I ignore her/him, just don't notice her/him at all.	226	I avoid her/him by being busy and alone with my "own thing."

Note. SASB = Structural Analysis of Social Behavior. The upper (friendly) 3 rows of the table describe Gifts of Love (GOLs) that support normative versions of separation as the developing child hatches from enmeshment (e.g., toddlerhood, adolescence). The lower 3 rows describe GOLs that support pathology in self-definition that derives from disrupted attachment. The middle row (120, 220) describes extremes of independence that are normative or pathological depending on context. Items with codes having the same last digit are complementary. Details for the SASB model appear in Chapter 3. SASB Intrex long form items are copyright © 1995 by University of Utah. Reprinted with permission.
[a]Prototypical parent = transitive action focused on another person. [b]Prototypical child = intransitive reaction focused on self.

Harlow's Descriptions of Minimal Conditions for Attachment

Harlow (1958) stripped attachment down to the "bare bones" by removing baby rhesus monkeys from their mothers at birth and housing them in bare wire cages equipped with surrogate mechanical "mothers" with varied attributes. An oft-cited version of his studies involved infants with one surrogate "mother" covered with cloth and a second surrogate "mother" with a bare wire trunk that could be grasped, but gave no option for soft ventral contact. Without question, babies preferred the soft mother. Some were fed on the cloth mother and some on the wire mother. Those fed on the wire mother would move back to the cloth mother immediately after feeding. Measuring attachment by time spent on the mother, all babies preferred to sleep and rest on the cloth-covered mother, regardless of which one provided the milk.

Harlow's cloth mothers also could provide a minimal "Secure Base" to the babies. When facing a "strange" object, such as an unfamiliar toy bear

TABLE 2.4
Extremes of Enmeshment as Defined by SASB Intrex Items

| Prototypical parent[a] || Prototypical child[b] ||
Code	Item	Code	Item
136	I put her/him down, tell her/him she/he does things all wrong, tell her/him my ways are superior.	236	I give in and do things the way she/he wants, but sulk quietly with resentment and anger.
137	I intrude, block, restrict her/him.	237	I just do things her/his way without much feeling of my own; I am apathetic.
138	I insist she/he follow my norms and rules so that she/he does things "properly."	238	I obey her/his-preferred rules, standards, routines.
140	I manage, control her/him, take charge of everything.	240	I yield, submit, give it to her/him.
148	For her/his own good, I tell her/him exactly what to do, be, think.	248	I feel, think, become what I think she/he wants.
147	Believing it's for her/his own good, I check on her/him and remind her/him of what she/he should do.	247	Pleasing her/him is so important that I check with her/him on every little thing.
146	I pay close attention in order to anticipate all her/his needs; I take care of absolutely everything for her/him.	246	I look to her/him, depend on her/him to take care of everything for me.

Note. SASB = Structural Analysis of Social Behavior. Items for the region of enmeshment describe hostile and friendly versions of patterns that support normative Gifts of Love for interdependence during times of crisis and for some types of learning. Items with codes having the same last digit are complementary. Details for the SASB model appear in Chapter 3. SASB Intrex long form items are copyright © 1995 by University of Utah. Reprinted with permission.
[a]Prototypical parent = transitive action focused on another person. [b]Prototypical child = intransitive reaction focused on self.

making loud noise by beating a drum, the mere presence of the cloth mother surrogate "calmed" the baby and gave it "courage" to face the threat. Without the surrogate mother in a strange room, some would curl up in terror even if there was no noise. An especially striking experiment with baby monkeys raised on cloth mother surrogates randomly subjected baby monkeys to an aversive blast of air (Rosenblum & Harlow, 1963). Those infants would spend even more time resting on the (punishing) mother surrogate. The authors did not interpret that result, but one might guess that these babies clung to the mother surrogate more often even though it was the cause of the problem because of greater insecurity. In other words, primates look to the familiar, huggable figure for security, regardless of history or consequences, and that

TABLE 2.5
Extremes of Hostility as Defined by SASB Intrex Items

Prototypical parent[a]		Prototypical child[b]	
Code	Item	Code	Item
123	Just when I am needed most, I abandon her/him, leave her/him "in the lurch."	223	I angrily detach from her/him, don't ask for anything; weep alone.
122	I leave her/him to starve, to get what she/he vitally needs all on her/his own.	222	I snarl angrily, hatefully refuse her/his caregiving, her/his offers to assist.
121	I angrily leave her/him out, absolutely refuse to have anything to do with her/him.	221	Filled with rage and/or fear, I do what I can to escape, flee, or hide from her/him.
130	I torture, murder, annihilate her/him no matter what she/he does just because she/he is "who she/he is."	230	I scream, agonize, protest desperately that she/he is destroying, killing me.
131	I approach her/him very menacingly, gather materials I can use to hurt her/him.	231	I am obviously terrified, very fearful of her/him; I am extremely wary.
132	I rip her/him off, gouge her/him, grab all can from her/him.	232	In a very grouchy, surly manner, I go along with her/his needs and wants.
133	I harshly punish her/him, take revenge, make her/him suffer.	233	I whine, protest, try to explain, justify, account for myself.

Note. SASB = Structural Analysis of Social Behavior. Items for the region of extreme hostility describe behaviors associated with psychopathology. Items with codes having the same last digit are complementary. Details for the SASB model appear in Chapter 3. SASB Intrex long form items are copyright © 1995 by University of Utah. Reprinted with permission.
[a]Prototypical parent = transitive action focused on another person. [b]Prototypical child = intransitive reaction focused on self.

is another form of evidence in support of the concept of Gifts of Love and the power of attachment whether the associated lessons are adaptive or not.

Harlow identified contact comfort, frequency, and proximity as essential to attachment, even though the soft clingable artificial mothers were not able to provide what biologists call the "average expectable conditions" offered by mother monkeys in the wild. For example, the laboratory mechanical surrogates could not retrieve the baby monkeys if in trouble, nor could they model fear in appropriate situations (e.g., poisonous snake) or demonstrate ways of finding food and shelter. Benjamin (1968) offered comments about possible clinical implications of Harlow's work. Readers who never have "known" a monkey or chimpanzee up close and personal will find engaging details that imply a sense of self and a lot else in Fouts and Mills (1998) and DeWahl (2009).

In sum, attachment is based on automatic primitive brain learning rather than logic or functionality. Attachment figures are the earliest version of safe haven for primates (and other mammals). They are the models, the teachers of the rules for threat and safety. To qualify as an attachment figure in childhood, the parent must be present often very early in life, offer contact comfort and food, and be relatively responsive to the infant's needs (e.g., hunger, pain, tiredness, curiosity; Bretherton, 1992). The infant cannot and does not test whether the lessons from its attachment figures are adaptive or not. Instead, the recorded rules for safety and threat are profoundly simple: In the presence of threat, see, feel, and do what caregivers see, feel, and do; or do what they direct you to do. The same process applies to learning about safety. Compliance with caregiver wishes activates the safety (parasympathetic) system and releases rewarding neurochemicals and hormones, discussed below. Attachment figures also can develop outside of the biological family and even in adulthood. They, too, can define safety and threat in the primitive brain. Examples include institutions such as residential schools, neighborhood gangs, churches, sports teams, and a closely knit military unit. Clearly, attachment is vital to survival of the primate. Its opposite is hostility, defined in specific forms by the SASB items listed in Table 2.5.

Developmental Stages That Follow Attachment

Starting with Freud (1959b), there have been quite a few descriptions of developmental stages in humans. Erikson (1959) provided a good example. He proposed stages of development that are more interactional than others and therefore more relevant to IRT. His stages are: trust versus mistrust, autonomy versus shame and doubt, initiative versus guilt, industry versus inferiority, identity versus role confusion, intimacy versus isolation, generativity versus stagnation, and integrity versus despair. In IRT, as for Erikson and most others, the first stage is about attachment, and the second is about differentiation. Only two stages follow in IRT. During Stage 3, peer play, social and cognitive skills are refined along with a consolidated sense of self that is both connected to and separate from the attachment figure. Stage 4 is adult bonding and continuing development of the ability to make competent contributions to the functioning and welfare of the community and of the next generation.

Some classical behaviorists might find mention of self in Stage 3 to be too inferential. They are invited to consider a video providing evidence of a self-concept in a gorilla, Koko (Brennan & Visty, 1999). Koko knows sign language because Penny Patterson, her companion and trainer for over 30 years, taught her. The video opens with Penny and Koko looking in a mirror that shows Koko's image. Penny touches the image and says and signs, using

American Sign Language, "Who is that?" Koko points to herself and signs "me, gorilla, animal." Then Koko initiates a request and shows evidence of attachment as she signs, "Koko love?" Penny signs and says yes, and Koko presents for a hug. Clearly, Koko has a sense of self. Differentiation of self from the attachment figure is an adaptive step toward competent adulthood.

Pathological Development

Stress has long been recognized as a correlate of mental disorder, though often it is thought to trigger inherited vulnerability to mental disorder rather than to be a primary factor, as conceptualized in IRT. Either way, it is important to review what is known about mechanisms that link stress directly to symptoms of mental disorder. For that, the work of Wong and colleagues is exemplary. Wong, Tai, Wong-Faull, Claycomb, and Kvetňanský (2008) provided important detail about the impact of epinephrine ("Epi"; associated with the sympathetic nervous system) on symptoms of mental disorder:

> Clearly, Epi is an important component of well-being in response to stress but excesses of stress and Epi can also be detrimental. Sustained stress and elevated Epi are considered major contributing factors in many illnesses, including cardiovascular disease, immune dysfunction and psychiatric disorders. Epi has pressor effects, increasing blood pressure and heart rate. The heart must work harder to maintain cardiac activity, and thus, sustained elevation of Epi can have dire consequence for cardiovascular function. Similarly, Epi affects many components of the immune system. If the latter is pre-activated, then it becomes more difficult to mount an immune response when necessary. Finally, altered Epi expression has been associated with behavioral disorders. Adrenergic cells in the C1, C2 and C3 regions of the brainstem send forward projections to the forebrain and midbrain, where Epi can be released to interact with alpha 1b receptors. These receptors lie proximal to dopaminergic, serotonergic and noradrenergic neurotransmitter centers that have been associated with psychiatric illness and are thought to modulate their function. These same centers are known targets for drugs effective in the treatment of behavioral disorders. (p. 250)

That analysis would support the hypothesis that perceived stress and epinephrine are primary factors in affective disorders. Evidence that relationships with attachment figures have a large impact on affective symptoms (diagnoses), brain development, and genes is reviewed below.

Unfortunately, this line of thought has rarely been approached directly because many believe it requires blaming parents. To the contrary, IRT theory is descriptive and based on natural science. Evolutionary theory, like any scientific theory about biology, is based on descriptions in relation to adaptation, not culpability. The more we understand and accept how we are constructed and how we work, the richer and more meaningful our lives and those of our fellow human beings can be. Psychotherapy can be more effective if mechanisms of symptoms are addressed directly; blaming is not a part of good psychotherapy. This effort to underscore the importance of learning about threat and safety from attachment figures is to help people make different and better choices for their own healing and, most especially, for nurturing the next generation.

As a child psychiatrist, Bowlby was well aware of the impact of attachment gone awry. He described three dysfunctional (insecure) attachment types in the child: avoidant, ambivalent, and disorganized. Huge numbers of studies have established that insecure attachments are associated with mental and/or physical illness in many forms (e.g., Cassidy & Shaver, 2008). Bowlby and his colleagues (e.g., Ainsworth, Blehar, Waters, & Wall, 1978) proposed that these types of insecurity derive from specific dysfunctional parenting styles: dismissive, preoccupied, and disorganized, respectively. Bowlby developed a productive collaboration with Harlow (1958; see also van der Horst, Leroy, & van der Veer, 2008), whose work with infant rhesus monkeys very much confirmed Bowlby's emphasis on attachment and Secure Base. An informative description of the history of Bowlby's work was provided by Bretherton (1992).

Many other research teams have found evidence showing that caregiver maltreatment of children is directly linked to psychiatric diagnoses. Cicchetti and Toth (2005) wrote,

> Maltreated children have evidenced elevated levels of childhood disturbance across a wide range of areas . . . including . . . depressive symptomatology, conduct disorder and delinquency, attention deficit hyperactivity disorder, oppositional disorder, [and posttraumatic stress disorder]. Maltreatment also is linked to adult disorders, including personality disorders, substance abuse, suicidal and self-injurious behavior, somatization, anxiety, and dissociation. (p. 427)

Choi, Jeong, Polcari, Rohan, and Teicher (2012) added that children who had not personally been abused sexually or physically but who were frequently exposed to parental violence had "increased risk for depression, posttraumatic stress disorder and reduced IQ scores" (p. 1071).

> Brain damage is a related consequence of child abuse. In IRT, child abuse is deemed a stress that usually is chronic. Bruce McEwen, a distinguished researcher on the impact of stress on the brain, concluded, "The brain is the key organ of stress processes. It determines what individuals will experience as stressful, it orchestrates how individuals will cope with stressful experiences, and it changes both functionally and structurally

as a result of stressful experiences" (McEwen & Gianaros, 2011, p. 431). Carpenter et al. (2009) noted "Quality of the relationship between infants and caregivers during stages of early brain development seems to be a critical determinant of life-long biobehavioral regulation, including HPA axis reactivity, in the offspring" (p. 69). Gunnar and Quevedo (2007) wrote, "Chronic stress can cause inhibition of neurogenesis, disruption of neuronal plasticity, and neurotoxicity. . . . increases the risk for physical and behavioral problems." They continue, chronic stress also affects gene expression in multiple brain structures, . . . "synaptic connectivity and neurogenesis and can increase cellular death, effectively altering the typical pathways and organization of the young brain" (p. 164).

Results from Stephen Suomi's primate laboratory at the National Institute of Mental Health about the impact of disrupted attachment also strongly support the theory that childhood stress results in brain damage that is relevant to affective disorders. For example,

> These findings suggest that exposure to an adverse early-life environment during infancy is associated with long-term alterations in the serotonin system and support previous studies suggesting that reduced 5-HT$_{1A}$R density during development might be a factor increasing vulnerability to stress-related neuropsychiatric disorders. Furthermore, alterations in the serotonin system seemed to be gender- and region-specific, providing a biological basis for the higher prevalence of affective disorders in women. (Spinelli et al., 2010, p. 1146)

Abuse need not be physical or sexual to damage the nervous system. In a comprehensive review of the literature, Teicher and Samson (2016) concluded,

> Parental verbal abuse, witnessing domestic violence and sexual abuse appear to specifically target brain regions (auditory, visual and somatosensory cortex) and pathways that process and convey the aversive experience. Maltreatment is associated with reliable morphological alterations in anterior cingulate, dorsal lateral prefrontal and orbitofrontal cortex, corpus callosum and adult hippocampus, and with enhanced amygdala response to emotional faces and diminished striatal response to anticipated rewards. Evidence is emerging that these regions and interconnecting pathways have sensitive exposure periods when they are most vulnerable. (p. 241)

Most people can agree on what physical or sexual abuse is. Agreement about what verbal abuse is might be less reliable. An example seen in IRT patients is shunning, or saying things such as "If you don't do what I say, you will be alone in hell forever" or "You are such a bother, I am going to send you back to the hospital." Such messages represent emotional or verbal abuse because they threaten separation from the attachment figure, which in the extreme is a death sentence for a primate. Other forms of verbal abuse attribute evil power to the child, and that can be internalized. An example is "You drive me crazy."

Conversations with parents about verbal abuse could be helpful because many do not fully appreciate the long-lasting impact of their words as well as actions. It is reasonable to conclude that abuse is more likely to have a lasting effect if by family than if by strangers. For one thing, abuse by family is more likely to be chronic. For another, the maladaptive cues based on abuse are backed by faith and credit due the caregivers: "You know what you know."[11]

FUNCTIONAL ANALYSIS OF ANGER, ANXIETY, AND DEPRESSION

It already is accepted that imbalances among the neurotransmitters and hormones (many of which are in the sympathetic and parasympathetic systems) are deeply implicated in psychiatric affective symptoms. What is not so commonly accepted is the interpretation in IRT that many of those miscued releases of neurochemical and endocrine imbalances reflect the individual's maladaptive attempts to cope with threat and find safety, symbolized by the sequence C1AB. For example, Joseph felt threatened when he sensed a loved one needed something (C1). His anxiety (A) mobilized him to see that they got what they wanted (B). That proved impossible, and with repeated perceived failure, he eventually collapsed into depression, angry with himself for his inadequacy. The IRT formulation method (Chapter 4) helps the clinician and patient identify such miscued sequences that account for affective symptoms.

In contrast to this evolutionary-based strategy of considering the adaptive functions of affective symptoms, in the official nomenclature, problem cognitions, affects, and behaviors are thought by many to represent defective mechanisms attributable to inherited vulnerability to stress with results described in separate sections of the *Diagnostic and Statistical Manual of Mental Disorders*, fifth edition (*DSM–5*; American Psychiatric Association, 2013), and the *International Classification of Diseases*, 10th edition (ICD–10; World Health Organization, 2017). To be sure, regardless of alleged cause, the categorical descriptions have successfully guided symptom management with medications and by psychotherapy that offers, for example, lessons in coping skills. Consequently, IRT case formulations do center on the *DSM–5* descriptions of affects related to threat and safety.

---

[11]Quote from Milton Miller, MD, chair of psychiatry at the University of Wisconsin–Madison in the 1960s and 1970s.

The affective categories involving anger, anxiety, and depression show substantial comorbidity (Chapter 9). That does not pose a conceptual problem when using IRT theory. Affective symptoms merely are the functional correlates of C1AB (primitive brain perception–affect–behavior) links designed by evolution to maximize adaptation.

Observations of contexts for aggressive behavior suggest that anger (A) has the adaptive purpose of predisposing behaviors (B) that support gaining control of perceived threat (C1) or getting distance from it. Anger feels better than anxiety or depression, perhaps because getting control or distance is an optimal solution to the problems posed by threat. Of course, in an advanced society not tied to the rules of the jungle, a friendlier solution is to negotiate an agreement that sets aside victory and complete control or complete separation and that instead resolves the issue in ways that address some needs of all parties. Such negotiations do not give immediate results or emotional "satisfaction" and they also require more control from the higher (cortical) brain than is allowed by the all-or-nothing strategies of the primitive brain. The ability to transcend all-or-nothing solutions that result in control or distancing is not restricted to humans. When carefully observed, and better yet when taught sign language, monkeys and chimpanzees have been seen to be capable of great tenderness, empathy, consideration, and fairness (DeWahl, 2009; Fouts & Mills, 1998).

If getting control or distance using anger is not possible or desirable, anxiety is a likely alternative. It (A) mobilizes the person to focus on and find a feasible way to respond effectively (B) to a perceived threat (C1). Anxiety is very uncomfortable and remains activated until the threat has been resolved. The discomfort helps ensure that the threat will not be ignored, which is adaptive. Then, if no solution is found, Depression (A) can serve as a defense of last resort. It follows perception of overwhelm without recourse (C1), and usually involves (B) giving up, withdrawing or hiding and in humans at least, "disallowing" self ("what I am, think, do is not adequate or acceptable or right"). Depressive defenses are passive, but do facilitate avoidance, or failing that, minimize one's threat value which can demobilize the predator (threat).

In sum: anger is the definitive response to threat in that it can support mastery of the threat or achieve distance from it. Anxiety takes over if the threat cannot be mastered or disposed of. Anxiety demands attention until the threat disappears. Depression supports behavioral defenses of last resort: demobilize, withdraw, hide, reduce one's threat value as much as possible.

Positive affects also have adaptive functions. They support gathering and processing food (enteric nervous system) that provide life-supporting energy. They also support safety system affects and behaviors such as relaxation, play, creative activity, and bonding to others. We are a group animal and such sociability is vital to our survival. Similarly, sexuality enhances bonds between parents and that helps assure protection of and caring for the young. Disturbances of positive affects are not discussed in this book, but IRT theory does apply to them.

EVIDENCE THAT SUPPORTS THE LINKING: C1AB

The SASB model, explained in detail in Chapter 3, assesses interpersonal relationships in terms of underlying dimensions called *affiliation* and *interdependence*. Each model point is composed of progressively varying proportions of the underlying dimensions of interpersonal space (explained at length in Chapter 3). As a result, when SASB-based measurements of interpersonal relationships (B) are related to a constant variable such as depression (A), their correlations (AB) show step-by-step changes in a "wave,"[12] as shown in Figure 2.2.[13] The figure presents correlations among 150 inpatient ratings of anger, anxiety, and depression (A is measured by the Symptom Checklist—90—Revised [SCL–90–R]; Derogatis, 1994) with their SASB-based descriptions of interpersonal patterns (B) with a significant other person (SO) when the relationship is at its worst (C1). C1 is not measured directly here, but threat (stress) is assumed because the behavioral ratings of SO are of an important attachment relationship at its worst, and for most people, that is a stress.

The wave in Figure 2.2 is a convincing demonstration of an orderly relationship between threat affects (A) and adaptive behaviors (B) assessed in relation to a stressful situation. The largest positive correlations in Figure 2.2 show that these threat affects sponsor interpersonally hostile behaviors and diminish friendly interpersonal behaviors. Anger shows the most powerful connections to interpersonal hostility; depression shows the least and anxiety is in between. The remarkably large negative correlations between depression and friendliness suggest that it actively inhibits friendly (attachment) behaviors. This thought is consistent with the fact that an active process is responsible for depressive symptoms. Serotonin (5-HT, a monoamine neurotransmitter) is a feel-good drug managed by the parasympathetic nervous system (right side, Figure 2.1). In depressed individuals, serotonin reuptake

---

[12]If you ride on a moving Ferris wheel and project a headlight on a screen moving at right angles to you, the result is a cosine or sine wave depending on the starting point.
[13]Data are from the Wisconsin database cited throughout this book. It was made possible by National Institutes of Mental Health (NIMH) Grant MH 33604 to L. S. Benjamin, supplemented by the Wisconsin Alumni Research Foundation (WARF). The project was called "Diagnosis Using Structural Analysis of Social Behavior," L. S. Benjamin, Principal Investigator, 1980–1982, $216,883. The sample includes a variety of very reliable assessments of 191 inpatient psychiatry patients at the University of Wisconsin Hospitals in Madison. The database has been loaned to many master's and PhD students and to several colleagues at other institutions. Not all have remembered to credit these sponsors. Many thanks are due NIMH and WARF.

NEGATIVE AFFECTIVE SYMPTOMS & TRANSITIVE ACTION WITH SO AT WORST (N = 150 INPATIENTS)

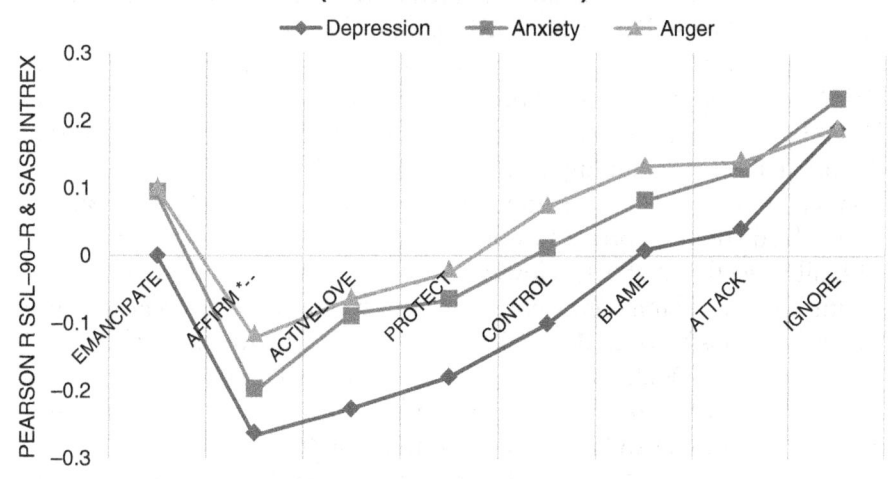

PATIENTS' INTRANSITIVE REACTIONS WITH SO AT WORST AND AFFECTIVE SYMPTOMS

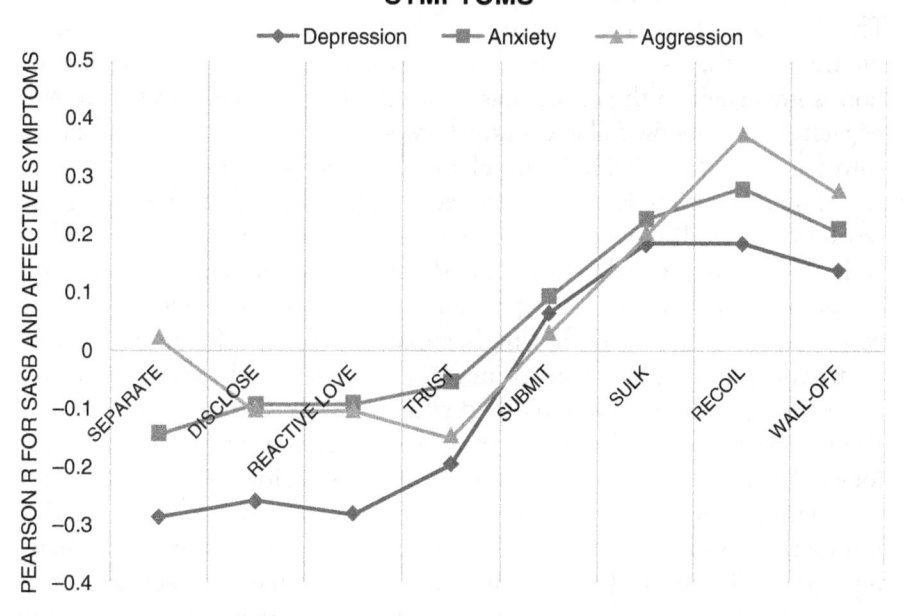

Figure 2.2. Anger, Anxiety, and Depression predispose hostile responses to significant other persons. Threat affects are inversely correlated with friendly interpersonal patterns and positively related to hostile patterns. Anger shows the largest correlations with hostility and depression shows the smallest. In fact, depression shows such large *negative* correlations with friendly behaviors that the conclusion is that it actively inhibits them. Magnitudes of effects of anxiety on behavior are, as predicted, in between those of depression and anger. SASB = Structural Analysis of Social Behavior; SCL–90–R = Symptom Checklist—90—Revised; SO = significant other.

from the synapse is too rapid; hence the shortage of feelings of well-being. Figure 2.1 suggests that a serotonin shortage not only accounts for affective symptoms of depression but also is related to (i.e., predisposes) active inhibition of friendliness. This is discussed again in Chapter 9.

Depression also has long been associated with helplessness (Seligman, 1975), but helplessness has not been a part of definitions of depression in the *DSM–IV* (American Psychiatric Association, 1994) or *DSM–5*. Honoring the original research findings, I have suggested that helplessness in depression represents a defense of surrender. However, data in the bottom panel of Figure 2.2 do not support that interpretation. Angry submission is associated with all three threat affects. However, there is a related result that is easy to misinterpret as submission. Depression is distinguished by significant negative correlations between depression and autonomy taking assessed by SASB as Separate and Disclose. The negative weight for Disclose ("I clearly and comfortably express my own thoughts and feelings to him/her") can be seen as defense by hiding and/or giving in to the other's view, while the negative weight for Separate (X "knows his or her own mind" and "does his or her own thing" separately from Y) marks lack of or inhibition of differentiation, a "disavowal of self." The normal senses of having positions of one's own are actively inhibited. It is not OK to have a "me," exactly as noted for Joseph. These data underscore that this disallowing of self is not the same as submitting—that is, "I think, do, become whatever she wants." The distinction is important in the clinic. Disallowing self (negative correlation with Separate) is an unobservable event, whereas submitting (positive correlation with Submit) reflects behavior in relation to someone else.

Finally, anxiety is the "in-between" activating affect that signals no resolution regarding what to do about threat—that is, try to prevail or actively leave or surrender. Figure 2.2 shows correlations between behaviors and anxiety midway between depression (hide, retreat) and anger (prevail or actively get rid of the threat). Whether anxiety is resolved by gaining control or distance, literal or psychic, or negotiated by setting boundaries in time or space depends on individual and situational differences. For example, Figure 3.8 (in Chapter 3) suggests that these links between affect and behavior can be affected by culture, presumably because culture affects parenting.

This demonstration that affective symptoms and behaviors go together in orderly ways in a threatening context is important enough to demand replication. To check that, here is a summary of what was seen when the same analyses were applied to a large sample with outpatient as well as normal raters (Rothweiler, 2004; $N = 234$), again rating self in relation to SO at worst. Affects in this study were assessed with the Millon Clinical Multiaxial Inventory–II (Millon, 1987). Using the same paradigm, Park (2005; $N = 313$) measured depression with the Beck Depression Inventory (BDI; Beck, Steer,

& Brown, 1996), anxiety with the Beck Anxiety Inventory (BAI; Beck & Steer, 1993), and state anger with the State–Trait Anger Expression Inventory (STAXI; Spielberger, 1999) in a normal sample. These two additional studies did not replicate the Wisconsin study exactly, but there were important similarities. Anger was associated with transitive hostile action (Blame, Attack, Ignore) or intense distancing (Recoil). Anxiety supported avoidant responses to the SO (Ignore, Recoil) in the two additional samples. Depression again was reflected by hostile avoidance (Ignore, Recoil), inhibited attachment behaviors (Affirm, Active Love, Protect; Reactive Love), and inhibited self-expression (Disclose). Together these analyses provide evidence that anger, anxiety, and depression do predispose specific behaviors and are adaptive responses to threat.

MECHANISMS THAT RECORD LESSONS IN SAFETY AND THREAT

Copy Processes

In addition to inherited proclivities for responding to threat such as the startle response, copying caregivers is a mechanism for passing information from one generation to the next about what to be afraid of (C1A) and how to be safe (B). Copying C1AB sequences is similar to what happens when RNA copies sequences in DNA and then directs the building of proteins according to those sequences.[14] Copying C1AB links is the way nature passes information from one generation to another about structure at the level of genes (DNA, RNA) and about defining threat and finding safety (C1AB) at the level of behavior.

There are three main copy processes that can be seen at the behavioral level:

1. identification—be like him/her;
2. recapitulation—perceive (C1), feel (A), and do (B) as you did with him/her in this situation; and
3. introjection—treat yourself as you were treated (inverse copy processes are defined in Chapter 3).

Copying is especially likely when the young child is in threatening situations because the threat system releases activating hormones: epinephrine, cortisol, and norepinephrine. Internal threat circuitry demands that the threat be addressed.

---

[14] I am indebted to my daughter, Linda B. Kidd, DVM, PhD, for this insight.

For Joseph, a threat would be disarray (C1) that might lead to parental fighting and divorce. Anxiety (A) about household disorder follows perception of disarray or someone's need. Do the dishes (B) is the safe response, and parasympathetic activity accompanies the perception of safety. The "reward" mechanism is release of serotonin, dopamine, oxytocin, or opioids. Gunnar and Quevedo (2007) and Charuvastra and Cloitre (2008) provided informative detail about such rewarding neurological and hormonal processes. The resulting affects are pleasant, relaxing, and reassuring. Such parasympathetic activity is salient when C1AB links reflect perceived safety, as in this example for Joseph.

Clinical experience confirms the theory that relationship with Family in the Head sponsors C1AB sequences that mimic what originally happened in threat situations. If the person complies with old rules (e.g., Joseph figures out how to please coworkers "before they know what they want"), it feels as it did when caregivers were pleased (e.g., house is neat and Mom and Dad are peaceful rather than doing battle about the kids). Such compliance with old rules about threat, whether adaptive or not, makes one feel safe. Patients who self-sabotage will say, "I know it is not good for me, but it feels right" or "I just *have* to do it."

The three copy processes described by IRT theory have been well validated at the behavioral level for interpersonal patterns (B) in one sample of inpatients and another sample of normal raters. The studies are described in Chapter 3. Another form of support for the claim that C1AB links are copied is in an article by Chartrand and Lakin (2013, p. 286), who described the adaptive functions of affective and behavioral contagion. In IRT the emphasis is on "contagion" of safety and threat patterns from parent to child during the formative years. Language learning is another form of early learning by copying, a skill that is not so accessible after the early years, as adults who learn a foreign language can testify.

Copying in the primitive brain is by associative learning (Reber, 1989). It appears to be facilitated by mirror neurons.

They were first discovered while one monkey watched another reach for a grape. The mirroring of that activity was recorded "at single-cell and neural-system levels" (Iacoboni, 2009, p. 654). The three types of copying would reflect activity by mirror neurons in different interpersonal contexts. For examples: In one context, father (Referent X) shows control in relation to Patient (Referent Y). In another context, the Patient (Referent X) shows control in relation to the spouse (Referent Y). Together, these copied connections define the patient's identification with the father: The patient's patterns with the spouse are like the father's patterns with the patient. Variations in this paradigm can represent all possible copy processes. Benjamin and Friedrich (1991) speculated about how patterns described by SASB could come to be represented in brain circuits developed by emergent processes.

Family in the Head: The Neurology of Internalized Representation

If copying is supported by mirror neurons, then the question becomes, How is that information stored, and how does it connect to and regulate affects? As noted already, John Bowlby (1969, 1977), a psychoanalyst, suggested that attachment figures provide "internal working models" for children, and object relations psychoanalysts call these *internalized representations*. In IRT, these internalizations are called *Family in the Head*, and they are important in affect regulation. It includes biological and/or adoptive relatives and other caregivers that offer safety and/or pose a threat. Examples include: instructors in a residential school, members of a neighborhood gang, important figures at church, sports buddies, or other members of a military unit.

There is evidence that Bowlby's internalized representations do exist. Suddendorf and Whiten, 2001 reported,

> . . . children begin to entertain secondary representations in the 2nd year of life. This advance is manifest in their passing hidden displacement tasks, engaging in pretense and means—ends reasoning, interpreting external representations, displaying mirror self-recognition and empathic behavior, and showing an early understanding of 'mind' and imitation. New data show a cluster of mental accomplishments in great apes . . . very similar to that observed in 2-year-old humans. (p. 629)

fMRI studies may have accessed mechanisms for these studies of perceptions of self and others. Martin (2007) wrote,

> Evidence from functional *neuroimaging of the human brain indicates that information about salient properties of an object—such as what it looks like, how it moves, and how it is used is stored in sensory and motor systems that were active when that information was acquired* [emphasis added]. As a result, object concepts belonging to different categories like animals and tools are represented in partially distinct, sensory- and motor property–based neural networks. (p. 25)

> . . . symbols for action are directly linked to circuits involved in that action . . . simply reading words denoting specific tongue (lick), finger (pick), and leg (kick) actions activated regions in premotor cortex that were also active when subjects actually made tongue, finger, and leg movements, respectively. (as cited in Hauk et al., 2004, pp. 32–33)

Martin also noted that internal representations have affective value:

> evidence is mounting that the amygdala also plays a prominent role in this circuitry, perhaps as a means of alerting the organism to a potentially

threatening predator or prey (e.g., Whalen 1998). Indeed, recent studies suggest that the human amygdala responds more to stimuli denoting animals than tools, irrespective of stimulus type including pictures, written words, associated sounds, and heard words. (Martin, 2007, p. 38)

and, *"remembering an action involves reactivating neural activity originally involved in that action: or . . . that occurred during learning. . . ."* Charuvastra and Cloitre (2008) noted, ". . . the feeling of trust involves an interaction between the amygdala and the prefrontal cortices (Adolphs, 2002; Winston et al., 2002) . . . (and there are) . . . neural processes linking social support to emotion regulation" (p. 313). Martin reminds, ". . . object concepts are not explicitly represented, but rather emerge from weighted activity within property-based brain regions" (2007, p. 25). Additional studies related to functions of internal representations are appearing with great detail, accuracy and credibility in journals such as: *Developmental Neuropsychology, Journal of Cognitive Neuroscience,* and *Infant and Child Development.*

Gifts of Love to Family in the Head

Family in the Head are "installed" by copying perceive–feel–act (C1AB) links and is stored as sketched in the preceding section. Whether they are adaptive or maladaptive, copied patterns (C1AB) reflect Gifts of Love to Family in the Head. Compliance or defiance is related to affect regulation because C1 (e.g., mother says "keep your room neat"), A (worry if it is in disarray), and B (clean it today) are linked. When Joseph succeeded in pleasing his parents, it brought "psychic proximity" to his Family in the Head and presumably activated his safety system as much as it did whenever real family hugged or praised him. As noted above, remembering an action reactivates the same circuits activated at the time of the action. Again, these effects are not dependent on whether the pattern "works" (i.e., is adaptive). Lessons in safety and threat are based entirely on frequency, proximity, and whatever attachment figures said and did regarding what to fear and how to be safe.

GOLs are copied patterns that bring a sense of "right" and "safe" because of associations with a caregiver's instructions or modeling, regardless of whether they are adaptive or not. If the copied lessons are maladaptive, so are the associated behaviors, even if they make no rational sense. Examples that demonstrate the power of GOLs include the following:

- Abused children who have been taken into protective custody nonetheless yearn for reunion with their original parents.
- Rosenblum and Harlow (1963) showed that baby monkeys abused by their surrogate "mothers" spent more time in prox-

imity to the abusers than did monkeys with huggable, soft, non-violent surrogates.
- SASB analyses of normal and patient raters showed that patients who had been treated with greater hostility by their caregivers nonetheless trusted them as much as did normal raters (discussed in Chapter 3).
- In Chapter 10, it is shown that therapists and patients who address GOLs in an adherent way (i.e., help patients acknowledge and relinquish the fantasies) have better outcomes.

WHAT ABOUT GENES AND TEMPERAMENT?

The emphasis on the impact on development of the nervous system of interactions with attachment figures raises the question, What about inheritance? The answer is that it is important, too. The sequences in DNA (genotype) are inherited, and they never change. However, even genes can be altered by learning that takes place within an "envelope of potential" set by the genotype (Kagan & Snidman, 2004). Temperaments probably define envelopes of potential for affective expression as well as for intelligence and musical, athletic, artistic, and other abilities. In other words, interactions with the environment have a lot to do with the phenotype, but only within the limits set by the genome.

As a simple example that illustrates the envelope of potential, the genome sets the potential for muscle size and strength. Suppose one identical twin exercises and works out a lot while the other leads a sedentary lifestyle. The exerciser will be closer to the top of his or her envelope, while the sedentary twin will be closer to the bottom. Their genomes remain identical, but their phenotypes will be different because of the impact of environment.

There are two ways that genes record the impact of environment. The first is by expression and silencing, and those changes are not heritable. The second is by epigenetic process, and that is heritable. Meaney (2010) advanced understanding about epigenetic processes that affect anxiety. Over many years, he conducted an exhaustive series of cross fostering studies of the impact of maternal licking of rat pups early in life on their anxiety as adults. Downgrading genetics studies based only on statistics that relate traits to consanguinity, he wrote,

> While there are indeed statistical relations between variation in nucleotide sequence . . . , in complex traits, at the level of biology there are no genes for intelligence, depression, athletic abilities, fashion sense, or any other such complex trait. Rather, there are certain variations in genomic sequences that can potentially alter either the DNA product

(RNA) or the degree to which the DNA is transcribed (i.e., actively producing its molecular product). There are multiple and complex cellular processes that lie between the DNA sequence and the functional outcome associated with the gene product. The relation between genotype and phenotype, even at the level of cellular molecules, is anything but direct. (p. 45)

Meaney underscored "the complexity of the processes that mediate genotype–phenotype relations even when considering the most fundamental aspects of gene function—the production of RNAs and protein products" (p. 45). He described epigenetic mechanisms as follows:

> The effects of maternal care on gene expression and neural function in the rat provide an understanding of how environmental events, including variations in parent–offspring interactions at the level of behavior, can become physically imprinted upon the genome. Maternal care can directly alter intracellular signals that, in turn, structurally alter the DNA and its operation. These structural modifications involve DNA methylation, a classic epigenetic mark that regulates gene transcription. More recent studies suggest that comparable epigenetic modifications associate with learning and memory (Lubin et al., 2008; Miller & Sweatt, 2007), chronic exposure to drugs of abuse (Renthal & Nestler, 2008), and psychiatric illness (Grayson et al., 2005; Ptak & Petronis, 2008; Tsankova et al., 2007). The dynamic genome is probably a slightly foreign concept to those who imagine the DNA as simply the repository of the sequence information that forms what is commonly referred to as the "genetic code." But the research of the postgenomic era, with its focus on the operation rather than simply the composition of the genome, reveals that the DNA is an active target for remodeling by cellular signals that are activated by environmental events. The reality of the functional genome does not admit to main effects of either gene or environment, but rather to a constant interaction between the DNA and its environment. (pp. 68–69)

Here is this layperson's (probably overly simplified) summary of the basic principles of genetics: DNA information is recorded by sequences in the genes that never change. Each cell in our body contains our entire genetic code (genome) in its DNA. The DNA code is used to make new cells that always include the original, inherited DNA. To make new cells, RNA copies the DNA by transcription. RNA then directs the building of proteins, the new cells. But different cells for the various body parts obviously require different information. Cell differentiation is implemented in different ways; expression and silencing are affected by environmental experiences but are not heritable. Heritable impacts of environment (epigenetic) happen at the point of copying by using a complex indexing process during which methylation "hides" the irrelevant information. The RNA then carries messages specific to the cell to be constructed.

Interactions Between Cortical Brain and Primitive Brain

Cortical or higher brain perception is the basis of comprehension and is symbolized by C2 in IRT, as it was by Reber (1989) and others. It is very different from perception in the primitive brain (C1). For one thing, C2 is not tightly locked to affects or behaviors, nor is it restricted to activity related to safety and threat. And unlike the primitive brain, the higher brain includes conscious decision making that involves choice, the "will," and a "decider." However, higher brain activity clearly can be impaired by primitive brain activity. For example, Jason may say he wants to accept a job, but his primitive fear of not performing perfectly and his uncertainty about how to please a new boss interfere with his attempts to stay employed.

Educators, economists, and others have been interested in studying mechanisms of cortically based learning and conscious decision making and in understanding how these are affected by primitive brain activity. An example of interesting research on this problem involved monkeys learning a stop-and-go task. Researchers at the Massachusetts Institute of Technology ("Primitive Brain Is 'Smarter,'" 2005) found that

> the striatum (the input structure of the basal ganglia) showed more rapid change in the learning process than the more highly evolved prefrontal cortex.... The basal ganglia first identify the rule, and then "train" the prefrontal cortex, which absorbs the lesson more slowly. (para. 5) ... The researchers speculate that perhaps the faster learning in the basal ganglia allows us (and our primitive ancestors who lacked a prefrontal cortex) to quickly pick up important information needed for survival. The prefrontal cortex then monitors what the basal ganglia have learned. Its slower, more deliberate learning mechanisms allow it to gather a more judicious "big picture" of what is going on by taking into account more history and thereby exert executive control. (para. 10)

Such research on interactions between primitive and higher brain surely also will lead to better understanding of mechanisms of psychotic and other forms of thought disorders.

A FINAL COMMON PATHWAY FOR MEDICATIONS AND PSYCHOTHERAPY

It is common to offer patients both medication to address mechanisms that support symptoms and psychotherapy to help them better manage their impairment. The distinction between methods and goals for psychotherapy and medications need not be sharp. According to IRT theory, there always is a final common pathway. Prescription of medications helps regulate hormones and neurotransmitters in the safety (e.g., dopamine, serotonin, oxytocin, opioids) and threat (e.g., cortisol, epinephrine, norepinephrine) systems. So does an IRT treatment that properly addresses activity of Family in the Head.

Given that psychotherapy and medications both access safety and threat systems, it makes sense to use both approaches. Randomized controlled studies have attempted to compare the effectiveness of each alone with combined uses (Elkin, Gibbons, Shea, & Shaw, 1996), but there is no consistent "winner" in that contest. As more is known about the genome, it is possible that future studies of genes will help predict who responds better to which approach (Fournier et al., 2009). In all cases, from the perspective of IRT, medications need to be available and used if needed to help keep the patient safe during crisis and functional during difficult stages of change as the patient is challenging Family in the Head and breaking old rules for safety and threat while installing new, more adaptive ones.

Medications and/or Psychotherapy Can Change the Brain

There is some evidence that medications can change the brain, possibly reversing environmentally caused damage: Gunnar and Quevedo (2007) observed, "Antidepressants and [corticotropin-releasing hormone] antagonists, for example, eliminate many of the behavioral disturbances that animals suffer due to early adverse experience; other pharmacologic agents also may be found to improve stress resilience among at-risk children" (p. 163). These authors noted that sometimes damage via stress can be reversed by psychosocial interventions:

> Maltreated preschool children placed in an early intervention foster care program (which promoted positive parenting strategies) showed both improved behavioral adjustment and more normative regulation of the HPA axis in comparison with children in typical foster care settings (Fisher et al., 2000). (p. 163)

Does Psychotherapy Bring Lasting Change?

Psychotherapy is sometimes alleged to provide lasting cure, whereas medications have to be maintained for a lifetime. Tests of effectiveness of psychotherapies, including IRT, do show reduction in symptoms, but symptom change alone does not define reconstruction that promises lasting change in the form of reliable Secure Base management of safety and threat.

To meet a medical standard for "cure," it makes sense to copy standard procedure in treatment of cancer, for which a cure is marked by 5 symptom-free years. There are psychotherapy studies that do follow up for as long as 5 years. For example, Lindfors et al. (2015) reported that longer term psychodynamic therapy resulted in more remissions by 5 years than did shorter term psychodynamic therapy. Lowyck et al. (2015) also followed up for 5 years but reported that most of their patients did have additional treatment during that time. They controlled for that by partialling out the number of months of additional treatment. It would be desirable to have more studies that follow up for 5 years and meet the same standard as those for cancer patients (i.e., do or do not have symptoms at the end of 5 years). Studies of psychotherapy that provide such clarity would better support the belief that psychotherapy has lasting effects.

APPENDIX 2.1
"THE SACRIFICE", BY MICHAEL MORAN[15]

In our darkened cellar,
lit only by the 60-watt shaft
coming down from the kitchen,
we three stand around
the open garbage can.
Father holds my plaited blanket,
a faded purple
no longer royal,
the silk border in shreds.
Mother's soft chant
limps through the damp,
cold basement:
"You're a big boy now,
You're a big boy."
In the palm of my right hand
I enfold my still wet thumb,
which is no longer
to be sucked.

Watching my blanket
drop into the trash,
I feel the soft fabric
like a phantom limb
and imagine it rotting
in the stench of the landfill.

---

[15]Michael Moran, psychiatrist extraordinaire, is fully and lovingly aware and accepting of the world, past, present, and future. I came to know him and others well when I was more of a participant than the alleged leader of a required multiyear group therapy for residents in psychiatry at the University of Wisconsin–Madison in the early 1980s. In those final days before the "decade of the brain," there still was emphasis on the impact of early development on adult psychopathology as psychotherapists tried to help damaged individuals repair themselves. Moran's poem captures the depth of an insecure child's terror in the face of an abrupt demand to differentiate from his transition object that had been serving as Secure Base in a threatening environment. From *The Fallen World*, by M. Moran, 2008, Monterey, KY: Larkspur Press. Copyright 2008 by Michael Moran. Reprinted with permission.

He claps me on the back.
She grabs my hand,
smiling weakly.
I hang back,
as they move slowly
to the bottom step.

Younger brothers
and sisters
cower silently
at the top
of the stairs.

Note. From *The Fallen World*, by Michael Moran, MD, 2008, Monterey, KY: Larkspur Press. Copyright 2008 by Michael Moran. Reprinted with permission.

3

STRUCTURAL ANALYSIS OF SOCIAL BEHAVIOR: THE ROSETTA STONE FOR INTERPERSONAL RECONSTRUCTIVE THERAPY CASE FORMULATION AND TREATMENT MODELS

Structural Analysis of Social Behavior (SASB) is a well-validated model for describing interpersonal and intrapsychic interactions in ways that are useful in the clinic as well as in research. Data are gathered by using the SASB-based Intrex questionnaires (Benjamin, 1995) to assess a rater's views of self and others (Benjamin, 2000) or by SASB coding that provides objective observer ratings of video of psychotherapy or other interpersonal situations of interest (Benjamin & Cushing, 2000). These SASB methods are theory neutral and have been used for assessing aspects of a variety of therapy approaches such as emotion-focused therapy (L. S. Greenberg, Ford, Alden, & Johnson, 1993), supportive–emotional (SE) therapy (Crits-Christoph, Connolly, & Shaffer, 1999), and psychoanalytic psychotherapy (Junkert-Tress, Schnierda, Hartkamp, Schmitz, & Tress, 2001). Barber and Crits-Christoph (1993) showed that SE therapy, which uses SASB to help describe core conflict relationship themes, is among the psychodynamic case formulation methods

http://dx.doi.org/10.1037/0000090-003
Interpersonal Reconstructive Therapy for Anger, Anxiety, and Depression: It's About Broken Hearts, Not Broken Brains, by L. S. Benjamin
Copyright © 2018 by the American Psychological Association. All rights reserved.

that have good interjudge reliability, internal consistency, and content, predictive, and concurrent validity. Reviews of a variety of other clinical and research uses by others of SASB appeared in Benjamin (1996b); Benjamin, Rothweiler, and Critchfield (2006); and in Constantino (2000).

Use of SASB-based concepts and data has been central to the creation and validation of the Interpersonal Reconstructive Therapy (IRT) case formulation and treatment models and the Natural Biology that supports them. A simple example of how SASB can be used to test theory appeared in Figure 2.2, where correlations between SASB ratings of behavior and standard ratings of anger, anxiety, and depression in a threatening situation showed distinctive patterns connecting these affects (A) and behaviors (B) as required by the Natural Biological concept of C1AB links discussed in Chapter 2. Some readers may not be comfortable with the level of detail and quantity of data in this chapter. They are invited to skip to Chapter 4, knowing that evidence is available here (and in selected places throughout this book) that uses SASB to validate concepts foundational to the IRT case formulation and treatment models.

SASB MODELS

Two versions of the SASB model respectively appear in Figures 3.2 and 3.3. Each is built on the 3 underlying dimensions that are pictured in Figure 3.1. They are (a) attentional focus, represented by the stick figures; (b) affiliation, represented on the horizontal axis in Figures 3.2 and 3.3 as well as in 3.1; and (c) interdependence, that is represented on all models by the vertical axes. The most complete SASB model appears in Figure 3.2 and is called the *full model*. Note that it has three planes that respectively represent (a) transitive focus on others (pictured in Figure 3.1 by the first stick figure), (b) intransitive focus on self (pictured by the second stick figure), and (c) transitive focus turned inward (called *introjection* and pictured by the third stick figure). For both models, the horizontal axis ranges from extreme hostility on the far left through zero to extreme friendliness on the far right. The vertical axis ranges from enmeshment (140, Manage, control or 240 Yield, submit, give in or 340 Control, manage self in Figure 3.2) at the bottom upward through zero to complete independence at the top (120 Endorse freedom or 220 Freely come and go or 320 Happy-go-lucky).

SASB-Based Dimensional Analysis of Interactions

An event, such as mother saying to her son in a matter-of-fact way, "You are stupid," is coded (i.e., dissected into the underlying dimensions) first by identifying the person to be coded, called X (mother), and then identifying

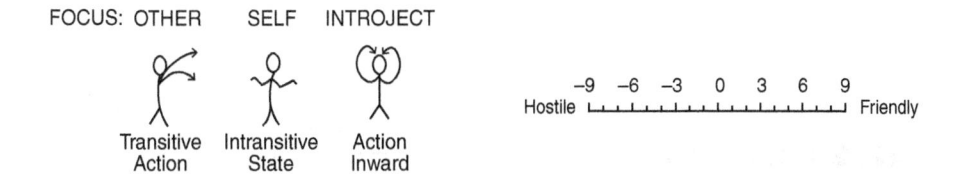

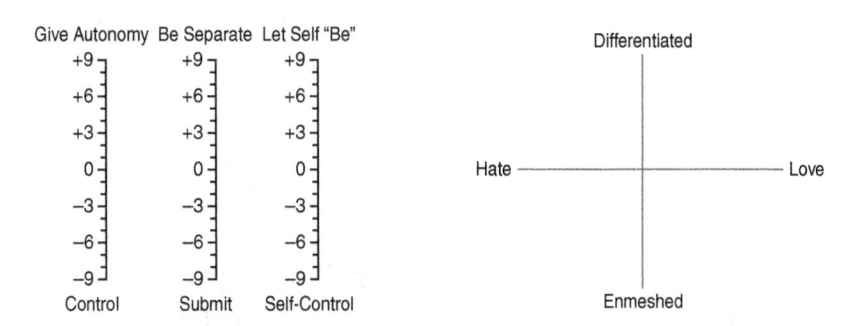

Figure 3.1. Dimensions of the SASB model. These are the basis of all SASB models, including those in Figures 3.2 and 3.3. Top left shows three types of attentional focus: transitive (on other), intransitive (on self), and introjected (on other directed inward). Top right shows the horizontal axis (affiliation) that ranges from extreme hostility to extreme friendliness. Lower left shows the vertical axis that ranges from interdependence (enmeshment) to independence (differentiation). Lower right shows that the horizontal and vertical axes combined define four quadrants. SASB = Structural Analysis of Social Behavior. Top left, top right, and lower left are from "Use of the SASB Dimensional Model to Develop Treatment Plans for Personality Disorders, I: Narcissism," by L. S. Benjamin, 1987, *Journal of Personality Disorders, 1* (p. 48). Copyright 1987 by Guilford Press. Reprinted with permission. Lower right is from "Structural Analysis of Differentiation Failure," by L. S. Benjamin, 1979, *Psychiatry: Interpersonal and Biological Processes, 42* (p. 5). Copyright 1979 by Taylor and Francis. Reprinted with permission.

the person with whom X is interacting, called Y (son). Three steps follow: First, determine X's focus ("You are stupid" is a transitive action directed toward Y). Next, identify X's affiliation (the remark clearly is hostile but not extreme; say, –3 units on the horizontal axis shown in Figure 3.1). Then identify interdependence (the statement is quite controlling; say, –6 units on the vertical axis in Figure 3.1).

Summing up, by the rules of plane geometry, "you are stupid" is coded at point (–3, –6) at about 6:35 o'clock on the top (transitive) plane of Figure 3.2. The name for the position is <u>136, Put down, act superior</u>. It is

INTERPERSONAL

OTHER

120 Endorse freedom
118 Encourage separate identity
Uncaringly let go 128
117 You can do it fine
Forget 127
116 Carefully, fairly consider
Ignore, pretend not there 126
115 Friendly listen
Neglect interests, needs 125
114 Show empathic understanding
Illogical initiation 124
113 Confirm as Ok as is
Abandon, leave in lurch 123
112 Stroke, soothe, calm
Starve, cut out 122
111 Warmly welcome
Angry, dismiss, reject 121
Annihilating attack 130 — **110 Tender sexuality**
Approach menacingly 131
141 Friendly invite
Rip off, drain 132
142 Provide for, nurture
Punish, take revenge 133
143 Protect, back up
Delude, divert, mislead 134
144 Sensible analysis
Accuse, blame 135
145 Constructive stimulate
Put down, act superior 136
146 Pamper, overindulge
Intrude, block, restrict 137
147 Benevolent monitor, remind
Enforce conformity 138
148 Specify what's best

Manage, control 140

SELF

220 Freely come and go
218 Own identity, standards
Go own separate way 228
217 Assert on own
Defy, do opposite 227
216 "Put cards on the table"
Busy with own thing 226
215 Openly disclose, reveal
Wall-off, nondisclose 225
214 Clearly express
Noncontingent reaction 224
213 Enthusiastic showing
Detach, weep alone 223
212 Relax, flow, enjoy
Refuse assistance, care 222
211 Joyful approach
Flee, escape, withdraw 221
Desperate protest 230 — **210 Ecstatic response**
Wary, fearful 231
241 Follow, maintain contact
Sacrifice greatly 232
242 Accept caregiving
Whine, defend, justify 233
243 Ask, trust, count on
Uncomprehending agree 234
244 Accept reason
Appease, scurry 235
245 Take in, learn from
Sulk, act put upon 236
246 Cling, depend
Apathetic compliance 237
247 Defer, overconform
Follow rules, proper 238
248 Submerge into role

Yield, submit, give in 240

INTRAPSYCHIC

Introject of
OTHER
to SELF

320 Happy-go-lucky
318 Let nature unfold
Drift with the moment 328
317 Let self do it, confident
Neglect options 327
316 Balanced self acceptance
Fantasize, dream 326
315 Explore, listen to inner self
Neglect own potential 325
314 Integrated, solid core
Undefined, unknown self 324
313 Pleased with self
Reckless 323
312 Stroke, soothe self
Ignore own basic needs 322
311 Entertain, enjoy self
Reject, dismiss self 321
Torture, annihilate self 330 — **310 Love, cherish self**
Menace to self 331
341 Seek best for self
Drain, overburden self 332
342 Nurture, restore self
Vengeful self punish 333
343 Protect self
Deceive, divert self 334
344 Examine, analyze self
Guilt, blame, bad self 335
345 Practice, become accomplished
Doubt, put self down 336
346 Self pamper, indulge
Restrain, hold back self 337
347 Benevolent eye on self
Force propriety 338
348 Force ideal identity

Control, manage self 340

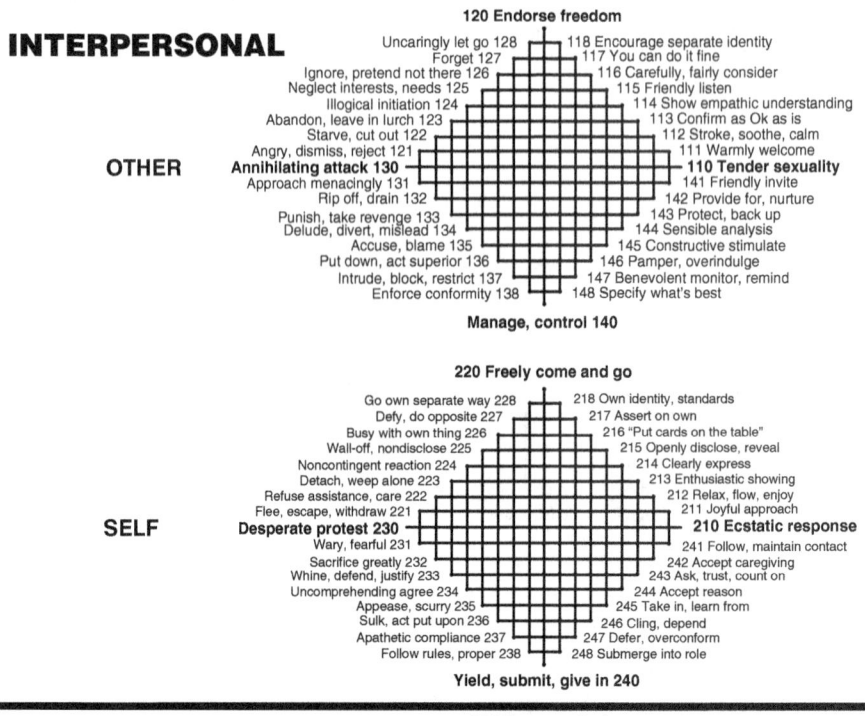

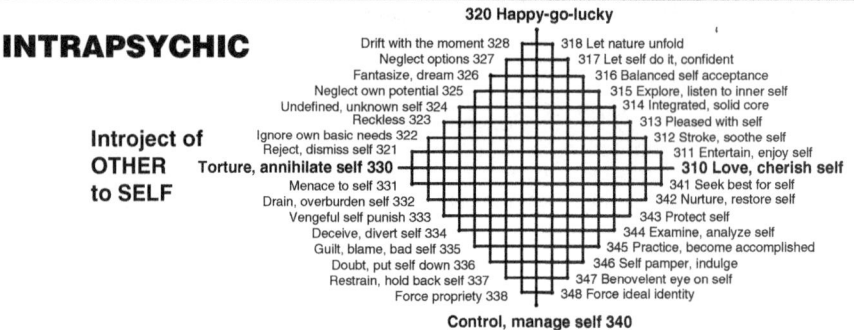

Figure 3.2. SASB full model. This is the most complex version of SASB, and it also provides the greatest degrees of resolution in describing interpersonal and intrapsychic events. SASB = Structural Analysis of Social Behavior. From "Structural Analysis of Differentiation Failure," by L. S. Benjamin, 1979, *Psychiatry: Interpersonal and Biological Processes, 42*, p. 6. Copyright 1979 by Taylor and Francis. Reprinted with permission.

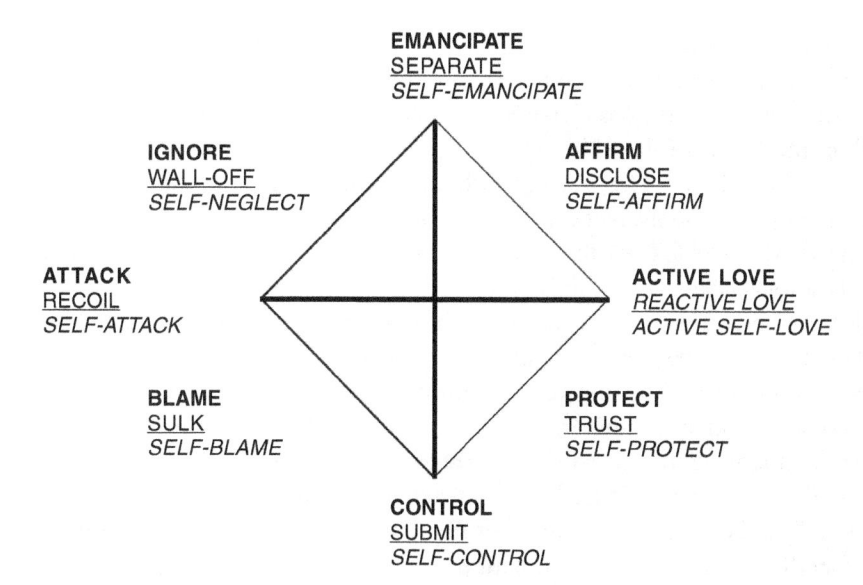

```
                    EMANCIPATE
                    SEPARATE
                    SELF-EMANCIPATE

    IGNORE                              AFFIRM
    WALL-OFF                            DISCLOSE
    SELF-NEGLECT                        SELF-AFFIRM


ATTACK                                          ACTIVE LOVE
RECOIL                                          REACTIVE LOVE
SELF-ATTACK                                     ACTIVE SELF-LOVE


    BLAME                               PROTECT
    SULK                                TRUST
    SELF-BLAME                          SELF-PROTECT

                    CONTROL
                    SUBMIT
                    SELF-CONTROL
```

Figure 3.3. SASB one-word model. The three planes in Figure 3.2 are represented here by three types of print: bold = transitive focus on other; underlined = intransitive focus on self; italics = introjection—transitive focus directed inward on the self. These points are ballpark summaries of events more exactly described by the full model in Figure 3.2. This simplest version is most convenient to use when describing an interpersonal event in text. From *Interpersonal Diagnosis and Treatment of Personality Disorders, Second Edition* (p. 55), by L. S. Benjamin, 1996, New York, NY: Guilford Press. Copyright 1996 by Guilford Press. Reprinted with permission.

transitive action that is moderately controlling and somewhat hostile. The number 136 indicates the event is on the first plane (1 = transitive) in the third Cartesian quadrant (Figure 3.1) and the sixth subdivision. These "codes" provide precise descriptions of interactions in terms of the underlying dimensions and make it easier to identify the predictive principles, discussed later.

Comparison of the Full and One-Word Models

The simplest version of the SASB model is the *one-word model*, shown in Figure 3.3. Events are coded by the same dimensional analysis, except the subdivisions on the axes are at larger intervals (labeled –2, –1, 0, +1, and +2 for the horizontal and vertical axes). Rather than representing focus by planes, focus appears in the one-word model as print font. bold = transitive focus; underlined = intransitive; italics transitive action turned inward (i.e., introjected). On this model, "You are stupid" is coded transitive (bold print), moderately hostile (–1), and moderately controlling (–1). The vector (–1, –1) on Figure 3.2 is located at 6:38 o'clock at the point labeled Blame. In this example, the full-model version of this event is <u>136 Put down, act superior</u> and conveys that there is more control than attack in the message compared to Blame, covering a broader area of possibilities and summing up with a name that implies control and hostility are present in equal measure.

The full model (associated with a long-form Intrex questionnaire) is best for fine-grained analysis of complex situations requiring maximal precision. The one-word model (associated with short or medium forms of the questionnaires) is best for quicker, "ballpark" analyses. Some situations require such fine-tuned distinctions; others do not. Naturally, the one-word SASB model is easier to use. The differences between the full and one-word versions might be illustrated by comparing the full model to determining the precise location of the plane with a compass and an altimeter, while the simpler judgments using the one-word model might be illustrated by naming locations according to a nearby city or other such landmark. The less exact judgments are easier to understand and often "good enough." On the other hand, there are situations where the more exact differentials (as in instrument landing during a fog) are important.

Measuring Relationships in Terms of SASB Models

In the observer coding system, interactions are dissected by dimension as described above to select a code or codes that best describe each interaction. In all questionnaires, items appear in a randomly determined order, and the rater gives each a score between 0 and 100 to describe aptness and frequency with which the item applies, with 50 marking the boundary between false and true. While writing items for the SASB Intrex questionnaires (and providing interpersonal detail needed for making objective observer codes), their structure was assessed by naive judges who rated them for the degree to which they reflected the underlying dimensions. Errors were corrected by revisions, and the new versions were tested with a new sample of judges. That process continued until judgments generated a reasonable facsimile of the models. More exacting comparisons of theory and data, including measures of angular placement and vector lengths, were provided in independent samples collected and analyzed by Rothweiler (2004). After the structure of items was confirmed by dimensional ratings, the SASB Intrex questionnaires and associated coding system were ready for clinical and research uses.

Gathering data using the real-time observer codes is more difficult but does reflect objective rather than subjective perspectives. Comparing them can be important. For example, Humes and Humphrey (1994) showed that adolescent females in family therapy rated their parents' interactions with them more accurately than did their parents. The objective codes also provide information about sequences that can have powerful causal implications. The SASB program Markov, explained clearly in Benjamin (1979b), can be used to describe sequential interactions with Family in the Head ("superego") and, for example, can demonstrate that current hostile interactions with attachment figures can be followed immediately by increased suicidal ideation (Benjamin, 1986). Skowron, Cipriano-Essel, Benjamin, Pincus, and Van Ryzin (2013) have used program Markov to show that maltreating mothers are calmer (feel safer) when their child is submissive while trying to complete a difficult task; by contrast, normal mothers are calmer when their child is appropriately engaged with the task on his/her own. That study provides compelling support for Bowlby's (1969, 1977) observation that parents who provide Secure Base conditions support autonomy as well as connectedness.

Whether the measure is by objective codes or by ratings on questionnaires, the data reflect interactions in specific relationships such as: *my spouse, me with my spouse, my son,* and *me with my son.* Questionnaire items can easily be used to assess different relationships in different states and times. For example, "Mom and me when she had a boyfriend" versus "Mom and me when she didn't have a boyfriend" was important for Jasmine, whose mother attended intensively to Jasmine when mother was getting another divorce, but mostly ignored her when mother was occupied with a new paramour. One result was that Jasmine as an adult was terrified to be "unpaired" and this seriously distorted the way she related to her partners. The Standard Series[1] usually provides a good overview of key relationships. It includes ratings of introject at best and worst; relationship with significant other at best and worst; relationship with mother when age 5 to 10; relationship with father when age 5 to 10; and mother with father and father with mother when age 5 to 10.

Informal (Subliminal) Uses of SASB Coding

"Informal" SASB codes, combined with principles from Natural Biology useful in sharpening clinicians' work with therapy process and content. For example, sometimes in therapy parents want to discuss their relationship with a child. Given there is no evidence the child is seriously disturbed and needs to be in his/her own treatment, simple discussions of the dimensions of Secure Base interactions can be very helpful to the parent and consequently the child.

Suppose a mother worries about a recent dustup with her 5-year-old son Sammy because he insisted on wearing a light jacket when going outside to play with a friend on a cold day. The therapist asked for a description of the event, and the mother offered: I said: "Jack's here and it's time for you to turn off that TV and get outside for some fresh air, so put on your big coat right now." Her message would be coded as **Control** on the one-word model

---

[1] The most frequently used SASB based assessment of self and relationships with key figures.

and 140 Manage, control on the full model. Sometimes it is necessary to use such raw control, but not usually under peaceful conditions. If he blew up in response to that, Sammy might be struggling with differentiation and resisting control as he explores having a separate self. Maybe the coat was the medium for Sammy's declaration of independence.

The therapist and mother might consider what would have happened if she said: "Jack is here and wants you to come out and play in the snow. Does that sound good?" An important part of that message (not the only) would be 116, Carefully, fairly consider (his separate wishes). If the son agrees, then mother would say: "You will need your big coat and mittens today because it's really cold outside, OK?" Here, mother offers 144, Sensible analysis, which is adjacent to 143, Protect, back up. If secure, Sammy is likely to respond with 244, Accept reason. But maybe he would have said, "I'd rather watch TV." In that, he asserts (216, "Put cards on the table"). Considering his perspective while holding firm with her support of peer play, mother might say, "I know. We can record the rest of that program so you can catch up with it later if you still decide to use today's (allotted) TV time that way. Right now, it could be lots of fun to play in the snow now with Jack." That would include the code 145, Constructive stimulate.

And the exchange would illustrate what Bowlby called the "dance between dependence and independence." That "conflict" is difficult to negotiate, even to understand. Without autonomy, self is compromised. Without control, self is undisciplined and asocial. Those patterns are shaped by many thousands of daily microinteractions such as this one. In this example, mother's dance is about "managing" the conflict between her son's independence via peer play versus passivity supported by TV watching. That simple exchange could go in many different directions, each one a version of the same struggle. Each should be guided by offering the child *Secure Base conditions*, defined as moderate amounts of control in support of developing autonomy. As always, context matters: Under extreme conditions, extreme parental behaviors (e.g., absolute control) can be required to provide safety and to facilitate development of a strong and sociable self.

Feeling the Structure of the SASB Models

If a clinician wants to build skill in recognizing patterns in the therapy process and content at the level of primitive brain, then repeated scanning of Tables 3.1 and 3.2 can help. Table 3.1 covers hostile autonomy on the left; its opposite, friendly enmeshment, is on the right. Table 3.2 covers hostile enmeshment on the left and its opposite, friendly autonomy, on the right (no shading). Developing the ability to sense/feel those four categories, friendly and hostile enmeshment or friendly or hostile differentiation, is a big step

TABLE 3.1
Relationships Among SASB Full Model Points: Degrees of Giving Autonomy

1 Track number	2 Transitive Hostile (T1S1)	3 Intransitive Hostile (T2S1)	4 Transitive Friendly (T1S3)	5 Intransitive Friendly (T2S3)	6 Track name
0	130 Annihilating attack	230 Desperate protest	110 Tender sexuality	210 Ecstatic response	Primitive Basics
1	121 Angry dismiss, reject	221 Flee, escape, withdraw	141 Friendly invite	241 Follow, maintain contact	Approach/Avoid
2	122 Starve, cut out	222 Refuse assistance, care	142 Provide for, nurture	242 Accept caregiving	Need Fulfillment
3	123 Abandon, leave in lurch	223 Detach, weep alone	143 Protect, back up	243 Ask, trust, count on	Attachment
4	124 Illogical initiation	224 Noncontingent reaction	144 Sensible analysis	244 Accept reason	Formal Logic, Communication
5	125 Neglect interests, needs	225 Wall-off, nondisclose	145 Constructive stimulate	245 Take in, learn from	Attention to Self-Development
6	126 Ignore, pretend not there	226 Busy with own thing	146 Pamper, over-indulge	246 Cling, depend	Balance in Relationship
7	127 Forget	227 Defy, do opposite	147 Benevolent monitor, remind	247 Defer, overconform	Intimacy–Distance
8	128 Uncaringly let go	228 Go own separate way	148 Specify what's best	248 Submerge into role	Identity
0	120 Endorse freedom	220 Freely come and go	140 Manage, control	240 Yield, submit, give in	Primitive Basics

Note. S = Step; SASB = Structural Analysis of Social Behavior; T = Trip. Complementary hostile points are in Columns 2 and 3; complementary friendly points are in Columns 4 and 5. Opposites are in Columns 2 and 4, and in Columns 3 and 5. The successive rows are arranged to show stepwise changes in Column 2 that reflect increasing degrees of giving autonomy. Tracks are numbered in the first column and their names are in the last column. This table is based on the SASB full model, which appears in Figure 3.2 and is described in Benjamin, L. S. (1979a). Structural analysis of differentiation failure. *Psychiatry: Interpersonal and Biological Processes, 42,* 1–23.

TABLE 3.2
Relationships Among SASB Full Model Points: Degrees of Control

1 Track number	2 Transitive Hostile (T1S4)	3 Intransitive Hostile (T2S4)	4 Transitive Friendly (T1S2)	5 Intransitive Friendly (T2S2)	6 Track name
0	140 Manage, control	240 Yield, submit, give in	120 Endorse freedom	220 Freely come and go	Primitive Basics
1	138 Enforce conformity	238 Follow rules, proper	118 Encourage separate identity	218 Own identity, standards	Identity
2	137 Intrude, block, restrict	237 Apathetic compliance	117 You can do it fine	217 Assert on own	Intimacy–Distance
3	136 Put down, act superior	236 Sulk, act put upon	116 Carefully, fairly consider	216 "Put cards on the table"	Balance in Relationship
4	135 Accuse, blame	235 Appease, scurry	115 Friendly listen	215 Openly disclose, reveal	Attention to Self-Development
5	134 Delude, divert, mislead	234 Uncomprehending agree	114 Show empathic understanding	214 Clearly express	Formal Logic, Communication
6	133 Punish, take revenge	233 Whine, defend, justify	113 Confirm as OK as is	213 Enthusiastic showing	Attachment
7	132 Rip off, drain	232 Sacrifice greatly	112 Stroke, soothe, calm	212 Relax, flow, enjoy	Need Fulfillment
8	131 Approach menacingly	231 Wary, fearful	111 Warmly welcome	211 Joyful approach	Approach/Avoidance
0	130 Annihilating attack	230 Desperate protest	110 Tender sexuality	210 Ecstatic response	Primitive Basics

Note. S = Step; SASB = Structural Analysis of Social Behavior; T = Trip. This table arranged exactly like Table 3.1 except that the successive rows in Column 2 are arranged to show stepwise changes from complete control to no control (and no giving of autonomy either). Again, complements are in Columns 2 and 3 in Columns 4 and 5. Opposites are in Columns 2 and 4 and in Columns 3 and 5. Antitheses are in Columns 2 and 5 and in Columns 3 and 4. This table is based on the SASB full model, which appears in Figure 3.2 and is described in Benjamin, L. S. (1979a). Structural analysis of differentiation failure. *Psychiatry: Interpersonal and Biological Processes, 42,* 1–23.

toward instantaneous recognition of patterns that matter. Armed with that skill, the clinician is less likely to miss differentiation failure, a problem that almost always is involved in one form or another in affective and some other disorders.

Another valuable exercise is to brush up on the meanings of *transitive* and "*intransitive*" by scanning and comparing columns with those headings. Early in the development of SASB, people complained that those grammatical words were "needlessly complex," and so the words *other* and *self* were used to distinguish transitive and intransitive focus. That works much of the time, but not always. For example, "You are the love of my life" might look like focus on other because of the word *you*, but the main message is about the speaker's state of being—that is, intransitive. In sum, the words *transitive* and *intransitive* are more precise than and preferable to *other* and *self*. Another advantage is that the words *transitive* and *intransitive* are not easily confused with the descriptions *I/me* or *he/she*.

A second useful exercise that contributes to intuitive use of the SASB model is to scan Figure 3.2, the full model, by starting at any point and progressing stepwise in either direction, continuing until returning to the starting point—that is, going full circle.[2] That same path can be followed with greater intensity by taking a round trip (going full circle) through the phrases in Tables 3.1 and 3.2. The trip through transitive items is marked by column labels T11, T12, T13, and T14 in Tables 3.1 and 3.2. T1 means Trip 1. The second digit is 1 or 2 or 3 or 4 and marks successive steps in T1. Trip 1 begins with full model point <u>130 Annihilating attack</u> in the first row of Table 3.1. Scan that column, and then find T12 for the second step. Continue through Steps T13 and T14, ending up at the starting point, <u>130 Annihilating attack</u> in Table 3.2, last row. Try to feel each step by imagining being in those positions in relation to important people you know. Repeat the process for Trip 2 (T2), which is about intransitive items.

PREDICTIVE PRINCIPLES

The SASB predictive principles of complementarity, similarity, introjection, opposition, and antithesis flow from the mathematical logic of the models. They link members of a pair by matching them in terms of the underlying dimensions of interpersonal space as defined by SASB.

---

[2]That round trip illustrates circumplex order, introduced to psychology by Guttman (1966), whose main point was to explain that factor analyses can use fewer numbers (i.e., scores on however many factors were extracted) to describe an individual. Items plotted within a 2-space defined by the first two factors would appear in a circle.

Complementarity

Complementarity happens when two people are matched on the affiliation and interdependence dimensions, with one person transitive and the other intransitive. For example, as Sammy agreed to go outdoors, he matched his mother's coordinates. His 244 Accept reason (+5, −4) matched her 144 Sensible analysis (+5, −4). Her transitive 116 Carefully, fairly consider (+3, +6) matched his intransitive 216 "Put cards on the table" (+3, +6). Complementarity works both ways: transitive to intransitive and intransitive to transitive, parent to child and child to parent, husband to wife and wife to husband. Going from transitive to intransitive seems familiar. If one person **Controls**, the other is likely to Submit. If one person **Ignores** another, the other will Wall-off.

Predicting from intransitive to transitive seems less obvious. Nonetheless, the reverse is true: If one Submits, others are more likely to **Control**. If one Walls-off, others will **Ignore** him/her. If a person walks fearfully (Recoil) through a dangerous neighborhood, he/she is more likely to be **Attacked** than if he/she walks confidently (Separate). Similarly, when Amy (Chapter 1) stopped appeasing family members, they gradually stopped abusing her.

The power of intransitive to draw transitive complementarity, like all other predictive principles, is adaptive in an evolutionary sense. It draws parents to infants as well as infants to parents. It also, as noted above, draws predators to victims; like sexuality, that principle is adaptive for the species but irrelevant or worse for an individual's survival. The prevalence of complementarity and the simplicity of its geometry tempt one to speculate about a mechanism for it. In Chapter 2, the idea of comparability to the inverse square law in physics was suggested.

Similarity

In contrast to the stability in complementarity, similar pairs (same focus, same location on affiliation and interdependence axes) can repel and make unstable matches, especially in the region of interdependence (lower half of Figure 3.2; Quadrants III and IV in Figure 3.1). Consider what happens when one dominant person interacts with another or what happens between two blamers, each certain they know what is right. How about between two submissive persons ("After you, Alphonse")?

Similarity in the region of hostile independence also is aversive but not so obvious. Similar members of a pair engaged in hostile autonomy may not notice each other, so repulsion is not detected. Similarity in the region of friendly independence likely is unstable because it is not easy to have both members of a dyad **Affirming** or Disclosing. On the other hand, the friendly independent pair is stable if they complement each other with one transitive and the other intransitive. For example, sometimes one **Affirms** the other <u>Discloses</u>. Then they exchange positions. Such time-dependent complementarity will keep them together even as they each have baseline positions of independence.

Introjection

Introjection is perhaps the most directly related to affective symptoms. It means treating yourself as you were treated by an attachment figure. If Dad **Blamed** you, *Self-blame* is likely. Joseph illustrated that. If your spouse **Affirms** you, *Affirming Self* is a likely result. Figure 4.2 (in Chapter 4) shows very clearly that parental transitive action directly parallels patterns in the introject. The introject, in turn, is very closely related to the threat affects: anger, anxiety, and depression.

Opposition

Opposites have the same focus but reverse the signs on the vertical and horizontal axes. That places them 180 degrees apart on the same plane. Columns 2 and 4 in Table 3.1 and Columns 3 and 5 in Table 3.2 describe opposites. Taking opposite positions can be useful in therapy when modeling or encouraging better options. A common example is for the therapist to listen (**Affirm**) rather than **Blame** or **Control**, which may be what the patient expects on the basis of his/her early history.

Antithesis

Finally, there is the principle of antithesis, which is the complement of the opposite. Antithetical points are different in every possible way. Antitheses are shown in Columns 2 and 5 of Table 3.1 and Columns 3 and 4 of Table 3.2. For example, the antithesis of <u>223 Detach, weep alone</u> is <u>143 Protect, back up</u>.

Julie's situation is an example of antithesis. She had a severely depressed mother who was virtually inaccessible to her (<u>Wall-off</u>). Julie tried to change Mother by taking care of her in every way possible (**Protect**, the antithesis of <u>Wall-off</u>), to no avail. She did the same with her children, explaining: "My children are not going to have to suffer because of an absentee mother as I did." Her antithetical indulgence and overprotection of her children unfortunately had its own unintended problematic effects on them because the greatest risk from overindulgence of children is narcissism and entitlement (i.e., introjected excessive self-love; inappropriate expectation of excessive submission and over-the-top nurturance).

Evidence-Based Tests of SASB Predictive Principles

Group means for complementary sets of eight-point profiles based on SASB Intrex short-form assessments of "father's transitive focus on me" and "my intransitive position with father" appear in Figure 3.4. The top panel is from a normal sample of 58 raters collected by C. Karpiak studying reliability of the SASB short form at an eastern U.S. university. It is important to know that the SASB Intrex short forms only use one item per model point. That is an extraordinarily demanding standard since most psychological tests use multiple items to assess a given concept. Yet comparable figures based on the SASB Intrex medium or long forms show the same patterns. The bottom panel is from 179 German patients (Mestel, 2012) with an *International Classification of Diseases* (ICD–10; World Health Organization, 2017) diagnosis of anankastic personality disorder (obsessive–compulsive personality disorder [OCPD] in the *Diagnostic and Statistical Manual of Mental Disorders* (fifth edition; American Psychiatric Association, 2013); chosen here because it describes Joseph, whose case is cited again in this chapter).

In the normal sample, eight-point parent transitive and rater intransitive profiles using the SASB short form appeared exactly as predicted by complementarity theory (rho = .91, p < .01). The behaviors rated with average scores of 50 or more, indicating they are "true," were **Affirm**, **Active Love**, and **Protect**. They are SASB model points that correspond to what Bowlby (1969) described as Secure Base conditions.[3] These conditions are complemented by Disclose, Reactive Love, and Trust in the normal sample. If the Secure Base conditions are introjected, they appear as *Self-Affirm*; *Active Self-Love*; and *Self-Protect*. All three of these Secure Base points are friendly, with moderate levels of independence and moderate levels of interdependence. As noted in Chapter 2, Secure Base is very important in sponsoring normal, adaptive behaviors and defining therapy goals.

In the patient sample shown in the lower part of Figure 3.4, as in many other patient samples, profiles peak with true ratings at fathers' transitive **Control**, rather than at **Protect**, as in normal samples. In addition, the profile for patients shown in Figure 3.4 is displaced in the friendly direction relative to fathers. Spearman's rho between fathers and patients in the figure was only .67 for the anankastic sample; it was even lower for some other disorders (such as rho = .37 for a histrionic group, also from the large German sample). This discrepancy always is in the direction of patients perceiving themselves as friendlier than their fathers; it is taken as evidence that supports the Natural Biological principle that the young reflexively attach to caregivers no matter what is offered.

---

[3]Also noted in Chapter 2, they are SASB codes of the behaviors of mother–child interactions that had been formally classified as Secure Base as defined by Bowlby (1969).

NORMAL RATERS N = 58

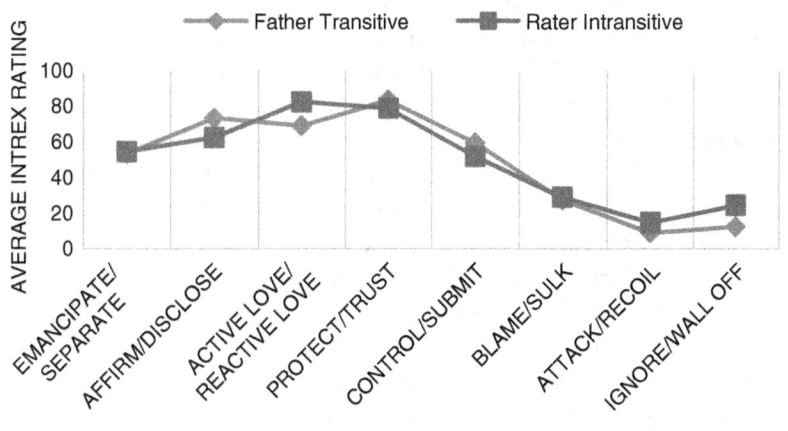

◆ Father Transitive ■ Rater Intransitive

ANAKASTIC PERSONALITY DISORDER N = 179

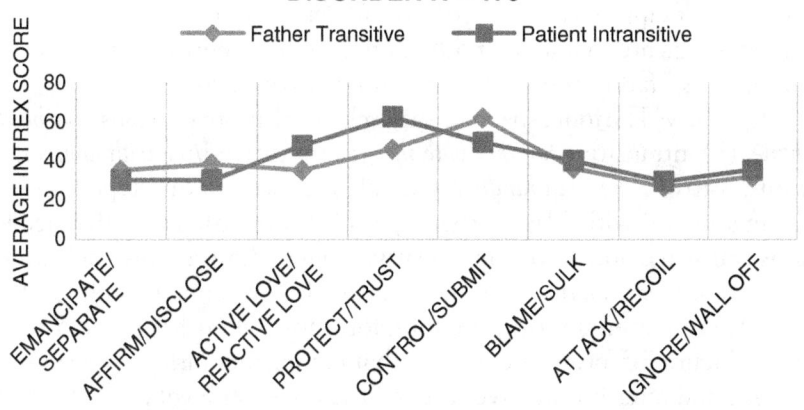

◆ Father Transitive ■ Patient Intransitive

Figure 3.4. Complementarity between fathers' transitive and patients' intransitive behaviors in normal (a) and patient (b) samples. In the normal sample, average ratings for fathers' transitive and raters' intransitive behaviors were closely matched, were very friendly, and supported autonomy; ratings for hostility were far below the *true* marker of 50. Profiles for anankastic (obsessive–compulsive personality disordered) patients and their fathers were markedly less friendly and more hostile than normal. Patients showed more attachment to their fathers than their fathers showed to them. That is another form of evidence that children attach, no matter what is offered.

Another method of testing the validity of predictive principles is to use canonical correlations between sets of eight points. That is illustrated here for complementarity using the total sample of 14,797 German patients from Mestel (2012). All Rao in the canonical correlations between parent and rater profiles were significant at $p < .000$. Principles of complementarity, similarity, and introjection (the most common connections) were tested, and each yielded $p < .000$, with all betas (weighting individual SASB model clusters) contributing to the prediction at $p < .000$. According to this and other methods, complementarity with father is the most powerful predictive principle (Rao $F = 520.438$); similarity was next (Rao $F = 192.152$) and introject was last (Rao $F = 41.505$). These relative frequencies likely are affected by interactions with other variables such as gender, psychiatric diagnosis, and culture.

With such large samples, highly significant results can be obtained even for weak effects. That means that no matter how powerful the effect, the reported trend does not represent all individuals in the sample. That is one reason reports of SASB studies are at the level of $N = 1$ whenever possible. A formal method for looking at predictive principles within individuals is to report selected Pearson rs among an individual's eight-point profiles. The parameter is called *within r*. If *within r* equals $\pm .71$ or more, the associated predictive principle is said to be present. *Within r* does not test "significance," but it does indicate that at least 50% of the variance between the two eight-point sets (e.g., father transitive, rater intransitive) is shared.

To review: The four aspects of each relationship are (a) transitive *him/her with me*, (b) intransitive *him/her with me*, (c) transitive *I/me with him/her*, and (d) intransitive *I/me with him/her*. Complementarity of one type is assessed by comparing (a) with (d); another type is (c) with (b). The difference is in who is transitive and who is intransitive. Figure 3.5 presents each *within r* for the *father with me/me with father* from the Wisconsin sample of 183 psychiatric inpatients rating the long form for "when I was age 5 to 10." Data in Figure 3.5 provide evidence that complementarity between father transitive and rater intransitive reached the criterion level of .71 for 51.9% of the patients. None met the criterion for antithesis. In the bottom panel, 36.7% of raters described similarity to father and 3.7% showed opposition.

Here, and in general, complementarity is the most common of the four predictive principles. It makes sense that complementarity would be the most common predictive principle, because by involving compatible matches on all three dimensions (affiliation, interdependence, and reciprocity of focus), it supports all features of attachment, which is foundational to primate adaptation. All other predictive principles involve one or more mismatches in underlying dimensionality. The weakest predictive principle is antithesis, and it involves discrepancy in every possible dimension (between planes, sign on affiliation axis, and sign on the interdependence axis). To

**Within r Complementarity (+) or Antithesis
(−) to Father transitive. Inpatient N = 183**

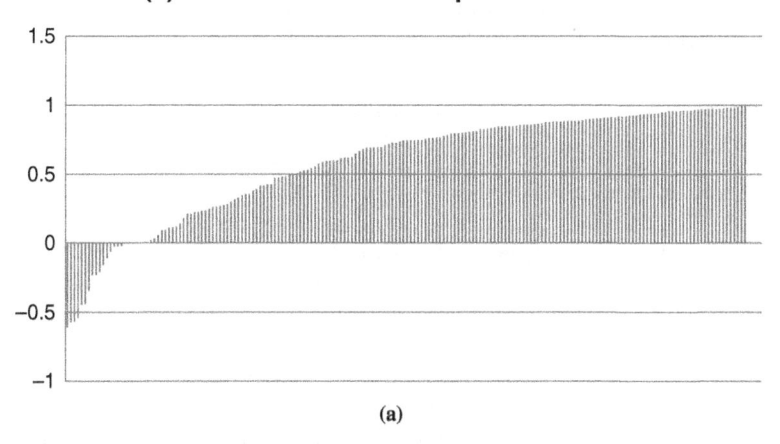

(a)

**Within r Similarity (+) or Opposition (−)
to Father transitive. Inpatient N = 183**

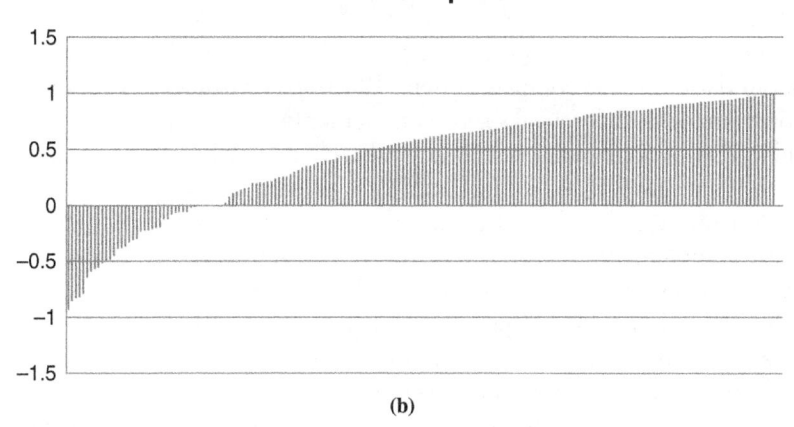

(b)

Figure 3.5. Testing for predictive principles by within-subject correlations for 183 inpatients. Data are from ratings on the SASB Intrex long form items that assess rater memory of the relationship with father when rater was age 5–10 years. Panel (a) assesses complementarity (right) and antithesis (left). Panel (b) tests similarity (right) and opposition (left). By this measure, (a) shows father–rater complementarity for 51.9% of the sample; only 2.7% showed antithesis. Similarity (b) met criterion for 36.7%, and 3.7% showed opposition. Here, and in general, complementarity is the most common and antithesis the least, and as explained in text, that is highly adaptive.

repeat: while complementarity supports attachment, antithesis opposes it in every way. Nature is successful in optimizing adaptive patterns of attachment.

Criticisms of SASB Predictive Principles

Long ago, I wrote an invited "target article" about SASB, followed by critiques from six colleagues (Benjamin, 1994). Some were highly supportive, some neutral, and some downright hostile. Widiger and Canyon (1994) implied that there are so many predictive principles, one is bound to turn up on a random basis. They wrote,

> A specific hypothesis regarding introjection might be refutable but not the SASB model from which the prediction was made because, if it isn't introjection, then it's complementarity; if it isn't complementarity, then it's imitative learning; and so forth. It would be helpful if Benjamin would specify what findings would occur for the model to be proved wrong. (p. 330)

The demonstration that follows shows that the predictive principles are confirmed in real databases but not in random ones. That contradicts the critics' hypothesis and proves it wrong. If the random distribution did "confirm" the predictive principles, that would prove the SASB model wrong. Here is the test: I created 14 samples of 1,000 "subjects" with means and standard deviations set to those for actual SASB data. Then I wrote the program CircumSteps to assess the predictive principles in actual data sets and in the random data sets and compared them. Illustrative results for 184 inpatients, reported in Figure 3.6, reveal strong complementarity in real data sets and none at all in the random data sets. Other predictive principles can be computed by this program simply by selecting data that represent the principle of interest.

For interested readers, here are the details of how the program works. To test complementarity, an 8 × 8 matrix of correlations between mother's transitive focus on the rater (on rows) and the raters' intransitive responses to mother (on columns) is compared to an 8 × 8 matrix of theoretical values that represent a perfect circumplex. If complementarity is perfect, the eight points on the diagonal (e.g., rater Disclose complements mother **Affirm**, rater Trust complements mother **Protect**, rater Sulk complements mother **Blame**) will average to 1. Circumplex order is tested by assessing whether all of the remaining correlations match predictions defined by a theoretical perfect circumplex matrix. If, for example, opposite points are matched (e.g., mother **Affirm**, rater Sulk; mother **Protect**, rater Wall-off; mother **Blame**, rater Disclose), the eight correlations should average to −1. And the average correlations at every step between exact matches (+1) and opposite matches (−1) will decrease or increase incrementally as prescribed by the perfect circumplex matrix.

The first line in Figure 3.6 presents the average r for the diagonal (exact match between mother transitive and rater intransitive) followed by average r

The 2 sets of 8 variables used in this analysis were:
C11(1) C11(2) C11(3) C11(4) C11(5) C11(6) C11(7)
C11(8) C14(1) C14(2) C14(3) C14(4) C14(5) C14(6)
C14(7) C14(8)

Obtained: Average r for 8 successive steps off the diagonal are:
  0.549   0.318   -0.023   -0.273   -0.461   -0.331   -0.066   0.288
Predicted: Successive values for a perfect circumplex matrix
  1.000   0.710   0.000   -0.710   -1.000   -0.710   0.000   0.710

Testing for circumplex order in the steps:
Product moment r between obtained & predicted values =   0.990
In 14 random samples of 1000 S each, Ave rho = .055, standard deviation = .335

Spearman rho between obtained & predicted values=   0.982
If rho = .643, then $p < .05$; If rho = .833, then $p < .01$
In 14 random samples of 1000 S each, Ave rho = .089 Standard deviation = .350

Figure 3.6. Testing for predictive principles embedded in circumplex order in a sample of 184 inpatients. The "Obtained" line presents the average *r* on the diagonal (exact match between mother transitive and rater intransitive) followed by average *r* at each successive step away from the diagonal until arriving at the diagonal again. The "Predicted" line presents the same information for the theoretical (perfect circumplex) model. Data and theory in these two lines are compared using nonparametric rho. Results show strong complementarity (rho = .98) that conforms to circumplex order. Random data do not replicate this result (rho = .09). Additional detail appears in text.

at each of seven successive steps away from the diagonal[4] until arriving at the diagonal again. The second line presents the same information for the theoretical (perfect circumplex) model. Data and theory in these two lines are compared using nonparametric rho. Results show strong complementarity (rho = .98) that conforms to circumplex order. Random data do not replicate this result (rho = .09).

Using an entirely different method to test copy processes (i.e., various predictive principles generalized from childhood to adult patterns[5]), Critchfield and Benjamin (2008) compared actual data to random scrambling of those same numbers. Copy processes: identification, complementarity, and

---

[4] Technical note: The data matrix, unlike the theoretical one, is not necessarily symmetric (e.g., data in cell for mother at Point 1, rater at Point 2 are not equal to mother at Point 2, rater at Point 1). That means that the process of comparing observed to perfect theoretical order has to be performed for Steps 1 to 7 from the diagonal within a fixed set of referents, such as mother transitive and rater intransitive.
[5] For example, mother transitive is compared with rater intransitive in this illustrative test of complementarity. A comparison of rater intransitive in relation to mother (in childhood) to rater intransitive with spouse (in adulthood) would test copy process recapitulation.

introjection appeared in inpatient, outpatient, and normal samples far more often than in the random scramble condition.

Finally, instead of using between-subjects correlations, as is conventional, that same strategy was applied to within-individual correlations. Again, the copy processes emerged significantly more often in real data sets compared to randomly scrambled sets (Critchfield & Benjamin, 2010).

These peer-reviewed studies could have disconfirmed the predictive principles and copy processes by finding evidence that they "exist" in random data sets or in real data sets scrambled to random order. To the contrary, the predicted order was never seen under the random conditions and always was seen in the real data sets. The predictive principles are not artifacts of faulty reasoning or methods. The unfounded, dismissive opinion about base rates for SASB predictive principles that appeared in an edited, peer-reviewed journal was unwarranted.

Another criticism of the SASB model is that factor analytic reconstructions of the model often assume the shape of an ellipse rather than a circle. That is true. The affiliation axis is longer than the interdependence axis in data sets provided by raters describing themselves and others. Ellipses also are generated by factor analysis of items that assess rater self-descriptions in terms of models of affect (examples appear in Park, 2005). An informative in-depth analysis of this and other issues was completed by Rothweiler (2004). Rather than indicating that the SASB model or the affect models are flawed, the result likely means that affiliation, whether in relation to behavior or affects, carries more variance than does the vertical axis assessed by the second factor.[6] The orbit of the earth, also expected to be a circle, turned out to be elliptical as predicted by Newton's inverse square law that provides (basically) that attraction varies as the inverse of the square of the distance between them. Quite possibly attachment is the same: The greater the affiliation, the greater the attraction, meaning the attachment axis will carry more variance than the interdependence axis, resulting in an ellipse.

Then there is the criticism that SASB is too complex (e.g., Benjamin, 1994, p. 319) and "unorthodox" (p. 320). If science must be orthodox, there is little chance for growth. If SASB is needlessly complex, the criticism is valid. But if the fine resolution in Figure 3.2 and the nature and relevance of supporting evidence and the clinical applications are sound, the complaint of needless complexity is not valid. Every time I hear it, I wonder how many physics or chemistry students or professors would complain that a theory is "too complex" and have that be accepted as a valid criticism regardless of supporting evidence.

---

[6]Results for SASB and also for affect models suggest a rotation off the horizontal. For SASB, the tilt may be secondary to joint influence of the two developmental goals mentioned in Chapter 2: attachment (intense levels) and autonomy taking (moderate levels).

The SASB model is reliable and has substantial validity (Benjamin et al., 2006), and yet it is radically simple relative to the full range of situations to which it can be applied. For example, ultimate complexity is posed by what Bateson, Jackson, Haley, and Weakland (1956) described as a "double bind." SASB codes can describe that (Humphrey & Benjamin, 1986) in ways that correspond well to what originators claimed it was and that make sense to experienced clinicians, especially family therapists. Complex coding also can help describe and understand mechanisms of "brain washing" portrayed in *The Manchurian Candidate* (Axelrod & Frankenheimer, 1962), Patty Hearst's kidnapping and "conversion" in 1974–1975, and in Shakespeare's (1988) *Taming of the Shrew*. This version of brainwashing is formally known as the *Stockholm syndrome* (Gale Encyclopedia of Medicine, 2008).

USE OF SASB TO TEST MAJOR FEATURES OF IRT CASE FORMULATION AND TREATMENT MODELS

This section focuses on uses of SASB to test major attributes of the IRT case formulations that guide every treatment intervention.

Secure Base as Normal and Therapy Goal Behavior

The idea that secure attachment is described by high ratings in the region described by SASB as **Affirm**/Disclose, **Active Love**/Reactive Love, and **Protect**/Trust has been confirmed for adults by others (Pincus, Dickinson, Schut, Castonguay, & Bedics, 1999) as well as for mothers and toddlers (Teti, Heaton, Benjamin, & Gelfand, 1995). Pincus et al. (1999) wrote, "The addition of interpersonal descriptors to the assessment of global attachment constructs adds precision to the description of 'internal working models,' increasing sophistication of attachment concepts for relational diagnosis and assessment" (p. 206). In IRT, Secure Base as described by SASB defines *normal*, and it is the therapy goal. That positive description of goal behavior guides therapists in the effort to build adaptive affects and behaviors more than focusing on symptom reduction that, in effect, defines normal as not "not normal."

Function of Anger, Anxiety, and Depression

Anger, anxiety, and depression have predetermined functions within C1AB links. Again, C1 = primitive brain perception of threat or safety; A = affect triggered by that perception; and B = behavioral patterns predisposed by that affect. Anger has the function of coping actively with threat by moderating control or distance. Anxiety mobilizes efforts to cope with threat that may resolve in any direction: fight, flight, or surrender. And depression is an adaptation of last resort, reducing threat value by giving in and/or withdrawal. That interpretation was discussed in Chapter 2.

Supporting evidence based on SASB was provided in Figure 2.2. All three threat affects were highly correlated with interpersonal distancing. Anger also was correlated with control. Depression inhibited friendliness and self-definition. The magnitudes of correlations between anxiety and various interpersonal behaviors supported the hypothesis that it is activated when the individual is "in between" anger and depression—conflicted about whether to downplay self, withdraw, hide (depression), or fight (anger) to prevail or repel/escape. Figure 3.8, to be discussed below, suggests that connections between patterns with attachment figures and threat symptoms can be affected by culture.

Threat, Symptoms (Disorders), and Autoimmune Disorders

If an attachment figure naturally is taken as safe haven by mechanisms discussed in Chapter 2 but actually is a threat, then the child is exposed to chronic threat by virtue of frequent contact. In addition, attachment to an abusive figure involves automatic learning in the primitive brain that records maladaptive details such as "Beatings are common and must be accepted without protest;" and/or "Betray your mother and your religion and be my sexual partner;" and/or "I am condemned to eternal suffering." Such attachments to a threatening figure, in effect, provide the basis for a form of autoimmune disorder. Normal defenses against threat are turned against the self, sometimes with deadly results.

The central role of perceived threat from caregivers is underscored by data in Figure 3.7 that link number of disorders to perceptions of threat and safety in relation to attachment figures. The dependent variable is the number of ICD–10 diagnosed disorders in the HELIOS Klinik database recorded as F3 or F4 disorder, excluding F3 bipolar disorder and F4 general personality disorders.[7] The sample therefore included five disorders: F3 depression; F4 anxiety; F4 post-traumatic disorder; F4 somaticizing disorder; or F4 eating disorder. Greater comorbidity is taken as a measure of severity of disturbance. At the clinic, staff were instructed routinely to make as many diagnoses as

---

[7]Bipolar and personality disorders were excluded from this F3 and F4 collection because they often are considered to be based on unique mechanisms. IRT theory is not consistent with that, but that view was used for this particular analysis to be more in line with contemporary beliefs. Further analyses including these and other diagnoses will be included in subsequent analyses and reported elsewhere (e.g., Benjamin, Critchfield, & Mestel, 2017).

**COMORBIDITY AND PERCEIVED
THREAT AND SAFETY WITH PARENTS**

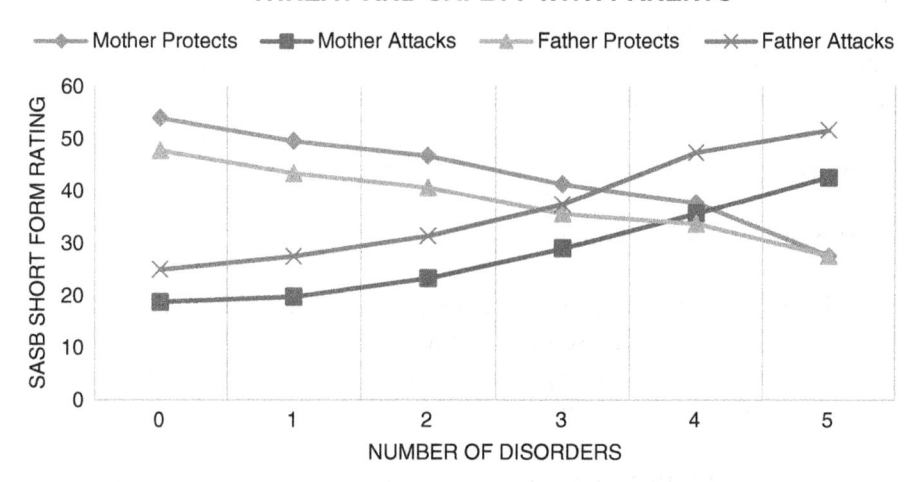

Figure 3.7. Paternal and maternal safety and threat ratings on SASB Intrex short form items for 14,829 German patients. Comorbidity (horizontal axis) increases with higher parental **Attack** ratings and decreases with higher **Protect** ratings of parents. Fathers are rated higher on **Attack** and mothers are rated higher on **Protect**. SASB = Structural Analysis of Social Behavior.

could be identified. Diagnoses are not up to German standards for "research quality" (personal communication, Robert Mestel, 2012), but the frequency of comorbid diagnoses suggests that in the matter of thoroughness, they represent the best of clinical standards for diagnosis. The intent to cover all possible issues is underscored by the fact that patients also were diagnosed by the European Operationalized Psychodynamic Diagnosis (OPD) diagnostic system. According to the OPD system manual, "seven reliability studies [of OPD] have been conducted in the German-speaking countries with scale kappas lying between .50 and .70. These values are as robust as those of any of the ICD–10 categories" (OPD Working Group, 2001, p. xi).

The independent variable in Figure 3.7, perceived threat from an attachment figure, was assessed by scores on a SASB short-form item describing **Attack**: "Without thought about what might happen, father (or mother) wildly, hatefully, destructively attacked me." Perceived safety was measured by SASB version 1 shortform item **Protect**: "With much kindness, father (or mother) taught, protected, and took care of me." The dependent variable is the percentage of patients who rated these items at 50 or more, meaning "true."

Results from 14,829 patients are simple and clear: Inspection of the figure shows (a) as the average ratings for **Attack** increase, so does the number of disorders per individual; and (b) as average ratings for **Protect** increase, the number of disorders per individual decreases. Perceived threat from attachment figures is powerfully associated with number of affective disorders, while perceived **Protection** (a Secure Base condition) is a buffer. More fathers were rated true (50 or more) for the **Attack** item, while more mothers were rated true for **Protect**. This theme of a direct connection between perceived threat from attachment figures and affective symptoms will be developed in depth in Benjamin, Critchfield, and Mestel (2017).

Impact of Culture on Symptoms

Different cultures have different definitions of what to fear and how to be safe. That reality has sometimes brought controversy and confusion to efforts to develop diagnostic systems. An example might be how to diagnose obsessive compulsive personality disorder when a person has been raised in a culture that places high value on compliance, control, and perfection above all else. If such a pattern is an ideal in the culture, should it be diagnosed?

SASB-based data suggest that cultural differences in interpersonal patterns do exist. Florsheim, Tolan, and Gorman-Smith (1996) used SASB to identify cultural differences in practices regarding letting adolescent sons go out in Chicago in the evenings. According to IRT theory, cultural norms likely are affected by lessons from caregivers who practice them. Cultural patterns, just like familial patterns, are "diagnosable" targets of treatment if they interfere with rather than support Secure Base and therefore are associated with symptoms. For example, Joseph (Chapter 2) "overdid" his allegiance to his cultural value to be considerate of the needs of others. He felt he was without recourse and defeated because he was so completely devoted to his impossible safety plan of anticipating and addressing needs of coworkers and friends as well as family before they knew they had them. His cultural value of consideration of others could support Secure Base behavior, but Joseph's interpretation of that norm was maladaptive and supported pathology.

Figure 3.8 offers data that show culture can affect symptoms. The figure compares two samples of inpatients at university hospitals, each group having interpersonal patterns assessed by SASB and symptoms assessed by the Symptom Checklist—90—Revised (Derogatis, 1994). One culture (Mountain West, Figure 3.8a) was politically conservative, and the other culture (northern Midwest, Figure 3.8b) was heterogeneous politically and ranked very high in the nation in levels of alcoholism, likely facilitated by the unabashed popularity of "partying."[8] The profiles have similar patterns, but

---

[8]Data for the Mountain West are from T. L. Smith (2002), and those from the northern Midwest are from the Wisconsin database described in Chapter 2.

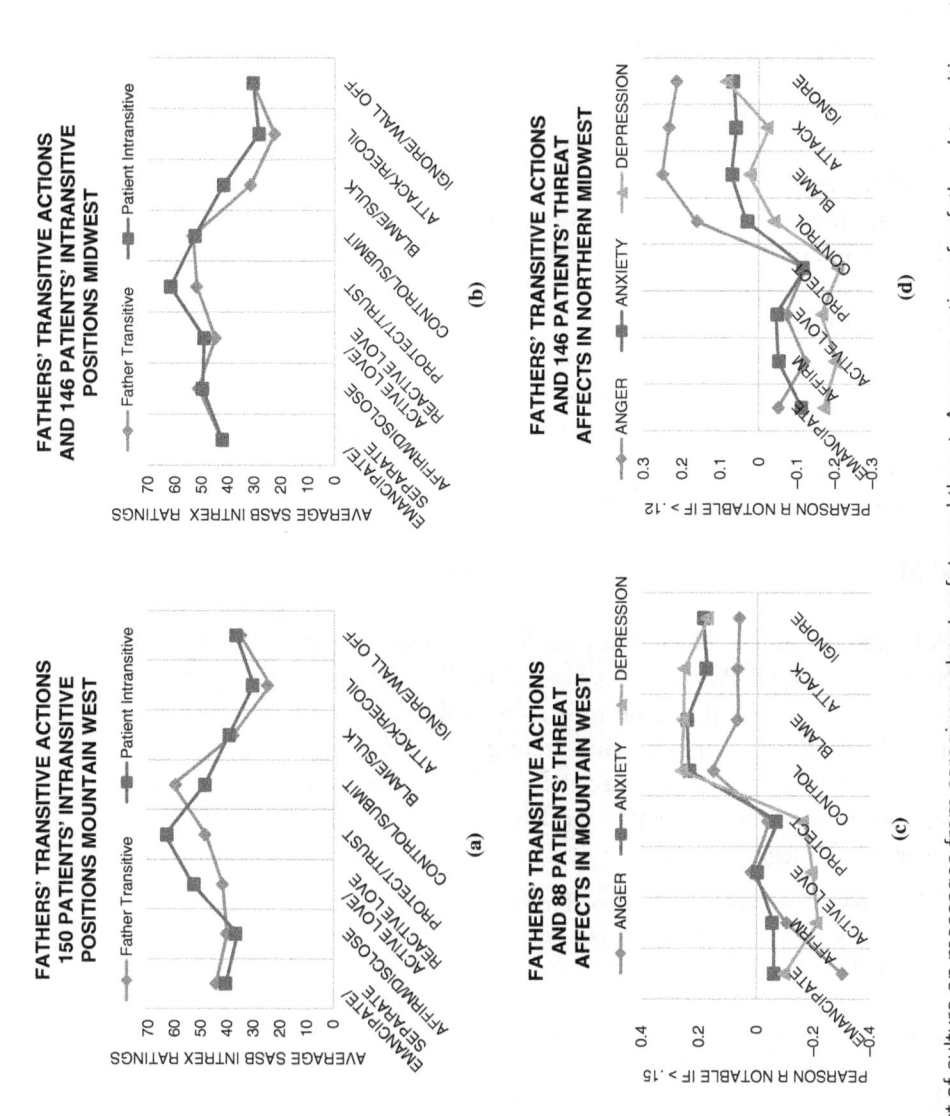

Figure 3.8. Impact of culture on messages from caregivers about safety and threat. Average ratings for fathers' transitive actions were similar in these two patient samples. The largest endorsements were for **Control** (a, b), with the trend more distinctive in the conservative (Mountain West) culture. Correlations between perceived paternal behavior and threat affects (c, d) were noticeably different in the two cultures. In the conservative culture, anger was likely to be punished and compliance with rules greatly rewarded. That could inhibit copying anger and account for the differences shown in (c) and (d): Paternal hostility was powerfully related to patient anger in the northern Midwest (d) but not at all in the conservative culture, where the largest correlation with paternal hostility was with depression (c).

fathers in the Mountain West (conservative) culture showed markedly more **Control** (60) than fathers in the northern Midwest culture (50).

Correlations between fathers' transitive behaviors and patients' levels of anger, anxiety, and depression were affected by culture, too. In the northern Midwest, hostility from fathers appears to have been copied by their children who became patients as adults. Identification with the aggressor may be experienced as a way to be safe in a culture that is relatively tolerant of such behavior but not in a culture that punishes anger. In fact, in the section of the Mountain West from which these data were gathered, overt hostility does violate a strong norm. Even differences of opinion are considered by some to be hostile and highly undesirable. In this setting, paternal hostility was correlated with anxiety and depression rather than with anger.

A reasonable guess that accounts for these particular cultural differences in the impact of patriarchal anger is that children are likely to be punished for anger but given support and medication for depression and anxiety. Gender also affects expression of affects and related behaviors. More complete understanding of cultural impact on affects is important and requires additional study, starting with clinical interviews and surveys that assess family reactions to expressions of affects and relating that to symptoms, if present.

Formal Models Linking Affects, Behaviors, and Cognition

A formal model for affect that parallels behavior (Structural Analysis of Affective Behavior [SAAB]) was proposed in Benjamin (2003b, appendix to Chapter 4). Using dimensional ratings as well as factor analytic reconstructions, Park (2005) explored the circumplex structure of two versions of the proposed affect model and assessed parallelism between them and the SASB (behavioral model) as well as models proposed by Russell (1980) and by Watson and Tellegen (1985). Park concluded,

> All models produced reasonably good to very good circumplex structure, particularly when ratings of self-reported affect in factor analyses were evaluated. There was strong support for the idea of parallelism between affect and behavior as all models evidenced rather good correspondence between affective states and social behaviors, point for point. This was true not only for the SAAB models that were developed specifically with the goal of parallelism in mind, but also with the extant affect models, which have historically been used to simply describe basic emotions that one might experience in everyday life. Correlations with measures of psychiatric symptoms indicated that the SAAB models were better able to predict relationships with symptoms of depression, anxiety, and anger than when using the extant models, suggesting that the SAAB models may be more useful clinically. (p. 5418)

Internalized Representations as Affect Regulators

Most of the SASB-based data presented in this book rely on the idea that raters' scores reflect their perceptions and memories of their relationships with attachment figures. These perceptions are related to symptoms because perceptions, more than "reality," drive affective and behavioral responses. The mechanism that connects interactions with attachment figures to affect regulation, as described in Chapter 2, is that children copy attachment figures under perceived conditions related to safety and threat. If parents offer Secure Base conditions, the child copies adaptive rules for safety and threat. Also noted in Chapter 2, there are brain circuits that record representations of objects, including living objects, and these circuits do have direct connections to affect regulators such as the hypothalamic–pituitary–adrenal axis. The circuits representing caregivers—that is, Family in the Head—also can reactivate the original scene with all of its perceptual (C1), affective (A), and behavioral (B) components. In effect, the internalized representations of attachment figures, first described by Bowlby (1969, 1977) as internal working models, are affect regulators.

If family provide working models, it is important to know whether patient perceptions of family interactions are accurate. Humes and Humphrey (1994) cited earlier, reported that objective observer SASB codes for interactions involving an identified adolescent patient during a family conference agreed more with the patient's ratings than with the parental ratings. An ideal way of exploring the accuracy of perceived patterns would be to generate SASB codes by observers of videos of parent–child interactions taken at regular intervals from birth to adulthood and compare them with ratings generated by family members. If the SASB emotion scales (Park, 2005) were fully validated, self-ratings with them could be included. Because SASB Intrex short- and medium-form items are at the sixth-grade reading level, by the time the child reaches that age, the child's perspectives could be added to the database. Comparing and contrasting these various perspectives at different times could identify misperceptions when and if they occur. That surely would have useful implications about with whom and how to intervene in family work.

Gifts of Love

In contrast to the several cited examples of research on the validity of copy processes, there is not much research that directly confirms the validity of GOLs. The concept centers on subjective goals that inspire adaptive and maladaptive C1AB links. Nonetheless, a creative and informative assessment of GOL activity was provided in a series of five carefully done experiments by Sohlberg and Birgegård (2003) and Sohlberg, Claesson, and Birgegård (2003). These investigators showed that a tachistoscopic flash "Mommy and I are one" could increase symptoms of depression, whereas the control condition, a flash of "People are walking," did not. Several measures of similarity between subjects and their mothers were used related to depression.

The role of SASB Intrex was to define the perception of mother during childhood under the heading of "relational schemas" that regulate affect and behavior (Sohlberg & Birgegård, 2003, p. 303). That would correspond directly to "Family in the Head." Findings were complex, but results with SASB were simple and consistent with the idea that activated Family in the Head (e.g., mother) can activate related (e.g., threat) affects. For the "Mommy and I are one" condition, the investigators reported, "higher correlations were found also between SASB Intrex . . . ratings of their mothers . . . and depression. In one case, the difference between groups was significant at $p < .05$" (Sohlberg & Birgegård, 2003, p. 305). In the groups exposed to the "Mommy and I are one" flash, the correlations were large for **Mother Blame** and moderately large for **Mother Ignore**, and that result did not obtain in the control group (Sohlberg & Birgegård, 2003, Table 1, p. 206). "With respect to memories of how mother acted (SASB), Table 1 shows that in two out of three cases, variables had more variance in common when correlations were computed in the experimental group than in the control group." This result was not significant, but the effect size was "moderate." In other words, when reminded subliminally of closeness to Mommy, individuals with internalization of a hostile mommy got more depressed. These effects persisted for at least 10 days. Sohlberg was so alarmed by the power of the effect that he and Birgegård stopped doing the research.

Their results are not surprising. The tachistoscopic flash was a subconscious activator of the relationship with mother, which if threatening, led to depression. This is consistent with the idea that symptoms can be increased as a person experiences a primitive brain reminder of his/her relationship with a hostile attachment figure, activating the automatic "loyalty" to the maladaptive rules and values of that figure. Acting on that reminder is supported by a pathogenic GOL, a sense of closeness to and safety in relation to that figure.

McCarty (1997) did a study of marital conflict that yielded findings that confirm the construct of GOLs in current attachment relationships. She performed sequential analyses of SASB codes[9] of marital interactions during a videotaped discussion of a conflict. Sequential analyses showed that wives classified as dissatisfied in the marriage mostly got friendly responses (consequences) from their husbands if they showed hostile submission (antecedent).

---

[9]She used the SASB software program Markov.

In short, resentful surrender (Sulk) was wives' route to **Affirm**ation and love from husbands. This suggests that a specific maladaptive behavior in the wife can be "rewarded" by loving behavior in the husband during a conflict. That is the paradigm for maladaptive GOLs: One complies with what is rewarded by love and affection from an attachment figure, whether or not it reflects Secure Base.

ADDITIONAL SASB-BASED DISSERTATION STUDIES OF PSYCHOPATHOLOGY AND TREATMENT

There are several other SASB dissertations by students who worked directly with me during my brief years as a dissertation advisor in academia after leaving the Department of Psychiatry at the University of Madison–Wisconsin and before returning to clinical work in a medical center in Utah. Here are examples: a study of the reliability and validity of SASB (Rothweiler, 2004), a parallel affect model (Park, 2005), and applications of SASB methods to studies of

- personality disorder (T. L. Smith, 2002),
- alcohol abuse (Moore, 1998),
- impacts of child sexual abuse (Schloredt, 1997),
- pedophilia (Strand, 1996),
- substance abuse (Sandor, 1996),
- marital conflict (McGonigle, 1994),
- Internet-based training about IRT case formulations (Davis, 2012),
- cross-generational factors in cocaine abuse (Cushing, 2003),
- performance anxiety in athletes (Conroy & Benjamin, 2001), and
- the impact of therapist affirmation (Karpiak & Benjamin, 2004).

Hopefully, in the next few years, I will be able to support the authors in submitting the unpublished SASB projects for publication.

II

THE CASE FORMULATION AND TREATMENT MODELS

II

4

THE INTERPERSONAL RECONSTRUCTIVE THERAPY CASE FORMULATION MODEL

The Interpersonal Reconstructive Therapy (IRT) case formulation and treatment models are grounded in the Natural Biology described in Chapter 2. That means the models are consistent with Darwin's theory of evolution and other well-established principles from the life sciences. Briefly, the IRT case formulation model identifies attachment-based psychosocial forces that account for much of the variance in affective psychopathology. The IRT treatment model helps the clinician address mechanisms that support attachment-related affective psychopathology in order to promote change during psychotherapy. Clinicians and researchers who understand the principles based in Natural Biology will be better able to use the IRT models in an adherent way, and adherence improves outcome (Chapter 10). Here is a brief summary of principles from Natural Biology that are central to clinical practice using IRT. This review is followed by application of the principles to the case of Pauline.

---

http://dx.doi.org/10.1037/0000090-004
Interpersonal Reconstructive Therapy for Anger, Anxiety, and Depression: It's About Broken Hearts, Not Broken Brains, by L. S. Benjamin
Copyright © 2018 by the American Psychological Association. All rights reserved.

HIGHLIGHTS OF NATURAL BIOLOGY

The natural mechanisms that ensure that the threat affects anger, anxiety, and depression assist adaptation were reviewed at length in Chapter 2 along with supporting logic and evidence. The Natural Biological principles apply to safety-related affects as well, but they only are mentioned briefly in this book. This section provides a brief review of the Natural Biological mechanisms of affective psychopathology and is followed by Pauline's story, a detailed example of an IRT case formulation.

The adaptive purposes of threat affects are as follows: Anger has the function of getting control of a threat or getting distance from it. Anxiety has the function of keeping the individual mobilized until he/she finds a solution to a threat. Depression is a defense of last resort and can sometime defend against the threat by withdrawing (retreating or hiding) or otherwise reducing one's threat value.

Affects related to threat and safety are managed by the subcortical "primitive brain" and the mechanisms of their adaptive functions are best understood by viewing them in the context of sequential links labeled C1AB. "C1" represents primitive brain (subcortical) apprehension of conditions of threat (or safety). A represents affects naturally released in response to primitive brain perceptions of threat (or safety); the threat affects include anger, anxiety, and depression (safety affects include feeling peaceful, relaxed, safe, and humorous). "B" represents adaptive behaviors that have been predisposed by the affects. Under threat, they include fight, flight, hide, or camouflage (when safe, examples of B include rest, relaxation, pleasure, curiosity, peacefulness, creativity). Threat-related C1AB links are supported by release of cortisol, epinephrine, and norepinephrine (safety-related C1AB links are supported by availability of serotonin, dopamine, oxytocin, and opioids).

The sympathetic nervous system (SNS) is a major component of the threat system, while the parasympathetic nervous system (PNS) is a major component of the safety system. In general, and for good adaptive reasons, they oppose one another. It is not, for example, easy to be creative (PNS) while under threat (SNS). Together with the enteric nervous system (ENS) that is in charge of obtaining and processing energy, the SNS and the PNS comprise[1] the autonomic nervous system (ANS). The ANS is the subcortical engine that runs constantly, managing the fundamental challenges (cope with threat and safety, find and process energy) of staying alive.

The primitive brain C1AB links connect directly to C2, the cortical, higher brain that integrates, coordinates, and decides. The threat system has

---

[1] As noted in Chapter 2, a more recent view does not include the ENS in the ANS.

more direct connections to the cortical brain and can trump higher level function when danger is detected.[2] Primitive circuitry for safety is less direct and less powerful, but not less important. The cuing of the SNS and PNS so that threat and safety can be recognized and managed is accomplished mostly by primitive brain lessons from interactions with early attachment figures.

C1AB sequences are installed simply by copying the C1AB sequences modeled by attachment figures under conditions involving threat or safety. Children (and adults sharing conditions of severe threat) absorb the whole picture: the threat; the affect of the proximal attachment figure; and what to do about it. The basic forms of copying are identification, recapitulation, and introjection. If the lessons in safety and threat are adaptive, the individual's affective expressions support Secure Base C1AB links. They are called *Green*, define normal, and are the goal of reconstructive therapy. Pathology is cued up by maladaptive lessons in safety and threat, and the resulting C1AB links are called *Red*. This means that pathological forms of anger, anxiety, and depression are miscued attempts to adapt that are based on dysfunctional lessons in safety and threat. Patients almost always prefer the terms *Red* and *Green* to *maladaptive* and *adaptive* when describing their recent states.

Adaptive and maladaptive C1AB links in the primitive brain are represented in the higher, cortical brain (C2) along with specific attributes of the attachment figures who provided lessons in safety and threat. The representations are so complete that it is reasonable to call these internalized representations of attachment figures "*Family in the Head.*" They are the affect regulators. The early, potent, and lasting primitive brain shaping is via an especially powerful form of associative learning, explored in laboratory studies of adults by Reber (1989). In children, it requires proximity, frequency, and gentle ventral contact with a familiar figure (Harlow, 1958). In adults, it requires perception of intense threat or intense connectedness. Responsiveness of the attachment figure is important, too, but this form of associative learning does not depend on adaptive function or whether the attachment figure is "nice."

The rule is stunningly simple: "See as they do, feel as they do, and do what they do, and you will be safe." That is why subsequent implementations of C1AB sequences support subjective feelings of safety and are called *Gifts of Love* (GOLs). This vital primitive brain learning about safety and threat is stored by gene expression and silencing and by epigenetic processes. The lessons start early and last a lifetime simply because lessons in threat and safety must never be forgotten. Another lasting version of this primitive form of associative learning is language learning by young children. The treatment

---

[2]Some politicians take advantage of this fact and scare people mindlessly into compliance.

implications of this analysis of affective symptoms are that if there is to be symptom change via psychotherapy, the individual's relationship with Family in the Head must be transformed so that the maladaptive lessons no longer misdirect the release of these natural affects.

PAULINE

Pauline was a 42-year-old depressed and anxious inpatient who came to the hospital for a second time saying, "I don't want to live anymore." She declared her burdens were too great; she would never change, and she had "let God down." Prior to her quite recent first hospitalization, in a fury she had destroyed her furniture and personal items and was planning to destroy herself, too, when the police arrived in response to neighbors' calls about the commotion. She was taken to the hospital and met criteria for bipolar disorder, a diagnosis she shared with her mother. She had a multiyear history of spending sprees and of alcoholism alternating with periods of sobriety. Pauline was a victim of sexual and physical abuse, but did well in school and had a good work history as a primary school teacher. But presently, she was unemployed and dysfunctional, living (unwelcomed) with various family members.

That description of Pauline will be familiar to most clinicians. It includes reason for hospitalization, presenting symptoms, present and past diagnoses, and a brief mention of social history, including a list of stressful events such as abuse and other forms of trauma. Medications appropriate to the presenting symptoms and diagnoses were offered by hospital staff, along with cognitive–behavioral therapy to help her change her negative thinking about herself and learn to better regulate her affect. Treatment for posttraumatic stress disorder was considered.

An IRT case formulation begins with such a standard description and enriches it by eliciting enough interpersonal information to explain why Pauline wanted to destroy her beloved condo and herself and why it happened when it did. The IRT treatment plan would include medications as usual, and the psychotherapy would draw on any and all treatment approaches. The choice of psychosocial interventions would be guided by a case formulation that includes attachment-based assumptions about what has gone wrong and how to facilitate constructive changes. Briefly, rather than assume the symptoms indicate a breakdown, as when a car's automatic clutch is broken, the theory in IRT is that she saw her destruction of her condo and intent to destroy herself, too, as adaptive. Such an interpretation draws on Natural Biology (Chapter 2) along with precise, reliable descriptions of interpersonal patterns (SASB in Chapter 3) that can link current stress-related patterns to past lessons in managing safety and threat.

During childhood, Pauline, the oldest of five children, cooked and cleaned and took care of the other children "because Mother worked outside the home." Mother would offer gifts to the other children and take them on outings, pointedly excluding Pauline. Mother called Pauline "dumb" and frequently said: "I wish I had flushed you down the toilet." When asked why her mother was so critical and rejecting, Pauline said, "There was no explanation; I guess I am just the different one."

Her father joined her mother in giving the other children gifts and privileges denied Pauline. He was physically abusive to all, but Pauline also was sexually abused when the other children were on outings with their mother. During that abuse, Pauline explained that she "would go numb" and did not resist "because I wanted my father's approval"—"I would do it if this is what made me get my love from my father." He threatened to beat her if she told anyone, so she kept silent until adulthood. She concluded, as children often do in such situations, "I was the bad one in the family" and that her abuse was due to her shortcomings. Despite all that, Pauline functioned well and was on the honor roll at school. Her solace was to withdraw to her room to play with her dolls in a fantasy family "like the family that I wanted."

When she was 18, Pauline married a kind man with whom she felt safe, and she completed college. However, she became uncomfortable with him and noted, "When things were going smoothly, I would push him away, or leave." Eventually she divorced him, kept a good job as a teacher for a few years, bought a nice condo, and furnished it very well via "spending sprees." Then she was in two successive abusive relationships, explaining, "It was almost like my father all over again. I was comfortable with that." She added, "It is too scary when everything is good." But one evening the boyfriend's abuse was extraordinary in undisclosed ways, and she responded with the attacks on her condo with the intent to destroy it, along with herself as well. The police came in response to the neighbor's calls, and she was taken to the hospital.

IRT CASE FORMULATION PARADIGM APPLIED TO PAULINE

In this section, Pauline's story illustrates the various steps in constructing an IRT case formulation. The very first step is to make any required disclosures regarding reporting laws and HIPAA privacy rules. Patients need to know as reliably as possible about any potential threats to and safeguards of their privacy, including the conditions under which the therapist might be required by law to disclose their protected health information. That said, it is helpful to explain that the purpose of the interview is to "see the world as you do. I will offer a summary of what I think is going on and why along with some thoughts about how psychotherapy might be helpful with that. It will be important that you correct any errors so that we can work with a plan that makes sense to you." An overview of the process is sketched in Figure 4.1, and Exhibit 4.1 helps organize detail for a case report.

Assess Symptoms

Pauline arrived at the hospital the first time because of the out of control destructive rage that included suicidality, followed by severe depression. She was diagnosed by hospital staff with bipolar disorder associated with a history of "excessive spending." After stabilization, she was discharged but deteriorated rapidly and was readmitted. As usual, the IRT case formulation began with identifying the current symptom profile and previous treatments, either by reading the medical record, being updated by staff, or by interview with the patient.

After the presenting problems are clear, the question "What do you most need help with?" is a good way to learn what most bothers the patient. Patients usually will name disorders or interpersonal problems such as marital difficulties or problems at work. With the stated problem "on the table," the IRT interviewer explains, as mentioned above,

> I would like to see the world as you do. If I can, I'll try to make some helpful suggestions to you (and your therapist, if appropriate). I'll ask a lot for specific examples, because with them I am more likely to be able to see things as you do. Think of this process as you would think of getting an x-ray. Maybe something important will turn up; maybe not. At the end of this interview, I'll give you a summary of what I think and ask if you think it makes sense. I'll ask you for any needed corrections in the summary.

Identify Current Stresses Linked to Symptoms

Suppose the patient names depression as the issue he/she needs help with. Looking for the current stresses, the interviewer asks, "What might you be depressed about?" Pauline clearly identified the precipitating stress as the dreadful evening in her home with her abusive boyfriend. She explained, "I put myself in bad circumstances and did things I don't want to think about; it is too painful." After the boyfriend left that night, she attacked and seriously damaged or destroyed as much as she could of her beloved condo, the place where her childhood fantasy about a loving home was to come true. Her suicidal intent had been derailed by the arrival of the police.

She was discharged shortly after the crisis but no longer had a usable place to live. Worse yet, the school district was reorganizing, and she was laid

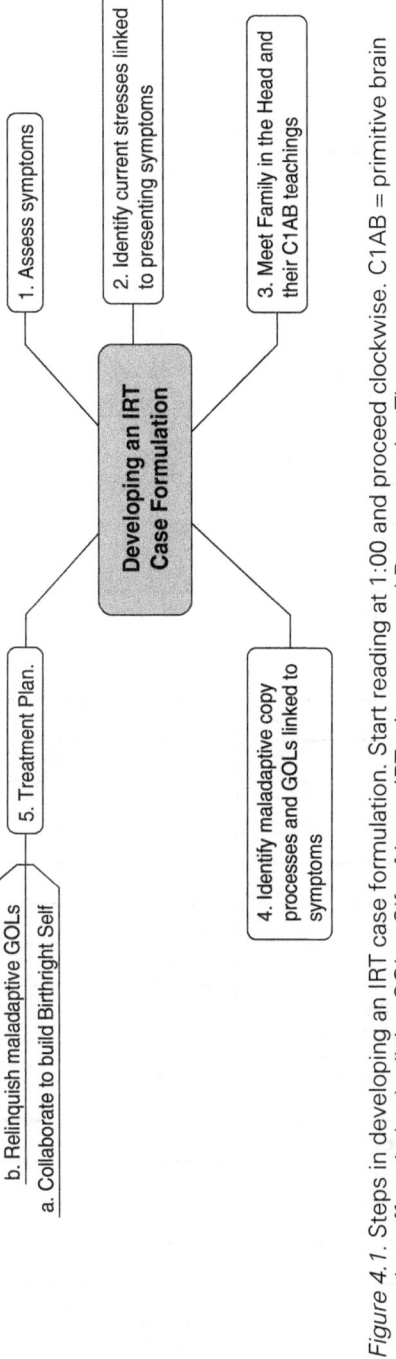

Figure 4.1. Steps in developing an IRT case formulation. Start reading at 1:00 and proceed clockwise. C1AB = primitive brain perception–affect–behavior links; GOL = Gift of Love; IRT = Interpersonal Reconstructive Therapy.

THE IRT CASE FORMULATION MODEL   91

EXHIBIT 4.1
Form for Collecting Information Needed for a Formal
Case Formulation Report

Presentation	
Actuarial description	
Symptomatic description	
Present Life Circumstances	
Current stresses	
Responses	
Conscious self-concept	
Significant other	
Medical History	
Family history of mental disorder	
DSM–5 Section I diagnoses	
DSM–5 Section II diagnoses (include criteria)	
Other noteworthy disorders (e.g., migraine, ulcerative colitis)	
Current treatments for Section I, II diagnoses	
Key Figures	
Mother	
Father	
Siblings	
School or work	
Peers	
Other key figures	
Case Formulation	
Copy process links between presenting problems and key figures	
Gifts of Love	
Treatment Implications	
[Presenting problem]	
[Presenting problem]	

Note. DSM–5 = Diagnostic and Statistical Manual of Mental Disorders (5th ed.; American Psychiatric Association, 2013).

off. She was utterly without direction. Her depression worsened, as did her suicidal ideation. Family brought her back to the hospital. The challenge during the consultation for this rehospitalization was to account for the destructive attack on all she held dear and her unremitting dysfunction and despair.

Identify Family in the Head and Their Lessons in Safety and Threat

According to IRT theory, presenting problems have been shaped by Family in the Head, a collection of internalized representations of attachment figures that sponsor rules regarding what to be afraid of and how to be safe. Of course, that is contingent on any impacts of inherited "envelope of potential" for responding to perceived threat. Temperamental factors might be such a factor that determines what is copied, but their impact cannot be assessed in an IRT case formulation interview.

Developmental factors that affected Pauline taught her that she was responsible for taking care of her father and siblings and that she was despicable and expendable. Her safest strategy was to comply with their views and demands and serve; she should not expect to be included, affirmed, and loved. Her baseline affects, behaviors, and primitive brain cognitions (C1AB links) were to avoid threat by pleasing others regardless of its impact on her (C1). Out of fear (A), she believed she should comply with their demands (B), and that (C1AB = GOL) was her best chance at receiving their approval and finding "safety." That sequence set the template for Pauline's attack on her dream home and herself (B), her rage at herself (A) over the perception (C1) that she had behaved in a way that caused her childhood incestual nightmare to return to haunt her despite her years of labor building her lovely condo. She took the sexual attack and her apparent collusion as "evidence" she would never be free of her horrible early experiences and fierce punishment and deprivation was her lot forever.

Identify Maladaptive Copy Processes and Gifts of Love Linked to Symptoms

During the precipitating episode, Pauline showed all three copy processes: (a) identification—she recklessly and ragefully attacked whatever she cared about; (b) recapitulation—she perceived, felt, and did what she did with them. That was to submit to sexual abuse, servitude, and isolation; and introjection—she had intense contempt for herself and reckless disregard for her own interests. All three were maladaptive copy processes and clearly were Red. By contrast, her history of high level of functioning in school and as she cared for her siblings was recapitulated by her work record, where she was well regarded and had good earnings, and was adaptive and Green.

Pauline's "spending" was devoted mostly to her passionate efforts to buy and install household items that contributed to her childhood fantasy of building a fine home in which there was to be "the family that I always wanted." In that house, she had submitted to sexual abuse once again to "earn the love." But afterwards, she introjected familial and conjugal vilification and concluded that she was contemptible and that she could never change. Identifying with her oppressors past and present, she set about destroying the home and herself. All of that—allowing degradation and exploitation and self-trashing—was a Gift of Love to the family in her head.

Her prior divorce from her kind and loving husband also was inspired by her loyalty to the old rules and values. She explained that kindness from her husband did not feel right, and she "did things" to undermine their good relationship. In so doing, she showed a copy process that recapitulated the message "I am different and do not deserve good treatment."

Explain the Case Formulation and Treatment Plan to the Patient

At the end of an inpatient consultation or after one or two outpatient therapy interviews, the therapist summarizes the case formulation and asks the patient for any needed corrections. The insight, understanding, and feeling that one's symptoms make sense often stabilize a person but do not bring lasting change.

After reaching agreement about the case formulation, the patient is offered a sketch of the treatment process clearly illustrated by his/her own story. For example, Pauline might be told,

> You allowed yourself to be treated so badly by (boyfriend's name) because that was what you had to endure from your father all those years. It was your safest choice at the time, and your primitive brain thinks it still is. So in therapy, you and your therapist can work together to dethrone the father in your head until he no longer is in charge of your primitive brain that manages anger, anxiety, and depression. If you can separate from "him" and from the mother in your head, who so often said she wished she had flushed you down the toilet, you could work on reprogramming your primitive brain to build a secure, Birthright Self. That could be the Pauline you would have been if you had Secure Base support at home.

It is a good idea to add warnings about how difficult the treatment process can be. For example, Pauline could be told,

> For you, the rules for safety are that you must expect to be abused and exploited and comply with that without complaining. Challenging those rules will be terrifying because if you defy them, Family in the Head will try to strike you down. It will be especially scary when you begin to make visible everyday changes in your life, like making new friends or doing well at work

again. Family in the Head will not like that at all. But you and the therapist will work on ways to resist the old rules, manage the fear, and teach your primitive brain new, more appropriate rules for how to be safe. After Family in the Head no longer runs your life, you can define your Birthright Self.

Occasionally, someone in an IRT workshop objects to this idea of describing the case formulation and treatment to the patient. Without debating related underlying theory, my response is: Participating in psychotherapy requires the patient to make a big commitment financially, emotionally, and socially, and the stakes are high. Patients deserve to understand the procedure, the rationale, and the risks and benefits. This is similar to the ethical disclosure one expects when contemplating having surgery or any other major procedure. One needs to know what the procedure is, how it is expected to affect one's symptoms, and what the risks and benefits are. An IRT clinician is not exempt from that ethical requirement.

REMARKS ABOUT THE INTERVIEWING STYLE FOR IRT

Whether constructing a case formulation or engaging in therapy process, the interviewing style matters a lot. Here, in italicized print, are some of the more important, not necessarily universal, features of interviewing in IRT.

Already it may be clear that *the IRT therapist is collaborative and transparent*. The process of gathering detail to build a case formulation in IRT is dominated by *helpful curiosity* and *advocacy*. *Specificity* and *trailing along with the patient's stream of consciousness* are the best way to access the primitive brain. A *question-and-answer style is rarely used* in IRT. One does not learn about connections between the present and the past by asking complicated or abstract questions such as: "How do these presenting symptoms reflect what happened in your family when you were a child?" Likely unproductive answers to that might include: "Not at all. I had a fine childhood" or: "I was abused, and that why I am so oversensitive" or: "What are you talking about? I inherited depression, and so did everybody in my family." *Avoiding vagueness and unfounded inferences (interpretations)*, the IRT interviewer seeks "raw data"—that is, *descriptions of specific interactions and feelings in the patient's own words*.

A good start most of the time is to *explore the contexts in which symptoms appear*. If asked "What might you be depressed about?" the patient will describe a current stress (C1) and probably include linked feelings (A) and relevant behaviors (B) in specific relationships. If the *C1AB links* are not apparent spontaneously, the interviewer should ask: "What started this (C1)?" "How did you feel about it (A)?" "What did you do about it (B)?" and finally: "What do you think about it? (C2)."

Connections between present and past and between copy processes and GOLs will be revealed if the clinician attends to the patient's *natural sequences of thought and related affects* while discussing current stresses and similar earlier stresses. Sometimes these C1AB links between the present and the past have to be invited by: "Have you ever felt (thought, acted) this way (or been in a situation like this) before?" The patient usually says yes and goes straight back to relationships with childhood attachment figures. If not, the interviewer can repeat the question, adding: "Thank you; can you also find this pattern further back in time?"

The original teachers of how to attend to the stream of consciousness to identify primitive brain processes were psychoanalysts. Reik (1983) explained it very well and provided many examples. While *tracking the free associative flow* in IRT, the therapist may be like a river guide riding the current of the patient's unconscious, judiciously using the paddle to avoid obstacles and turning as needed to get to the destination of identifying connections between current patterns, feelings, and thoughts to relationships with attachment figures.

Another essential feature for interviewing that accesses the primitive brain is that the clinician uses what Sullivan (1953) called *peripatetic empathy*. One interpretation is that as the interviewer tracks the patient's stream of consciousness, he or she *reflects what the patient thinks, feels, does, or wants to do* using an *interactional frame* using *as much primitive imagery as possible*. For example, if the patient says, "I had to wait my turn and hear the others scream as he beat them," the interviewer does not say something stilted, such as "That must have been frightening." A more engaged version of empathy might be: "That is so terrifying I cannot even imagine how one could bear it." Such a comment better conveys that the interviewer is listening and understands the intensity of that experience.

Before the end of the interview, *key attachment figures should have been mentioned*. To be sure no key figure was overlooked, the interviewer can ask about "any others" who might be related to (presenting symptoms). Order comes out of chaos toward the end of the session, when the interviewer *organizes the information* by using the IRT case formulation model (Figure 4.1) and *asks the patient to confirm or correct it*. That integrative process is put in terms the patient can understand, modeled by the narrative for Joseph at the beginning of Chapter 2.

Eliciting traumatic material along with affect can be overwhelming and is *offered all at once only to inpatients*. It is rare to offer a full case formulation to an outpatient after one interview. The reason for caution is that *backlash from Family in the Head is likely*. Patients who have been programmed to keep family secrets will feel they have been disobedient and disloyal by disclosing things that never before have been so clearly said out loud, especially to others. This can lead to internal punishment sponsored by a hostile internalized representation. Patients who are identified with the aggressors of course, will lash out at others, including the interviewer.

Inpatients are asked to talk to hospital staff if their Family in the Head gets mad at them and they need some support after the consultation. Outpatients would have to monitor and manage this themselves on their own and that is why *case formulations go at a slower pace* for them. Lower doses of exposure to unfriendly Family in the Head allow *more time for the therapy relationship to develop to the point where there is trust that supports security* strong enough to help the patient stay stable between sessions.

Another feature of IRT interviewing is explicit *reference to Natural Biology*. That perspective permits the clinician to *explain how "everything makes sense."* Many patients are convinced they are irrational, even "crazy." They often stabilize as they learn that what they have been doing is entirely understandable, given their lessons in safety and threat, and that copy processes are as natural as copying DNA by RNA.

It also is important to *review the normal developmental sequence* with the patient. The IRT version of development was described along with supporting evidence in Chapter 2. It The sequence includes (a) *Secure Base attachment* that (b) supports curiosity and the development of friendly and safe autonomy taking (i.e., *differentiation*), (c) *peer play* to develop social skills and culturally relevant education to develop cognitive skills, and (d) by adulthood, there is *pair bonding and constructive participation in the "group"* (society) with contributions to the next generation. As with all IRT terms, the interviewer uses examples from the patient's own story when explaining the developmental sequence. *Differentiation failure typically is the major problem.*

When describing the case formulation to the patient, the *interviewer often asks: Is that accurate? Does it make sense?* If affirmed (which almost always happens), a brief description of Gift of Love fantasies (GOLs) can be added toward the end of the explanation of the case formulation, though if the patient is fragile, description of these fantasies might better be delayed for later.

REVIEW OF PAULINE'S STORY

Given freedom to tell the story, Pauline provided details about her incest that drew a synecdoche for her life. She was rejected by her mother and could only guess the reason was that for unknown reasons, she was "different." The incest with her father happened when her mother was out and about with the other children. The experiences were frightening not only because she was "alone" but also because her father was dangerous as he threatened her and others at times, as well. Lonely, helpless, and frightened, she submitted to the sexual abuse because, as she explained: "I would do it if this is what made me get love from my father." During childhood, her response, her only solace, was to withdraw to her room and engage in the fantasy home she would build and live in some day.

But on the fateful evening, the repetition of incest patterns happened in the fantasy home she had built with her spending sprees. Again, in adulthood, she was alone socially except for *him*. She again gave herself the blame and said: "I put myself in bad circumstances and did things I don't want to think about; it is too painful." The incident "proved" to her that she never could change and that her dream home was not to be. She flew into a rage (identifying with her father) at herself and her dreams and concluded that all was lost.

It is no surprise that she fell into despair and demobilization after all that. Being able to see that it all makes sense, including the horrendous violence Pauline showed toward and all that she had worked so hard to build. Understanding their case formulation helps normalize and stabilize patients. It is not a cure, but it can allow them to reset their internal compass and begin the journey of rebuilding self in a more secure form.

CASE FORMULATIONS DO NOT INDICT

Many patients, especially those who have been severely abused, are reluctant to discuss family and tell about abuses. They need reassurance that the goal in IRT is to describe how things work, not to hold judgment. In fact, the method can generate considerable sympathy for parents, too, given that they likely were replicating their own histories in some ways. The main treatment implication of developing and sharing an IRT case formulation with patients is that it helps them see that their symptoms are evidence of normal mechanisms that have been shaped by abnormal circumstances. That is a great relief usually.

It is important to add, however, that there are times when blaming is a temporary part of an IRT treatment. For patients crippled by self-blaming, a helpful initial step is to change the focus and blame others within reasonable limits. But shifting blame is not the final resting point for anyone. Letting go of the corrective time machine fantasy, separating from family in the head, and moving on toward building better relationships with self and others is.

EXAMPLES OF COPY PROCESSES AND GIFTS OF LOVE IN MOVIES

Although not a part of psychological or psychiatric theories of pathology, copy processes and GOLs have been represented by artists in movies and plays for quite a while. Some older examples are listed below. Readers can find their own examples if they concentrate on interpersonal patterns in stories about the growth or decline of a main character. However, it will not be possible to construct case formulations if a movie or story does little more than envelop the viewer in primitive images and sounds.

The Aviator

The Aviator (Mann, Climan, King, Evans, & Scorsese, 2004) tells a story allegedly about Howard Hughes that begins with his mother bathing him as a young adolescent in the library of their home. She is very concerned about germs. He grows up to be a wildly successful, daring entrepreneur, but ends up locking himself in a hotel room, wherein for years, he runs around naked, alone, and terrified of germs.

The General's Daughter

In *The General's Daughter* (Neufeld & West, 1999), a very talented, successful female graduate of West Point is brutally raped by her peers in a war game exercise. Near death, her father, a general, visits her and tells her to forget about it. Eventually, she develops a pattern of extraordinary promiscuity among all the officers on her father's staff. She stages a replication of the rape scene in a way that allows her father to see what it was like and, perhaps this time, rescue and take care of her. He does not; he walks away, leaving her there. Shortly thereafter, she actually is raped and killed.

Jude

In *Jude* (Eaton & Winterbottom, 1996), a poor stonemason and his wife struggle to find work, shelter, and food. They travel through the countryside in Europe, with the son from his first marriage in tow. Two more children are born, and it becomes even harder to make ends meet. The oldest boy often is charged with caring for the two younger ones. Rejection of the family's requests for lodging because of the children is a recurrent theme. One day, the parents come home to find the two younger children stabbed to death, apparently by the oldest son, who had hanged himself. He left a note indicating that times would be better for them now without the children. He seemed to have introjected his treatment as an unwanted nonentity and given his parents what he thought they most wanted. Of course, it was not, and the loving couple separated.

EVIDENCE BASE FOR THE IRT CASE FORMULATION AND TREATMENT MODELS

Evidence that validates the IRT models is reviewed in Chapter 10. Here is an illustrative test of the validity of the case formulation model that is relevant to Pauline's case formulation. Figure 4.2a shows that

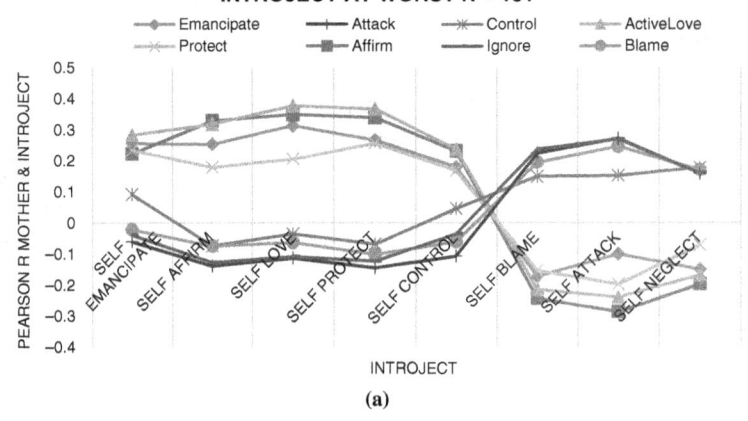

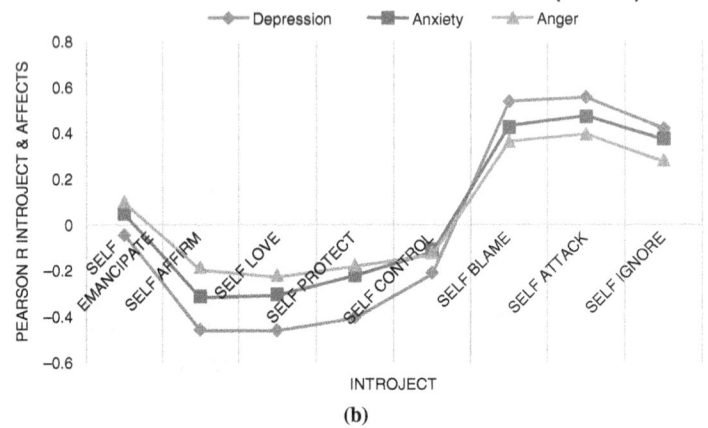

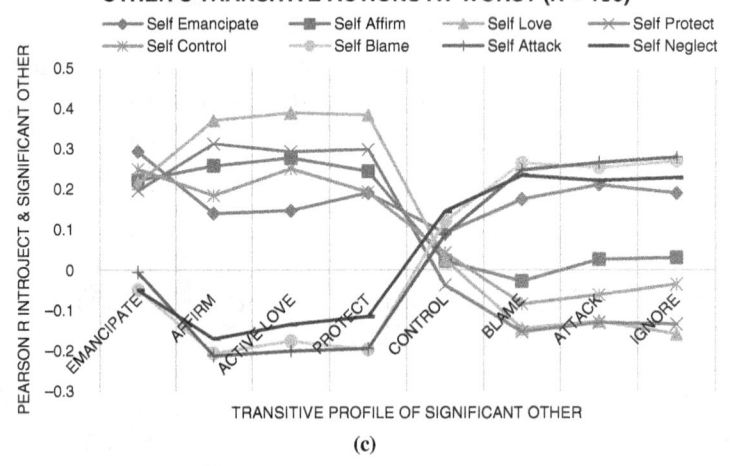

Figure 4.2. From hostile parent (a) to hostile introject and threat affects (b) to the choice of significant other (c). These correlational data do not carry information about sequence, but theory provides that attachment figures' patterns come first; introject (copy process) and affects follow. They predispose copy processes when choosing an adult attachment figure. Sequential data are the only way to check that interpretation.

inpatients'[3] views of mothers' transitive actions were introjected in patterns that follow circumplex order. Love from mothers supports self-love and caring. More hostility from mothers is reflected in more self-attack. Figure 4.2b shows that introjected hostility is directly related to threat symptoms of anger, anxiety, and depression as predicted by Natural Biology: If the caregiver is a threat, then maladaptive cuing of threat affects follow. Figure 4.2c shows that choice of an adult partner can match the negative affects and structure of the introject. A hostile self-concept and threat affects can mediate choice of an adult attachment figure. Pauline, who suffered chronic abuse and exploitation, described the subjective mechanism: "Having a nice boyfriend or husband did not feel right." Her recapitulation of being with an abuser restored the original "order." If the procedures used to create Figure 4.2 are used on ratings of fathers, results are similar.

IRT CASE FORMULATIONS AND MAINSTREAM MEDICAL VIEWS OF PSYCHOPATHOLOGY

The data in Figure 4.2 support the foundational principle of IRT case formulations, which is that perceived interactions with attachment figures have a major role in shaping symptoms of affective disorders, self-concepts, and personality patterns (C1AB). That might seem to contradict two well-established facts about mental disorder to the effect that symptoms are based on brain chemistry and circuitry that is different from normal; that these differences run in families and statistics suggest that mental disorders are inherited. On the other hand, the IRT theory of copy process is supported by recent research on mirror neurons and by studies of the structure, neurochemistry, and functions of threat (sympathetic) and reward (parasympathetic) systems and their interactions. It also is supported by the science of epigenetics, which has made it very clear that critical early interactions with attachment figures change genes in ways that are related to affective disturbances in adulthood, and those changes are heritable. Supporting detail and citations appeared in Chapter 2.

RED GOLs AND AUTOIMMUNE DISORDERS

The counterintuitive nature of the suggestion that GOL fantasies support symptoms and maladaptive behaviors suggests that affective symptoms/disorders may be akin to autoimmune disorders. Self-sabotage is a direct result

---

[3]These data are from the Wisconsin database.

of misdirected attempts to protect the self. Pauline gave an extraordinarily clear explanation: "It is too scary when everything is good." As in autoimmune disease, normal behaviors are attacked as "not self" by hostile Family in the Head. Autoimmune disorders will not remit until and if the natural protective mechanisms that have gone amuck can be reoriented to support self-care rather than self-destruction.

The concepts of autoimmunity and of (Red) Gifts of Love that support self-destruction are extremely counterintuitive. To buttress the argument, a dramatically clear example is offered here. It comes from Jason, described in Chapter 1, who left IRT angrily and later sent friendly reports about his progress on his own. Here is a message from him about the validity of GOL. It was his response to a newspaper account of a boy who had been kept in a cage, was severely abused, and eventually beaten to death. Jason wrote:

> He had a sister, but the sister's treatment was more normal. One day the Father beat the boy particularly badly and put him back in his cage. According to the account of the sister, in the morning he was lying dead in his cage. The parents buried him in a shallow grave under a slab of concrete and erected a prefabricated steel shed on the slab. The family then moved away. Some years later, the death of the boy came to light somehow, and the grave was found. Also found, and published in the present, were some letters or musings the boy had written about his life: about how he was unhappy that his behavior was such that everyone disliked him, and that he wished he could do better. There were some photos of him in the newspaper. He seemed to be kind of a sweet, mild-tempered kid. There was no mention of serious misbehavior in any of the accounts. He does not seem to have been violent, or exceptional in any way.
>
> The interesting aspect of the story to me is that I can imagine, easily, the boy accepting the judgment of his family that he was being put in the cage for his own good. When I was small, there was a (isolated place in the house) where I felt safe and liked to spend my time. The floor was rough concrete. It was not particularly clean. . . . I actually chose this space . . . for my own. So I can easily imagine the boy accepting the cage as "his" space. [Jason then described his own severe beatings.] However, basically I did accept, on some level, that I was being harassed, diminished, and hit because my behavior was unacceptable to others. And that what was being done to me was, if unpleasant and often arbitrary, basically a consequence of this inadequacy on my part. I devoutly wished to be a better person, yet I did not know how to effect the change, whatever it was, which would make me acceptable to others. After reflecting on my own life, I can easily imagine the boy in the newspaper story going into his cage without complaint. I can even imagine him choosing the cage over other options because of the sense that he will be accepted by his parents if he embraces his prison. In this phase of my life, I am trying not to choose the "cage" anymore.

5

THE INTERPERSONAL RECONSTRUCTIVE THERAPY TREATMENT MODEL

In the first book on Interpersonal Reconstructive Therapy (IRT; Benjamin, 2003b [paperback ed., 2006]), which is the IRT treatment manual, interventions for common clinical dilemmas, such as stalled treatment and challenging crises, were described in detail organized by flow charts, tables, and diagrams. In this book, Natural Biology is added to give a very clear, science-based rationale for choosing interventions. That grounding in a consistent and valid frame of reference enhances descriptions of how to sponsor change, even in patients with long records of treatment resistance.

FROM FREUD TO TODAY:
A LONG JOURNEY OVER A SHORT DISTANCE

> The discovery that we made, at first to our great surprise, was that when we had succeeded in bringing the exciting event to clear recollection, and had also succeeded in arousing with it the accompanying affect, and when the patient had related this occurrence in as detailed a manner as possible and had expressed his feeling in regard to it in words, the various hysterical symptoms disappeared at once, never to return. Recollection without affect is nearly always quite ineffective; the original psychical process must be repeated as vividly as possible, brought into *statum nascendi* and then "talked out." In the case of excitation phenomena—contractures, neuralgias, and hallucinations—the symptoms appear again during this repetition in full intensity and then disappear forever. Defects in functioning, paralyses and anesthesias disappear in the same way, the transitory exacerbation not being of course perceptible in these cases. (Freud & Breuer, 1893/1959, p. 28)

Except for the stilted language of translation, a modern clinician might think this description of treatment for symptoms of mental disorder refers to prolonged exposure therapy for posttraumatic stress disorder (PTSD; Foa, Hembree, & Rothbaum, 2009) or emotion-focused therapy (L. S. Greenberg, 2004) or perhaps to dialectical behavior therapy (Linehan, 1993), cognitive processing therapy (Resick, Monson, & Chard, 2014), or supportive–expressive therapy (Luborsky, 1984).

The Fundamental Algorithm

A one-sentence summary of the process Freud described is this: Change in psychotherapy requires accurately identifying and fully expressing trauma-related emotions, thoughts, words, and behaviors, reexperiencing and repeating that process many times in the therapy setting. That likely is related to the psychoanalytic terms *abreaction* and *working through*, now sometimes called *processing*. From the perspective of Natural Biology, the word *reprogramming* seems more apt because it captures the dumbly mechanical, robotic nature of the primitive brain cuing of affects and includes the idea that repetition is central to changing the connections. The word *algorithm* from computer programming describes a series of steps or procedures that are to be rerun again and again as many times as needed. When referring to the repetitive process in therapy described by Freud, it will be called *Freud's algorithm*.

It is amazing that a method described so long ago in the context of treating "hysteria" now is at the heart of many important contemporary psychotherapy approaches for such a wide variety of mental disorders. That, of course, raises the question of what has been added and how do the additions improve on what he said? Here follows a review of illustrative contemporary therapies and some of their uses of Freud's algorithm.

Progress After Freud

Freudian psychoanalysis was revised in important ways by object relations psychoanalysts. They rejected Freud's primary drive explanation that aggression and sexuality are primal energies present from birth that need to be contained by social forces represented by the superego, with the ego assigned the task of mediating between these social and unconscious primal forces. Object relations theorists shifted the focus to the impact of important social relationships on the self, and that change was monumental. Bowlby (1969, 1977) was an object relations psychoanalyst who made attachment front and center in research and practice in developmental theory, psychotherapy, and more. Therapist readers interested in learning more about object relations psychotherapy would appreciate reading a clear, sensible, useful, authoritative book by Thoma and Kachele (1991), two distinguished German psychoanalysts. Scholars unfamiliar with the history of psychoanalysis will appreciate the accurate, succinct reviews of major versions of psychoanalysis in J. R. Greenberg and Mitchell (1984).

IRT training and practice draw heavily on the wisdom of object relations psychoanalysis. Many of the ideas and methods from psychoanalysts are irreplaceable. It has long been accepted that human intelligence in general and science in particular move forward faster if theorists and practitioners build on past accomplishments of others rather than reinventing the wheel. To be consistent with that perspective, it is really important that young therapists have exposure to the work of a variety of skilled therapists in readings and in person (Benjamin, 2015a).

Psychoanalysis of one kind or another prevailed as the treatment of choice in psychiatry until the 1960s, when effective medications became available. Ultimately, they became the standard of care along with electroconvulsive therapy (ECT) and deep brain stimulation, all supplemented by lessons in coping offered by various revisions of cognitive–behavioral therapy (CBT; Beck, Rush, Shaw, & Emery, 1979). To this day, psychiatrists continue to seek more effective surgical, neurochemical, and genetic ways to treat mental disorders (Insel, 2010) with physical or chemical interventions. The hope is that such treatments will be more rapid, effective, and lasting than anything presently available.

Meanwhile, there are significant numbers of psychiatrists skilled in prescribing medications who also practice psychotherapy. They, like practicing psychologists, social workers, and others almost always put Freud's algorithm to good use. One type of psychotherapy is called *prolonged exposure*, a highly structured way to reactivate the trauma memory as vividly and intensely as possible (flooding) and repeat until it extinguishes. L. S. Greenberg's (2004) emotion-focused therapy contributes to self-organization by emotion coaching that helps people "become aware of, accept and make sense of their emotional experience" (p. 3). Dialectical behavior therapy (DBT; Linehan, 1993) offers trainings that help people regulate their emotions by enhancing skills in mindfulness, health and fitness; distress tolerance; emotion regulation; and interpersonal relationships. It should be added that procedures in DBT are unusually clear, and the emphasis on self-help via DBT apps for phones is exemplary. Eye movement desensitization and reprocessing (EMDR; Shapiro, 2001) features an intervention using specific eye movements while recalling trauma; the procedure reduces the vividness of traumatic memories and associated affects. Transference-focused therapy (Yeomans, Clarkin, & Kernberg, 2015) reactivates and transforms residuals of earlier problem feelings, thoughts, and patterns as they appear in the therapy relationship.

Relationship of IRT to Freud's Algorithm and Other Psychotherapies

The process described by Freud and Breuer in 1893 is very important in IRT, but his primary drive interpretation of why it works is not. In IRT, Natural Biology provides the rationale for focusing consistently on what Bowlby called the "internal working models" that regulate affect. The strategy of focusing on Family in the Head more than on symptom management is that working with the source is more effective than working primarily on the consequences. The encounters with internalized versions of relationships with attachment figures necessarily reactivate the original scenarios, as in Freud's algorithm. Within any and all of these approaches, greater depth of experiencing (C1 function) while accurately connecting the original stress with appropriate words (C2 function) is, as Freud suggested, correlated with better outcome (M. H. Klein, Mathieu-Coughlan, & Kiesler, 1986).

In IRT, the clinician begins with a case formulation that accounts for all presenting symptoms in terms of attempts to adapt. It is not a check box approach that recommends Technique X for Symptom Y. "Tough love" is an example of how a technique can apply to one person but not to another. "Tough love" is often recommended for the purpose of challenging substance abusers to take responsibility for themselves. If tough love works, it must mean that the message "nobody is going to take responsibility for you any more" has been received. That means that tough love can be appropriate for individuals for whom there have been perceived safe base persons, called *enablers*.

However, some addicts have a history of consistent neglect and abuse, either in reality or within a facade of normality. Tough love is not news for them. Using is not for pleasure or relief from malaise; it is for escape from unbearable pain (not including pain about loss of a caregiver) or internal terror. They don't expect help. For them, tough love from "an enabler" might be experienced as shutting off the last ray of hope. Continued self-neglect or worse would follow. In sum, the IRT case formulation is essential to uses of the IRT treatment model because it addresses each presenting symptom in terms of the individual patient's view of how to cope with threat and achieve safety.

COMPARING AN IRT TREATMENT WITH FOUR WELL-ESTABLISHED TREATMENTS FOR BORDERLINE PERSONALITY DISORDER

Use of the IRT case formulation and treatment models helps the clinician organize a patient's information in ways that guide the choice of treatment models that address a given purpose at a given time. To show what the integrative approach looks like in the clinic, interventions with an individual with borderline personality disorder (BPD) in my outpatient practice are compared with interventions recommended by four therapies for treating cases with BPD, a diagnosis known to be difficult to treat, that are supported by randomized controlled trials (RCTs).

Melissa

Melissa was referred at age 18 to my part-time private practice following discharge from the hospitalization for her first and only suicide attempt, accompanied by the BPD label. Hers was a very long term, often-interrupted treatment. She did show continual growth and make profound personality change, albeit short of "perfect" Secure Base. From childhood to adulthood, Melissa had a complex, intimate, and somewhat stormy relationship with her father. She thought it may have been sexual but did not recall any confirming specific evidence; if it happened, it may have been pleasurable. She knows that before she was born, he had a hospitalization for threatening behaviors, but he never attacked her physically and was quite generous with her. Still, he could get quite angry verbally and was very controlling. Melissa fought back in kind. Overall, she had considerable influence with him, especially if she was needy. Her mother was quiet and unassuming. Melissa was fond of her mother but rarely spoke of her.

Melissa had sexual encounters initiated by an older male babysitter and later by a teacher when she was in high school. Because of the inappropriate gaps in age and status, all of her incidents of sexual encounters prior to age of majority were abusive; hers did not involve physical violence. Melissa had done well in high school but did not go to college. She married early and had remained in this supportive relationship with a talented man who had his own history of abuse and disability. She was unemployed until late in her 20s.

Initially, her comorbid problems were depression and food and drug abuse. Of her BPD symptoms, dramatic instability, cutting behaviors, and suicidal fantasies were most salient. Various medical symptoms emerged later in treatment and are described below as possible evidence of "symptom substitution."

Like patients in RCT effectiveness studies of BPD cited below, Melissa showed improvement in her ancillary and initial comorbid symptoms during the first year of treatment. This improvement included no rehospitalizations, diminished depression, and no additional suicide attempts or cutting beyond suggestive scratches, although she continued to think a lot about all of the above. Also like some RCT-certified effective treatments for BPD, her symptoms of personality disorder per se did not improve much.[1]

Melissa's dramatic events regarding reckless intimacy–distance struggles continued for at least 2 years and abated slowly after that. As the BPD-like crises diminished, medical crises—that is, emergency room visits for medical problems involving stress-related physical disorders of the heart and the nervous system—became salient. Psychoanalysts in the 1950s and 1960s might call that *"symptom substitution."* RCT designs do not require looking at whether there is symptom substitution; studies only measure changes in symptoms of the targeted diagnosis along with the oft-seen comorbid symptoms and ancillary problems that do not qualify formally as "symptoms" (e.g., rehospitalization, emergency room visits).

At about 3 years, Melissa started dropping in and out of therapy. In IRT, it is recognized that this will happen, so patients are allowed to return if ready to collaborate in therapy tasks. Patients can be dismissed if they violate a specific contract not to engage in alcohol or substance abuse or any other such practices that are grossly incompatible with therapy process. Melissa was dismissed because she had joined an organization that sponsored values and practices that were clearly counter to therapy goals.

After 5 years, having left that organization, she was ready to resume IRT and participated once a week for about a year, and then she moved to once every 3 weeks and maintained that pattern for several more years. During this lengthy "low dose" period, her former BPD features, such as episodes of blowing up, taking off for parts unknown, lability in her views of self, losing

---

[1]Of the four well-known treatments for borderline personality disorder reviewed in this chapter, only two (Kernberg, Selzer, Koeningsberg, Carr, & Applebaum, 1989; Young, Klosko, & Weishaar, 2003) reported improvements in symptoms of BPD per se.

time or dissociating, and other such forms of intense experiencing came to mind far less often and never were acted on. She reliably used choice not to engage in BPD patterns. Her functioning improved markedly as she moved from unemployment to become a skilled and valued part-time employee as an events planner for a large Rocky Mountain resort. She began to work on and succeed at reducing abuse of her prescription medications.

The Late Mini Crisis

Quite late in this story, Melissa had a mini BPD crisis. I had just reset limits regarding her recent increases in between-session contacts by telephone and email. Melissa reacted to the limit setting with an angry email explaining how hurt and rejected she felt. She was critical of herself, too, and said she despaired about achieving lasting recovery and felt suicidal again. She wondered if she might need electroconvulsive therapy treatments. In this verbal "crisis," BPD-like features included fear of abandonment, unstable relationships, unstable self-image, suicidal threat as a favored go-to solution, affective instability, and inappropriate intense anger. Those proclivities were weak; the salient remaining problem pattern was her external orientation, which is not mentioned in the *Diagnostic and Statistical Manual of Mental Disorders* (5th ed.; American Psychiatric Association, 2013). Within that, her welfare, she believed, was still in the hands of others. Her executive skills, which were significant, often were devoted to getting others to take care of her. That is illustrated in this mini crisis as she suggested an intervention that would be done to her and fix things. Her rapid resolution of the mini crisis is described later in this chapter after comparing her treatment to other BPD approaches.

Interestingly, one of Melissa's more debilitating medical disorders unexpectedly disappeared when a laboratory test came back normal, puzzling everyone. The negative results were confirmed again later. It is possible they were correlated with her personality changes. Her enmeshment and dependency on her father was a major subject in therapy, and the details of how she related to him were consistent with the specific mind–body connections described for that disorder by Graham's (Graham et al., 1962) extension of a psychosomatic theory (first published by Grace & Graham, 1952).[2]

---

[2]For each of 18 medical disorders, Graham et al. (1962) described chronic attitudes activated the week before hospitalization (What happened, and what did you want to do about it?). For example, if a person is preoccupied with a particular threat, elevated blood pressure is natural, and if it is maintained intensely and chronically, essential hypertension is diagnosed. It will be exacerbated when something happens to heighten perception of that particular threat. Graham's paradigm suggesting that symptoms of the selected 18 medical disorders reflect natural defenses gone awry is foundational to the IRT case formulation method for interpreting affective disorders.

Presently, Melissa still comes to IRT about once a month and takes a variety of medications but does not abuse them. In sum, she relates to others with Secure Base behaviors and performs well at work except for absences related to medical problems. For years, she has not engaged in signature BPD behaviors or the familiar ancillary events (e.g., cutting, hospitalizations, emergency room visits). Residual maladaptive wishes occasionally rise up and can result in seducing a new health caregiver into offering to fix her. We are working on termination from IRT, which is terrifying because it raises the challenge of crossing the Rubicon of disability status and taking on the burden of full self-support and the rewards and dangers of independent, healthy adult functioning.

Comparison of Melissa's Treatment With Four Others

IRT is integrative and has much in common with well-known treatments for BPD. For example, my use of Kernberg's (Yeomans, Clarkin, & Kernberg, 2015) use of transference as in transference-focused psychotherapy (TFP) was salient throughout. During the mini crisis, a transference-focused therapist might say that Melissa split off negative from positive representations of self and others (e.g., therapist), theoretically because of lack of accurate mirroring during childhood. The TFP treatment plan would use the therapy relationship to integrate views of self and others into a coherent, realistic, stable whole. Melissa did work hard in IRT to see herself as an integrated, whole person, separate from others, including me.

Linehan's (1993) dialectical behavior therapy likely would suggest that Melissa's views and feelings had been invalidated during development, leading to unmodulated affect regulation. A DBT therapist would validate Melissa's feelings and shepherd her through the dialectic between acceptance and change (or control and warmth, as in Bedics, Atkins, Comtois, & Linehan, 2012), offering help via DBT skills-training exercises in mindfulness, distress tolerance, emotion regulation, and interpersonal effectiveness. All that was included in Melissa's IRT. Validation (as distinct from indiscriminate praise) is implicit in accurate empathy. Regulation was guided mostly by the very useful "DBT self-help" apps (https://www.dbtselfhelp.com). DBT includes group therapy, and Melissa did benefit greatly from a version of "group therapy" available to her within her religious practice, which values personal responsibility taking.

Mentalization treatment (Bateman & Fonagy, 2004) would emphasize the ability to link inner experiences to accurate representations of others and to develop emotional skills needed to establish real relationships. The idea would be that Melissa lacked accurate mirroring as a child and therefore did not learn to modulate and accurately interpret her feelings and those of others. In mentalization therapy, she would learn about her impact on others and understand another person's perspective as well as her own as she develops a more coherent sense of self and a secure attachment style.

IRT theory also recommends focusing on relationships with others as they are affected by internalized representations of attachment figures. IRT users do not assume that the BPD patient lacks ability to understand affective states of others. Quite the opposite: From early life, Natural Biology ensures that all moving animals can sense the states and copy the behaviors of familiar others under conditions of safety and threat. Melissa had uncanny skill in sensing the states of others and often used it to elicit care. As she developed a sense of boundaries between herself and others, she was better at self-care and -management. In addition, she offered effective help to others and was greatly appreciated for it.

A therapist using Young, Klosko, and Weishaar's (2003) schema-based therapy would note that Melissa's needs for security, nurturance, empathy, and more were not met because her parents were experienced as cold, detached, unpredictable, and abusive and failed to provide adequate nurturance, empathy, or protection. As a result, the theory would suggest that she had schemata that led her to expect abandonment and instability; to mistrust and expect abuse; to feel defective and ashamed; to be dependent and incompetent; to be vulnerable to harm or illness; to be enmeshed and have an underdeveloped self; and to feel like a failure and inadequate (Young et al., 2003). Schema treatment helps a patient modify these beliefs through exploratory and experiential strategies.

Although Melissa's developmental history did not include detachment, physical abuse, or lack of nurturance, she certainly was affected by her developmental experiences. And the general idea that adult symptoms directly reflect early experience with attachment figures and that treatment requires work with the resulting distortions is shared with schema therapy and most other such derivatives of psychoanalysis. IRT is different from schema therapy and most other therapy approaches in that with the use of Structural Analysis of Social Behavior (SASB) to describe interactions and internalizations and the Natural Biological perspective demands highly specific connections between early stress and symptoms and points to mechanisms of attachment that support those connections.

This review of Melissa's treatment demonstrates the integrative nature of IRT in that interventions from other therapies are used regularly. Not surprisingly, at the end of Year 1 of Melissa's therapy, her progress in IRT matched the results for these four proven effective psychotherapies regarding reduced hospitalizations, less depression, and fewer suicide attempts and parasuicidal behaviors. Definitive change in her BPD behaviors required 2 more years. To be clear, Melissa's treatment did not end at Year 1; in fact, her multiyear treatment still has not ended (more about that later). Her extraordinarily long, sporadic treatment documents the aforementioned need to have follow-up before implying that a psychotherapy has lasting effects.

IRT TREATMENT GOAL

In the research literature on effectiveness of treatments, as well as in clinical practice, the therapy goal is symptom reduction. If the reduction is great enough to be within normal limits (WNL), therapy is successful. Unfortunately, effectiveness studies only are required to show that symptoms were reduced more in one group than another. Reducing symptoms to WNL is not required. Even if it were, WNL amounts to defining *normal* as "not not-normal." It is better to characterize normal populations in terms of what is the case rather than what is not the case. What is the case in normal populations, is Secure Base intrapsychic and interpersonal behaviors. These behaviors have very large negative correlations with symptoms, and Secure Base patterns are the ultimate goal in IRT treatments.

PROCESS SKILLS IN IRT

The IRT treatment model is shown in Figure 5.1. Five process skills[3] (P) are shown in the upper left-hand corner, and they are needed during each and any of the five therapy steps (S) that are shown in the lower part of the figure. There follows a review of each therapy process and step in the figure.

Process Skill 1. Accurate Empathy

Empathy, emphasized as a core healing force by Carl Rogers (1951), is important in any psychotherapy and just about any health care intervention. Empathic statements are friendly and convey understanding, caring, and interest; they accurately reflect what the patient is saying, feeling, doing, or thinking. Crits-Christoph, Cooper, and Luborsky (1988) showed that outcome in psychotherapy was better if empathy was accurate. In their study, *accuracy* was defined as consistent with their case formulation about the patient's core conflict relationship themes. A similar result for accurate empathy was seen in IRT (Karpiak, Critchfield, & Benjamin, 2011).

---

[3]These five process skills were called the *core algorithm* in Benjamin (2003b [paperback ed., 2006]).

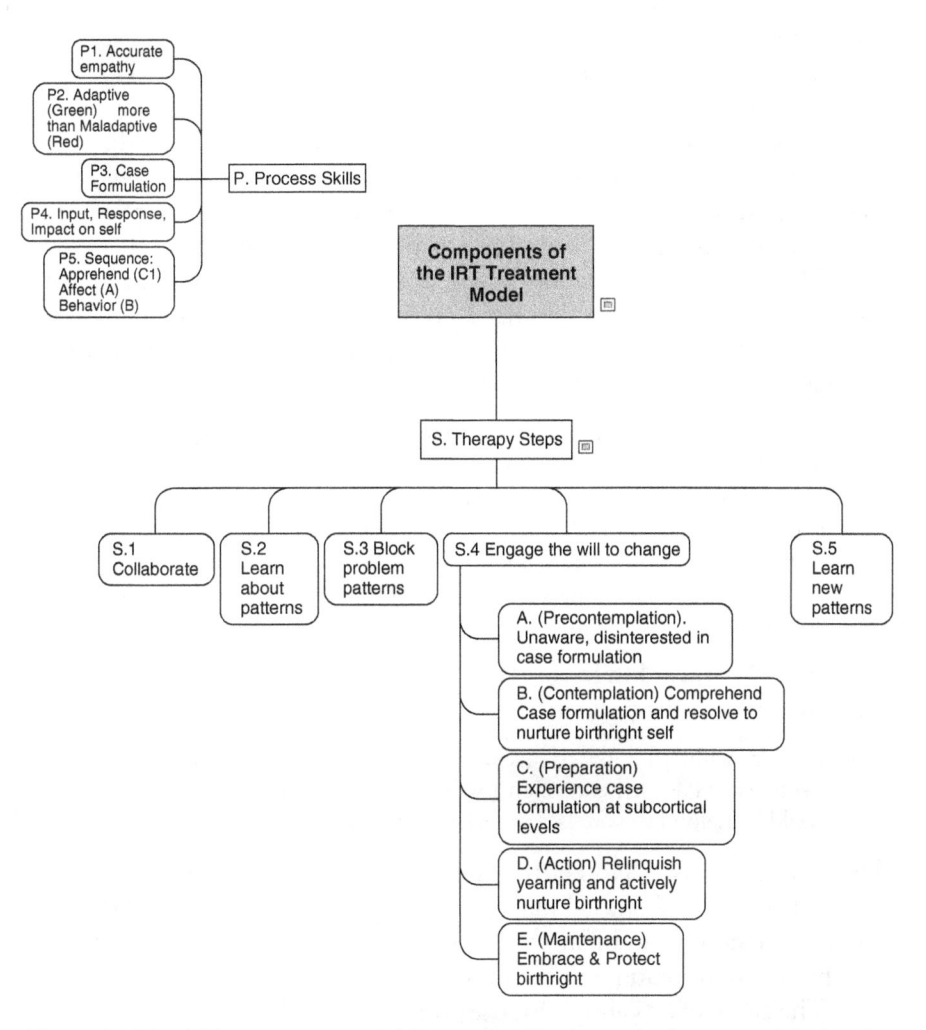

Figure 5.1. The IRT treatment model. Process skills shown in the upper right-hand section are used at all five steps of therapy, shown in the lower section of the figure. The steps describe sequences in general, but there is much going back and forth as the patient makes overall progression toward reprogramming C1AB links where C1 = primitive brain perceptions of threat or safety, A = affective responses to perceptions of safety or threat, and B = behavioral patterns predisposed by the affects to support safety. This figure is a summary and enrichment of text and a figure (Figure 3.1, Therapy Steps and Tasks) in Chapter 3 in Benjamin (2003b [paperback ed., 2006], pp. 72–116). The 2006 concept of the *Growth Collaborator* is renamed *Birthright Self* and the 2006 concept of the *Regressive Loyalist* is renamed the *Yearning Self*. IRT = Interpersonal Reconstructive Therapy.

Empathy also helps the IRT interviewer track activity of the primitive brain. For example, Melissa loved to imagine dramatic rescues by me. Rather than attempt to suppress such fantasies lest they become action, it was important to invite her to elaborate on her fantasy and track its imagined consequences. In tracking her fantasy, she could see that such acting out was a recapitulation of an old pattern that brought her closer to her father (gave psychic proximity) and was a GOL to him/me. The example also illustrates that emphasis in IRT is on motivation more than on containment of symptoms, and with resolution of motive, symptoms disappear.

The reverence for staying close to what is on the patient's mind, regardless of any emergent "chaos" surprises observers and deserves emphasis. As noted by a student at a well-known training program for psychotherapists who also attended a series of IRT workshops,

> . . . there is much more 'going on' (that you are doing on tapes) than the text (Benjamin, 2003b [paperback ed., 2006]) explicates . . . and what you're doing differs considerably from a large number of the mentors I have observed in psychotherapy. . . . The distinct difference between your 'stance' with the client and the other psychologists that I see is that your focus upon collaboration is both friendly and respects the patient's autonomy.

She cites a "critical difference" (Benjamin, 1996a) in the therapist's introduction of IRT to the patient:

> If you're willing I'd like to talk with you a while and see if I can see the world as you do. If I can, then I will try to make some suggestions that could be helpful to you. Is that alright? (p. 77)

This student noted, "No control, no judgment of patient by therapist.—patient has choice about talking (freedom respected)—patient and therapist are separate and have different ways of seeing things, and the therapist try very hard to understand him/her accurately."

The chaos of traveling with the primitive brain by honoring free association and tracking images and their meanings during IRT has to be organized at some point. That happens some time before the end of an interview as the IRT therapist provides the patient well-organized feedback and checks the validity of summaries by asking, "Does that make sense?"

For many years, the consultative interviews ended with a summary that included all elements of the case formulation except GOLs. More recently, I have added descriptions of GOLs. "Outing" GOLs is quite a bit more difficult than simply identifying copy processes, and it can be dangerous. In an inpatient service that is not so much of an issue; with outpatients, it is wise to go slowly and carefully with reference to GOLs because GOLs hold the ignition key to maladaptive C1ABs.

After hearing details of their case formulation (as did Joseph at the beginning of Chapter 2), patients (and therapists) typically say, "I see how it works. But how do I change?" Unfortunately, "insight" offered by the case formulation is only the beginning of therapy; I say again and again, "Insight is the road map, not the journey." Attempts to answer "How do I change?" are the main theme in Chapter 6.

Process Skill 2. Emphasize Adaptive (Green) More Than Maladaptive (Red) Statements

Expressions of empathy can support primitive brain perceptions (C1), the affects (A) that follow, and their predisposed behaviors (B). If C1ABs are adaptive (Green), they are associated with the Birthright Self. If they are maladaptive (Red), they are associated with the Yearning Self. The need to consider the context in which empathy is offered was identified in a cognitive–behavioral and as well as in a time-limited psychodynamic therapy (Karpiak & Benjamin, 2004). In both of those treatments, the therapists' expressions of empathy following adaptive statements improved outcome, while expressions of empathy following maladaptive statements detracted from outcome.

But as usual, such a general principle can be valid statistically and yet not apply to every individual. For example, on a clinical basis, I believe patients who suffered abuse and were punished and mocked for expressing feelings about it likely do need empathy, and plenty of it, for their pain and suffering. But if victims of chronic abuse have adopted a passive–aggressive pattern designed to punish the therapist caregiver/parent for perceived default (as described in Benjamin, 1996a, Chapter 11), then lasting empathic focus on ongoing misery can enable further suffering.

Worse yet, such patients can use the defense of projective identification supported by the fantasy that making the therapist feel as bad as he/she does is key to recovery because if the (defaulting) therapist personally experiences the misery deeply enough, maybe he/she finally will do something that actually helps. That pattern, like all patterns, has a history; this one likely is preceded by conspicuous and cruel withholding of acknowledgment or solace by an attachment figure. Typically, that would be the mother who knew her daughter (the patient) was being abused by the mother's husband. Such a daughter likely will feel guilty as well as confused, hurt, and angry and will have kept the secret for years, yearning for someone to understand and help, even as she trusts nobody. Difficult patients have difficult histories, and eliciting collaboration with them is understandably difficult and not for the faint of heart.

Empathy is most effective if it directs the patient's attention to adaptive behaviors and any potentially interfering maladaptive primitive brain activity. Many patients prefer to use the simpler language of *Red* and *Green* instead of "*maladaptive*" or "*adaptive*." Notes from Amy's last trainee therapist illustrate:

> When asked if her Green voice was thinking at all about possibly working again, she was really surprised and stated that she was just thinking this past week for the first time in years that she might be able to handle going back to work. We talked about Red and Green and how all of this Green is going against her IPIRs,[4] and this is igniting her Red. Once she had an understanding of all of this with regard to GOLs, she was very motivated to move out and even look into jobs.

Process Skill 3. Use the Case Formulation

An adherent IRT therapist considers the case formulation for every intervention, starting with the very first exchange in a session. For example, suppose the patient says, "I didn't want to come today because there is nothing to talk about." The IRT therapist might reflect that with "Nothing to talk about today?" If affirmed, the therapist might say, "Are you willing to say how you feel about our work last time?" That could lead to discovery that Family in the Head had been saying to the patient: "We don't like what you are doing there; this so-called therapy is a waste of time." From there, work can begin on what likely happened last session that would have offended Family in the Head. Such an exchange traditionally would be called *analyzing the resistance*.

In IRT, using the case formulation is the key to treatment resistance. Note that the "resistance" was identified by taking the patient's words ("nothing to talk about today") very seriously. Asking the higher brain "Why not?" in such an instance is too abstract and likely will yield little that is relevant because early in therapy, C2 is not aware of C1 tricks. Assuming that the primitive brain is operative when the therapy process goes off track, the therapist can use sequencing to identify links between a problem (nothing to talk about today) and activity of Family in the Head. The process is called *deep tracking*. In psychoanalysis, it might be called *uncovering the unconscious*.

Process Skill 4. Input, Response, Impact on Self

The simple words *input, response, impact on self* mark a profound difference between IRT and many other versions of psychotherapy. In IRT,

---

[4]IPIR means "important person and his or her internalized representation." In this book, IPIRs have become *Family in the Head*. That new term is less accurate and precise, but many psychologists did not like the formal language and many acronyms in the Benjamin (2003b [paperback ed., 2006]) IRT book.

events are viewed in interactive context because of the assumption that affective symptoms are miscued attempts to adapt to threat. Identifying the "input" identifies the perceived threat. For example, the sad patient might be asked, "What might you be depressed about?" The angry person might be asked, "What might be bothering you today?" That sounds like simplicity itself, but the "stimulus and response" perspective in IRT challenges the dominant "trait" paradigm that is content with describing a person as "depressive" or "anxious" or "borderline" without routinely considering context.

To illustrate the difference between the interactive (input, response, impact on self) perspective and trait theory, suppose Melissa was admired for something she did at work—as often was the case—(input). She does not feel well and calls in sick the next day (response) and gets another black mark for unreliability (impact on self). Trait theory might lead to correcting her BPD pattern of unpredictability and recommending a sensible structured plan for how to keep to a work schedule even when she does not feel like going to work. Although teaching her to be reliable supports goal behavior, an IRT therapist first would focus attention on her motive for calling in sick rather than on her need to be reliable. Melissa's primitive brain would tell her that success at work is dangerous. If she continues to be competent and reliable, the father in her head won't help. She needs to regress to the safety of disability as a GOL to achieve closeness to the father in her head. Reliability at work is unlikely to be sustained until Melissa becomes less terrified of autonomy and differentiation from the father in her head.

Understanding the case formulation, even just practicing the process skill of working with interactions, is not easily accomplished. Davis's (2012) dissertation study used interactive online video training based on enacted vignettes from cases in the IRT clinic to teach clinicians or potential clinicians (undergraduate and graduate students plus a few licensed mental health workers) to note details about current input, response, and impact on self as portrayed in a clinical vignette. There also was instruction about copy processes, but the primary outcome was based simply on recalled details of input, response, and impact on self for a case in the video. The highly structured training was more effective in helping clinicians attend to and remember interactive detail. But even for the licensed clinicians, the task was perceived as difficult, and the average performance was not impressive. After training, the high-structure group got 67% of the details correct about input/response/impact on self; the low-structure group, only 53%.

To relate these results to Melissa's responses to being praised at work, consider this: Usual practice would direct clinicians to focus on her BPD patterns and affective symptoms (instability and unreliability, depression, self-criticism). Those are "traits" that presumably account for her calling in sick, and they are the treatment target. But the trait perspective misses her threat-based motivation to fail (If I am competent and autonomous, he will not take care of me, and what will happen to him?). Again, in IRT, first address the motive (perceived threat/safety), and when the patient can feel safe enough to dare to change (differentiate), reliable behavioral change is more likely.

Process Skill 5. Link Primitive Brain Perception (C1), Feelings (A), and Behaviors (B)

Hopefully by now, readers are interested in contexts that activate sequences of primitive brain apprehension (C1), affect (A), and behavior (B). In response to my limit setting, which she perceived (C1) as abandoning, Melissa became angry (A) and told me so (B). According to her internal rules, that should have caused me to relent and return to "normal." As noted above, her disability was a GOL to maintain closeness to her internal father.

FIVE STEPS IN IRT

The five therapy steps in IRT are outlined in the lower part of Figure 5.1. The therapist is a guide, a coach, and a potential benevolent internalization who helps the patient free himself or herself from maladaptive internal rules and values and build new, more adaptive ones. Detailed descriptions of therapists' interpersonal styles and technical interventions appeared in several tables and flow charts in Benjamin (2003b [paperback ed., 2006]). Those charts are the basis of the IRT adherence scale that is used to test whether the IRT model is used and whether the components affect outcome in predicted ways (Chapter 10).

The center of Figure 5.1 reviews the steps, which progress from S1, establishing agreement to work toward a common treatment goal of Secure Base, to S5, learning new Secure Base (Green) patterns. The steps in between (i.e., S2–S4) prepare the way for behavioral change at S5. At S2, there is learning about patterns and understanding how the case formulation applies to what happens every day. Again, this insight provides a road map, but it is not the journey to change. At S3, early in therapy, dangerous behaviors are blocked. Much later on, this step becomes important again in S4 and S5 while actively replacing maladaptive behaviors with more adaptive ones. S4, engaging the will to change, is the most difficult step and the place where most dropouts occur. Here, the motive to realize fantasies of the Yearning Self has to be left behind and replaced by efforts to realize what is possible in the Birthright Self. After committing to the Birthright Self and taking initial actions to enhance it, new learning and reprogramming take place at S5. Behavioral methods for improving self-regulation and building more adaptive behaviors become central.

Progression through the steps does not happen in a rigid sequence. There is a lot of back and forth and jumping around. The sequencing in Figure 5.1 is about general trends that are volatile.

Therapy Step 1. Collaboration

Amy, Jason, and Melissa did have chemical imbalances, but they were stress related. They did respond to medications, as do all IRT patients, but that was not enough to resolve their discomfort and malfunctioning. For that, they needed to recue their safety and threat systems so that their beliefs about what to fear and how to be safe were more adaptive. Recuing begins with collaboration at the higher brain level (C2) to work to achieve Secure Base. Later on, the collaboration committed to change also has to be at the primitive brain level, C1, and that is much harder.

To review, Secure Base is described by the SASB model as transitive and intransitive behaviors that are friendly, moderately enmeshed, moderately differentiated, and balanced in focus on others and self, as described in Tables 2.1 and 2.2. Those friendly transitive behaviors also will be directed inward to create an inner Secure Base. Secure Base reflects adaptive cuing of the safety and threat systems, and if achieved, there will be minor symptoms, if any. The most difficult part of working toward Secure Base is finding the courage to differentiate from Family in the Head who sponsor the maladaptive rules. If that is managed, then regulating can happen by repairing, creating, and internalizing more benign attachment relationships. The therapist is part of, but by no means all of, that effort. If there is success in reregulating Secure Base, Natural Biology will provide the psychoactive neurotransmitters and hormones needed for normal affect regulation, and the therapy goal will be realized.

The part of this that is least understood, even by professionals, is the need to practice skills in friendly autonomy giving and taking. In a study of executive functioning (EF, working memory, impulse control, and set shifting) in 80 children aged 12 to 15 months, Bernier, Carlson, and Whipple (2010) measured maternal sensitivity, mind-mindedness (i.e., parent's tendency to use mental terms while talking to the child), and autonomy support. They found that "autonomy support was the strongest predictor of EF at each age . . . independent of general cognitive ability" (p. 326). Ulberg, Høglend, Marble, and Sørbye (2009) used SASB codes of a successful treatment to show that increases in friendly complementarity and autonomy taking were accompanied by decreased depression. In the IRT clinic, we found it extremely helpful to all of these severely disordered individuals to give them SASB-based descriptions of friendly autonomy (Table 2.2) and to use that as a guide to finding alternative responses in situations with family that had been difficult. It also is illustrated by many of the examples of "nonaggressive assertiveness" in the book *Your Perfect Right* (Alberti & Emmons, 2017). Reading that book often was assigned as homework for IRT patients.

Although collaboration in working toward Secure Base may seem easy, leaving old ways behind typically is terrifying and depressing. For example, Jason had to accept that he was a hated and extruded child and give up the idea he would ever be loved by Family in the Head. That was a long and painful process because he had learned that the greater his cleverness, the worse the attacks from his father and mother. Most certainly he could not call attention to himself by visible excellence. Yet he was so clever, the secret escaped with but minimal effort. It was a mark of significant progress when he sat in a restaurant writing about the day that had included constructive, highly competent exchanges with colleagues and friends as he enjoyed his plate of curry, anticipating his pleasant, scenic drive home.

When developing collaboration, as already noted, it can help patients move forward to remind them that the case formulation is a descriptive, not a blaming process. IRT therapy is not about judgment and justice. Rather, it is about understanding developmental processes accurately in order to help patients make better choices. Interventions that convey that perspective include "Please know I am not questioning what you say; I am trying to be sure I understand it." Or "I am guessing your family would not like you to be talking about this." Or "This is not to judge them as good or bad; they have their own Family in the Head to cope with, too. Our focus right now is to talk about stresses that might relate to why you are hurting so much." Actual confrontation of parents is not encouraged in IRT. The reason is that parents likely are damaged, too, and attacks on them are unlikely to enhance the family system to which the individual patient belongs. The system can be changed with family therapy, but that subject is far beyond the present scope.

Despite all these efforts to help people collaborate to work on managing fear of challenging Family in the Head, some individuals—especially those with patterns of borderline personality disorder—will angrily quit and then want to come back and repeat that cycle a few times before they commit to genuine collaboration working toward abandonment of old fantasies and a more benevolent and realistic view of who they are and who they can be. In DBT there is a rule: Patients who quit therapy are out of therapy. That is totally understandable and may help some people truly engage with treatment later on. Although there is no such rule in IRT, it would be IRT adherent for an IRT therapist to use that rule, especially if there is reason to think the patient is too fragile to tolerate the reconstructive process.

Therapy Step 2. Learn About Patterns, Where They Are From, and What They Are For

Here are some examples of maladaptive messages that patients bring to therapy; an early task is identify the links to the attachment figures who delivered them, shown here in parentheses:

- I am helpless, ashamed, and alone. (You are good for nothing, and nobody loves you.)
- I am incompetent and destined to fail. (Can't you ever get anything right?)
- I am the lowliest of the low. (I am going to thrash you within an inch of your life because you think you are so high and mighty.)
- Everything has to be perfect or I can't stand it. (If the house is not in perfect order when I get home, there will be hell to pay.)
- I don't trust anybody, including myself. (Ha ha! You thought I would catch you when I said jump into my arms!)
- I hurt others before they hurt me. (I will get you, little brother, no matter what you do.)

Such messages from attachment figures are reflected by copy processes, and whether they are adaptive or not, they represent GOL fantasies that bring feelings of safety. That is because primitive brain learning is based on frequency of proximity to attachment figures, and it has nothing to do with adaptive value.

Having a clear vision of a "healing image," an antidote to such messages to self, helps keep collaboration intact. It is not easy for patients to conjure up healing images that need to be closely related to Secure Base. Many have been immersed in interpersonal warfare and have no models to suggest what Secure Base would be like. This problem is illustrated by a highly functioning liberal arts professor who privately suffered from self-loathing and struggled with suicide. She had a history of severe abuse and had repeated that in a marriage she could not leave. One day, a friend repaired a broken kitchen appliance for her. The professor was astonished because she had learned that "when things go wrong, you just accept it and make do however you can. Your best bet is to anticipate others' needs so they don't get upset and create mayhem." It never occurred to her to do something directly to address her own needs. She had to keep focus on avoiding disaster. With thought about all this, she chose fixing the mixer as her near-term healing image.

A very good way to learn new patterns is to discuss current problem interactions, relate them to the case formulation, and try simple adaptive alternatives. For example, the professor's research assistant was failing to perform well, and she was thinking about how to transfer him to someone who might ask him to do things that were more interesting to him. There was a discussion about who he reminded her of; it was a talented brother who seemed self-centered and only did what he wanted to do. With the image of fixing the mixer in mind, she decided to initiate a meeting with the research assistant, tell him in great detail what she needed, and require him to meet in a week with the task completed, or else they would discuss his transfer to another professor, provided there was one who would accept him. If no one would accept him, this issue would be brought up in the next faculty review of students. In a week, he returned with the task done well. Apparently, he needed more clarity and assertiveness from her regarding what she wanted and needed. Of course, that might not have worked, and then the student's fate ultimately would be determined by the administrative system.

Transference analysis is another way of learning about patterns. For example, if a patient was overindulged, because of inappropriate expectations he may find the therapist to be neglectful. Relating that distortion to the case formulation might be called *transference analysis*. Connolly et al. (1996) studied transference by identifying relationship episodes (RE) in treatments of 35 male opiate addicts, some with cognitive therapy and some with supportive emotional therapy. By comparing core conflict relationship episodes in interactions with the therapist as well as with significant others, including mothers, the researchers confirmed the existence of transference within both treatments. Importantly, they noted that "transference" could be seen in relation to adult significant others (e.g., spouse, friends) as well as with the therapist. In IRT, transference is described by any copy process that involves the therapist. As the Connolly et al. study confirmed, there are copy processes in relation to other attachment figures, too.

Patients say they feel less crazy when they learn that messages from Family in the Head reflect a natural process and that what is unnatural is not the patient, but rather the rules family had for threat and safety. One person put it this way: "The language keeps you from falling into family chaos; instead, it gives it a container, a physical explanation. It's not like there are wiggling people in there, even though that is how it feels." Another said,

> It is easier to say to myself, "that is your lower brain operating" rather than "I am hearing voices." It demotes them, takes away their power. It makes the experience of hearing them more like an effect rather than a cause.

Copy Processes

As noted in Chapter 4, free association is key to making critical links between present and past. It reliably reveals copy processes because associative links are set by proximity in time or space without regard for logic or consequences.

For example, Jasmine, in her late 20s, had been immobilized by depression for over a year when she came to IRT. Treatment included some sessions with her mother and father and with her mother alone because there had been some family disagreements over Jasmine's lifestyle choices. In one session with Jasmine's mother, we spent time talking about her mother's own painful history. She felt that my descriptions of her patterns and how they were reflected in her treatment of Jasmine were accurate but made her feel guilty. The gist was that the mother had been disappointed in this child, and Jasmine had internalized this view and became a major disappointment as she did things inconsistent with her family's culture and her own welfare.

I reassured Jasmine's mother that the case formulation was descriptive, not judgmental; I said I realized she was only copying her own developmental experience, as we all are likely to do, and thanked her for her honesty. I added that the reason for talking about links between the past and present is that it can increase awareness, and that supports different choices.

Jasmine listened quietly to all this and after a while said, "I am sick of bottom feeding. I am almost 30, and it is time to move on. I don't want to smoke anymore; I want to get a good job and a different boyfriend." That was a higher brain choice and did not bring immediate changes. But that declaration set the agenda for change, and with once-per-week meetings in Year 1 and sporadic sessions in Year 2, Jasmine followed through with major, positive, life-changing, courageous decisions. I never again saw a need to discuss goals and motivation. Therapy was all about what she was confronting and where she wanted to go.

Aggression as a Primary Drive?

The Gift of Love (attachment gone awry) theory might rankle those who are convinced that aggression is a primary drive, suggesting that as a given energy, it must be properly channeled or else it will generate symptoms. It is not difficult to find evidence in the public domain that might seem to support that perspective. Examples include accounts of a young man taking a machine gun into a preschool and mowing down several teachers and 20 or so little children and a group of men sending into a marketplace children wired with bombs that are detonated by remote control. It is easy to believe those incidents reflect primary aggression uncontained, if not evil incarnate. How can such situations possibly reflect Gifts of Love?

The first response to that question is that naturally reared animals do not show such decontextualized aggression. Their fighting has obvious connections to survival of the individual or the species. So, from an evolutionary perspective, there is no such thing as raw primitive aggression as an end in itself. Approaching this uniquely human problem from an evolutionary perspective, there are two possible interpretations, and both suggest that those bizarre incidents manifest severe psychopathology. One type of pathology is Klute syndrome (Benjamin, 2003b [paperback ed., 2006], pp. 288–290), in which sexuality has been associated in the primitive brain with extreme aggression against helpless victims. The programming might have been auto-erotic activity connected with violent video games involving helpless victims. Alternatively, such pathological acts could be GOLs to attachment figures or identification with a violent parent or even a religious leader.

There are other possible scenarios, too. Unfortunately, there is no way to know because the perpetrators in the examples were killed while on their murderous suicidal missions. The point here is that IRT does not invoke primary drive theory as in classical psychoanalysis, but then it must account for such events. The assumption is that copy processes and GOLs to attachment figures are involved.

Gifts of Love

Understanding that affective symptoms are miscued affects serving as Gifts of Love is the part of IRT theory that is most difficult to understand. And yet the idea that the nervous system records what appears to please internalized attachment figures has been around for quite a while. I cited Fairbairn (1952) when first describing GOLs in Benjamin (1993). More recently, the idea was indirectly supported by Linehan and colleagues (Brown, Comtois, & Linehan, 2002) in a study that showed that suicide attempts were made on behalf of someone else.

In an example of self-sabotage supported by GOLs during IRT, a very competent, highly placed woman was attacked by trolls on the Internet and could not dismiss them as just that: disgruntled cowards spewing venom anonymously. Asked why she allowed that to get to her, she associated to ruminating as a child on how to get her mother's attention. She knew from experience that it was not OK to do well; only the boys could do that. Then she developed the theory that if she was hurt, she would be allowed to succeed. So she had a strong tendency to allow herself to be victimized. And she was. There were times when suicide seemed to her to be a solution to it all. I noted that suicide would make her the ultimate victim and please the haters. Reflecting on that, she said, "I need to realize that being hurt is not going to make her (mother in the head) like me."

Use of Sensory–Motor Imagery to Show Empathy, Facilitate Discovery, and Encourage Change

David Graham, cited earlier, spoke about connections between language and sensory–motor perceptions/actions. For example, *manufacture* means "make with your hands." *Travel* means "traverse, go across." I have found that German is most likely to be precise in this way. But there are plenty of evocative words and phrases in English, and I love to use them often. Here is just one: A patient was talking about how she had waited far too long to leave an abusive relationship. She said the process of leaving had been so unnecessarily long and tortured. I wondered aloud if it was like cutting the dog's tail off three times, and it was still too short. The patient began sobbing and after quite a long time, she repeated, "It was so humiliating. I was so tortured." This exchange was part of grieving and letting go. As Freud said, enhancing the depth of the experience with compelling imagery is a very effective therapy intervention. The stark image of repetition of useless painful efforts deepened her grief and helped her consolidate her understanding and will to change.

Poetry is the ultimate medium for effective use of words to express primitive brain activity. Mary Oliver's poem "The Journey" (Oliver, 1986, pp. 38–39) explains how and why differentiation from enmeshed families is so painful and difficult.

Therapy Step 3. Block Problem Patterns

Becoming able to block problem behaviors directed toward self or others is especially important when the behaviors are dangerous. Early in therapy, blocking may involve standard methods for handling emergencies known to many practitioners; they are important and are reviewed in Chapter 7 of Benjamin (2003b [paperback ed., 2006]). Very briefly, the clinician always is alert to evidence the patient might be suicidal, assesses and addresses intent and availability of means, and then elicits some form of agreement to a safety plan. Failing that, commitment is considered and used if necessary.

If the patient is collaborative, an IRT therapist can use the case formulation to contain dangerous behaviors. The therapist reviews the threat in terms of the case formulation, engages the will to resist giving this GOL to "them," and negotiates a promise to protect the Birthright Self. The therapist then adds a request to contact the therapist if the patient is losing that battle and in danger of acting on self-destructive thoughts between sessions. If the therapist is contacted, he or she tries to schedule an emergency session for the next day if the patient can pledge safety until then. Again, if there is little collaboration, more coercive methods, such as having family take the patient to the hospital or calling the police, may be necessary.

Jason's therapy provides an example of how the case formulation can be used to block a presenting symptom. Early in therapy, Jason was vulnerable to bursts of aggression. One day he got into a confrontation with a drunken man about access to a doorway. He described his intense anger and detailed how he could have seriously hurt the man. He recognized that his rage was an old pattern and said that despite working hard in therapy, this event showed he had made no progress. He added that with my focus on the positive, he was not allowed to learn from negative instances. I underscored his point: Therapy is failing. Jason agreed and added that I had said I had no new tools. I responded,

> True. But please let us use the tools we have. These are: recognize that your difficulties are derivatives of your early trauma, that you continue to suffer in life as you did then, and that at times you use their negative strategies on yourself and on others.

I asked what percent of him reflected belief that the difficulties he had were residuals of family damage. He said, "Quite a bit." I said "Good. Then let's use these tools to unpack the family in your head in action."

I suggested that we "walk the cat back," like the CIA after a job gone bad. Jason reviewed the offender's behavior and concluded there would be no point to going over it again. I said, "Please. I insist you hear me out on this." Then I reviewed the story of the fight as he told it, adding endorsement of his good judgment in that he had not decked the guy as he easily could have. I said,

> What needs to be changed is the intensity of your internal responses, including your self-talk after the event. The bottom line here is that you did not act with the street person as your father did with you, but you condemn yourself as if you had.

After some discussion, he agreed to try harder to stick with the plan of learning to acknowledge his strengths, an act that would have unleashed his father's rage. Not only would it be a crime to acknowledge the self-restraint; the father in his head might mock him for not decking the offender. So Jason was damned if he aggressed and damned if he did not. He very much needed differentiation from the father (and mother and siblings) in his head. Reconstructive work requires many such reruns of episodes in a safe relationship.

Therapy Step 4. Engage the Will to Change

The biggest difference between walking the walk and talking the talk in IRT appears during attempts to engage the will to change. Therapy Step 4 in Figure 5.1, engaging the will to change, is subdivided in the Prochaska, DiClemente, and Norcross (1992) stages of change. The first three, precontemplation, contemplation, and preparation, reflect the process of moving from (a) being completely unaware of how to explain symptoms using the case formulation to (b) understanding copy processes and GOLs and the normal developmental sequence, plus thinking about defining and nurturing the Birthright Self and give up the Yearning Self, then (c) getting ready to do something about it, challenge old loyalties, and experience resistance from Family in the Head with a plan to push on.

The fourth stage, taking action, is so difficult and so important that all of Chapter 6 is devoted to engaging the will to change. The key to reconstruction is turned when the Yearning Self finally is relinquished—for example:

> Mother will never stop hating me, and Dad will never stop attacking me. They will not acknowledge, affirm, and protect me, no matter how faithfully I conform to what they seemed to think and expect of me. Instead of worrying about and following those old rules, I will stop undermining myself and enjoy my gifts. I will move on and take my chances on my own merits.

The last stage of Prochaska et al.'s (1992) stages of change is maintenance, which entails resisting any regressive pull to go back to the familiar, maladaptive rules of the Yearning Self. It means shoring up the Birthright Self and not despairing if there occasionally is regression back to old yearning.

Therapy Step 5. Learn New Patterns

The last step in the IRT model—"the bottom line"—entails two types of new learning: one for the primitive brain and one for the higher brain. Learning at Therapy Step 4, engage the will to change, is primarily in the primitive brain. Learning at Therapy Step 5, learning new patterns, also involves primitive brain teaching (C1), but ordinary adult learning (C2) is more relevant.

Behavioral technologies used to treat PTSD are recommended for Therapy Steps 4 and 5. They include EMDR (Shapiro, 2001) and DBT (Linehan, 1993), which introduces psychotherapists to selected Buddhist practices in mindfulness combined with behavioral principles. The Buddhists are geniuses at mastering the primitive brain, so it makes tremendous sense to benefit from their wisdom in this challenging task. Linehan's (1993) contribution to mastery of affects and thoughts during psychotherapy is monumental. Emotion-focused therapy (L. S. Greenberg, 2004) teaches patients to recognize, label, understand, and 'downregulate' emotions to alter maladaptive memories, invoking the neurological perspective of LeDoux (2002) and zeroing in on Freud's algorithm. L. S. Greenberg (1983) also effectively used Gestalt two-chair techniques to help patients act out and experientially learn to relate differently to internalized representations.

Using the two-chair technique with the patient in various roles is a potent way to work with Family in the Head and to teach alternative responses by switching roles. Examples of "dangerous" but constructive acts while addressing Family in the Head could include self-validation and a declaration of independence. Patients often balk at this assignment and that should be honored until they become strong enough to do it. It can be wise, before engaging in such an exercise, to agree on a signal to end the exploration and return to the present. Therapists should prepare a method explicitly to send the Family in the Head back to where they were in the patient's childhood (i.e., temporarily restore the status quo).

Approaches that are more directly focused on higher brain mastery include rational emotive therapy (Ellis, 1973) and cognitive–behavioral therapy (Beck, Rush, Shaw, & Emery, 1979). The latter appears to be evolving to include more interventions at the primitive brain level.

New behaviors can be practiced as homework. For example, after leaving IRT, Jason wisely chose self-care as his first challenge. On his own, he implemented and followed through with health regimens, some of which included social interactions with colleagues and new friends. It was quite a while before he had developed the confidence needed to tackle what likely felt most dangerous, namely allowing himself to be more productive at work, his ultimate therapy goal. Melissa addressed her financial dependency on her father by getting a part-time job, gradually assuming more responsibility, and putting in more hours at work. This was short of independence from him, but it was an important beginning. Amy needed to move out of her parents' house, refuse to be a slave for family or friends, take some classes to explore what line of work she might like to pursue, and date kind men. She did all that one step at a time, first simply saying no to requests to take on huge unreasonable tasks. Later on, she took bigger steps, such as going away for a weekend with a friend. Finally, she moved out and started to claim her independence in full.

Another behavioral intervention is to ask parents who are having difficulty with their children to identify the copy processes manifest in their own parenting methods and decide if they want to do things differently. If they do, then parent–child interaction training (PCIT; Eyberg & Robinson, 1982) can be unusually efficient and effective. Parents are the main attachment figures and have the most power, so if they can learn to deliver Secure Base conditions, virtual miracles can occur. Readers again are invited to look at the child welfare website sponsored by the U.S. government (https://www.childwelfare.gov/) and reflect on how they might use the PCIT principles in practice (Child Welfare Information Gateway, 2013). It is all about Secure Base parenting.

Homework in IRT

Most of therapy change happens outside the therapy room, and so IRT therapists work with patients to develop homework assignments appropriate to the patient's case formulation and stage in therapy. An especially challenging homework assignment is to practice Secure Base as described in Tables 2.1 and 2.2. Family in the Head will not approve, but the patient needs to find the courage to try to get better anyway. Examples of homework appropriate to the theme of a therapy session were offered in this chapter's discussion of the therapy steps in IRT. Common assignments are to practice affect management, change in self-talk, and so on in relation to issues such as sensitivity to rejection, anger when others don't submit, lack of assertiveness, vulnerability to an oppressive loved one, and so on. Assigning movies about problems similar to those faced by patients at the moment can help normalize their experience by showing them at the primitive brain level (as when the viewer is immersed in the experience of the story) that they are not alone and that there can be good outcomes in life. For examples, *The Judge* acts out a GOL fantasy as a young lawyer takes care of his failing father who has gotten into big trouble (Downey, Gambino, & Dobkin, 2014). *Gaslight* shows how one can be brainwashed by an exploitative marital partner who wants complete control (Hornblow & Cukor, 1944). Brainwashing also is demonstrated in *The Manchurian Candidate* (Axelrod & Frankenheimer, 1962). The evolution of different forms of healthy but not idealized relationships is suggested in *Arranged* (Crespo & Schaefer, 2007) and *Elsa & Fred* (Ehrenberg et al., 2014). And so, with a selective eye and good luck, one can find profound wisdom in many forms of the arts, whether in novels or movies or opera or editorials.

Sheer Grit: Using the Five Rs

If secure in the therapy relationship, it is easier for patients actively to make change happen first in relation to Family in the Head and then in behavior. The grit of making change happen is summarized as the Five Rs:

1. Recognize specific instances of problem patterns,
2. Review their historical roots,
3. Resolve to change them,
4. Resist urges to repeat them, and
5. Rebuild the agreed-upon Secure Base alternatives.

Readers might understand the difficulty at this step by recalling what it was like just to break a simple, visible behavioral habit such as quitting smoking or losing 10 pounds. Change of automatic habits requires effort from within. As is true for quitting other addictions, giving up GOLs as required for change in psychotherapy cannot happen simply by "showing up."

Treatment of Melissa's Crisis

The regression reflected in Melissa's email probably was associated with her increasing apprehension (C1) that her parents were ill and mortal. Given Melissa's ability to Recognize, Review, Resolve, Resist, and Rebuild, the following email "reminder"[5] was all that was necessary to reorient her; a concerned phone call could have enhanced regression to externalization by giving the therapist a greater role in resolution of the crisis:

> I am very sorry you are feeling so much worse. But to the extent you can work on internal directedness, please try to look within yourself and generate your own answers here. I do not imagine that seeing me more often would solve this dilemma. That would just be repeating the old pattern of merging with a Big Other Person. The same applies to your questions about ECT. You have enough information to provide a Green and a Red answer for that and make your decision. Some people truly need to rest on others/external forces. You get to decide whether you are one of them. I hope you choose to get back in the driver's seat. I know that by now, you know how to take control of yourself!

In her next session, the mortality of her parents and the therapist were discussed, and Melissa returned to her focus on differentiating from her father and working on her inner sense of competence and security.

WHY AMY, JASON, AND MELISSA?

The stories of Amy, Jason, and Melissa, all very long term cases, were chosen to illustrate IRT case formulations and therapy steps because it is important to know that some outpatients need therapy for that long or they will be written off as chronically mentally ill (CMI). In IRT with "standard outpatients" in our private practices, Ken Critchfield and I have known many

---

[5]Present rules provide that if patients initiate a confidential conversation, providers may respond to an email. That may change. In any case, readers are reminded that email is not secure, and patients need to be reminded continually of that. I prefer to encrypt messages if patients will purchase the same system I use (AxCrypt Premium; AxCrypt AB, Stockholm, Sweden). Presently, a fax that is initiated from paper, not a computer, to a private number is a means of communicating that complies with the Health Insurance Portability and Accountability Act of 1996 (HIPAA). Of course, it is wise to minimize this and any other form of therapy work outside of in-person sessions. And if an email implies an emergency, then the more complex procedures described in chapter 7 of the IRT manual (Benjamin, 2003b [paperback ed., 2006]) are recommended.

more rapidly reconstructed cases. Here are a few examples from my practice; there are more in Chapter 6.

Barbara participated without hesitation in the IRT therapy process, and it was very intense. One day, after what turned out to be the last of six sessions, Barbara had to drive her car to the curb and park because she was awash with realization of the exact nature of her Yearning Self and how completely it had taken her over. She felt so overwhelmed that she chose to take a break from therapy, as some do. After a couple of months, she wrote,

> I really feel like this time without conversing with you has been beneficial. As you know, so much progress was made so quickly in my visits to you, and I really have benefitted from letting things 'settle'. The insights seemed to come fast and furious for many weeks after my last appointment, as my conscious mind mulled over and dealt with all of the realizations I've had, and the many deep insights I became aware of with your help.

Janet is another example of a high performer who made short work of reconstruction. She, too, was accomplished in many domains but had become embroiled in a highly adversarial divorce. Her history was so full of trauma one might expect her to become CMI or even to die by suicide. Her anxiety was extreme despite help from medications. She responded immediately to IRT, with little time needed to differentiate from Family in the Head. She said, convincingly, that she was fully aware of the details of her abuse, that it was beyond inappropriate, and that she wanted nothing to do with them, fantasized or real. She saw what the abuse had done to her siblings, and it was not for her. She had read about Secure Base parenting, knew that was far from what she had experienced, and was able to provide Secure Base for her own children. After 36 weekly IRT sessions spaced at irregular intervals later in the treatment, she drifted away for a couple of months and then wrote,

> I am doing well: working hard, losing weight, having nice times with my husband. I don't feel anxious or desperate any more. Everything you tell me reverberates in my mind. I want to thank you for helping me get to this place of strength.

Janet may or may not return for "booster shots" as some people do, but she will not again feel overwhelmed and without recourse.

So there have been examples of extraordinarily long treatment, some of extremely brief reconstruction of long-standing problems, and some in between. There are many who get to Therapy Step 4 and decline directly or indirectly to go further. As noted earlier, some say in a healthy way that they just don't want to go through the pain of differentiation.

More quit after mastering the initial crisis and more serious symptoms such as suicidality or unmanaged rage. An example is Anita, who was attractive, bright, and functional. At some time during 20 widely spaced sessions working on whether she should get divorced, she entered a colorful relationship with John, a charismatic and passionate but quite self-centered man. She accepted the idea that her pattern was to lead men around by the nose (her husband) or vice versa (John). She knew she did not like John's complete control, and she wanted him to be more loving. So she had gotten out of the frying pan (declining couples therapy with her husband and deciding to carry on with her wish to get divorced) and landed in the fire (with John, who had been silently in the background all along).

We had a few couples sessions with John, which did not change anybody. I agreed that John was quite controlling but also noted her similarities to him, all rooted in her family history. I suggested that her patterns, including whom she found attractive, could be the focus in our individual work in IRT. She agreed to try that but did not call and make additional appointments. I suppose she is still on-again, off-again with John or someone similar.

CAN BRAIN DAMAGE BE REVERSED WITH PSYCHOTHERAPY?

Given that maladaptive brain circuits supported by gene changes do amount to "brain damage," some may wonder how in the world such brain "damage" can be reversed by talking. McEwen and Gianaros (2011) provided hope. A brief summary of their research with colleagues at Rockefeller University is available on McEwen's (n.d.) website, where it is noted, "Stress-induced remodeling is largely reversed once the stress is removed, although gene expression patterns continually *change with experience* [emphasis added] and resilience declines with aging" (para. 4).

The idea that brain changes can happen during psychotherapy was noted explicitly by Karlssen (2011), who cited a host of neuroimaging studies. Another promising perspective on reparative brain plasticity comes from studies of brain recovery after physical injury; for example, Kleim and Jones (2008) wrote, "The existing data strongly suggest that neurons, among other brain cells, possess the remarkable ability to alter their structure and function in response to a variety of internal and external pressures, including behavioral training" (p. 225).

These studies are promising but not definitive. Future studies on what enhances reparative brain plasticity will be important to psychotherapy as well as to rehabilitative medicine.

6

PHASES OF THE ACTION STAGE OF CHANGE

I understand, but how do I change?

After hearing their case formulation, patients virtually always ask, "But *how* do I change?" The Interpersonal Reconstructive Therapy (IRT) clinician is charged with responsibility to say more than "You have to work it through." It is good if the clinician's language includes detail that makes the process, including risks and benefits, clear:

> We will work with your Family in the Head to help you dare to find ways to be safe that will grow your Birthright Self, however you may decide to define that. I am sorry to say that the process is frightening, because nature does not want you to break the old rules for safety. It also is sad, because you will be reminded of all the losses you have had because of the old unhelpful rules. But it is possible to change all this, and if you want to try, I'd be glad to be your coach, working to help you reach that goal as fast and as completely as possible.

---

http://dx.doi.org/10.1037/0000090-006
Interpersonal Reconstructive Therapy for Anger, Anxiety, and Depression: It's About Broken Hearts, Not Broken Brains, by L. S. Benjamin
Copyright © 2018 by the American Psychological Association. All rights reserved.

CONNECTING THE CASE FORMULATION TO TREATMENT

One of the main points in Chapter 5 is that an IRT clinician focuses more on instructions about safety and threat from Family in the Head than on the symptoms per se. That ensures that most of the work is with cause (the motivation that supports symptoms) rather than with effects (symptoms decontextualized). Said another way, it means that when working with Freud's algorithm, the reactivations and discussion of affects necessarily will lead to a focus on relationships with attachment figures.

For example, if Jason (Chapter 1) nearly gets in a street fight, the review of the episode would include a verbal "rerun" of the encounter from start to finish, with detail about thoughts and actions along with reexperiencing of feelings during the event. Along the way, if he does not make the connection himself, the clinician might say, "So this guy was totally out of line, and it was all you could do not to just let him have it." And after some conversation about that, the clinician might ask, "What does it remind you of?" That would lead to one of the many violent episodes with his father and all the pain and yearning about rapprochement with him.

This GOL territory is where the work on "cause" can happen. Unfortunately, the GOL is the "sore spot" and patients are not eager to work with it; they can get upset and even angry about being led there. Slowly, carefully, maladaptive parts of the grip of Family in the Head on the primitive brain can be addressed and, yes, "worked through" as defined by Freud's algorithm.

Higher Brain Motivation

The emphasis on motivation in relation to copy processes and GOLs is not the same as motivation addressed in motivational interviewing (Hettema, Steele, & Miller, 2005; Substance Abuse and Mental Health Services Administration, n.d.) in prolonged exposure therapy (Foa et al., 2005) or addiction treatments (Prochaska, DiClemente, & Norcross, 1992). In those well-known approaches, the motivational focus is on the costs of not changing compared to the benefits of change. For example, "Your anger is threatening your marriage and your job. If you could get free of the effects of it, you might save your marriage and do better at work." That certainly is true. It is based on good higher brain logic (C2) and can be helpful in IRT as a part of Step 1, developing collaboration at the level of the primitive brain. Unfortunately, that is not enough, because the primitive brain forces rule over logic. That is nature's intent: It makes little sense to allow the luxury of higher brain processes to rule over perception of threat that has been defined early in life by the previous, surviving generation.

Primitive Brain Motivation

To repeat: While the higher brain arguments make sense, the primitive brain is more compelling. Because links among maladaptive perceptions of threat and safety (C1), affects (A), and behaviors (B) are supported by GOL fantasies, they are the ultimate treatment target.

Initially, patients can be passively aware of and agree to the therapist's description of GOLs. But they rarely are aware of how powerful GOLs are until starting to change. For example, neither Amy (Chapter 1) nor Jason was fully aware of the impact of GOLs on their life choices. Amy's GOL was to serve abusive boyfriends to appease her internal cousin, which might finally bring affirmation, love, and protection from her internal mother. At first, she simply could not resist outrageous requests for service. Jason's GOL was to not let himself succeed at work lest his internal father strike him once again. They were trapped in the fact that they had coped with daily terror, sometimes near mortal danger, using their GOLs, which were repetitions of self-sabotage that led to feeling safe because that is what "they" (father, mother) thought was right. The primitive brain held that therapy plans to change those patterns were just plain wrong. The strategies of self-sabotage (Amy's abject, humiliating services; Jason's ongoing failure to use his enormous talent more productively) had served them "well" in that the old views of danger (C1), related affects (A), and behaviors (B) presumably continued to activate neurotransmitters or endocrines such as dopamine, serotonin, oxytocin, and opioids[1] to generate positive affects as directed by evolutionary forces to facilitate safe behaviors as defined by caregivers.

This process is not dependent on logic or effectiveness in reality. C1AB links, whether miscued or properly cued, are "rewarded" by safety system activities. As a result, highly intelligent patients like Amy and Jason, with their miscued affects, could implement acts of self-sabotage with conviction and expertise.

In an IRT treatment, *Freud's algorithm* refers to reprogramming affects that have been miscued by relationships with attachment figures. Attachment-based stresses can be physical, sexual, verbal, emotional, and/or behavioral. Attachment-based trauma surely includes physical beatings or rape or banishment. But attachment-based trauma also can be less obvious. An example

---

[1] This claim could be tested more directly by identifying episodes of work with GOLs in a session video accompanied by measures of safety and threat system activity. Therapy scripts and simultaneous physiological measures were created in the 1980s but were not helpful. One problem was the lack of knowing what to look at in overwhelmingly large data banks. If the texts could be marked for relevance to GOLs, specific predictions could be tested using SASB codes in the resulting smaller samples. A model for a sharply focused approach to analysis of selected critical interactions appears in Skowron et al., 2013.

would be perpetual silence from an important caregiver that is interpreted as rejection or judgment as being unworthy.

The ultimate measure of adaptive meanings of any parental action or "intervention" is, "What did the child learn about him/herself and the world (represented by the attachment figure) in this experience?" If it was a sensible lesson in socialization that was specific to an offense and not about the child in general, it probably was helpful. If the message created a sense of "What I am is profoundly offensive, inadequate, worthy of condemnation, and a blight on the face of the earth," the message is damaging. Even unrealistic positive messages can be damaging: "You are so gifted, I am sure you will be famous" said often in relation to everyday events is sure to support a hugely maladaptive case of narcissism. The next section zeros in on exactly how to try to undo the damage from such maladaptive internalizations.

IDENTIFYING AND BREAKING THE LOOP OF PSYCHOPATHOLOGY

In Figure 6.1 there is a summary of the reprogramming or "working through" in IRT. It begins, as suggested at the top right of the figure, with identifying a precipitating stress, a primitive brain perception of a threat or loss of safety (C1). That activates current affective symptoms such as anger, anxiety, or depression (A) that will predispose behaviors that are supposed to be adaptive (B). The patient who comprehends his/her case formulation will realize that these C1AB links reflect all aspects of copy process in relation to an attachment figure whose "voice" can be "heard/sensed." This is consistent with and builds on Freud's algorithm. As understanding deepens, the patient will see that the sequence is supported by the fantasy, the hope that the internal attachment figure will reward the copying (GOL behaviors) with affirmation, love, and protection. The case of John provides an example.

John's Revelation

John, a university professor who completed reconstruction in about seven months, sent me a note after he had been in IRT for about four months:

> I have found myself in this place since grade school. I am tired of trying to get a grip on myself, to hold myself together, to do a good job, not to ruminate. I understand I am biologically predisposed to see good things as a threat: to see myself as unworthy. I do see myself as unworthy. Now I am likely to get a big award. What would Dad say? "That is a joke." He would long for me not to get it. He would resent it if I did get it. There is no changing him. My heart feels that. My heart is profoundly dumb,

Identifying the Loop of Psychopathology

- Precipitating stress (C1)
- Current anger, anxiety, depression (A)
- Related maladaptive behaviors (B)
- Identify messages from Family in the Head
- Detect copying of C1AB links as identification, recapitulation, introjection.
- Target Gifts of Love (GOLs) = copied C1AB links supported by fantasies of Affirmation, Love and Protection from internal working models

Breaking the Loop of Psychopathology

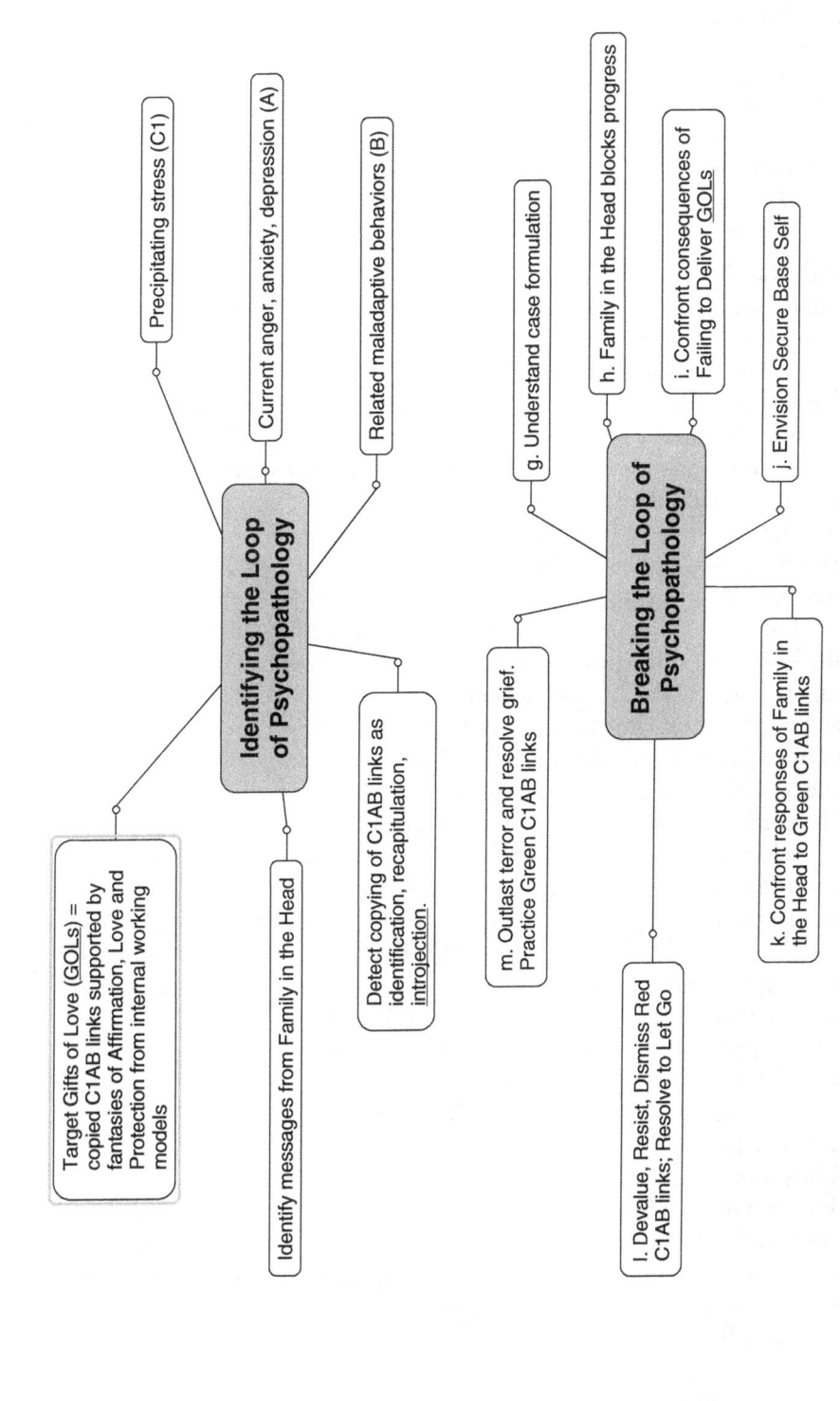

- g. Understand case formulation
- h. Family in the Head blocks progress
- i. Confront consequences of Failing to Deliver GOLs
- j. Envision Secure Base Self
- k. Confront responses of Family in the Head to Green C1AB links
- l. Devalue, Resist, Dismiss Red C1AB links; Resolve to Let Go
- m. Outlast terror and resolve grief. Practice Green C1AB links

Figure 6.1. Identifying and breaking the loop of psychopathology. The top panel unpacks the steps in connecting stress to symptoms and symptoms to messages about threat and safety from attachment figures. The bottom panel shows the sequence that supports differentiation from maladaptive aspects of family in the head and clears the way for reprogramming with standard behavioral interventions. Steps k, l, and m are reviewed in greater detail in Figure 6.2.

impervious, relentless in its convictions. So archaic. It is an ancient religion. The furies in a Greek play won't let me rest, be satisfied, enjoy my life. It is a curse. Now I am safe in my life, and yet I feel fear. This fear I feel is wretched. "You furies, you had a place in that world. You have no real warrant in my life since I left home." The catastrophe of that truth is that we have reason and reason is constantly tricked by emotion. Before I was aware of the emotion, I found a reason for it. I was on the lookout, making things wrong. "Things must be wrong because I feel wrong." This is an addiction.

With that brief statement, John fully and passionately confronted his case formulation. He identified his stress; it was the threat of an award. In response to this threat of success, he clearly felt fear, was weary of his history ("tired" suggests depression), and had anger for distance ("you furies . . . have no real warrant"). He linked all this to problem behaviors ("I was on the lookout, making things wrong"; "reason is constantly tricked by emotion"). He alluded to copy processes of introjection ("I see myself as unworthy") and recapitulation ("making things wrong"). He could "hear" his father saying, "That is a joke." He described the rationale for failing, the support for his self-destructive Gifts of Love, as he added that his father "would long for me not to get it."

The lower part of Figure 6.1 sketches the sequence for actually breaking out of the loop of psychopathology, and John's note exemplified this sequence. Drawing on clarity about his case formulation, John noticed that Family in the Head was blocking development of his Birthright Self: "He would long for me not to get it. He would resent it if I did get it." John confronted the consequences of failing to comply with his father's negative expectations of him ("The furies in a Greek play won't let me rest, be satisfied, enjoy my life. It is a curse."). Then, in a major leap forward, he envisioned his Secure Base self; he wanted to "be satisfied, enjoy my life." Immediately, recognizing that his father would mock his positive achievements ("that is a joke"), he took critical action: He "talked back" to the father in his head ("You have no real warrant in my life since I left home") and devalued the old responses, labeling all this "an addiction" and "a curse." Most importantly, he resolved to let go of his maladaptive wishes as he said, "There is no changing him," and commenting on how hard it is to let go, he notes, "My heart is profoundly dumb, impervious, relentless in its convictions [thinking father would change and become loving]. So archaic."

The primitive mind cares little about reality. John's father actually was dead. But the father in his head lived on, behaving as usual. That fact underscores why such discussions with Family in the Head are critical to success in reprogramming. After sending that note, John spent some time on his grief, but also became more open to taking in the affirmations in his present life. He terminated IRT a few months later.

About the Will to Change

The processes in Figure 6.1 are all about the fourth step in the IRT treatment model (Figure 5.1), called *engaging the will to change*. John's note was an extraordinarily succinct description of the process of a critical phase of "working through," of opening up to reprogramming. John had been an abused, abandoned child but was blessed with massive talent. He had learned to make his own way, to take care of himself, and so he did not linger in IRT. Most patients will stay longer after reaching this point and participate in reprogramming while still in therapy.

John is not the only one to leave shortly after such a deep-seated revelation. I assume he took advantage of my routine prescription of a dialectical behavioral therapy app that walks people through the repetitious work of reprogramming that is needed to complete reconstruction of the primitive brain. If that did not suffice, then help with L. S. Greenberg's (2004) emotion-focused way of implementing Freud's algorithm likely would be needed to reprogram John's ancient curse.

It could be said that "enabling the will to change" involves provocative language for a therapy that aspires to adhere to values and procedures from the basic sciences. But there has to be something beyond mechanics. Even brain researchers have had to acknowledge will when trying to explain "fire or don't fire" at the neurological level. Some use the term *decider* (e.g., Saaty & Vargas, 1993). Here is the how the dilemma of will strikes IRT: If the will to change is the "decider" of whether or not to let go of GOLs, how do we enhance it if we don't know what it is?

Once again, physics offers a model: Consider the challenge of defining dark matter. What is it? No light, not a single proton, can escape from a black hole, so we can never see dark matter directly. But we know dark matter exists because of the interactions (behavior) of objects near a black hole. And some day, we may have a theory that will predict other interactions that will test the theory of what a black hole is. Of course, there will be an infinite regression of new questions that follow those answers. But along the way, as usual, the study of interactions is the best method we have for saying things exist and learning more about how they work (interact).

So, by analogy, let us say that at the action phase of engaging the will to change, the patient faces a no-go versus a go decision. He/she is a "decider." There is "I see, but I don't want to change and I am not going to change" versus "I see, and I am sick of this so I want to work as hard as possible to liberate and define my Birthright Self." The second choice tilts the scale, but we only know what "the will" did by observing what the patient does or doesn't do. We are left with specific suggestions for how to enhance that outcome, and they are summarized in Figure 6.2.

a. Resist Red voices. Defy with green action.

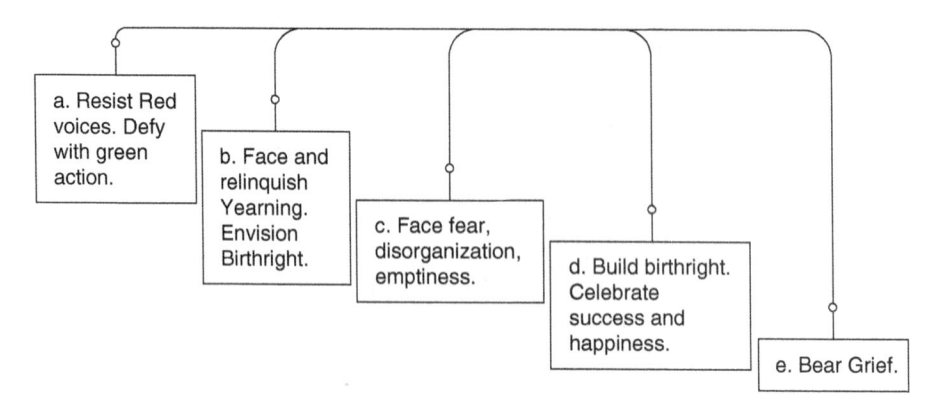

b. Face and relinquish Yearning. Envision Birthright.

c. Face fear, disorganization, emptiness.

d. Build birthright. Celebrate success and happiness.

e. Bear Grief.

Figure 6.2. Phases of the stage of action while engaging the will to change. This is the make-or-break stage of reconstruction. Activities shown from Steps a to e are "sequential," with a lot of going back and forth.

PHASES OF THE ACTION STAGE OF ENGAGING THE WILL TO CHANGE

John blasted through the action stage of change requiring very little work from me. He did not show much of the usual fury, fear, and depression, even though "outing" GOLs as he did is terrifying, demoralizing, and depressing. Again, the problem is that change demands disobedience, betrayal, and renunciation of rules and values from important members of Family in the Head. And if the separation is mastered, there follows deep, seemingly bottomless depression over losses of irretrievable dreams and of paths not chosen. Nonetheless, breaking the old primitive brain rules for safety and enduring the disorientation, fear, and despair while working on installing new rules and values are required.

Before beginning this definitive stage of action, Jason and Amy needed a lot of time to collect themselves, largely through becoming grounded in understanding their case formulation and by being "heard" and supported until they decided they could be safe enough to risk change. Amy took advantage of support from the IRT team for that. Jason did not risk doing it during therapy. After terminating IRT sessions, he deliberately, patiently, and skillfully reprogrammed himself by himself, spontaneously reporting about his progress as the years went by. So John and Jason went through the stages shown in Figure 6.2 by themselves. Most people benefit from guidance through the phases in the figure. John's solo trip through them is described below, along with examples from other patients who traveled this stepwise route in a variety of ways. At every step, Freud's algorithm was used.

Action Phase a: Resist Red Voices, Defy With Green Action

When the patient is ready to take action against the maladaptive rules and values, the first step in that process is to resist the voices of Family in the Head that disapprove of any deviation from standard operating family procedures. Threatened by promotion, John had to resist, set aside, dismiss, and downgrade messages from the father in his head, such as "That is a joke." John countered that with "You furies, you had a place in that world. You have no real warrant in my life since I left home."

Stacey, an anxious woman who had been raised as a "service animal," eventually declared she was worn out by the demands of her husband, adult children, neighbors, and all the community service committees. Then she was stricken with severe anxiety. The mother and sister in her head hissed, "You are selfish; you never think of anybody but yourself." Stacey capitulated and resolved to redouble her efforts to serve. Then she got depressed, concluding there was no way for her to be happy. It took a while before she was ready to begin to take action again.

When ready for action, the first thing to do is to notice when a symptom is worse and identify the precipitating perceived stress. This can be subtle, as in Stacey's case. Like Amy, even just thinking about doing something she wanted to do (take a weekend trip to a desert resort) rather than what she should do (cooking, housekeeping, gardening, church services, babysitting, and other such never-ending everyday acts of service) would terrify Stacey. The defiance reliably activated critical voices of Family in the Head: "You are selfish. You are unworthy. That is stupid. Poor you, feeling sorry for yourself. Why don't you just buck up? You are a hopeless case. You are wrong."

Stacey and Amy spent a very long time repeating loops as shown at the bottom of Figure 6.1 and in Phase a shown in Figure 6.2. It seemed impossible for them to dare to do something they wanted to do, which always was quite modest. They were very frightened about breaking the mold. Jason and Melissa, by contrast, were more defiant and moved on to the next step rapidly.

Action Phase b: Face and Relinquish Yearning, Envision Birthright

As patients begin to break the old rules, just like addicts, they are strongly drawn to scurry back to patterns of self-sabotage to cover their bases and demonstrate loyalty to and wish for the love of Family in the Head. Mary showed this in an unusually clear way. As she described recent unfair accusations about an action she had taken as an administrator with a lot of responsibility for public affairs, I noticed she was smiling. I asked how she felt about the criticism of her in the press, and she said, "exposed and mad."

Therapist: Exposed and mad?

Mary: I get mad a lot. You know that.

Therapist: That usually means you are in a Red state.

Mary: You don't see how serious this is.

Therapist [ignoring Mary's anger]: I can think of some reasons you might turn Red now. [lists elements in this particular challenge that resembled challenges in her childhood situation, when she was given responsibility for out-of-control men who were "bad actors"]

Mary: I do feel I am being like Anna Karenina before she threw herself in front of the train.

Therapist: I hope you do not do that.

Mary: I am not going to do that.

Therapist: Good. She did it because she thought he would know she loved him.

Mary: I am just thinking about her thoughts.

Therapist: I repeat: It would show she loved him. I am asking who you might be loving as you smile at the thought of you and your department going down over this.

Mary: When I am persuaded I will be brought down, I am happy and smile?

Therapist: Yes.

Mary: Now that you have said that, I see that I jump on the side of caution and negative expectations when things start to feel optimistic. Why do I do that?

Therapist: I can associate to that. Can you?

Mary: No.

Therapist: Kitten. [Her father had killed a kitten that she was very excited about and dearly loved.]

Mary: Oh. Yeah. Last night I was wishing we had not brought all those things up last time [therapy session]. If I think about them, I have such vivid memories of the losses. That makes me smile an evil, mean smile. I am going home from school to see the kitten, and when I get there, she is gone. Not there. I am told she is dead. [She smiles.]

Therapist: You are them when you smile now.

Mary: Then I would want to kill myself.

Therapist: No, I mean you treat yourself as they did.

Mary: I cannot stand to be that sad.

Therapist: You have to. I will help.

Mary: They don't allow it. I never got to be sad about any of it. That little kitten was so cute. I had trained her to do so many things. She was so . . . so little. [sobs] So you say I am possessed by them? Then I am like them?

Therapist: You treat yourself as they did. That is the problem. We are trying to change that.

Mary: Then there is such evil in me.

Therapist: We are trying to get rid of these feelings.

Mary: I have to move. I can't stay where I am. I can't take it.

Therapist: You have done it for years.

Mary: I am angrier.

Therapist: That can be good.

Mary: I am less patient. I have this mocking "na na" presence. It is just them. This morning I was going to send you a note and say I could not come.

Therapist: I am glad you did come.

Mary: Me, too. I can be haywire. It is really hard to be mad at you.

Therapist: Do you want to?

Mary: No. But I was this morning. It made me feel completely nuts, like I have flown off the radar. You think their part of me wants me to be mad at you. The other part of me can't bear being mad at you.

Therapist: You have a right to be pissed off at me sometimes.

Mary: I can't think of any examples.

Therapist: Well, you were mad at me this morning, probably for pushing hard on "them" last session. That is normal because we are breaking major internal rules. Those neurons will try to bring you, me, our process down.

Mary [abruptly shifting mood]: Speaking of having a life . . . It is such a relief right now to be out of the Red.

The next day, Mary sent a note about that session:

> I was laughing with them and against myself, against the people now that I am charged with protecting. I was smiling and becoming animated as they would have: my father, my brother, and my mother with their angry sneering smiles and cackles. I have never associated that smile with the devils in me. I see the defeatism, the pleasure in it. Is this what masochism is? Taking (their) pleasure in one's own pain, in one's own demise. Sharing the pleasure of the abusers in order to be (like) them? Oops. They don't want me to use that word—abusers.

Although Mary often was praised for her work, the Internet trolls sometimes hurt her if they joined Family in the Head. With anonymity themselves, such trolls up the ante when the target person is doing well and highlight any possible flaws. The mistake in question here had occurred at a low administrative level, but as the division director, she was held responsible. That was too similar to the way the family worked, which was to hold her responsible for the misdeeds of others, including those of her father. To get a semblance of control, she joined the trolls and Family in the Head who possessed her as she mocked and criticized herself. It seems to be a case of "if you can't beat 'em, join 'em."

Action Phase c: Face Fear, Disorganization, Emptiness

It was fear that led Mary to "join 'em." Holding steadfast to the current benevolent truth about oneself is not easy for victims of chronic stress from caregivers. It is hard to bear the reliving of it all and then, when breaking free, to find it is painful to lose GOL fantasies that Family in the Head eventually will change and become loving and accepting. As progress becomes more apparent objectively, the realization of the costs of past GOLs is followed by disorganization, emptiness, and in the end, deepest grief. Here are specific examples, each from a different person: "I am stepping off a cliff without my father's foundation." "I can't bear the loss of my imaginary world." "Who will I be if I am not who I have been?" "How do I kill part of myself?" "When I begin to want things for myself that they would hate, I have to retreat to an internal monastery." "I don't want to have to choose because I do not want to have to grieve. I feel the enormity of the grief I know I will feel. I sense it."

Responding to the fear and emptiness, patients may become passive in the face of escalating symptoms. Or they may be angry they have been led to this point and don't see a way out. Feeling defeated and in a sense abandoned, they may let the symptoms escalate and report them with ever-increasing frequency and desperation. Emails, telephone calls, and therapy sessions announce symptoms, disorganization, emptiness, and anger, all cries for help. Empathy is desired but, at this late stage, usually should be restricted to acknowledgment of "message received." Confrontation may be required to knock the process back on track as patients cling to regression and hope that Family in the Head will relent. At this stage, sometimes I will complain that I am the only one on the patient's Green side and ask,

> How about some help? Anybody but Red in there? Your passivity seems to call for me to quit withholding and fork over my powers to heal. Of course, if I could fix you, I would. I can't, and I see that you are showing lingering loyalty to "them" as you, in effect, leave me on the sidelines to conduct a Star Wars with them all by myself. I need you to take part in this struggle. I need you to fight for your right to make your new, more adaptive choices. Just last week, you had a marvelous time with [name two social situations] and prevailed nicely in [provide example of a work situation]. Today, you ignore all that wonderful progress and despair, saying you are stuck and have no idea why.

After one confrontation of that sort, I received a note that connected this pattern to incest:

> Your request that I be less passive and expect less of you has helped me clear my head of the stupor a little. It's as if I am still calling for her [negligent mother who never rescued the patient from incest in the night] through you. Waiting. Wondering whether she will come, or send him, or feign sleep while he wanders. I lie there waiting. Then . . . I give in to the inevitability and to the pleasure that cannot be separated from it. I cannot distinguish the pleasure from the giving in. It comes with hate; I am mocking myself all the while, connecting pleasure and rage to giving in, to momentary pleasure, to joining, to shame. Passivity is a salvation.

During this phase of action, there also is a need to meditate and to "be with" the emotions of fear, loss, disorientation, and overarching sadness, all about so much that has been wrong and lost. Emotion-focused therapy (L. S. Greenberg, 2004) can be especially useful at this and the next stage:

> The goals of emotion coaching are acceptance, utilization and transformation of emotional experience. This involves awareness and deepening of experience, processing of emotion as well as the generation of alternative emotional responses. In emotion coaching a safe, empathic and validating relationship is offered throughout to promote acceptance of emotional experience. An accepting, empathic relational environment provides safety leading to greater openness and provides people with the new interpersonal experience of emotional soothing and support that over time becomes internalized. (L. S. Greenberg, 2004, p. 6)

L. S. Greenberg (2004) offered helpful, specific suggestions for enhancing Freud's algorithm: use positive imagery of emotion to counter negative imagery, use enactments of emotion (psychodrama), have the patient recall another situation in which a particular emotion also was present, change the patient's view of a situation to activate a different emotion, express the therapist's own emotion about the patient's situation, and guide the patient to experience a new emotion in interaction with the therapist (p. 13). As always, any technique imported to IRT requires timing determined by the case formulation, the patient's progress in therapy as assessed by the therapy model, and the current context. Emotion processing, which can be helpful at any time, seems especially important in IRT when the focus is sharply on reprogramming the primitive brain.

Action Phase d: Build the Birthright, Celebrate Success and Happiness

As the patient becomes better able to accept, be with the losses, and dare to think he or she can manage the future safely in new ways of being, IRT becomes increasingly like standard outpatient practice. The new self is buttressed by exploration of new ways of being and, of course, consistent use of relearning technologies to program the old brain more adaptively. Here is a wonderful example of a list of alternative activities one patient created to distract herself from Red ruminations and actions:

> Music, mostly classical; the yoga I can do, especially the breathing; reading great writing; reading things I have avoided reading and thinking about; poetry; natural beauty; conversation with smart, kind, thoughtful, funny people; watching sports, live and on TV; solitude; taking the risk of being with people; taking the risk of seeking appropriate forms of help from colleagues; playing with the dog or just watching him invent games for himself or run joyfully through the house; the sun; the beauty of the house; the beauty of the landscape; eating well; solving problems or trying to come up with solutions; exercising, to the extent I can. Makes me feel clean; laughing with friends, especially old ones with whom I feel safer; thinking about you and the therapy process; feeling at home where I am.

Another useful technique is to engage in interpersonal coaching. Discourage blaming and model more constructive ways of asserting with friendly differentiations. Help patients take risks by disclosing more about their situation so others can better understand them. Encourage patients to listen well to others and remember what they say to strengthen the relationship. When patients have had the habit of overwhelming others with demands and complaints, encourage them to rein those in, listen better, and tell more interesting, less self-centered stories. When patients have been compelled to control all the time, encourage them to do more "letting" and less "making." Alternatively, when patients have been passive and dependent, encourage them to do more "making" and less "letting."

Patients may also need to be encouraged to envision their goals and their healing images in more detail. Some may be able to embrace aspects of their mother that were adaptive without having to identify with her in ways that have been problematic. The joys of choice and openness to new experiences can be discussed in some detail as time is taken to "sit in the psychological sun" and consolidate gains.

Action Phase e: Bear Grief

Stages d and e are closely related and maybe should be described together. In reality, every phase of change involves little steps toward building the new Green self. That is what upsets Family in the Head so much. As the new patterns grow stronger, realization that this better condition could have, should have evolved sooner brings anger sometimes, and always, grief. The reason grief comes last is that full apprehension of loss can only happen after the potential of now is more fully apprehended. New benefits become clear, and the person can fully experience what has been lost. One can't really know what one has lost until one has had something better. The contrast brings huge grief: "I don't want to believe this is the life I have had." "I find myself surprised at how grief stricken I am that I have not been able to spend more time with the things I love, that I have not been able to choose them." "I am going through a lot right now, evidently. I don't fully understand." "There is a lot of regret in it, a lot of grief, some occasional, newfound calm, and some hope."

Natural Biology again explains what is going on: Grief comes with loss of an attachment figure. The internalized representations are truly lost after there has been action embracing the Birthright Self and after the benefits of that are better apprehended. When a loved one has died, funeral ceremonies that include viewing, burying, or cremating the body are very important to successful grieving. Those procedures are more than hygienic; psychologically, they make it clear that it is over. The grieving ones must fully apprehend that the person, the relationship will never return. It is finished. Grief, especially between parent and child, is never easy, even in monkeys. Some mother monkeys have been seen to carry the body of a dead infant for months until finally it is left behind. Finally, all hope of revival is lost. A similar pattern is seen in grieving the loss of GOL wishes, which amounts to loss of an attachment figure. Consider this:

Joan: How do I get past the sadness?

Therapist: Societies that provide for a viewing of the deceased person confront the grievers with the reality: It is over. Helped to believe it, they are then free to let go and move on.

Joan: Last week, I almost went to the cemetery where they [family of origin] are buried.

Therapist: What would you have done there?

Joan: Said goodbye. I realize I don't have the sense that they are dead. Every now and then—no, a lot of the time—I say to myself, She did not love me. She hated me, I think. She did not want me. She did not love me. And then I feel amazed by it. It is amazing. Trying to get it to feel real. To the degree it does, I feel, *Wow*. Damn. I am taking it in more.

REVISITING THERAPY STEP 5: EMBRACE AND PROTECT BIRTHRIGHT (MAINTENANCE)

This last therapy step, discussed in Chapter 5 (Figure 5.1), overlaps the final phase of the action stage. It is when people finally seem to "cross over" and are no longer so vulnerable to slipping back into Red states. If they do slip, they recover quickly. They recognize regression and are better able willfully to declare they won't give in to it. This stage can include statements like "I don't want them anymore" or "I no longer want to pretend I am one of them." And after having good days, they can say, "I plan to have many more days like these!"

The main marker of completed reconstruction is the presence of an inner secure self. Interpersonal and intrapsychic features of secure self behaviors are described, again, as Secure Base in Tables 2.1 and 2.2. The items in the tables describe resting, relaxing, bonding, and curiosity. According to Natural Biology, these positive states are supported by adaptively released safety system endocrines (dopamine, serotonin, opioids). Under safe conditions, there is no perceived threat, and therefore threat system symptoms disappear naturally. Of course, as is the case for an old back or leg injury, there is a potential for regression when extremely fatigued, ill, or otherwise stressed in ways that can reactivate old destructive patterns. With good self-care, regaining the recovered state is rapid at that late stage.

Reconstructive therapy for individuals is difficult for patients and therapists alike. To learn to be adherent to the IRT version of psychotherapy, patients and therapist trainees need lots of practice, with periodic review by an IRT expert. Adherence, or purity of treatment, is vital. Our small-sample research shows that adherence to the model is directly related to symptom change and other measures of outcome (Chapter 10). The components that are most directly and significantly related to outcome are empathy and collaborative focus on GOLs. These components do not function in isolation. Every aspect of the treatment model in Figures 5.1, 6.1, and 6.2 is important to every other aspect. Everything organizes around the challenge of creating and maintaining collaboration to relinquish old GOLs and build Secure Base (Birthright Self). That is another, more explicit level of explanation for Freud's algorithm, and it is founded on a rationale offered by Natural Biology: Secure Base defines adaptive normalcy for a primate. GOLs are the anchors to pathology if rules for safety and threat are maladaptive, or GOLs are the inspirations toward health if the rules for safety and threat are adaptive.

Is reconstruction in IRT worth all the training and time it requires to recue the affect regulators by changing signals from Family in the Head? In the IRT clinic, we (Ken Critchfield, Thomas Woolf, and I) decided the answer is yes. Rehospitalizations of our treatment-resistant group were reduced significantly, and we believe, on the basis of clinical evidence, that there were beneficial multigenerational effects for those patients who had children.

IRT AND FAMILY THERAPY

IRT is an integrative approach, and so individual IRT therapy sometimes is combined with family therapy, illustrated with the case of Joyce in Chapter 7. IRT and family therapy are closely related simply because the case formulation and therapy plan for working with Family in the Head involve the same "interactive" processes as family therapy. Family in the Head are copies of what happened in the formative years, and unless family has changed in the meantime, family sessions in the beginning will be "déjà vu all over again." Change, whether in individual or family therapy, depends on helping each person find Secure Base in some form: loving connections that unambivalently support friendly autonomy.

It is wise for therapists to have training and experience with family therapy before trying to use it as a supplement to IRT with individuals. As a supplemental treatment, everyone understands the limits. The identified patient is the focus, not the family system as a whole. The goal in this limited form of family therapy is to facilitate mutual understanding and friendly differentiation. If that goal is not possible (often it is not), then it can be helpful to have made a recording of the session (with everyone's permission) that can be used later to help the individual IRT patient come to terms with the fact that nothing is going to change. Listening to that "evidence" can help him/her let go of GOL fantasies and move forward from there.

III

APPLICATIONS TO AFFECTS PRECIPITATED BY THREAT

7

ANGER

In the next three chapters, the Interpersonal Reconstructive Therapy (IRT) models are applied to anger, anxiety, and depression, respectively. According to Natural Biology, all three signal that threat has been detected by the primitive brain (C1), and they predispose behaviors that address threat in different ways. Anxiety and depression have diagnostic categories of their own, but anger does not.

DIAGNOSES AND EXPLANATIONS FOR ANGER FROM THE LITERATURE

Intermittent explosive disorder (IED) is one of the very few if not the only official *Diagnostic and Statistical Manual of Mental Disorders* (fifth ed.; DSM–5; American Psychiatric Association, 2013) diagnostic category that

---

http://dx.doi.org/10.1037/0000090-007
Interpersonal Reconstructive Therapy for Anger, Anxiety, and Depression: It's About Broken Hearts, Not Broken Brains, by L. S. Benjamin
Copyright © 2018 by the American Psychological Association. All rights reserved.

centers on anger in adults. Kessler et al. (2006) estimated the prevalence of IED at 3.9% and 7.3% in U.S. households on the basis of a representative sample of 9,282 national (USA) households. Only 28.8% ever received treatment for their anger.

In the diagnostic manuals, anger is described as irritability in some psychotic disorders, bipolar disorder, depression, generalized anxiety disorder, schizophrenia, alcohol or drug abuse and dependence, and domestic abuse. Forensic psychologists are sometimes tasked with predicting violent behaviors. Douglas and Skeem (2005) performed a meta-analysis that suggested that the likelihood of angry action is affected by diagnosis, gender, past success with violence, current level of stress, use of drugs and alcohol, and lack of available support.

Anger is implicated in physical health, too. For a long time, it has been well known that cynical hostility is correlated with higher risk for coronary heart disease (e.g., T. W. Smith & Brown, 1991). T. W. Smith, McGonigle, and Benjamin (1998) linked differences in cynical hostility within pairs of identical twins to differences in remembered relationship with the same attachment figure. Carlisle et al. (2012) showed that priming negative relationships by reminding subjects in discordant relationships of their marital partner was associated with greater threat, lower feelings of control, and higher diastolic blood pressure reactivity during stress. And T. W. Smith, Uchino, Berg, and Florsheim (2012) showed in a sample of 150 healthy older couples that self-reports of marital adjustment and anxiety and anger during a discussion of a marital disagreement correlated with coronary artery calcification, which is a powerful predictor of coronary arterial disease.

Despite its large presence in mental and physical disorders, there are not many evidence-based treatments for anger as a primary focus. A common recommendation for treatment of anger is for practitioners to help patients recognize, label, and "be with" their anger. Some encourage patients to "get out" that anger by yelling and "telling off" offenders in fantasy exercises during therapy. Some recommend that the patient "get it out" actually by telling others how angry they are. This strategy of recognizing, labeling and "getting it out" is based on primary drive theory from psychoanalysis; that perspective suggests that sexuality and anger are basic energies that must be expressed but have been suppressed or misdirected because they are forbidden by social norms represented by the superego. As noted many times in this book, IRT theory does not draw on primary drive theory in psychoanalysis.

However, given the popularity of the cathartic model, it is reasonable to consider whether it is helpful to express (get out) anger in fantasy if not reality. Do movies, videogames, or stories about violence reduce or increase the likelihood that viewers will act on such primitive impulses?

Some evidence, especially in the child development literature, has suggested that rather than diffusing aggression, exposure to aggressive models increases viewer aggression.[1] For example, Krahé, Busching, and Moller (2012) showed that after controlling for initial levels of aggression and other likely confounding variables, watching violence in the media predicted subsequent violence in adolescents.

Clearly, one's belief about the cause of a symptom, anger in this case, affects the choice of treatment interventions. There are quite a few interpretations of anger other than the one based on cathartic theory. Many are reviewed in a thoughtful and well-documented book about anger by DiGiuseppe and Tafrate (2007). The following list offers examples of interpretations of anger: Sometimes it is attributed to frustration. Others speak of "schadenfreude" (i.e., pleasure in the suffering of others). Some suggest that anger is the result of poor self-esteem, and in fact, insecure attachment styles have been related to anger: "Secure persons scored lower in anger-proneness, endorsed more constructive anger goals, reported more adaptive responses and more positive affect in anger episodes, attributed less hostile intent to others, and expected more positive outcomes than insecure persons" (Mikulincer, 1998, p. 513).

There also are theorists who suggest that problems with anger are inherited, making the common assumption that if there is a physical mechanism involved, a behavior must be "biological," meaning "inherited." Joyce et al. (2009) found that "the 9-repeat allele of the dopamine transporter is associated with angry–impulsive personality traits, independent of any link to mood disorder.... This could form the basis of a dopaminergic neurobiological model of angry–impulsive personality traits" (p. 717). Bishop and Lane (2002) proposed that problems with rage have "roots in emotional deprivation in childhood, especially when the child was used as a narcissistic extension by parents.... If a patient is overtly angry, he or she is more likely to be diagnosed with personality disorder" (p. 739).

Personality disorders having highest trait anger include passive aggressive, borderline, narcissistic, antisocial, dependent, and depressive personalities (DiGiuseppe & Tafrate, 2007, p. 204). Whatever the causes, DiGiuseppe and Tafrate (2007) are persuasive in their observation that anger is so prevalent and so important that it surely should be diagnosable as a standalone clinical problem, along with anxiety and depression.

---

[1] Older readers will remember the Bobo the Clown studies, during which children watched a favorite character being hit by a dominant or admired adult model. Later, when left alone, the children were aggressive toward Bobo. The variables that enhanced imitation were dominance and warmth of the model, which of course are features of attachment figures (Drabman & Thomas, 1977; Johnston, DeLuca, Murtaugh, & Diener, 1977; Plomin, Foch, & Rowe, 1981; Walters & Brown, 1963).

TREATMENTS FOR ANGER

There is suggestive evidence that some antidepressants may reduce aggression (Bond, 2005). Antipsychotics also can be effective (Buckley, 1999), which is not surprising because they appear to shut down "caring." Anger is treated by catharsis and by anger management training. The training teaches patients to recognize "triggers" to their anger and offers a number of techniques to contain it. Some are relaxation, thinking reasonably (e.g., not in all or nothing terms), enhancing communication skills, learning to practice empathy, meditation, distraction, deep breathing, and more. A meta-analytic study by DiGiuseppe and Tefrate (2003) reported a significant moderately sized effect from anger management training. Massad and Hulsey (2006) also focus on "cognitive restructuring" for people with PTSD, which often includes problems with irritability. Their emphasis is on changing causal attributions about the trauma by offering "attribution-based" treatments. Another treatment related to anger is empowerment therapy, in which victims of sexual violence are counseled to express their anger as a way of empowering and making them feel less responsible and helpless (Van Velsor & Cox, 2001).

According to a meta-analysis by Bratton, Ray, Rhine, and Jones (2005), play therapy, especially humanistic play therapy, is an effective treatment for children with problems, including "behavior" and "personality" problems, that often include anger. Treatment of domestic abusers is more effective if the offender can be motivated to participate in a working alliance. Individuals with antisocial personality disorder are especially reluctant to enter a working alliance and are prone to treatment resistance for interpersonal violence. However, Krampen (2009) showed that violence in this group can be reduced by enhancement of social–emotional skills, empathy, and morality by modeling and operant training techniques, role-playing, homework, guided imagery, development of life projects, and other techniques from anger management treatments. In sum, anger and aggressiveness clearly present problems for clinicians, and a number of treatments have been offered for it. However, clinicians have little guidance about when to use which approach, with whom, and how it works.

UNDERSTANDING AND TREATING ANGER USING IRT

In IRT, anger is an important component of the primitive brain chain C1AB that reflects the following sequence: sense threat (C1), release affect (A), and implement predisposed adaptive behaviors (B). It has long been accepted that anger predisposes the adaptive responses of "fight or flight." According to IRT theory, anger facilitates adaptation by implementing control of or creating distance from the threat. Anxiety and depression offer very different solutions. The choice of which threat affect is activated in a given context depends on lessons from attachment figures and usually represents identification with an angry caregiver.

For example, Jill came to IRT because she was very distressed by her adolescent daughter's detachment and uncaring attitudes. Her response to it, she explained, was to yell and scream and say things she knew were inappropriate and damaging. Her intent was to change her daughter (control) to make her do what was right. Jill's diagnosis was intermittent explosive disorder. Predictably, the effect of her anger was to drive her daughter away and to create distance. As the very intelligent, highly competent CEO of a successful business, Jill was able to tell her story in a way that led to rapid development of her case formulation. Briefly, she had been very close to her mother, who was prone to similar temper tantrums if Jill was inattentive and noncompliant. In response, Jill had spent her lifetime trying to please her mother. Jill's rages at her daughter represented identification with and love for her mother. She verbally attacked her daughter, although she knew in her higher brain that her anger was not appropriate or effective.

What was news to Jill was that it was less about her daughter and more about a Gift of Love (GOL) to her internal mother. Jill had had previous treatments that had helped her manage problems with depression, but now she faced unfinished business about how to be a better mother. It had not helped Jill in previous therapies to "feel and get rid" of her anger at her daughter. IRT theory directed that Jill needed to let go of her belief that all would be well if she gained control of her daughter using her mother's methods to re-create the intimacy she had with her mother.

As she differentiated from the mother in her head, Jill could let go of her wish to maintain enmeshment with her daughter and instead develop a well-bounded relationship with her child; in addition, perhaps that would free her to develop a more intense intimacy with an adult partner. The idea of letting go of this fantasy connection to her mother made Jill very sad and afraid. She terminated IRT abruptly and obviously was angry because she never made good on her promise to send payment. It is all but certain that she resumed her old patterns with her daughter, remaining loyal to the mother in her head.

Here are the steps in the IRT treatment model (Figure 5.1) as they typically would appear in a treatment for anger.

Collaborate

Collaboration at first means that the patient, who is aware of his/her case formulation and understands that changes are needed in relation to

Family in the Head, agrees at the higher brain level (C2) to work to build inner security that supports a secure self, the Birthright Self. But as therapy begins, collaboration at the level of the primitive brain becomes more and more important. In most IRT consultations and supervisions about "stuck" cases, the issue almost always is that primitive brain collaboration has been compromised. According to the primitive brain, the patient's agenda is to stay safe by old rules as the therapist works toward an approximation of Secure Base as described in Tables 2.1 and 2.2. Absent acute awareness of the fact that at the primitive brain level, the patient is not on board with the therapy goal, the clinician is reduced to ritualistic choices or trying this and that "technique" and hoping for the best.

Here is an example of what happens if that is the case. Emily's anger did not remit despite the therapist's efforts to try a number of "techniques." She was furious with her mother, who wanted Emily to take her mother's side in a long-lasting, still ongoing battle with her father. The therapist was frustrated as he tried and failed to help Emily progress despite his good suggestions that were focused on changing the patient's angry behavior. Emily refused to practice friendly assertion with her mother in an empty chair exercise. She refused to talk about her relationship (i.e., anger) with the therapist. She was recapitulating her long-practiced reactive defiance of her mother's expectations that she take her mother's side in disputes with her father. She felt criticized rather than understood whatever the therapist attempted to do to start a dialogue about interactive patterns.

But then the trainee therapist landed on a "technique" that worked because it struck at the underlying issue as defined by Natural Biology: differentiation and self-definition. Addressing Emily's underlying motivation rather than appearing to be trying to manage her, the therapist told Emily that he wanted to help her find her own self, her real self. She started to cry and then sobbed. After that, collaboration began in earnest, and meaningful work on change began. When perceived demands stopped, and advocacy for her differentiation was introduced, Emily's Birthright Self sensed the wisdom of it, and genuine therapy work toward Secure Base began.

Emily was willing to accept descriptions of how to practice friendly differentiation or "nonaggressive assertiveness"—for example, "Mom, I am sorry about your fights with Dad, but I love you both and do not want to be a part of them." She also found a collaborative way to suggest that her mother and father seek marital counseling. Whether that suggestion succeeded or not was not as important as the fact that in sticking with that solution, Emily made it clear to herself that she was not responsible for the parental marriage. Teaching friendly differentiation is a splendid way to replace maladaptive angry habits with ones that work better. Everybody wins. Nobody loses.

Learn About Patterns

Patterns in the primitive brain chain (C1AB) are easiest to see at the behavioral level, especially for clinicians who have learned to use the clarifying lens of Structural Analysis of Social Behavior (SASB). As noted many times before, context always matters. For example, anger for control is likely in a person with borderline personality disorder (BPD) when he or she feels rejected or abandoned (Benjamin, 1996a [2nd ed., 2003a], Chapter 5). Robert provides an example of how to start with learning about patterns in a patient who has major problems with anger.

Robert was in his early 50s when he came to the hospital following his third suicide attempt, this time an overdose on several of his prescription medications. He had been depressed for more than 20 years and believed that death "is a nice sleep" followed by nothing. This attempt was precipitated by rage about being undermined by two coworkers that resulted in demotion to a lower paying job after he had worked long and hard making many important and obvious contributions to the growth of the company. He believed, "People you work with turn on you." He did not know how he would support his family, and suicide seemed like a good way to take care of them because of his life insurance policies. He had a history of domestic abuse that included breaking some of his wife's bones.

Robert did well in high school and athletics and was proud to have been known as a tough guy, which he attributed to his harsh upbringing. He often was beaten by his mother and father with a large willow switch and/or was punched in the face, stomach, chest, and arms with closed fists. He was the only child of six who was punished; sometimes he was beaten for something a sibling had done. But the most frightening punishment of all was to be sent to a dark shed to spend the night alone.

Identifying with both parents when he attacked his wife, Robert also introjected parental attack in serious suicidal attempts. His wife was aggressive, too, so in marrying her, he recapitulated his relationship with his mother. Being a victim was his lot at work, too. Despite heroic efforts to please important others over a long period of time, he was punished and rejected there. With that, he just plain gave up and turned to suicide, which led to the current hospitalization.

Introjection is the copy process easiest to connect directly to symptoms. There are many published studies that show hostile introjects measured by SASB connect powerfully to self-attack and to threat-based symptoms. Data in Figure 4.2 demonstrated: (a) that remembered transitive hostile maternal behavior was mirrored in hostile patient introjects; (b) that introjects directly correlated with affective symptoms, with anger having the largest detrimental impact on hostility toward self; and (c) that hostile introjects were closely connected to hostile transitive actions by adult partners, recapitulating the hostile relationship with mother. Data in Figure 4.2 also suggest the opposites: that maternal friendliness during childhood optimized self-concept, minimized threat affects, and enhanced the choice of a significant other in adulthood.

Block Problem Patterns

Blocking anger in its many forms rarely is easy. Probably the reason anger is so hard to transform is that it is the most comfortable negative affect. For most people, it feels ever so much better to be outraged than to feel anxiety or depression. Nature encourages anger, probably because if you are under actual threat, fighting supports an optimal outcome: You prevail, and the threat defers, is destroyed, or leaves. When anger is a symptom and expressed with loved ones in the absence of credible threat, it is a disaster because threat is injected into an important safety system. Even worse, if sexual aspects of the safety system are activated during aggressive behavior, there is sadism and/or schadenfreude, both of which are unnatural, uniquely "human," and extremely difficult to treat because the reward in the pathology is sustained by GOLs plus intense pleasure. Other blockers to progress include therapist failure to adhere to the IRT treatment model, patients' fear of challenging GOLs, and erotization of misery or failure or self-destruction (i.e., Klute syndrome; Benjamin, 1996a [2nd ed., 2003a]; Benjamin, 2003b [paperback ed., 2006]).

Blaming

Blaming is an angry behavior that is based on feelings of outrage, of being right while others "obviously" are wrong. Here is an example of a common version of anger during psychotherapy. Like Jill, this patient was prone to "melt downs" and screaming rages. She recognized that as a problem but felt helpless to curb it.

Martha: It takes a long time to break this habit. It sneaks up when I am not looking. It is still the attachment thing. I still want to scream at them [her parents]. I want them to listen. I just want them to know. To hear me without saying back that the problem is all me. I want them to hear it without interrupting me every other second.

Therapist: You cannot imagine your parents listening to you?

Martha: Not unless I am calm and saying it's all my fault.

Therapist: What is it that you want your mother to hear?

Martha:	About the stuff inside me that makes me sick and depressed. Something in me as a little kid saying, "It is *your* fault!"
Therapist:	You are very hurt by all the blaming, and it feels better and right to blame back. You have done this in family sessions in previous therapies. Again, how did that work out?
Martha:	They just got angrier. We would stop speaking for months.
Therapist:	So raging at them does not change them. It does not make them become more loving.
Martha:	Right. I can see that.
Therapist:	Well, your anger is intended to control them and make them more loving, but it actually brings distance. How do you feel about that?
Martha:	I think that getting angry at them is a waste of energy.
Therapist:	I agree. I think we might better stay focused on helping you lower your expectations of them and your understandable wishes that the past was different. It is tragic it was so bad for you. But it seems that your anger about it, your copying of the family style of blaming, is keeping you stuck there.

This patient was passionate, smart, and talented. She understood this completely and decided to contact her parents much less often and sharply curb her self-destructive impulses that she recognized were messages to her parents regarding how badly she had been treated. When she did visit, she tried hard to have no expectations other than that there would be no changes and that she would remain civil to them. To help with this, she took a friend on visits and stayed in a hotel rather than in the small family home. Lowered expectations diminished her rage immensely. She began to focus on her own education and career and current social network and eventually reconstructed a new lifestyle and identity and built a comfortable and valued relationship.

Suicide

Suicide is a version of anger that requires immediate blocking. Remembering that anger has the function of creating control or distance can be especially helpful in blocking suicidal action. Here is an example: Betsy was a professional female who performed very well but was exploited by her boss. The small company was under financial pressure because of a big unexpected loss, and she was taking up a lot of the slack that had resulted from the departure of two employees. In addition, she had not been paid for 2 months and was hard pressed to meet her expenses. She was furious about the overload and the exploitation. Given that her mother still did not value her except when mother wanted Betsy to buy her something, and given that her father had been physically and emotionally violent with her until she left home for college, Betsy usually turned her anger against herself as she introjected her father's rage and her mother's dislike of her. She had cast her lot with her husband, who, of course, often flew off the handle. With alienation from her family of origin, a husband who angrily pressured her about bringing in more money, plus the impossibly large workload, she was feeling very angry (identification with her father), but also worthless and disenfranchised (introjection of father's messages). She saw suicide as a good response to her stresses.

She had lost her sense of mastery at work, the center of her adaptation. Knowing that she was an extremely competent, hardworking, and valued employee, I felt confident suggesting homework that forced her both to value herself and to learn a more adaptive way of dealing with exploitation:

> So how about talking about using your anger to try to get your boss to stop being so unreasonable? What would happen if you told him you need to be paid now and you need an assistant to help with the added burden or you will be looking for another job in a few days?

The patient was thoughtful about this, and we spent a little bit of time role-playing different outcomes of such a conversation. She decided to try this plan and promised, regardless of what he said, to be safe until the next session and to call for an extra appointment before then if she needed help maintaining safety.

The following week, she reported she was interviewing candidates for a new assistant and had a paycheck. Skillful assertion had elicited the reasonable treatment she deserved. The anger and the suicidality were gone. She also was asserting more with her husband, and he was responsive. This was an instance in which addressing a situation, more than internal processes, was adequate to resolve the crisis. Although it seems likely that Betsy needed internal change to avoid repetition of the pattern of being exploited, she was content with this encounter. I believe the patient should be the judge of when to terminate therapy, provided they understand what that might mean in relation to their case formulation and the next possible steps in reconstruction.

Gifts of Love

The term *Gifts of Love* refers to the motivation that supports copy processes. That motivation is the wish to find safety—that is, affirmation, love, and protection—through loyalty and adherence to the rules and values of attachment figures. GOLs are identified by "walking the cat back" from the symptom of behavior (B), to the associated symptom of affect (A) that predisposes the behavior, to misperceptions of threat and safety (C1), and finally to the related lessons from specific members of Family in the Head (copy processes). Because copy processes are directly associated with subjective feelings of safety, the GOL aspect of this process that supports self-sabotage rather than self-protection is the target of interventions in IRT. This focus on misdirected attempts to adapt can be seen as an analogy to correcting mistakes in identification of normal self-cells as not-self when treating autoimmune disorders (Chapter 2).

Here is an example of how GOLs that support anger appear in an outpatient treatment. Fred was a highly functional, very successful professional man who had been arrested for being the aggressor in a street fight. As we discussed this distinctly self-sabotaging behavior, I asked Fred what his father would have to say about it. He said,

> There is idolization of violent elements in my father, and he was violent. I want to make him proud. I think he will have conflict between saying, "My boy stands up for himself" versus "this is destructive." I was in my 30s before my dad ever said he loved me. He never gave me advice; he was emotionally distant, conspicuously absent.

With unmistakable clarity, Fred was describing identification with his father's violence and the GOL that supported it. It took Fred quite a while to let go of the primitive brain idea that being successful in fights was the way to his father's love and was worth the associated costs to his career and marriage. A major factor in his change was the fact that he truly loved and wanted to stay with his wife, and she became very skillful in asserting during marital counseling.

Joyce provides another clinical example of how to work in therapy with the idea that current symptoms of anger replay ancient history with Family in the Head. Joyce suffered from chronic anger and anxiety, and both would become worse following a success:

Joyce: I can't go on with this job. It is too stressful, and I am not good enough for it anyway.

Therapist: You feel unable and unworthy right after receiving that award?

Joyce: I really feel worried that I can't keep this up. I am thinking of quitting.

Therapist: What does the family in your head say about the fact that you are doing very well in your job, and you just got a big award?

Joyce: They would say, "You are getting stuck up. They don't know you like we do. You will get your comeuppance soon."

Therapist: I see. So you agree with them?

Joyce: Yes.

The conversation with Joyce then turned to discussion of early experiences during which success was followed by degradation and beatings from attachment figures. Introjecting those lessons, she declared herself not good enough and unable to stand the stress of the job. Her internally inspired anger was devoted mostly to self-attack, although at times subordinates could experience it, too. Given the modeling of anger and her lifelong experience of constant threat, it is not surprising that Joyce suffered from anxiety as well. The treatment for both symptoms, as always, was to progress through the steps in the treatment model and engage in Freud's algorithm via repetition of the detail provided in Figure 6.2.

Engage the Will to Change

It is not surprising that therapy often comes to a halt at the action stage of engaging the will to change. As noted in Chapter 6, it is here that the sacred rules for safety and threat must be broken, leaving the patient bereft of defenses with little idea of "what next." But those who proceed to take action through the phases of the action stage can cross the boundary between self-study and self-change. The clinician's job is to help them make this difficult journey safely. Here, the phases of the action stage of engaging the will to change are reviewed as they can apply to treatment of anger. It is not easy.

Jane was her violent father's favorite child. He often told her she was beautiful and brilliant and he loved her very much. If she got in trouble with her brothers, he would back her up. She learned that if she made a fuss when they did not comply with her expectations, she could escalate until her father would come and settle things in her favor in a hurry. She carried this stance into adulthood and picked partners who would scurry to avoid her rages despite the fact her demands frequently reflected an attitude of extreme entitlement. She was pretty and witty so she could get new partners, but each partner eventually grew weary of the burden and moved on. She was perpetually miserable and eventually settled on demanding special care from physicians and a very sad life of loneliness. Although many of her friends and partners had suggested she try psychotherapy, she never stayed more than a few sessions, saying she knew all there was to know about psychotherapy and nobody was up to being helpful to her.

Jane's father's favoritism did not support her development as a contributing member of the community. Sadly, this admiring relationship that engendered raging and entitlement may have been cemented into her psyche by an intimate, pleasurable form of incest. Jane was not interested in change. After her father's death, she found that going to doctors for her many symptoms and using alcohol were reliable enough as ways to activate her "safety" system. Despite all the losses she had suffered because of her rages, which were of psychotic proportions when she was drunk, she saw no reason to attend Alcoholics Anonymous. Jane illustrates how failed entitlements often are found in narcissistic personality disorder, as described in the *DSM–5* and with interpersonal detail in Benjamin (1996a [2nd ed., 2003a]).

Another form of recapitulation of angry behaviors is seen in passive–aggressive personality disorder, as described in the *DSM* (fourth ed., text revision; *DSM–IV–TR*; American Psychiatric Association, 2000), *International Classification of Diseases* (ICD–10; World Health Organization, 2017), and Benjamin (1996a [2nd ed., 2003a], Chapter 11). It is marked by demanding dependency combined with provocative oppositionalism (copy process opposite), usually in response to perceived defaulting and negligent caregiving alternating with demanding micromanagement and punitive interactions.

One of many examples comes from a consultation at an institution for severely dysfunctional adults. The treatment had been focused on restoring function and getting the patient out of the institution and back to work. Staff had chosen, reasonably enough, to set an initial goal of getting out of bed and dressed by himself in the morning. After a year of behavioral management, he was dressed by 1 p.m. rather than 5 p.m. On exploring the commentary of the patient's Family in the Head, it became clear that he felt he was punishing his parents for having been so busy working when he was little. Now he was too damaged even to get out of bed, and they had to pay for his extended treatment. IRT theory would predict that any and all interventions would yield no change until and if he no long saw his disability as a "victory." People in this group have a strategy of "winning by losing."

In IRT, the first task would be to elicit collaboration in working toward winning by winning for himself—that is, by working to enhance his Birthright Self on his own behalf. This might start by considering whether his victory is much fun compared to what he might be doing if he were not trapped into doing the opposite of what his parents want. Such framing of his defiance, which he interprets as a marker of independence, as a predetermined mirror image of abject compliance can sometimes strip oppositionalism of its glory. Being compelled to do the opposite hardly is free choice. Why let his parents compromise his right to a life of his own design? Work with people with passive–aggressive personality disorder, who consistently "speak in tongues" (i.e., send self-contradictory messages), requires quite a lot of skill and a tremendous amount of patience.

Resist Red Voices, Defy Them With Green Action

Anger is adaptive in therapy if it is expressed in the service of distance from toxic internalized representations of family. But angry patients, like all others, are vulnerable to rejection by Family in the Head, and so they need help resisting the "defenses" of Family in the Head. Here are typical versions of that: "This therapy is wrongheaded." "I am a fool if I go along with it." "The therapist does not know anything." "The therapist does not care."

Consider Paula, a highly effective and well-liked executive:

Paula: I am feeling pretty hopeless today.

Therapist: Right after we have just celebrated your playful, relaxing weekend?

Paula: I am mad at you.

Therapist: Why now?

Paula: You want me to reject them [Family in the Head]. You are so direct about it.

Therapist: Yes. That is a problem?

Paula: I have ways of protecting myself. Not being in reality is one. And you cut though them. Lately you have been especially blunt. You have been going after me. I mean *them*. What am I talking about? I forget.

Therapist: Anger at me for talking about them in ways that lead to anger at them and possible loss of the family in your head.

Paula: That's right.

Therapist: Do you want me to stop doing that?

Paula: Stop making me angry at them?

Therapist: Stop trying to help you get free of their dreadful grip.

Paula: No.

In this example, the dialogue was brief, dense, and focused sharply on the mechanisms of change: There was attentive listening, accurate reflection, collaborative framing of the problem in terms of the case formulation and treatment goals, and exploration of whether Paula wanted to proceed with this or not. There was everyday, jargon-free, efficient use of language. There was no lecturing, confrontation, therapist defensiveness, or demandingness. Paula was given structure, information, and choice. Her anger was diffused by offering the option of distance from the therapy task of defying Family in the Head. Collaboration in continuing to do the therapy work was restored by reminding her of why she needed to confront and change her old brain rules and values.

Externalizing patients may choose, more often than others, to attack the therapist when confronted with the task of challenging Family in the Head. IRT therapists are not expected to be masochists or martyrs, and if the patient is relentless in attacking the therapist and unwilling to consider the possibility of transference distortion (a psychoanalytic term meaning inappropriate perception of the therapist as a replication of the parent), it is recommended that the patient be given the option of switching to another model or possibly to another therapist.

As usual, context matters, and there is no rule of thumb about it. I choose to be confrontational probably more often than many others because I saw it modeled so often by master therapists in the 1960s (Benjamin, 2015a) and because I believe that people who adapt by relentless intimidation are unlikely to give it up until they meet someone who can speak their language framed in ways that support constructive change. This belief reflects the observation that violent street kids are most open to change if guided by somebody who knows their ways, who has "street cred." If the therapist stands up to tough patients in credible and knowing ways, some, but not all, of the hardened ones conclude there might be something worth considering here.

This is illustrated by an example from a tough-as-nails woman who was close to her highly controlling and often outraged mother, who was the hub of the family wheel. Josephine, like her mother, was quite comfortable being aggressive. They often had big dustups but easily made up, assured that they loved each other. The aggression served Josephine well enough in her work, where intimidation was adaptive, but not so well in relationships, including the therapy relationship. For example, Josephine had made good progress as she acknowledged that she was like her mother, and remembering what that was like when she was a child, she said she would like to change. She understood that change meant being less aggressive in service of dominance of those near to her. But her resolve in that was undermined by ambivalence. She continued to have stressful encounters, and when I would try to help her focus on her loyalty to her mother's ways, she would become anxious and deny the connection. She would declare that I simply did not understand how awful the problem person of the moment was.

At one point, when less aggressive interactions would have served her especially well, I suggested again that she check and try to work with the interpersonal effectiveness and emotion regulation sections of the dialectical behavior therapy self-help app. A few days later, she declared that my suggestion comprised neglect and abuse of her:

> You've broken me down, and perhaps I needed it. I've taken it; I am taking it. I'll go back to that website, but, frankly, I wasn't impressed. . . . But if you see me as needing to change like that, I do feel pretty awful. And yes, I've got to change those things.

Her statements directly reflected ambivalence about change, and she did not notice the contradictions. She was overtaken by the conflict between holding on to her internal mother and their ways of being together and becoming more agreeable with friends and colleagues. I tried to connect with her as I acknowledged that reconstruction does begin with deconstruction and that it often does leave one feeling disorganized, panicky, and empty. Leaving old, safe ways behind felt disloyal to her mother in the head, and the loss of her approval and support was nearly unbearable. Then, pressing toward change, I noted that change can bring present-day gains in satisfaction in relationships and the joys of releasing her truly gifted Birthright Self that had gone dormant. But Josephine remained ambivalent and, unfortunately, moved to another state before we finished our work. I fear the mother in her head prevails to this day.

When patients become angry with the therapist, along with thinking about how that relates to the case formulation, another possibility that is important to consider is whether the anger is legitimate and to try to repair any breach in the relationship related to a therapist mistake. For example,

> You are right; you told me about that before, and I should have responded then. I was very tired that day and may not have been as alert as usual. I am sorry. If you sense that I am not attentive enough again, would you please bring it up on the spot so we can work with the issue right then?

In the example of Josephine, it could be argued that she had inappropriately exacting and unrealistic expectations of the therapist and that, rather than apologize, her unrealistic expectations should be "interpreted." That very well could be correct, but I do not recommend such a confrontation until later in therapy, after the patient understands the case formulation and the reconstructive process more completely. Before there is strong collaboration based on experiences working together on difficult subjects, it seems unfair to invite people to speak from their primitive brain and then right away "confront them with reality."

Face Fear, Disorganization, Emptiness, and Despair

After patients decide to stop fantasizing that allowing endless repetition of old maladaptive habits will bring love and reconciliation with symptom-relevant attachment figures, the question "Now what?" looms large. While relinquishing the implicitly learned paths to safety, patients get frightened, disoriented, and disorganized. Without the GOL as the center of hope and the court of last appeal, patients speak of feeling a "hole" within. The feeling is extremely unpleasant and variously includes anger, despair, anxiety, panic, and apathy. They can't decide what to do, what to choose. And yet they must.

And that is not their only challenge. As they start to separate, the Family in the Head goes into outrage over the defection. This may be introjected as a period of self-loathing. There are rumination and regret over maladaptive choices and undesirable behaviors, all inspired, paradoxically, by a quest to be loved. Patients can be reminded of how natural, how inevitable it was that they would do what they did, and yet their ownership of it should not be negated. Their emptiness and despair can be normalized. As they begin to let go of GOLs, they more fully apprehend how much needless pain and waste there has been.

Build the Birthright and Face Grief

Toward the end of the stage of action, the sadness that has waxed and waned throughout therapy becomes deep grief. It centers on loss. Giving up GOLs as one builds the Birthright Self does compare to recovering from the death of a loved one. Kübler-Ross (1969) identified five stages in grief when learning one is going to die soon or after the death of a loved one: denial, anger, bargaining, depression, and acceptance. Those same stages were later used to describe responses to many other forms of loss, including coping with the breakup of an important relationship and giving up an addiction.

There are stages of grief in giving up GOLs, too. In psychotherapy, first it is important that patients clearly see, sit with, and be with the truth of how it really was. This often means recognizing the terror of beatings, the fury of the parent and the introjected self-loathing, the helplessness, and the ineffably deep sadness that followed. If the abuse was sexual, there is all of that plus the complexity of added pleasure and the feeling that one has a sense of some importance to someone, no matter how degrading and shameful the details.

Taking such things in is not easy, but it must be done to master the natural press to deny and preserve the fantasy of love and reconciliation that has been so sustaining for all these years. The process of fully acknowledging it should support the will to be free, the will to let go. The IRT therapist tries to keep the focus on motivation to let go and changes the therapy process if it seems that reviewing the trauma is stoking the yearning. For example, if the patient regresses after such a session, I will say something like this:

> I guess we went there too soon. It is important to be able to review all this from the perspective of an adult who wants to be free and move on. If revisiting the trauma excites old wishes to try to redo history, we need to stop doing this until later, when you are more convinced you want to let go of all this.

Here is an example of such a patient who walked up to the issue and turned back, declining to go forward. Jordan had just returned from a visit home for Christmas:

> *Jordan:* I quit. I don't want to do this visit home very often.... They do not see much about me other than my faults. I see my own faults. I left there feeling really discouraged. I am just a very different person. The way they live and the way I like to live are just different. I went to all this effort trying to get their love or approval. What a waste. What a stupid thing.
>
> *Therapist:* You want something from them they can't, or won't, give?
>
> *Jordan:* "Can't," I think. It is not there.

This realization helped Jordan lower her expectations of family and relieved her chronic state of anger and dissatisfaction. That was because she stopped imagining that her anger would get them to change as desired. But not long afterward, Jordan stopped coming to therapy, declining to leave a message of explanation. I believe that such a clear realization of the futility of the GOL wish had a lot to do with that decision. Her prior history of going in and out of alcoholism suggested to me that she had returned to alcohol as a way of coping with this loss. I also expect that quitting IRT reflected her disappointment that therapy had taken her to such a painful realization. Therapists need to acknowledge that you can lead a horse to water, but you can't make her drink.

Patients who press on beyond the pain of giving up GOLs and experience more moments of enjoyment usually move from terror to sadness about losses. There is noticeable conflict about having looked at the facts clearly:

> I feel grief-stricken that I have not been able to spend more time with the things I love, that I have not been able to choose them. I am going through a lot right now. Evidently, I don't fully understand all of it. There is a lot of regret in it, a lot of grief, some occasional, newfound calm, and some hope. I am breaking all those false beliefs I had, such as everything is heaven *or* hell. The God I used to believe in I don't like. I will do what is correct and what is right regardless of the system I grew up in. I do believe in God. This one gave life to me, and I am going to live it.... In

the process, I lose insanity, and the quality of my life goes through the roof. And all I had learned growing up is further behind me. That is what hurts. I fought the mourning process. But if you don't mourn something, you do not acknowledge it for what it truly is. Then I am removed from the truth. I lie to myself. People who lie shut out only themselves!

Learn New Patterns

As old, destructive habits become less sacred and interest in learning more adaptive ways of being increases, comprehension of the case formulation continues to help motivate behavior change. Patients do not go from one state abruptly to another. It is too scary and sad to change. It has to be approached gradually, like making contact with a wild animal. There are strategies that help. First and foremost, the therapist remains ever alert for motivational relapse, meaning that the patient "slips" back into the old addiction because it just plain too frightening or sad to move forward.

For example, one patient in the IRT clinic was distressed about being critical of her daughter just as her mother had been critical of her. She understood copy processes but could not stop being so critical. The supervisor recommended that the therapist begin with interventions that might disrupt automatic loyalty to Family in the Head:

> Help her see that she is being controlled by her mother's ways. She won't like that. Help her say to herself, "Stop: I don't want to treat my daughter like my mother did. I want to be my own person as a parent, and I certainly do not want my daughter to suffer as I did."

That strategy did help but more often is effective with better functioning mothers whose abuse of their children is not so severe.

After patients begin to be comfortable with the idea of letting go of their ancient GOLs, they are open to learning new patterns. For example, William decided he truly did not want to honor his father's hostility, and that meant he would stop intimidating and yelling threats when his employees did not do what he wanted. With full awareness of copy process and determination to renounce GOLs to his aggressive father, simple behavioral coaching became effective. The therapist suggested that William start the change process by giving himself a time-out before he exploded. Then he should reengage with intent to train his personnel specifically about what he wanted of them. With some practice, the explicit time-out was no longer needed, and he could go directly to telling employees about what was expected. When threat was required, William practiced offering clear contingencies such as "If this does not improve in 3 months, we will not renew your contract." William agreed to have regular meetings to let his employees know how they were doing.

The purpose was to educate and reward them. After the first run-through, William agreed to the program and needed no further remarks to carry it out to good effect.

Parents who decide to let go of their family tradition of violence need instruction in positive alternatives. As noted earlier, parent–child interaction therapy (http://www.pcit.org/) can help new learning. The power of parental affirmation when the desired response is emitted was demonstrated in a study of night training (Benjamin, Serdahely, & Geppert, 1971). In that study, results suggested that punishment delayed learning to stay dry all night long, while praise for success accelerated the learning.

New learning should include teaching about how to offer Secure Base conditions. Patients without it in their history have no idea what to do. It is helpful to give them descriptions of key parental Secure Base positions offered by the SASB model as Affirm (friendly autonomy giving) and Protect (friendly structuring), described in Tables 2.2 and 2.1, respectively.

Another helpful strategy is to give parents an individualized imaginary experience of what it is like to be on the receiving end of Secure Base conditions. They can be invited to recall a difficult moment with an abusive parent and explore how it feels with the therapist role-playing a "benevolent parent," modeling friendly autonomy giving and benevolent structuring specific to that moment. And to help patients manage their own affect, as noted before, all available learning technologies are appropriate at this step of learning new patterns as well as near the end of Step 4, engaging the will to change.

When treating anger and many other symptoms, repairing old relationships or developing new ones always is helpful. That idea is conveyed well in the movie *My First Mister* (Baum et al., 2001). A furious adolescent becomes transformed by an asexual relationship with a benevolent older man. Watching movies that illustrate a therapy-relevant point can be very helpful in modeling and motivating change, even with a difficult symptom like anger.

Jack demonstrated how anger is gone, not just contained or suppressed, after differentiating from symptom-relevant members of Family in the Head: He did not become furious with his wife last Saturday night, even though she had been quite provocative:

> I thought about what we said about this being just like my Dad and about our conclusion that my getting so mad never works anyway. So I just didn't take the bait. The next morning, I was warm and supportive. It worked out really well.

The therapist celebrated this use of functional analysis of anger with hearty affirmation. Jack needed distance from ancient rules and loyalties; with that achieved, his anger dissipated.

Such successful movement toward therapy goals can be exhilarating. One patient wrote, "Happiness and joy are becoming more familiar." And then, she sank back into Red:

> But still, anger is safer. It has always been safer. That is why I always went into rages. It is easier to hurt myself and others than to feel the feelings. If I feel, I might get swallowed by them; I might not be able to come back from feeling them.

Eventually a patient at this stage will need to weigh the costs and benefits of joy and vulnerability versus the fantasy of control with rage and the certainty of misery. As she has more episodes of joy and happiness, she will become less afraid of them.

A final issue has to do with relationship with family in the here and now after revising the relationship with Family in the Head. That is simply described as *friendly differentiation* (Table 2.2). Here is an example offered by a patient who mastered it: "I feel so grateful I can be around my parents and not fall apart. I am proud of myself. I am not going back to them for dark secrets. I am just going back and trying to have a good time."

8

ANXIETY

Fear demands "All hands on deck" when there is a perceived threat. That is adaptive because it mobilizes the person to address the threat. And because of specificity when there is fear, it is possible to identify the source and master it, to control, repel, or escape from it. By contrast, anxiety is activated when there is a sense of threat but the source is diffuse or hidden or expected to materialize unpredictably. Both fear and anxiety are pathological when there is no credible threat, whether overt and specific or covert and generalized. According to Interpersonal Reconstructive Therapy (IRT) theory, maladaptive lessons from attachment figures about safety and threat are a major cause of pathological versions of anxiety. This chapter is about how to assess and treat anxiety using the IRT case formulation and treatment models.

---

http://dx.doi.org/10.1037/0000090-008
Interpersonal Reconstructive Therapy for Anger, Anxiety, and Depression: It's About Broken Hearts, Not Broken Brains, by L. S. Benjamin
Copyright © 2018 by the American Psychological Association. All rights reserved.

ANXIETY, TEMPERAMENT, AND GENES

To review: As with most attributes, there likely is an inherited "envelope of potential" to experience anxiety, and an individual's position within that envelope is affected by interactions with the environment (Kagan, 1994). Temperament surely is a part of "envelope of potential." Impacts of attachment-based stresses may be moderated by temperament. Heritability studies that examine the relative contributions of "genome" and "environment" disagree about the relative magnitude of the impact of environment and heritability on anxiety. For example, Hettema, Neale, and Kendler (2001) used meta-analysis of monozygotic versus dizygotic twin studies of panic disorder, generalized anxiety disorder, and one of the phobias to assess this issue and concluded that heritability across the disorders is "modest." But Craske and Waters (2005) observed that "generalized anxiety disorder, and to some extent panic disorder, loads most heavily on broad underlying factors, whereas specific life history contributes most strongly to circumscribed phobia" (p. 197). New technology may help sort all this out by working at the level of specific genes. That is likely to be inordinately complicated. For example, Sharma, Powers, Bradley, and Ressler (2016) found

> robust [Gene] × [Environment] interactions . . . involved in major signaling systems in development and neural function. However, an important point is that tens, if not hundreds to thousands, of different genes and gene loci are likely involved in genetic heritability underlying part of the risk for stress- and anxiety-related disorders. (p. 257)

Meanwhile, the use of IRT case formulations systematically addresses developmental factors related to anxiety and other threat-related affects in adulthood. The impact of attachment figures is revealed by connecting symptoms to specific, reliably identifiable patient perceptions of activity of Family in the Head. The perceptions of patterns with attachment figures are measurable by ratings on Structural Analysis of Social Behavior (SASB) Intrex questionnaires and are illustrated at the group level by various SASB-based figures in this book. In clinical practice, relevant patterns usually are identified during interviews that focus on patients' views of specific interactions with attachment figures. Abstractions such as "He is not comfortable with negative affects" are not considered meaningful until illustrated by specific descriptions such as "He is afraid to talk about himself or his views of the marriage if his wife is present because he knows she will attack him for anything that does not put her in an ideal light." Such a statement contextualizes this patient's reluctance to say anything negative about his wife. The detail touches on his primitive brain perceptions (C1) and the associated affects (A) and predisposed behaviors (B) that are stored as messages from his "Family in the Head." The "insight" into his anxiety about expressing angry thoughts is that as a child, he was severely beaten by older brothers if there was any evidence that he might have thoughts and feelings that disagreed with or somehow put them in a bad light. With his choice of a demanding, punitive wife, he recapitulated the maladaptive pattern with his brothers and remained anxious about the dangers of speaking up.

In Chapter 2, possible mechanisms for how such experiences are recorded so that the associated "lessons" help the patient recognize threat (e.g., to disagree) and find safety (e.g., to keep silence) were reviewed. Important mechanisms include gene expression, silencing and epigenetic processes identified by Meaney's (2010) work on anxiety in adult rats and work by Suomi and others with chimpanzees (Ichise et al., 2006). Such laboratory studies make it clear that attachment-related stress in the young mammal has a powerful impact on adult expressions of anxiety.

STRESS AND ANXIETY

IRT case formulations are founded on the argument that perception of conditions of threat and safety are fundamental to affective expressions that appear as symptoms of anger, anxiety, or depression. Because a threat is a stress, studies of stress during development are quintessentially relevant to understanding the development of affective symptoms of anger, anxiety, and depression. The connection between threat and hostile behavior is most obvious for anxiety, but functional analysis of these symptoms (and the data in Figures 2.2, 3.8, and 4.2) shows that their connections to behavior in the face of threat are interrelated, with anger sponsoring transitive action in relation to the threat, depression reflects intransitive retreat while anxiety is a mobilized state poised between those two options.

A Natural Biological paradigm that connected stress to pathology was established long ago in rats by Hans Selye (1946, 1950). He showed that lasting physical stress leads to what he called general adaptation syndrome (GAS). There are three stages to GAS: First is an alarm stage that provides bursts of energy, and second are attempts to resist or adapt to the stressor. The third stage is exhaustion. His work primarily was about the impact of stress on physical mechanisms, but there are implications for behaviors, too. McEwen (2005) described impacts of stress on brain development in compelling detail.

The simple functional analysis of anxiety and depression in IRT theory is consistent with Selye's (1946) description of responses to stress. First are the stages of alarm plus resistance, and they are associated with anxiety (generalized fear) and anger (resistance). Depression is a passive defense of last resort. Demobilization and the behaviors of withdrawal and hiding seem comparable to the stage of exhaustion described by Selye as the end point of GAS. Similar parallels have been drawn by others.[1]

Some may object to this generalization of Selye's work to humans. (a) They might note that the stresses he used mostly were physical (chemical anatomical) rather than psychosocial, and anxiety in humans is not necessarily preceded by physical injury. (b) Others might say that he worked on rats, not humans. Those concerns are addressed by noting that physical damage is a stress, but it is not the only version of "stress." Perception of threat is a stress, too, because it can activate the sympathetic nervous system in mammals. Also, studies of the rat have contributed much to modern medicine. It is a convenient laboratory subject, and its genome matches the human genome at approximately the 90% level, while that of chimpanzees is 95% like humans (Chapter 2). In other words, principles established in rats and chimpanzees are very likely to be valid in humans.

(c) Still another reason to remember Selye's work is that the number of research studies in psychiatry and psychology that explore connections between stress and affective symptoms in humans is massive. In April 2017, a search of the American Psychological Association's database with key words "stress" AND "anxiety" yielded 58,262 articles, of which 17,315 were about PTSD, 10,812 were directly focused on stress and anxiety, and 5,471 were focused on stress and anxiety and depression. The range of variables related to stress and anxiety was wide; they included alcohol abuse, substance abuse, disturbance of sleep, religious beliefs, trauma (e.g., combat, accidents), bullying, and more. By contrast, an independent search for "anxiety" AND "heritability" yielded 241 studies, which is less than 1% (.04%) of the number of articles studying stress and anxiety. Clearly there is substantial interest in evidence about the link between stress and anxiety, and it far outweighs the contemporary focus on heritability of anxiety.

Even more relevant to the present discussion of anxiety and stress is a stunningly clear analysis of circuits involving epinephrine by Wong, Tai, Wong-Faull, Claycomb, and Kvetňanský (2008); a summary appeared in

---

[1] An Internet search of "general adaptation syndrome and anxiety" yields many results. One result criticized Selye personally and suggested his views are not backed by much evidence. That is puzzling, given that his legacy 1946 article on GAS was 112 pages long with impressive graphs, figures, and tables. His 1950 article was likewise very scholarly. Legitimate criticism would have to do with the suffering almost certainly inflicted on the rats. That is a profoundly difficult ethical issue that applies to a shockingly large number of medical studies. The issue always comes down to a conflict between human needs versus the greater good, and most of us are guilty of putting humans first while trying to minimize damage to other creatures and the environment.

Chapter 2 of this book. Holsboer and Ising (2010) also linked stress, brain function, and symptoms of anxiety (and depression):

> Different peptides, steroids, and biogenic amines operate the stress response within the brain . . . [and] act as neuromodulators in the brain, affecting higher mental functions including emotion, cognition, and behavior. . . . These central neuropeptides elicit corticotrophin into the periphery, which activates corticosteroid release from the adrenal cortex. These stress hormones are essential for the adequate adaptation to stress, but they can also evoke severe clinical conditions once persistently hypersecreted. Depression and anxiety disorders are prominent examples of stress-related disorders associated with an impaired regulation of stress hormones. (p. 81)

The IRT clinician would expect hypersecretion is the result of unrelenting perception of threat; the treatment implication would be to try to work with the misperceptions, assuming the patient is not actually living under threatening conditions.

WHY DISCUSS STRESS AND HEREDITY?

This point about the impact of stressful environments on development of affective symptoms is reviewed here because it is foundational to the treatment strategy in IRT. Here is why it matters: The prevailing perspective accepted by most clinicians is that affective symptoms are the result of inherited vulnerabilities triggered by stress. That diathesis–stress model leads directly to efforts to control symptoms that untoward heredity has sponsored. To be sure, symptom control is good, sometimes essential. But the Natural Biological perspective directs the IRT clinician to focus more directly on the cause of threat symptoms: namely, inappropriate activation of the threat systems by misperception of threat. That cause can be addressed by psychotherapy that changes the patient's relationship with Family in the Head, the affect regulators. If successful, Secure Base is achieved, and there are no symptoms that need to be controlled.

TREATMENTS FOR ANXIETY

Medications

"Antidepressants, anti-anxiety medications, and beta-blockers are the most common medications for anxiety disorders, including obsessive compulsive disorder (OCD), post-traumatic stress disorder (PTSD), generalized anxiety disorder (GAD), panic disorder and social phobia." This information about mechanisms of and treatments for various anxiety disorders appears online (http://www.nimh.nih.gov/health/topics/anxiety-disorders/index.shtml). Because drugs that treat anxiety are widely abused (see Drugs.com), some physicians have been prescribing antipsychotics for anxiety disorders (Comer, Mojtabai, & Olfson, 2011). That has the advantage of blocking anxiety without risk of abuse because patients and street drug users are not interested in them. The National Institute of Mental Health (NIMH) site reports that risk factors for anxiety disorders are shyness or behavioral inhibition in childhood, being female, having few economic resources, being divorced or widowed, exposure to stressful life events in childhood and adulthood, anxiety disorders in close biological relatives, parental history of mental disorders, and elevated afternoon cortisol levels in the saliva for social anxiety disorder (NIMH, 2016). It is possible to interpret most of these findings using concepts from Natural Biology, but that is beyond the present scope. The Natural Biological arguments would address disrupted attachments associated with social, financial, or physical vulnerability—all natural reasons to be anxious.

Psychotherapy for Anxiety

Cognitive–Behavioral Therapy and Other Psychotherapies

Newman et al. (2011) conducted a randomized controlled trial that treated anxiety with cognitive–behavioral therapy (CBT) plus supportive listening (*n* = 40) or CBT plus interpersonal and emotional processing therapy (*n* = 43). Earlier results had suggested CBT could be enhanced by combining it with interpersonally focused interventions, and this study sought to confirm or disconfirm that finding: "Using blind assessors, participants were assessed at pretreatment, posttreatment, 6-month, 1-year, and 2-year follow-up with a composite of self-report and assessor-rated GAD symptom measures" (p. 171). Although both approaches yielded significant change, there was no difference between groups. The implication is that CBT for anxiety was not enhanced by adding these other approaches, and the conclusion was that the previously reported enhancement of CBT may not apply to every individual (Newman et al., 2011, p. 171).

Elliott (2013) performed meta-analyses on treatments for anxiety disorders and noted that most studies involved CBT, which consistently had larger effect sizes than the compared approaches. Elliott's focus was on humanistic (person-centered experiential [PCE]) therapies, and he noted that despite inferior performance relative to CBT at the group level, PCE was better for some individuals. Both Elliott and Newman et al. (2011) commented that identifying individual (or diagnostic group) differences may be important to choosing optimal treatments.

Symptom Containment or Redirection

There are many additional therapy approaches designed to contain symptoms of anxiety. Variations on the CBT paradigm are common. Franklin and Foa (2011) recommended a response prevention procedure that asked patients with OCD to invoke a range of personally distressing images (starting with the least frightening and progressing to the most) and to refrain from their usual ritualistic responses and/or engage in alternative activities. Foa, Hembree, and Rothbaum (2009) recommended prolonged exposure (a form of extinction) for treatment of posttraumatic stress disorder.

A newer method of reprogramming the primitive brain is cognitive bias modification (CBM; MacLeod & Mathews, 2012). CBM treatments are quite brief and appear to be effective in reducing anxiety in normal subjects and in individuals with diagnosed anxiety disorders and depression. For anxiety, this computer-based procedure briefly presents two images or words that respectively evoke negative (e.g., a threatening face) and neutral attributions (e.g., a neutral face). More anxious people focus more on the threatening image. The computer program draws the subject's attention from the threat to the neutral image by providing an engaging task such as asking the subject to identify letters appearing in place of the neutral face. Repeating the procedure around a thousand times, over a total of 2 hours, changes the user's tendency to focus on the negative image/word. This effect of diminished bias toward negativity generalizes to other situations.

Behavioral Antidote to Anxiety

A fascinating animal study suggested that anxiety can be relieved if the subject has some control over exposure to the threat. Joseph E. LeDoux (2013), a distinguished neuroscientist, explained this in an article describing how rats learn to respond to cues associated with danger. His basic procedure was to put rats in a box, play a tone, and shock them mildly. The rats' natural response was to freeze in response to the shock and, later in a different box, to the tone alone. It was very difficult to extinguish the freezing to the tone by using what might compare to "exposure therapy."

But LeDoux (2013) and his colleagues found a different "treatment method" that was quite effective: They repeated the trauma training as before, but this time progressively conditioned the rat to run to the other side of the box, at which time the tone was turned off. In other words, the rats had a way to turn off the signal of a threat. After learning that, they stopped freezing in response to the tone that was no longer associated with threat. From the perspective of Natural Biology, one could say the new procedure gave them a way to control the threat signal. LeDoux said the rats used "proactive" avoidance to get over their fear of the tone. Whatever the choice of language, the research suggests that anxiety will abate if the sufferer has the ability to avoid reminders of impending stress. That might compare to the clinical practice of helping patients learn to avoid "triggers" to memories linked to threat from related members of Family in the Head.

IRT: Address Attachment-Based Causes

As mentioned above, in IRT the focus primarily is on the adaptive purpose of the anxiety. Recall Joseph (Chapter 2), who believed he had to, in effect, read peoples' minds and give them what they wanted, or else disaster was sure to happen. That was, of course, impossible, so he was worn out by his failure to serve people what they wanted before they knew they wanted it. The treatment issue for Joseph was this: If he was treated again with medication and lessons in coping skills, he might recover, but returning to work, his strategy of pleasing others was likely to fail again, and he would be back in the hospital. Why not focus on the stress he experienced during childhood that convinced him his job was to keep everybody satisfied and allow him to reexperience and reconsider it and its current relevance using Freud's algorithm while going through the steps of enabling the will to change, listed in Figure 6.2? As he started to get free of the old mandate, he could work on new coping and social skills, and after they were mastered, he should not have another regression back to the toxic rules he constructed during childhood.

Prevention and Resilience

Studies of resilience in children in response to traumatic events (e.g., fire, earthquake, shooting, other extrafamilial event) have suggested that duration and age of exposure matter (Masten & Narayan, 2012). The impact can be minimized by avoiding separation of children from caregivers and reuniting separated families; carefully monitoring children's media exposure to images of the event; and more rapidly restoring routines, schools, and opportunities to play and socialize with peers. These findings are consistent with the idea that being with (normal) family and peers offers natural antidotes to anxiety, namely safe base.

Offering training in effective parenting promises to have long-lasting beneficial effects in preventing anxiety and other affective disorders by facilitating development of normal, Secure Base patterns in relation to self and others. McGilloway et al. (2012) offered their Incredible Years Basic Parent Training Program to 149 disadvantaged children who had high scores on behavior problems on the Eyberg Child Behavior Inventory (Eyberg & Pincus, 1999). Subjects in the program ranged from 32 to 88 months of age and were compared with 46 children in a wait-list control group.

Significant impacts were seen on behavior problems (effect size of .77), child hyperactive–inattentive behaviors (linked to anxiety), and social competence, as well as on parent competencies and well-being. The idea of treating anxiety in children by teaching parents how to offer Secure Base conditions received support from a study by Leonardo and Hen (2006), who noted the serotonin system has a big role in maintaining normal levels of anxiety. According to Natural Biology as applied in IRT theory, serotonin is associated with Secure Base, which encourages parasympathetic activity that opposes threat-system chemistry.

CASE FORMULATIONS FOR ILLUSTRATIVE SUBTYPES OF ANXIETY

The literature on treatment of anxiety sometimes offers different treatments for different subtypes of anxiety. IRT treatments can accommodate subtypes via case formulations that address each symptom. For any and all case formulations, the IRT therapist uses the process skills and therapy steps listed in Figures 5.1, 6.1, and 6.2. To illustrate the flexibility of the case formulations that direct the progress through the standard treatment steps, here are IRT case formulations for two subtypes of anxiety: phobia and agoraphobia.

Phobia

Phobia involves fear of something specific that causes dysfunction. According to IRT theory, a phobia represents inappropriate perception of and response to threat based on maladaptive signals from Family in the Head. Anthony was afraid to drive on busy streets because his demanding and critical father had convinced him he would make mistakes that would result in disaster. Anthony had introjected his father's criticism and recapitulated his role of fearful, incompetent driver; maintaining these patterns was a GOL that kept him close to his father and his father's views of who he was. The IRT treatment for Anthony would center on helping him dare to separate from the rules sponsored by the father in his head.

Agoraphobia

Patsy, a home decorator with a fine reputation, was afraid to go out of her apartment lest she see a currently defaulting, blaming client. Patsy had just finished a large job for this wealthy woman, who frequently got drunk and would be beside herself with fury. In this project, a very expensive modification of the kitchen had to be redone because the client did not like it, even though she had approved the plan. A new wood floor had to be replaced because the client was not satisfied with how it looked. A recreation room had to be repainted because it was not bright enough. The subcontractors were amazed at all this but continued to rework the project to please the client. Patsy had to pay the subs out of pocket, and the client was supposed to reimburse her but did so only in part because she was not yet satisfied with the project. Sending the account to collections was an option but sure to trigger a lawsuit because the client had a stable of lawyers, and her history suggested that she relished legal fights. So far, the client had said she was going to do all that she could to ruin Patsy's reputation. The time and money required to try to recover her costs seemed not worth it to Patsy, who wanted, most of all, not to have to interact at all with this woman any more.

Despite the fact that her performance had been good in the opinion of all parties except the client, Patsy felt she had done something wrong because the client was not pleased. Her developmental history had shaped her belief that whenever something went wrong, it was her fault. Her main copy processes were introjection and recapitulation. Her family had viewed her as incompetent, even as they expected her quietly to support and "clean up" after her entitled, critical older siblings. So when Patsy encountered a disapproving, exploitative, and explosive female figure, she was reminded of an oppressive sister and fell victim to the old injunction that she was at fault and should set things to right. Patsy could not stand up for herself at all.

To escape her agoraphobia, Patsy needed to realign her relationship with Family in the Head so that she could honor her own abilities and needs rather than feel that when a dominant female was inappropriate and displeased, it was her job to solve the problem, quietly and behind the scenes. Treatment for Patsy required that she let go and grieve the loss of hope finally to be affirmed and protected by her mother and then proceed to make the most of her relationship with her current attachment figure, her spouse.

IRT TREATMENT OF GENERALIZED ANXIETY DISORDER

Collaborate

The process of change, as always in IRT, begins with addressing the motivation that has been holding the patient back and then defining and agreeing on therapy goals. In a brief version of family therapy guided by IRT case formulations, the focus was on Joyce, in her late 20s, who was living at home, not working, anxious, angry, and depressed. Quite feisty and confrontational, Joyce had trouble keeping friends and often found herself in abusive situations. She had a traumatic history with her abusive father but now was living with her mother and her mother's new husband, a kind man. Her mother was thoughtful, understanding, warm, and supportive. After a few IRT family sessions, Joyce fully grasped that she was identified with her biological father and realized that was not at all how she wished to be. On her own, she began to think about all of the scrapes she had been in because of acting like him. She began to change how she related to her friends and her stepfather but still was terrified to think about leaving home, away from immediate access to mother. Joyce was an only child and felt, "She will always be there to take care of me when I need it because of the abuse [from biological father] I have suffered." Fear of leaving her mother's nest was a major block to Joyce's progression toward an adult level of autonomy. She was not willing to collaborate to work toward the goal of IRT, friendly autonomy, and internal Secure Base.

As family sessions continued, mother more clearly came to join her husband, who wanted Joyce out of the house, and acknowledged the very real need for Joyce to become independent. Joyce was frightened by this perspective, but she stopped fighting with her stepfather using her old confrontational, defiant style. She practiced "walking away" so that she could cool down and come up with a reasonable way of asserting with him. Understanding that autonomy taking was an important developmental stage that was supposed to happen in a healthy person rather than evidence that her mother was defaulting, she began to think more actively about finding a different living arrangement and moving toward self-support. That was not easy, but it turned out that she was helped by some old friends in a nearby town who had identified an open part-time job and offered to share housing with her. Despite anxiety about such a big change, Joyce accepted their offer.

Recognizing that she might have difficulties after she moved to the new town, Joyce continued in family therapy while preparing to leave. She identified situations that might set off her Red, fatherlike patterns, and she resolved to work hard to use her new skills in nonaggressive assertiveness (Alberti & Emmons, 2017). When she came close to letting loose with the old rages, she repeated, "I am done with this." After about four more sessions, she set off for the new town, determined to succeed. Although she was not living far away from home, she visited only on important occasions and did not return to live at home again. She was practicing peer play merging into the stage of adult development.

It is unusual that such "insight" translates directly into the action stage of change. It likely was facilitated by the facts that (a) Joyce had her own individual therapist, (b) that her mother was so caring and supportive, and (c) made it very clear that she agreed with her husband that Joyce needed to move on. Collaboration about the nature of the therapy goal by Joyce and her mother was the key to their progress toward healthy, friendly differentiation. It still took about a year to accomplish.

Learn About Patterns

Identifying C1AB links that connect patterns in current relationships to interactions with attachment figures is a major step toward engaging the will to change. In this step, the patterns that need to be identified are those that have to do with primitive brain copying of perceptions, affective and behavioral links (C1AB) under conditions involving threat or safety. Here are some examples of symptom-relevant copy processes involving anxiety.

Copy Process: Identification

As noted earlier, patients see the copy process of identification quickly with higher brain skills (C2) if they are interviewed with emphasis on interpersonal detail. Mary, for example, knew she was quite anxious unless she was in control. She knew her need to control represented identification with her stepfather, and she felt safe by assuming that if she was like him, she would never again be a victim. After realizing that her need to control had caused her a lot of difficulty in her adult intimate relationships, she vowed to try to change it. She accepted assignments to monitor herself and immediately noticed, "Talking like him feels real. Anything else feels unnatural." Accepting that her primitive brain was in charge, she resolved to update it.

Using her iPhone recorder, she began to practice talking to her lover about a difficult issue without dominating. She played it back and thought about what she said and how she said it. Recognizing her father in action, she would try again, making a new recording until she was showing friendly differentiation, as had been modeled by the therapist plus assignments to read self-help books under the heading of nonaggressive assertiveness. Mary repeated the exercise until she became good at making "clean" statements about her own views without being coercive. She agreed that it would be good for her to maintain her skills in control because she was a highly placed executive in a large company.

"Mission creep" can be an example of misdirected anxiety. If a person requires everything and everyone to be in order and in its place, any noticed deviations in the order of things or the behavior of others must be addressed immediately else the anxiety about disarray arises. Eleanor said,

> Morning is my best time. I think more clearly then. But I delay getting to professional work because of other things that need to be done. There are so many little decisions that are laying waste to my life: Millions of tiny ants are stinging me to death. Wow, that sounds exactly like my

mother. Her experience of her life is of never-ending little stuff. Everything is insignificant, but there is so much of it that it takes over. Like her, I tolerate too much digression. Mother was a manager, but a really bad one. I am, too. She would try to make me do it this way or that, like I try to make my husband do things. I have my mother's stick-oriented way of behaving that makes life miserable if you don't do what she wants.

This, of course, includes patterns characteristic of OCPD (Benjamin, 1996a [2nd ed., 2003a], Chapter 10), which is predictably comorbid with anxiety disorders because of the need to stay mobilized to keep things and people in good order.

Copy Process: Recapitulation and GOLs

Generalized anxiety disorder (GAD) often is preceded by a history of unpredictable, severe violence and/or credible threats of abandonment for alleged crimes attributed to the person with GAD. Marcia's GAD was based on severe physical violence: "When Dad was a jerk, I could not say he was an asshole. You just sit there and politely eat his shit, saying nothing unless you have a death wish." But that did not assure safety. One time when she was an adolescent, she came home at a time he decided was too late, and so he

> beat me 'til I peed my pants. I had to miss 3 days of school waiting for the bruises to clear. There is no room for error. My childhood was miserable. I would rather die than have to live it again. . . . I had to anticipate all the time. It was unpredictable. For all those years, I had to dodge bullets. I'd try to keep everything perfect so he would not attack.

Most tragically, and not uncommonly, some mothers fail to support, and sometimes even collude with such abuse. Marcia continued, "At age 10, I took care of my infant brother completely. I shopped, cooked, cleaned, took care of him. I did everything. Sometimes Mother helped. And sometimes Mother would lock me in the basement with the dog." Scary fairy tales may not be so popular any more, but Marcia's story shows their scary substance still holds true. The copy process of recapitulation leads abused people to pick abusive partners, and the tale repeats. After several years of work in IRT, Marcia and her husband managed to differentiate in friendly ways from their families in the head and, most importantly, chose to learn to relate to each other in far more loving ways. Her anxiety abated noticeably.

Copy Process: Introjection and GOLs

Almost every anxious person is self-critical, and that criticism reliably speaks the words of one or more attachment figures. Here is a brief conversation about the inner life of Doris, whose AA sponsor told her that she "goes overboard in criticizing herself." She accepted this description of herself during her first IRT interview:

> Life is a trial, and you are sure to be gonged. The world is populated by judges, ready to gavel you down at the first word. But what actually is happening is that you are talking to yourself as if you are your mother.

Doris agreed with this and noted, "I criticize myself as a defensive maneuver. It is a way to prevent her litany." That explanation applies to quite a few self-critical people: They bring themselves down before the Family in the Head does. It is very difficult for them to practice friendly self-talk. Saying "I am a good person" can itself elicit intense anxiety. In response to that, Family in the Head likely would counter,

> You think you are so great. Well, you didn't tell the half of it. You are completely selfish and you only pretend to be honest and fair. You are a liar, and nobody who really knows you as well as we do will ever want to be with you. Wait and see; you will get your comeuppance.

Battling the roots of such anxiety-inspiring introjections is a main agenda in IRT.

In another example, Ann had struggled with bulimia for many years along with GAD. She had been making progress with eating when she became enraged by a situation at work in which an officer of the law had engaged in unlawful behavior on the job. Ann was responsible for this person and had called him in and managed the situation in appropriate ways. That night, she binged and then screamed at herself about messing up, believing "nothing ever is good enough."

Therapist: What would Mother say about all this?

Ann: She would be critical in some way. Nothing ever is good enough for her.

Therapist: So you scream at yourself for her?

Ann: Absolutely. I am bound to fail.

Therapist: Well, does the screaming have a purpose?

Ann: Yes. If I shred myself, I pacify the ugly fates.

Ann's fury at herself, then, was to control herself and possibly appease the ugly fates (her mother). Her bulimia reified the conflict between complying with her overweight mother's modeling of overeating versus having a normally weighted self. Her treatment for anger and bulimia centered on comfortably differentiating from the never-pleased mother in her head.

Gifts of Love

Gifts of Love are probably the most difficult of all IRT concepts to understand. How can it be that trashing one's self-interests is evidence of love? But one can see it in myths (casting treasured young women into the volcano), heroic acts in war, taking controversial political positions, and internal GOLs in relation to Family in the Head. Joyce had acted like her violent father as testimony to him, as a way of being closer to and possibly currying his favor, and finally as a way of feeling safe simply because she was copying a powerful attachment figure and doing what he seemed to think was appropriate. It makes us feel safer because nature's rule is "do what they do, say, feel." Such compliance makes one feel safe.

This means that children treat themselves as they have been treated, and the principle applies to perceptions, affects, and behaviors (C1AB). If they have been threatened, they are going to be anxious. Abused children are anxious and, as an associate once said, willing to turn themselves into pretzels to get approval from the abusing ("internal" if not external) parent. There are lots of data that connect perceptions of hostility from an attachment figure to hostility against the self and hostility against the self creates anxiety, among other things. Figure 4.2 showed direct connections among hostility from caregivers, hostility toward the self, and symptoms of anger, anxiety, and depression. In addition, that figure showed how directly the self-concept maps onto the relationship with a significant other person in adulthood.

Again, the theory is that copying happens by automatic primitive brain learning. But that is not enough. Copying alone is not permaglued. It is sustained by a subjective feeling of safety even if the pattern is not adaptive ("I know it is bad for me, but it feels right."). Here is how a therapist can find evidence of such GOLs during an interview if it does not emerge spontaneously. First, be sure of collaboration and patient interest and readiness before exploring GOLs. The subject is explosive, and poking at it can be dangerous unless the patient is feeling secure and in control of the process. If the decision is to proceed, then invite the patient to participate in a thought experiment involving a series of questions and imaginary answers. The therapist invites an imaginary scenario in which the patient is, for example, anxious or self-critical. First, the patient repeats the self-criticism out loud. The therapist reflects that and then asks (waiting for answers after each question): "Who might say something like that to you? When was that? How would you feel? What is the message you are supposed to get? What if you disagreed with it? What if you agreed with it? What did you think about it? What did you feel about it? What did you want to do about it?" In other words, get a clear, concrete picture of the behavior, the feelings, and what set it all off; in other words, get the C1AB elements of the originating events. After that is clear, run the same procedure on the patient's response to his/her own self-talk. Together, summarize the results, something like this:

> So when you blame yourself, you can, if you listen well, hear father in your head blaming you. That frightens you. Sounds like he would agree with your self-criticism and believe that it shows that you got his message. And you feel you have done the right thing by trashing yourself.

After reviewing the internal process as the patient has described it, say something like, "But in reality, you disagree with all this. Is it more like an ancient curse than a summary of reality now?"

The main ideas here are for patients to see that their self-attacks are not inevitable or "out of the blue" but rather copy processes that reflect messages from loved ones. They are supported by love of those attachment figures. They need to be updated. Freud's algorithm is the ultimate method of becoming free of old rules for safety and threat. After that, learning new C1AB patterns is relatively rapid.

Block Problem Patterns

According to Natural Biology, anxiety is a mobilized state suspended between fight and surrender on the continuum of options for how to respond to threat. Chronically anxious people often are ambivalent: Go or no-go; do it and undo it; think for it and think against it. After identifying the ambivalence and the role of Family in the Head, the deadlock can be bypassed to some degree by reframing the current struggle as tension between normative adaptive function and allegiance to ancient maladaptive rules. Jayne provided an example:

> At work, if I am ahead, I have to talk to myself and explain what is going on and let myself win. In a while, I will know it is okay for me to be the best I can be. I am not responsible to diminish myself to make someone else feel better.

Changing self-talk in this way helps block anxiety about doing well if that has been the issue.

Usually patients can make such changes at their workplace first, because it compares psychologically to school, where for them things were more predictable, reasonable, and rewarding. Such deliberate scripting of friendlier self-talk can sometimes make a big difference at work. But in intimate relationships at home, resolve to use a more adaptive view of oneself easily dissipates. In that context, the idea of defying maladaptive rules is experienced as especially dangerous, likely because intimate relationships are where the primitive brain is more dominant.

Here is another of many examples of a person who functioned well at work but not at home and not in relationships. Penny was paranoid, and like other paranoid people, she was anxious; paranoids have a lot to worry about. Penny had tried all her life without discernible success to please her mother. Her mother actually was quite dependent on Penny even as mother was critical of her and freely expressed her preference for Penny's sister. Penny held a good job, supported her mother and also often bought her mother generous gifts, as she deprived herself.

After working for a while in IRT on developing the courage to allow some self-nurturance, she finally began to buy needed items for herself. As she survived doing small things for herself, she escalated by buying a much-needed car for transportation to work, which was not near a bus line. Yet her mother attacked her by calling herself indulgent for buying the car: "Why couldn't she keep on riding her bike or walking? There are hundreds of much better, less selfish uses for that money." Shortly thereafter, Penny's paranoia convinced her that her coworkers disapproved of and spoke badly of her. She also convinced herself that I was secretly displeased that she had become so allegedly self-indulgent.

Penny's paranoia was addressed early in therapy by reviewing her history with her mother—how Penny had been neglected, denigrated, and attacked as being unlovable and selfish, with the only acceptable activity for her being to serve others with maximal effort and competence. Her paranoia and anxiety were normalized by noting that her self-talk reflected her mother's criticism for buying the car and that her belief that her coworkers disapproved of her recapitulated her relationship with her mother. That intervention helped Penny change her self-talk so she became able to arrange once to get together with a friend from work. But that last step of building loyalties to friends outside of the family was too difficult for her to contemplate, so Penny decided she had progressed far enough and stopped IRT.

Engage the Will to Change: Phases of the Action Stage

In Figure 5.1, Prochaska, DiClemente, and Norcross's (1992) stages of change were applied to engaging the will to change. Recall that (a) *precontemplation* applies if the patient is not aware of or interested in his/her case formulation. (b) *Contemplation* emerges after the patient understands the case formulation enough to engage meaningfully in collaboration to work toward building a secure self. It is not difficult to elicit higher brain (C2) collaboration to work toward Secure Base. Lower brain collaboration (C1) is the real challenge. (c) *Preparation* is a good description of process after the patient feels committed to relinquishing yearning, letting go of maladaptive GOLs, and becoming ready to work toward the Birthright Self. Joyce clearly was there when she said, vehemently, "I am done with this." Prochaska et al.'s fourth stage is (d) *Action*. This critical stage is broken into the five phases shown in Figure 6.2 and was discussed at length in Chapter 6. The reprogramming of the primitive brain happens at that phase and is followed by continuing effort to (e) *Maintain* the new patterns.

The action stage is maximally stressful because it is here that the patient must behave in ways that defy ancient rules for safety, and everyone feels anxiety then, whether that is a presenting symptom or not. The pivotal point in reconstruction is when the patient comprehends (C2) and apprehends at the primitive brain level (C1) the futility of GOLs and begins to break the ritual of self-sabotaging loyalty to maladaptive rules and values.

For example, Francine was chronically anxious because of a compulsion to please others. To become more peaceful, she had to accommodate to an accurate description of her deceased mother, whom she still longed to please:

> Mother is not going to understand how much I hurt and how faithful I have been to her rules for me [the behaviors inspired by her GOL]. She will not come hold me and protect and love me at long last [the GOL wish]. She was not there for me, and she will not be there for me [the GOL behaviors won't work]. I understand that my addiction to repeating these thoughts and actions makes me miserable and is based on wishes about Mother that never can [and never could have been] realized. I don't want this anymore [will to change is engaged]. I might as well pick up the pieces, take better care of myself, and move on.

In behavior, Francine must defy her maladaptive rules for safety that were desperately needed when she was a child; she must acknowledge that the dreadful abuse experiences and neglect were inappropriate, survive the terror associated with change, deal with ineffable grief that comes with apprehending what actually happened and accepting that the plans and dreams long held will never be realized. She must resolutely take control by continuing to talk back to Family in the Head, daring to affirm and take care of herself in visible ways. She must make herself engage with the boring, repetitive exercises in reprogramming (e.g., meditation, distraction) to recue her primitive brain. No wonder quite a few people decide not to pursue the action stage.

These internal difficulties are called *add-ons* to actual stresses an individual might have as an adult. Many people suffer clear and present environmental threats as adults. In that case, stress responses are normal. IRT therapists do try to strategize with such patients about stress management, but that is not always successful. After current reality is addressed optimally, the add-ons from maladaptive learning become the focus. For example, Pauline (Chapter 4) was unemployed and homeless, and that was a severe stress in itself. But she had "add ons" from Family in the Head that said she was different and bad and did not deserve to have nice things—especially not the fantasy home she had always dreamed of and actually created. For her, the noise from Family in the Head, the ancient add-ons, "justified" extreme violence against her realized fantasy of a nice home and herself.

Resist Red Voices, Defy With Green Action

An early form of action is to begin to "talk back" to Red aspects of Family in the Head, denying oneself the "security" of sinking into old, familiar, but destructive ways of being and doing. At the same time, one also needs to look forward to goals consistent with the Birthright Self and trying out more adaptive behaviors even though they feel strange, not right, and even dangerous. Moving forward can begin with choosing a specific assignment of working on a small but psychologically significant task that makes the patient inordinately anxious because of pushback from Family in the Head. For example, try something new with the children as suggested by parent training and then say to oneself: "I think I did a really good job with the children today." Family in the Head will start mocking both the training and the self-praise. The therapist and patient can discuss ways of getting them to subside. Maybe, if the family is dominated by lawyers, it would be to tell the family "judges" that court is not in session.

Ways of talking back are chosen by whether they will block Red behaviors and/or enhance Green behaviors. Any and all modern strategies for symptom management discussed in the preceding section "Psychotherapy for Anxiety" could be adapted for use in IRT at this stage. Self-management activities (http://www.DBTSelfHelp.com) can be very helpful, especially after the will to change is fully engaged. Possibly a version of cognitive bias modification could help by presenting images of specific, personalized, threatening attachment figures and images of specific, personalized, safe attachment figures and rewarding attention to the positive one. But given the experiences of Sohlberg and Birgegård (2003) when working with attachment-based subliminal stimulation, the procedure would need to be carefully monitored for safety and the patient debriefed afterward.

Sleep problems usually accompany anxiety in IRT because it is a mobilizing affect and mobilization disrupts sleep. Many times patients with sleep difficulties suffer from dangerous intrusions, such as memories or nightmares of beatings and/or sexual abuse in the night. In addition to medications, they can be helped by imaginary conversations or fantasies or actions that put up a "barrier." They might say, out loud, "Shut up and get out of my house, Dad. You are not in charge here." Maybe they can think of fantasy ways to lock out intrusive abusers. "Imagine huge steel bars across your doors that can be opened only from the inside by you." Or "Tell him to go back to the grave." Or "I live here, far away from you. Go back to your own city." For these victims, it can also help to encourage them to recall any available images of safe figures from childhood and bring them into the present: "I am going to recall and visualize everything and every feeling I can remember about my grandpa and the wonderful things we did together." Sleep meditations and/or peaceful music available on the Internet can help, too.

Sometimes sleep disruption is due to anxiety about real current stresses. In this case, addressing the stresses directly and temporarily can help. For example,

> Anxiety means you are mobilized to do something. What did you ruminate about last night when you woke up? Next time, try to write down all the things you are trying to cope with, and promise yourself to look at your list in the morning. Then let it go until morning. You will deal with the list then.

Alternatively, "if you think of a doable solution, just get up and implement it" or "write down the approach you want to use and make an appointment with yourself to deal with it the next day." The idea is that if anxiety is the reason for trouble sleeping, finding a solution and recording it frees the primitive brain of its duty to keep the person on alert; having a definite plan may allow the person to go back to sleep.

Face and Relinquish Yearning, Envision Birthright

The logical mind (C2) asks, How can people yearn for the love of an abusive attachment figure? But they do, and Natural Biology explains why. A few words about the perspective of the abuser might be in order. They, too, have copy process as suggested by the fact that typically, as they abuse their child, they are loving their own abusive parent. Copying prevails and seems just and right in Red mind. It can be supported by ideology, too: "Family is blood; we are the only ones who love you no matter what. This is for your own good." One only needs to lead the patient to these waters, listen, and learn from what they say.

Here is another example: Heather is a highly accomplished, much beloved social activist who suffers a lot from anxiety. Over the years, her mother has sent her the nastiest emails imaginable. Mother has vehemently refused generous, useful gifts from Heather. At family gatherings, mother pointedly will not speak to Heather. Mother's venom for Heather seems unbounded. And yet, she complains that Heather never visits. Heather concludes,

> As in a cartoon, my mother eats her young and then complains her days are empty. I see her as a spider with glowing angry eyes, waiting to get me. I've thought about being angry at her but am mostly afraid. If I criticize myself, I recognize where it comes from. She is devoted to disliking her children. Part of me wonders if after she dies, I will wish I had reconciled

> before then. But how do you like loving someone who does not love you? Every time she calls, I want to tell her, "Don't call again." And yet, as a dead person, she will be stirring around in me after she dies.

Fortunately, Heather eventually did overcome her yearning and differentiate from mother. She was able to be kind to mother and peaceful about her death at the very end, even as her mother was still filled with venom.

Sometimes the will to let go of GOLs can be enhanced by primitive but accurate imagery that makes the internalized figure less desirable. Adele, a woman with a distinguished career in journalism, excelled in her profession, in beauty, and a lot else. Despite all of her assets, Adele was very anxious about any flaws in her appearance or behavior. She suffered from generalized anxiety disorder. Her mother was an albatross, following her physically and psychically everywhere she went, including into her marriage and her relationships with her children. Adele knew she needed to separate from mother, but she experienced monumental verbal assaults whenever she tried to distance from mother. Adele did love her mother very much but was perplexed about how to be friendly with her and still have a life of her own.

We set up a simple behavioral program for helping mother become less demanding and intrusive. Basically, the idea was that Adele announced she would withdraw in some way whenever mother had a meltdown. That stopped the big scenes. However, mother still intruded in amazingly creative ways. One day, I offered an image that seemed to summarize mother's impact: "As I think about your mother, I visualize a lamprey." "A what?" said Adele. "A lamprey: a primitive fish that dwells at the bottom of a pond and affixes itself to other fish and sucks the life out of them." Adele was aghast but agreed that was how mother felt to her. The image was offensive and accurate enough that Adele resolved to set even firmer limits on her mother and wholeheartedly commit her time and energy to her marriage. Interestingly, the relationship with mother improved, and Adele's obsessive–compulsive tendencies abated significantly.

Sometimes the loyalty to abusive parents seems intractable. If symptoms escalate and suicidality intensifies, it may be necessary to take harsher measures. But do not lead the patient into a traumatic past without a clear purpose and agreed-on signals for returning to the present. For example, after a brief verbal excursion into the trauma, say, "Let's return to the present now. It is 2018, not 1972. Everything is different. Look around this room. You are not there anymore." After return is established, ask the patient to take the perspective of a hypothetical social worker or some other outside observer. Summarize what has been discussed without evocative imagery:

> So here is this tiny house with virtually no soundproofing. He raped this little girl [the patient] often and was physically violent as well. Mother

had to have noticed but still failed to protect the child and talk about what was happening. Then she criticized the child and blamed her for whatever went wrong in the house.

Ask the patient, "What you would you do about this as an outside observer?" Patients often know when it was a reportable situation but did not feel they could tell about it and survive. They may be right. But in the therapy office, it is safe, and reframing the trauma by asking the patient to see himself or herself through the eyes of a responsible other (e.g., a social worker) can contribute to the task of distancing from crippling signals from Family in the Head.

Sometimes ambivalence about betrayal of the attachment figure can be softened by mentioning mother's likely abuse and her own copy process. Be careful with this, however, because if the patient is still stuck in the "who is to blame" mode, empathy for the abuser "equals" guilt on the patient's part. The purpose of empathy for the abuser is not to blame the patient or the parent. The purpose is to depersonalize the scenario. If patients can comprehend that the abuse was a pattern coming down through the generations, the false belief that the abuse was caused by the patient's allegedly evil or seductive or disobedient nature is weakened. This helps vitiate the impact of toxic signals from Family in the Head.

Visualizing the Birthright Self is a huge challenge for some. The overall plan can be sketched by showing them the full SASB model (Chapter 3) and/or the items in Tables 2.1 and 2.2, which describe Secure Base Green interactions under safe conditions. A very effective way of communicating different ways of relating is to role-play, with the therapist modeling the all-important but likely unfamiliar patterns of friendly differentiation. Further discussion about building the Birthright Self comes in Action Phase d (build the Birthright, celebrate success and happiness).

Face Fear, Disorganization, Emptiness

Nature does a good job of assuring that everyone is afraid to give up the GOLs. As noted in previous chapters, those who face the fear and begin to defy the maladaptive rules often become disoriented and disorganized. Here is a sample of that process. I had been emphasizing for quite a long time that I was not able or willing to join in a symbiotic relationship with Maxine, replacing her father, thereby enabling a presenting problem. She finally had begun to believe I meant it. Maxine wrote,

> It was amazing that we could talk about my attachment to you last session. This is really important now because I am feeling "aimless." I sit at my computer and stare because I feel like I should be doing something. I wander around my house for the same reason. I know that this is a large

part of truly feeling the "void" that we talk so much about. I think that it is being caused by us dealing with our attachment, with my dad attachment, and with losing hope for mom attachment. If I am not who I have been, then who am I?

At this phase, many describe a deep black hole of nothingness. Some flounder around dangerously trying to "fill" the hole. They might leap into a new but ill-advised relationship that seems to meet their current hunger. That leads inevitably to disappointment, and the terrible anxiety resolves to grief as they surrender to the reality that their childhood cannot be relived. There is no substitute for what should have been. One patient explained, "I don't know where I am. It feels as if I am on a precipice. In my chest, I am about to do something like drive the car into the wall." It helps if the therapist shows that he/she understands the intensity of the stress and accurately explains Natural Biology to reassure the patient that this is normal because his or her threat system is on emergency alert.

Therapy as safe base is especially important during the action stage. However, if the patient starts to think of the therapy relationship as The Solution, as the relationship he or she should have had as an infant and toddler and a relationship that must last forever, there is a major transference problem. Evidence that the patient's anxiety is related to fear of loss of the therapy relationship includes the following: "You just want me to turn Green in order to get rid of me." "You got me to challenge 'them,' and now you are not there for me." Behavioral examples that mark a transference problem include inappropriate requests to meet more often and/or at odd times, demands for more personal information about the therapist, and panic if the therapist fails to respond to a text or email or phone message as desired. It is quite common for patients to project their disappointment and rage about loss of the GOL fantasy onto the therapist as they yearn for the therapist to become the new and better parent.

To contain such transference problems, the therapist should appeal to the case formulation and concepts from Natural Biology to help restore collaboration in working toward therapy goals instead of regressive ones. It is vital to maintain clear boundaries that make clear the professional nature of the relationship, else the fantasy will bloom and sabotage the therapy. For example,

> It is totally natural you would want me to be your all-time Secure Base, and in fact internalizing our relationship will be a part of your recovery. But the idea I must be physically present makes sense for an infant and toddler, but isn't natural or adaptive for an adult. Certainly having a secure relationship is optimal for adults, too, but only if they each are

well differentiated and not enmeshed, as is normal for infants and toddlers but not for adults. So let's talk about ways you might begin now to build and/or find new benign relationships in your own world. We'll start small, and not go any faster with this than you feel ready for.

Build the Birthright, Celebrate Success and Happiness

As must be clear by now, work on the Birthright Self cannot begin in earnest until the horrible costs of the Yearning Self, the Red GOLs, and the old loyalties are fully understood and absorbed. Here is an unusually clear description of the big picture in reconstructive change. Charlene was a chronically anxious, highly accomplished and articulate service professional.

> I need to accept the fact that I am the person who experienced the horrors of my childhood and adolescence. I am not separate from that history; do not have my being in the alienated narrator or disdainful critic, or in the one who is crushed by the weight of it all. Those positions belong to them and are my way of keeping them and my need for their love alive. When I try to live in those positions, I live at a distance from myself and cannot rest. When you talk about my identification with my father, when you explain that I cannot resist the impact of films or books because of the duration and extent of trauma, when you tell me that I was victimized in the way you have been saying it lately, I seem to get calm or calmer, and, ironically, to feel less like a victim. I guess I feel "seen," and I settle into an understanding of myself that makes me want to take better care, rather than to destroy her/myself. I hear inside myself a kind of quiet "yes," and a wish to choose things that acknowledge the truth, stop judging myself by the standards that they set or ones derived from the belief that I should be able to live as though none of this ever happened, or happened to someone that I can choose to ignore, attack, and question, as though she were not quite real, or not really important. It seems odd that becoming one with her or simply accepting the effects of my past on my present would lead me to feel less anxious in the present, as though the hovering outside of her and the frequent swooping attacks on her have been less protective and more victimizing, even if I (Red) have imagined that the distance from her is a kind of safety. I no longer want to pretend that I am one of them, disdainful of my "weakness," my "sensitivity," guilty of all the heartache and of "feeling sorry for [my]self." They managed to get me to distrust most everything about myself, except the things I buried. I have to be inside those truths in order to feel that I exist.

Such a statement does not mark the end of yearning. There follows more back and forth between Red and Green, with yearning invading the psyche again and again, like the memories of a long-lost lover. But over time, it recedes, and the Birthright Self is more and more often present. The transition to health is marked by subtle but important changes. For example, after providing this summary, Charlene had a genuine life crisis and during it observed, "I thought about letting myself slip back into misery, but didn't." Her new brain, her comprehending system, finally was able to override the angry screams of her ancient safety system. She understood she now had choice. She no longer had to believe there was little she could do other than anxiously try to anticipate anything and everything until inevitable failure materialized and then sink into depression and defeat.

Face Grief

Sadness and grief lurk behind every phase but dominate only after the new patterns begin to consolidate. Kimberly had the following exchange with her IRT therapist:

Kimberly: I don't want to have to choose because I do not want to have to grieve. I feel the enormity of the grief. My wand is broken. No way around it. If I cannot make them be happy with me, I may as well make me happy. I realize, I accept that I am orphaned the way I always thought I was. It is true.

Therapist: So alcohol no longer helps with the pain of not belonging to the inner family circle?

Kimberly: Yeah. That sucks. But alcohol just does not work on this anymore.

Kimberly then became clean and sober but was diagnosed with cancer a few months later, suggesting that her sense of loss was profound.[2] The body sometimes speaks louder than the new brain. Fortunately, she was treated properly and has been symptom free for several years.

Learn New Patterns

Serious change, major reconstruction, follows after letting go of GOL wishes. At that phase, behavioral instruction can have rapid impacts. Laura, an anxious victim of chronic sexual abuse by her father, had a difficult husband. After finally letting go of her GOL to her father, she easily learned to avoid uproar by saying something like this in a potentially dangerous situation: "Honey, I'd rather drop this and have a pleasant Sunday. But if you

---

[2] The literature on the mind–body connection is fast growing and fascinating. My own approach to that problem is completely dominated by the views of David Graham (Graham et al., 1962). I hope to have a chance to write more about somatization in the near future. For now, let it be clear that loss of attachments can be a death sentence for animals and people. This is an understandable problem, and I believe Graham's perspective is the best way to explain it.

keep that up, I will leave for the day." The strategy was effective. If it had not been, she was prepared to carry out her threat, despite the possibility that he was capable of escalating and becoming violent if she threatened to leave him. She had a plan for her safety if that happened and was determined that if he did not behave responsibly, then she would leave and would look at her action as practice for good new ways of relating that would help her make better choices in an eventual new relationship.

Shirley was chronically overwhelmed by an iron rule that the other person must agree with and feel good about her actions or she would become beside herself with anxiety. We traced its origin to parental fantasies about needing complete control of children. If the child is not happy about the parent's management, the parent is shown to be bad. Such a parent might try to seduce the child into compliance: "It is *great* fun to do the dishes. Try it. You'll see." As the child cries, howls, has a meltdown, and does not do the dishes accurately, declaring it is not fun, the child acquires the label of an entitled, tantrum-prone, irresponsible child who has to have her own way. To avoid that kind of attribution, Shirley accepted and carried into adulthood (recapitulated) her assignment of making others feel good about whatever she did and felt she must be happy with whatever that brought.

Of course, children must learn to participate in household chores as a part of their learning to be good "herd members." The problem with expecting a child to be chronically happy (compounded in this example by the corollary that the parent will then be happy about herself) violates Natural Biological principles. Instead of requiring the child be happy to do dishes, principles of Natural Biology would suggest that modeling, offering benevolent structure for how to do the task, and providing immediate feedback for good performance, praise for mastery, and praise for contributing to household functions is a better lesson for adaptation to adulthood than any form of ruse or manipulation.

Despite her understanding that her iron rule was inappropriate, Shirley still was reluctant to lower her impossible expectation that she could keep everyone happy; she remained anxious. It was not until 3 years later, after a tumultuous struggle with differentiating from Family in the Head, that she became able to see others as responsible for their own choices and settle for focusing mostly on her own choices. That helped her demobilize, and her anxiety abated.

REMARKS ABOUT ABUSE OF TREATMENTS FOR ANXIETY

Anxiety may be responsible for rampant problems with alcohol and drug addiction that increasingly plague Western society. While anger has no drug specific to it and depression is treated by drugs that have no street value, the treatments for anxiety, such as benzodiazepines and opioids, have tremendous street value. In response to abuse of antianxiety drugs, prescriptions have become so highly restricted that quite often, pain is undertreated.

This problem of misuse of treatments for anxiety with medicine leads to accidental overdose and significant impairment of functioning. It sponsors neglectful parenting that will reverberate for decades to come. Solutions to the problem begin with better understanding of the perspectives of drug abusers and with assessment of the user's relationship with the drug. My experiences with users, plus some SASB studies, suggest that benzodiazepines are preferred for anxiety because they block inner voices and "noise." Opioids may reduce anxiety by fostering a sense of protection, a loving antidote that shields the user from threats. Everything is "way cool, great." Alcohol has a related effect on anxiety in that it, too, promises love (Moore, 1998). That idea was famously represented in a cartoon by illustrator Boris Artzybasheff that showed an adult male curled up in the lap of a full-breasted bottle of alcohol. Sandor (1996), using SASB Intrex ratings, learned that cocaine addicts perceive cocaine as submissive to them (implying they are in control). It appears that cocaine and alcohol provide relief from anxiety by altering perceptions of love and enmeshment. A sense of loving enmeshment is, of course, the affective state that is supposed to result from GOLs—from compliance with attachment figures' rules and values for safety and threat. In sum, substance abusers have found a "shortcut" to perceived security.

9

DEPRESSION

The Natural Biological interpretation of depression builds on the fact, reflected in the items in the *Diagnostic and Statistical Manual of Mental Disorders* (5th ed.; *DSM–5*; American Psychiatric Association, 2013), that depressed patients feel overwhelmed, helpless, and without recourse. Typically, they withdraw and seem to have given up. All that is quite natural if they perceive a threat that is impossible to control or repel and from which there is no escape. In that situation, depressive responses can be adaptive, a defense of last resort. In the jungle, depressive positions such as withdraw, hide, and be still can avoid detection or deter a predator by reducing the individual's threat value. But if the perception of threat is inaccurate, then the depressive responses are maladaptive and symptomatic.

Threat affects, including depression, are cued or miscued by lessons from attachment figures about what to fear and how to be safe. The mechanism by which lessons in safety and threat are acquired is copying primitive brain perceptions (C1), affects (A), and behaviors (B) linked together (C1AB)

http://dx.doi.org/10.1037/0000090-009
Interpersonal Reconstructive Therapy for Anger, Anxiety, and Depression: It's About Broken Hearts, Not Broken Brains, by L. S. Benjamin
Copyright © 2018 by the American Psychological Association. All rights reserved.

and supported by Gifts of Love (GOLs). These linked responses are adaptive if they have been cued by Secure Base interactions between caregiver and child. Impacts are recorded by gene expression and silencing and by epigenetic processes within the "envelope of potential" determined by the genome. This chapter is about how to apply this Natural Biological view of depression while using the IRT case formulation and treatment models. It starts with a review of the "state of the art" from other perspectives.

DEFINITIONS OF DEPRESSION

Depression in general is defined as major depressive disorder in the *DSM–5* and the *International Classification of Diseases* (10th ed.; ICD–10; World Health Organization, 2017). There are many subtypes of depression, and some investigators (e.g., McCullough et al., 2003) have recommended ignoring them because there are few differences among subtypes in treatment response variables. Indeed, the ratings of depression (and anxiety and anger) used in the analyses presented throughout this book make no distinctions among subtypes of depression.

However, in the clinic, it could be important to attend to them because some patients require referrals to psychiatrists or internists for medical help. Examples include medication-induced depressive disorder, premenstrual dysphoric disorder, and depressive disorder due to another medical condition. Nonphysician IRT clinicians regularly should make referrals for medical assessment. There may be a need to identify and treat relevant medical issues, such as thyroid dysfunction or anemia or other illness that could account for low energy experienced as depression; in addition, medication may be needed to keep patients safe from activation of their threat systems before the therapy alliance is strong and again later, during reconstructive work, when the rules for threat and safety are being challenged and patients become more angry, anxious, and/or depressed.

Throughout all steps in IRT, no matter what the diagnosis, patients often need extra help to contain therapy-interfering symptoms while they are transforming their relationship with Family in the Head. Preferred methods, in addition to referral for medications, are to encourage patients to use dialectical behavior therapy (DBT) apps and/or meditation apps, enroll in yoga classes, and use other resources for self-help and self-management.

TEMPERAMENT AND GENETICS OF DEPRESSION

Certainty that depression is based largely on a defect in a genotype that is triggered in response to stress has diminished recently. The diathesis–stress model per se has to be correct. But the applications of it, as mentioned in

Chapter 8, have been misleading because they have given too much weight to the destiny-via-genes interpretation and showed too little concern for the impact of attachment. More caution about assigning weight to the inherited component (envelope of potential) was raised by an analysis published in *Biological Psychiatry* and summarized by Sanders (2013): "By combing through the DNA of 34,549 volunteers, an international team of 86 scientists hoped to uncover genetic influences that affect a person's vulnerability to depression. But the analysis turned up nothing" (para. 1).

New ideas for how environment can affect genes have emerged. One is epigenetics, reviewed at length in Chapter 2. Still another consideration is clearer realization that many patterns in infancy are patterns for life. Bornstein (2014) summarized a current perspective on the gene by environment interaction as follows:

> The developmental changes that take place during the first year of life are as dramatic—or more dramatic—than any others in the human lifespan. The most remarkable involve the changing shape and capacity of the body; the complexity of the nervous system; the dawning of sensory and perceptual capacities; the increasing abilities to make sense of, understand, and master things in the world; the achievement of communication; the emergence of characteristic personal styles; and the formation of specific social bonds. At no other time is development so fast-paced or thoroughgoing in so many different spheres of life. Yet, at the core of the infant, and later the toddler, child, adolescent, and adult, is the same individual, and some stability and predictability from infancy—whatever their dynamic endogenous and exogenous origins—can be supposed. (p. 144)

Clearly, both environment and heredity are important, and Bornstein also reminded readers, interestingly, that the relationship is reciprocal: Inherited features of the infant affect the environment, too. Anyone who doubts that is invited to examine the internal discomfort that bursts into awareness when an infant cries.

The Natural Biological perspective assumed in IRT is that details of interactions with attachment figures must be considered during psychotherapy treatments for depression. Again, the idea is to focus more on the maladaptive definitions of safety and threat that inspire the depressive symptoms than on efforts to control or contain symptoms. This perspective is wholly compatible with what is known about the natural functions of the nervous and endocrine systems. For example, Pizzagalli (2014) focused on anhedonia as the "cardinal symptom" of depression (p. 414) and speculated that "stress sensitivity" affects dopamine pathways to "interfere with brain reward systems" (p. 403) implicated in incentive motivation and reinforcement learning (p. 403). The language "interfere with brain reward systems" is important. Recall that in Figures 2.2, 3.8, and 4.2, there are large, orderly, and significant negative correlations between depression and friendly interpersonal interactions. The conclusion was and is that depression is not just a matter of "running out of gas." Rather, the accelerated reuptake of serotonin actively inhibits attachment behaviors.

The perspective from Natural Biology includes an explanation for why that is adaptive. If one is defeated and helpless and without recourse, damping down interactive activity is a way to avoid attention, to hide. The abused and depressed wife stays in bed all day, minimizing encounters. The impaired chimpanzee avoids the juvenile male gang; the baby monkey who got left behind hides until the mother returns and rescues him.

STRESS AND COMORBIDITY OF DEPRESSION AND ANXIETY

Stress likely interacts with inherited attributes, whether they support vulnerability or resistance to developing depressive symptoms. As noted in Chapter 8, it is proposed in IRT theory that the first two stages of Selye's (1946) general adaptation syndrome include valid descriptions of anxiety. Here, it is proposed that Selye's descriptions of the third stage, exhaustion, are reasonable ways to describe depression. The exhausted stress victim and the depressed patient both can be described as demobilized, having given up, given in, and withdrawn. With that context in mind, consider the following aspects of items that describe depression in the *DSM–5*: diminished activity, fatigue, loss of energy, and hypersomnia.

However, additional items for depression, such as irritability and insomnia, suggest the opposite—mobilization. According to principles discussed in Chapter 8, they can be interpreted as evidence of comorbid anxiety more than components of "depression." Such variability is reasonable if one views anxiety and depression (including angry spikes) as equally viable options to respond to perceived threat. The difference is that anxiety indicates that the person is at the moment trying to find a response to the threat, while depression signals exhaustion and defeat. Individuals under long-term stress might well wobble between trying to cope and giving up. This interpretation is only possible if the idea of depression and anxiety as discrete categories is abandoned in favor of viewing them as natural and immediate responses to perceptions of threat interacting with perceived resources for coping with it.

That interpretation could be extended to the comorbidity of anger with depression as well. Careful interviewing could reveal that an angry outburst from a depressed person had the function of pushing someone away while the depressed person wanted to be alone. Or maybe a child did not obey, and the depressed mom wanted more control. Family in the Head also are factors that contribute to bouts of anxiety or anger when a person is in a lasting depression.

Maybe an irritable mom got mocked by the mother in her head when her son ignored her request. Comorbidity is natural as different situations intrude on the defenses of demobilization and withdrawal characteristic of depression.

EVIDENCE THAT INTERACTIONS WITH FAMILY IN THE HEAD SPONSOR DEPRESSION

Family in the Head have a lot to do with the rise and fall of depressive states as current stresses reactivate primitive brain memories about what to fear and how to be safe. The relevance of Family in the Head is supported by evidence reviewed in Chapter 2 linking depressive states to internalized representations of a depressed mother (Toth, Rogosch, Sturge-Apple, & Cicchetti, 2009). Another form of evidence is the "Mommy and I are one" studies by Sohlberg and Birgegård (2003), who found that subliminal exposure to mother in the head was followed by more than a week of marked depression. Blatt (2004) also linked remembered childhood experiences and negative internal representations to depression; he identified two subtypes: anaclitic (related to perceived loss of attachment figures) and introjective (related to self-criticism). Allen et al. (2006) interviewed 143 seventh and eighth graders and their mothers twice, a year apart. They recorded each mother and her adolescent discussing an issue about which they disagreed and also considered peer reports. They concluded, "Dysfunctional interaction patterns with parents and peers [combine] additively to account for substantial change variance in depressive symptoms over time" (p. 55).

Altogether, studies like these mean that negative (hostile) actual and internalized relationships with attachment figures and current relationships, including those with peers, contribute to ups (activated as anxiety or anger) and downs (deactivated as depression) of threat affects. Differences depend on the envelope of potential and on copy processes that define an individual's primitive brain perception (C1), affects that follow (A), and behaviors that are predisposed (B). Any discoveries about activation, deactivation, or inhibition of brain reward systems should correlate directly with these behavioral, attachment-based descriptions of the mechanisms of depression.

IMPACT OF CULTURE ON DEPRESSION

Culture affects parenting, and parents provide lessons in threat and safety. For example, Methikalam, Wang, Slaney, and Yeung (2015) noted that Asian cultures value achievement and support perfectionism. In a study of 174 Asian Indians, they assessed whether subjects were from perfectionistic or non-perfectionistic families. A conclusion was that perfectionism is characteristic of Asian families, but only is pathological (associated with symptoms) when the individual's perception is that he/she did not meet family expectations. To address that, these investigators suggested the clinician help the patient

> differentiate between having high standards and a tendency to never be satisfied with their performance. The latter seems to suggest working on coping with the internal critic and helping the client to understand the internalization of familial norms rather than lowering standards. (p. 220)

This example regarding the impact of culture on pathology and consideration of how to address it by addressing impacts on Family in the Head is wholly consistent with theory and practice in IRT. Notice that the recommendation did not challenge the culture; it focused instead on a pathological mechanism that did not accurately represent the cultural values in this case. When that is true, therapy work need not clash with the culture.

However, some cultures have values that do not support Secure Base behaviors, and there is a potential clash between that culture and IRT advocacy of Secure Base as a goal. For example, a culture might sanction severe physical punishment for children or rigid extremes of dominance and submission. Those interactions mean that the attachment figure is a severe threat and autonomy is suppressed. Secure Base does not follow chronic threats to and chronic domination of the child. Given that normalcy and therapy goals are clearly defined in IRT, it follows that a member of a culture that finds those goals unacceptable should not be treated with IRT. Based in Natural Biology, it is important for the IRT clinician to disclose the evolutionary basis of the case formulation in a way that allows the patient clearly to decide whether to participate in this treatment that places such a strong emphasis on attachment and friendly forms of individuation.

ASSESSING SUICIDE

According to the National Institute of Mental Health (n.d.), suicide is the 10th leading cause of death in the United States, with the rate of successful suicide in males being four times that of females. It is standard practice to refer outpatients for hospitalization when they become dangerously suicidal, so it is not surprising that suicide rates peak immediately after admission. Less expected, perhaps, is that suicide rates also are quite high after discharge, especially if the hospitalization time was short (Qin & Nordentoft, 2005). Meehan et al. (2006) used the British national database to identify cases of suicide during a 4-year period. Sixteen percent had committed suicide as inpatients, and 23% more had committed suicide less than 3 months after discharge, with most on the first day of discharge and next most within 2 weeks of leaving the hospital.

Bryan, Corso, Neal-Walden, and Rudd (2009) described a brief questionnaire assessing warning signs of suicide according to a consensus of experts. These signs include substance abuse, purposelessness, anxiety, feeling trapped, hopelessness, withdrawal, anger, recklessness, and mood change. They added a few items, such as command hallucinations about self-harm. Examples of standard interventions include determining whether there is a specific plan and means, limiting access to means, securing short-term contracts for safety, and hospitalizing the person.

COMORBIDITY

Large correlations among symptoms of anger, anxiety, and depression are shown in Table 9.1. Natural Biological reasons for comorbidity between depression and the other threat affects were reviewed above. In addition,

> Multiple studies have demonstrated that depression . . . is a robust risk factor for the development of cardiovascular disease in healthy populations, and is predictive of adverse outcomes (such as myocardial

TABLE 9.1
Four Studies of Comorbidity Among Anger, Anxiety, and Depression

Study aspect	Park (2005)	Smith (2002)	NIMH Grant MH33604	Rothweiler (2004)
N	313	82	154	227
Population	College students	Utah inpatients	Wisconsin inpatients	Outpatients and trade school students
Anger measure	STAXI–2	SCL–90–R	SCL–90–R	MCMI–II Sadism trait
Anxiety measure	BAI	SCL–90–R	SCL–90–R	MCMI–II Anxiety trait
Depression measure	BDI	SCL–90–R	SCL–90–R	MCMI–II Dysthymia trait
r, anxiety and depression	.636**	.653**	.737**	.658**
r, anxiety and anger	.385**	.456**	.595**	.324**
r, depression and anger	.399**	.306**	.495**	.223**

Note. BAI = Beck Anxiety Inventory; BDI = Beck Depression Inventory; MCMI–II = Millon Clinical Multiaxial Inventory—II; NIMH = National Institute of Mental Health; SCL–90–R = Symptom Checklist—90—Revised; STAXI–2 = State–Trait Anger Expression Inventory—2. Despite different measures, populations, and locations in time and space, all three threat affects are comorbid at levels better than $p < .01$ or better by the Bonferroni test. The association between anxiety and depression consistently is the highest, and the connection between anger and depression is the lowest.
**$p < .01$.

infarction and death) among populations with preexisting cardiovascular disease.... Poor health behaviors, such as physical inactivity, medication nonadherence, and smoking, strongly contribute to this association. Small randomized trials have found that antidepressant therapies may improve cardiac outcomes. Based on this accumulating evidence, the American Heart Association has recommended routine screening for depression in all patients with coronary heart disease. (Whooley & Wong, 2013, p. 327)

As noted before, comorbidity has inspired controversy about diagnosis, but most often diagnostic controversy has centered on personality disorders (*DSM–5*, Section III). The perspective offered by Natural Biology in IRT makes comorbidity among affective disorders and with personality disorders a nonissue. The natural connections are shown in Table 9.2. The table marks reasonable, adaptive connections between threat affects and personality disorders. In other words, comorbidity involving anger, anxiety, and depression is natural, adaptive, and common; it is supported by the structure and function of the autonomic nervous system and its connections.

Comorbidity does have treatment implications. In practice, antidepressants that address depressive symptoms often are prescribed alongside anxiolytics that address symptoms of anxiety. Some medications treat both of these disorders. In practice, patients who have treatment-resistant depression can end up taking medications from all four major categories: antidepressants, anxiolytics, mood stabilizers (lithium), and even antipsychotics. In other words, comorbidity in the clinic is well recognized by prescribing clinicians.

The IRT case formulation method addresses each presenting symptom for an individual in reliable, specific, and sensitive ways (Critchfield & Benjamin, 2008, 2010). The treatment goal is always the same: achieve friendly differentiation from maladaptive messages from Family in the Head and replace them with Secure Base practices. Achieving Secure Base does result in significant reduction in symptoms.

Variations in Comorbidity Among Individuals

In IRT research as well as in practice, the individual is the focus. Group data are suggestive of important trends, but they never apply to every individual in the sample. It is vital that clinicians who apply significant research results to an individual recognize that research results rarely characterize 100% of the sample. With notable and welcome exceptions (e.g., Losada et al., 2015; Cunha et al., 2012), the reader of effectiveness studies does not learn what percentage of individuals in the sample actually showed the reported effect.

TABLE 9.2
Comorbidity Between Threat Affects and Behavior in Personality Disorders

Personality disorder	Anger (r)	Anxiety (r)	Depression (r)	Interpersonal description
Borderline	.516**	.410**	.358**	There is a **morbid fear of abandonment** and a wish for protective nurturance, preferably received by constant physical proximity to the rescuer (lover or caregiver). The baseline position is friendly dependency on a nurturer, which **becomes hostile control** if the caregiver or lover fails to deliver enough (and there never is enough). There is a belief that the provider secretly if not overtly likes dependency and neediness, and a vicious **introject attacks the self** if there are signs of happiness or success.
Antisocial	.369**	.173	−.001	There is a pattern of inappropriate and unmodulated desire to control others, implemented in a detached manner. There is a strong need to be independent, to resist being controlled by others, who are usually held in contempt. There is a willingness to use **untamed aggression** to back up the need for control or independence. The person usually presents in a friendly, sociable manner, but that friendliness is always accompanied by a baseline position of detachment. He or she doesn't care what happens to self or others.
Histrionic	.066	−.047	−.242	There is a strong **fear of being ignored**, together with a wish to be loved and taken care of by someone powerful, who nonetheless can be controlled through use of charm and entertainment skills. The baseline position is of **friendly trust** that is accompanied by a secretly disrespectful agenda of forcing delivery of the desired nurturance and love. Inappropriate **seductive behaviors** and manipulative suicidal attempts are examples of such coercions.

(*continues*)

TABLE 9.2
Comorbidity Between Threat Affects and Behavior in Personality Disorders *(Continued)*

Personality disorder	Anger (r)	Anxiety (r)	Depression (r)	Interpersonal description
Narcissistic	−.031	−.229	−.495**	There is extreme vulnerability to criticism or being ignored, together with a strong wish for love, support, and admiring deference from others. The baseline position involves **noncontingent love of self and presumptive control of others**. If the support is withdrawn, or if there is any evidence of lack of perfection, the self-concept degrades to severe self-criticism. Totally lacking in empathy, the person treats others with contempt and **holds the self above and beyond the fray**.
Dependent	.301*	.474**	.648**	The baseline position is of **marked submissiveness** to a dominant other person who is supposed to provide unending nurturance and guidance. The wish is to maintain connection to that person even if it means tolerating abuse. The person believes that he or she is instrumentally incompetent, and this means that he or she **cannot survive without the dominant other person**.
Obsessive–compulsive	.374**	.382**	.303*	There is a **fear** of making a mistake or being accused of being imperfect. The quest for order yields a baseline interpersonal position of **blaming** and inconsiderate control of others. The person's control alternates with blind obedience to authority or principles. There is excessive self-discipline, as well as restraint of feelings, **harsh self-criticism**, and neglect of the self.
Avoidant	.256	.358**	.545**	There is **intense fear** of humiliation and rejection. Feeling flawed, the person **withdraws** and carefully restrains himself or herself to avoid expected embarrassment. He or she intensely wishes for love and acceptance but will become very intimate only with those who pass highly stringent tests for safety. Occasionally, the person loses control and explodes with rageful indignation.

				Interpersonal Description
Passive–aggressive	.401**	.371**	.323*	There is a tendency to see any form of power as inconsiderate and neglectful, together with a belief that authorities or caregivers are incompetent, unfair, and cruel. The person agrees to comply with perceived demands or suggestions but fails to perform. He or she often complains of unfair treatment and envies and **resents** others who fare better. His or her suffering **indicts** the allegedly negligent caregivers or authorities. The person **fears** control in any form and wishes for nurturant restitution.
Paranoid	.432**	.370**	.200	There is a **fear that others will attack to hurt or blame**. The wish is that others will affirm and understand. If affirmation fails, the hope is that others will either leave the person alone or submit. The baseline position is to wall off, stay separate, and tightly control the self. If threatened, the person will **recoil in a hostile way or attack to countercontrol or gain distance**.
Schizotypal	.368**	.366**	.347*	There is a fear of attacking, humiliating control; the wish is that others will leave the person alone. His or her baseline position is one of **hostile withdrawal** and **self-neglect**. The person believes that he or she has a capacity for magical influence that can be implemented directly (telepathy) or indirectly (control through ritual). Usually the person imposes these "powers" from a distance. He or she is aware of **aggressive feelings** but usually restrains them.
Schizoid	.084	.093	.199	There are **no fears or wishes** about others. The baseline position involves active and passive autonomy. Underdeveloped in social awareness and skills, the person nonetheless has instrumental skills and can meet expectations of formal social roles (parent, boss, employee). He or she may be married but does not develop intimacy. There may be an active, but not necessarily bizarre, fantasy life.

Note. Bold print in the Interpersonal Description column marks patterns that explicitly or implicitly relate to anger, anxiety, or depression (interpersonal descriptions are from Benjamin, 2003a). Significant correlations between threat affects and behaviors and personality disorders therefore support the hypothesis that threat affects predispose specific behaviors, as hypothesized. The sample included 124 inpatients who rated symptoms on the *Symptom Checklist—90—Revised*. The Minnesota Multiphasic Personality Inventory—II was used to describe personality disorders according to the Morey et al. method (Colligan, Morey, & Offord, 1994).
$* p < .05.$ $** p < .01.$

This unacknowledged problem regarding the gap between group data and application of research results to individuals is illustrated in Figure 9.1 by the comorbidity between depression and anxiety (left) and depression and anger (right) in a sample of 154 inpatients. At the group level, both analyses yielded rs with $p < .001$, Bonferroni tested. Most readers will recognize that $p < .001$ means that the observed effect (correlations with depression and

Comorbid Depression & Anxiety
N = 154 Inpatients SCLM ratings

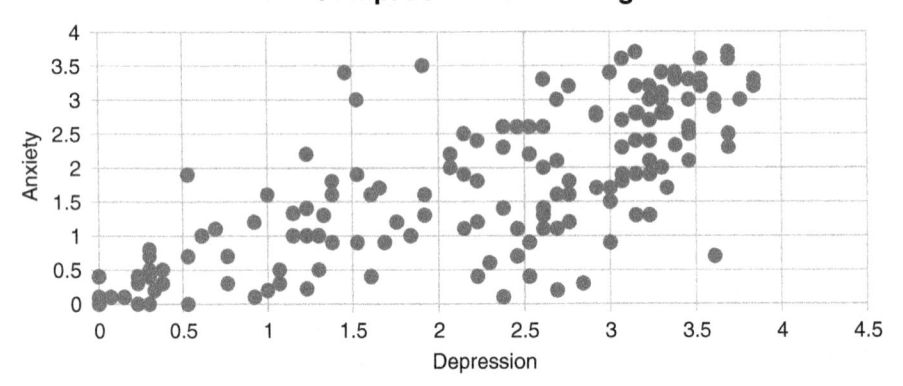

Comorbid Depression and Anger

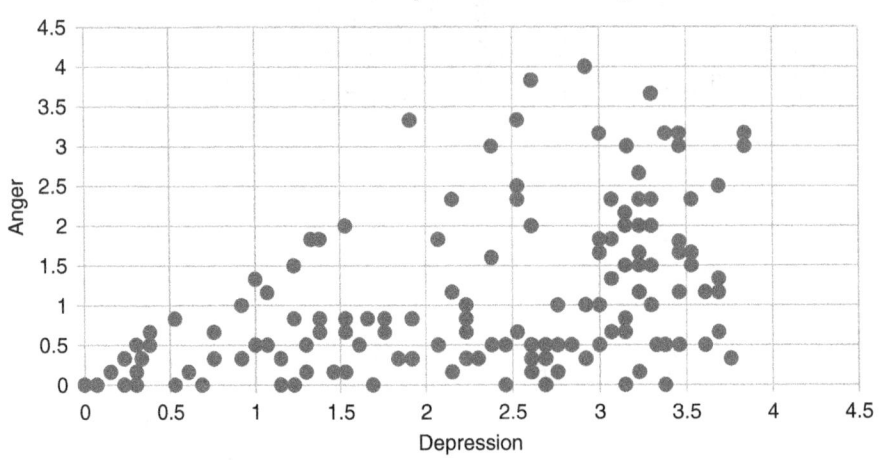

Figure 9.1. Individual scores showing comorbidity of depression with anxiety (top) and with aggression (bottom) in 154 inpatients. A perfect correlation would be shown by a line from the lower left to the upper right, with most data points close to that line. The correlations for each figure were significant at $p < .000$ by Bonferroni tests but are much clearer for the one at the top. The differences between these two figures demonstrate why a "significant" association may (top) or may not (bottom) apply to a majority of individuals in the sample.

with anger) would be obtained in only 1 of 1,000 repetitions of the experiment if the data are from a randomly distributed population. But that does not mean that there is covariance between depression and anxiety—for example, for 999 of 1,000 patients. It does not even mean that the overwhelming majority of individuals were comorbid for depression and anxiety.

Unhappy reality is shown by the scattering of data points in Figure 9.1. For both types of comorbidity (top and bottom), a perfect correlation would be shown with every data point landing on a diagonal line from the lower left to the upper right. There were quite a few inpatients who did come close to that line, but many others landed a noticeable distance from it. Notice a large band along the horizontal axis of the figure at the bottom: It shows that many patients scored very low on aggression, no matter what their level of depression. Another "band" on the vertical axis of the bottom figure runs counter to the significant correlation between depression and hostility. Everyone in that group was extremely depressed, but they varied a lot in their levels of aggression. If one imagines that a severely depressed individual feels like a fatally injured animal, then lashing out if anyone approaches would not be a surprise. The analogy might account for this finding.

The reality that there are many variations in comorbidity to be seen in the clinic is managed explicitly by the IRT case formulation method. The clinician is expected to address the entire affective symptom profile, including anger, anxiety, and depression (sympathetic), as well as positive (parasympathetic) disturbances such as mania and eating and sexual disorders (not discussed in this book). Personality disorders are included, too, using the interpersonal descriptions in Benjamin, 1996a [2nd ed., 2003a].

The task is simplified by remembering to relate salient presenting symptoms to primitive brain perceptions of safety and threat (C1), affect (A), and behavior (B), summarized as C1AB. Copy processes and GOLs will naturally emerge if the process skills (Figure 5.1) and case formulation procedures (Exhibit 4.1, Figure 4.1) are used. Explanations for comorbidity will relate to perceived threats and associated responses. For example, a patient may be depressed because of failure to be perfect as the mother in the head demanded and anxious because the father in the head was likely to administer beatings unpredictably. Another patient may be comorbid for depression and aggression because his beloved father was famously aggressive toward him while his mother abandoned the patient when she left his father when the patient was age 5. He identified with his aggressive father and suffered depression whenever he was reminded of the loss of his mother. These examples illustrate the general idea that all variations on comorbidity among affective symptoms can exist for knowable reasons if relevant clinical information at the level of $N = 1$ is elicited by the interviewer guided by Natural Biology.

Personality Disorders and Depression

There are important advocates (e.g., D. N. Klein, Kotov, & Bufferd, 2011) of the view that comorbidity between personality and depression sometimes is built into a "depressive personality" that reflects "temperamental risk factors." As noted repeatedly, temperament is a predisposing consideration, but interactions with attachment figures have a natural predisposition to have a huge impact on the individual's view of what to fear and how to be safe. Earlier in this book, data showing links between perceived interactions with caregivers and symptoms were presented (e.g., Figures 2.2 and 4.2) and illustrate orderly links among affects (Symptom Checklist—90—Revised; Derogatis, 1994) and behaviors (ratings of Structural Analysis of Social Behavior [SASB] points) and interactions with attachment figures. Another form of AB links is shown in Table 9.1. On the left-hand side, there are correlations between affects and behavior when B is defined by *DSM–5*-related definitions of personality disorder (using the Morey et al. translation of scores on the Minnesota Multiphasic Personality Inventory—II validated by Jones, 2005). In the table, quite a few significant correlations between anger, anxiety, or depression and the *DSM–5* personality disorders appear in bold.

Another connection between threat affects and personality disorder is shown on the right-hand side of Table 9.1. The far-right column presents interpersonal descriptions of *DSM–5* personality disorders. They were generated by SASB coding each of the personality disorder items (Benjamin, 1996a [2nd ed., 2003a]). In Table 9.1, words in bold in the interpersonal descriptions for a given disorder match a significant correlation on the left-hand side, also in bold. For example, borderline personality disorder (BPD) was significantly correlated with anger, anxiety, and depression, and all three correlations appear in bold. Bolded words in the interpersonal descriptions of BPD are hostile control matching anger, morbid fear of abandonment matching anxiety, and self-attack matching depression. The Natural Biological perspective requires that personality disorders (interpersonal behavior, B) be linked directly to affects (A) and primitive brain perceptions (C1) of threat or safety.

IMPACT OF DEPRESSION ON SIGNIFICANT OTHERS

Figure 9.2 shows that, in addition to affecting one's own behavior (Figure 2.2), threat affects also have an impact on the behavior of important adult attachment figures. Along with showing the familiar patterns of circumplex order, the data in Figure 9.2 suggest that anger (A) is associated with perceived submission of the significant other person, perhaps via anger that supports efforts to control (intimidation). The figure also shows a large

THREAT AFFECTIVE SYMPTOMS & INTRANSITIVE ACTIONS OF SO AT WORST (N = 150 INPATIENTS)

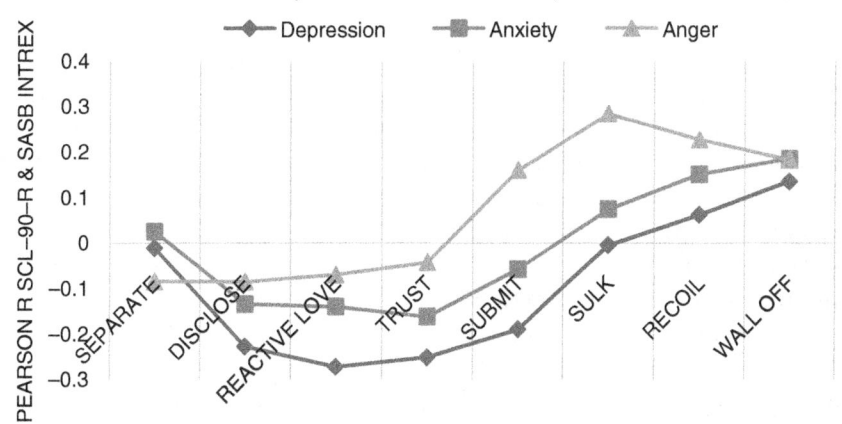

Figure 9.2. Perceived impact of patients' threat affects on intransitive responses of their significant other person. More depressed patients perceive greater deficits in friendliness from their significant other person, whereas more angry patients perceive greater submission and recoiling from their partners. Possible meanings of this finding are discussed in text. SCL–90–R = Symptom Checklist—90—Revised; SO = significant other.

correlation between patients' depression and inhibition of friendliness in significant other persons. That could be a result of affective contagion or reactive depression in significant other persons who despair after living with walled-off, unavailable, sometimes irritable spouses. Adding ratings made by significant others could refine understanding of the meaning of Figure 9.2. For now, the inference is that patients' anger, anxiety, and depression affect their views of, and quite likely the behavior of, significant others.

Recognition of such effects on relationships can be useful clinically. For example, depressed patients often feel disenfranchised, that they don't matter. One depressed patient was ready to give up on life when she was confronted with the fact that her partner was devastated by her suicide attempt. The patient was jolted into this reality as she realized that she mattered, and that helped her reengage with life. But calling attention to the patient's negative impacts on others can backfire if the patient takes such information as blaming. Worse yet, a passive–aggressive suicidal patient might be egged on by such information because he/she wants the partner to suffer along with other "deficient caregivers." That strategy is common enough to have a name; it is called *projective identification*. As usual, context matters when it comes to understanding symptoms and choosing related interventions.

TREATMENTS FOR DEPRESSION

Medications

There is a large array of medications for treating depression. They all affect mechanisms that activate the patient and/or increase positive affectivity either directly or by blocking or slowing reuptake of endogenous chemicals that support positive affectivity or help activate the person. A few examples include selective serotonin reuptake inhibitors, which slow reuptake of serotonin in the brain synapses; dopamine reuptake blockers, which can help the pleasant affects associated with dopamine reappear; and selective norepinephrine initiators, which slow reuptake of norepinephrine, an activator. That these drugs help control symptoms of depression by, in effect, making natural system neurochemistry more available is consistent with the Natural Biological analysis of depression as withdrawal via inhibition of sociability or by deactivation. For treatment-resistant cases of depression, psychiatrists sometimes use electroconvulsive treatment (Depping et al., 2017) or transmedial deep brain stimulation (Mayberg et al., 2005). Their mechanisms are still under study.

Psychotherapy

The sections that follow provide an illustrative review of the vast literature on psychotherapy treatments for depression.

Cognitive–Behavioral Therapy Variations

Cognitive–behavioral therapy (CBT) is taken to be the standard of care when it comes to psychotherapy in general and depression in particular (Beck, Rush, Shaw, & Emery, 1979), having been shown by the randomized trial method to be effective in reducing symptoms of depression and anxiety. CBT also has been adapted in a large number of ways. For example, Fiske, Wetherell, and Gatz (2009) reported that variants of CBT, such as bibliotherapy, problem-solving therapy, and life review or reminiscence therapy, were both effective and underutilized for treatment of older adults. Fournier et al. (2009) found CBT superior to antidepressants for outpatients who had experienced "marriage, unemployment, and . . . a greater number of recent life events" (p. 775). Hayes, Villatte, Levin, and Hildebrandt (2011) offered a summary of a variety of CBT-based psychotherapies that included assessment of outcomes. Their historical account begins with behavior therapy and moves to cognitive–behavioral therapy. Important outgrowths from there include mindfulness-based therapies, metacognitive therapy, motivational interviewing, behavioral activation therapies, integrative behavioral couple therapy, functional analytic psychotherapy, and some additional integrative approaches.

Hayes et al. (2011) classified this collection of CBT approaches in three clusters using language at a high level of abstraction. The first cluster of treatments addresses "acceptance, detachment, metacognition, defusion, emotional regulation, and the like" (p. 160). That is accomplished by techniques to "reduce the automatic behavioral regulatory power of thoughts, feelings, memories, and bodily sensations . . . producing . . . greater psychological openness" (p. 160). The second cluster of CBT treatments enhances "pure awareness, perspective taking, theory of mind," and the third "deals with motivation to change, values, commitment, and behavior activation" (p. 160). They summarized the results as follows: Patients develop "a more open, aware, and active approach to dealing with the psychological barriers to effective living" (p. 160).

Additional therapies are not considered variations of CBT but nonetheless use similar therapy processes. They, too, are somewhat directive, focused on current challenges and states. A well-validated example is interpersonal therapy (IPT; Klerman, Weissman, Rounsaville, & Chevron, 1994). IPT treatments address interpersonal relationships and encourage work on loss, conflict in relationships, social isolation, and adjustment to life changes. Patients learn to link their moods to interaction in relationships, to express their feelings and expectations, and to problem solve. IPT is an empirically supported, effective treatment for depression (Dunn, Trivedi, Kampert, Clark, & Chambliss, 2005).

Acceptance and Commitment Therapy

A cousin of the CBT family of therapies, acceptance and commitment therapy (ACT) helps the patient achieve psychological flexibility by working with six key processes: defusion, acceptance, attention to the present moment, self-awareness, values, and committed action. Losada et al. (2015) pitted ACT against CBT in a randomized controlled trial of treatment for depression in caregivers of a family member with dementia; a control group (CG) was offered minimal support:

> At postintervention, 23.33% in CBT, 36.36% in ACT, and 6.45% in CG showed clinically significant change. At follow-up, 26.32% in CBT, 36% in ACT, and 13.64% in CG were recovered. Significant changes at postintervention were found in leisure and dysfunctional thoughts in both ACT and CBT, with changes in experiential avoidance only for ACT. (p. 760)

Their conclusion, modestly stated, was, "Similar results were obtained for ACT and CBT. ACT seems to be a viable and effective treatment for dementia caregivers" (p. 760).

These modern behavioral therapies, CBT and its derivatives, complete the transition from strict behavioral observation to heavy emphasis on study of the mind, a development that Skinner (1987) decried in his swan song. Back in the age of differentiation from psychoanalysis, Rogers (1951) had emphasized joining and tracking the patient's inner life with deep empathy. He rigorously avoided giving patients instructions or directions; he considered that kind of control to be disrespectful and to interfere with self-discovery. Existential therapies (Gendlin, 1999, a philosopher who worked with Rogers) had a voice then, too. Presently, the Hayes et al. (2011) overview of CBT seems reminiscent of Rogers's empathy, positive regard, and congruence and ways of being described by existential philosophers. The earlier versions of this approach were shown to be effective by M. H. Klein, Mathieu-Coughlan, and Kiesler's (1986) Experiencing Scales that reliably assessed depth of experiencing in therapy and predicted better outcomes. That measure likely could capture some of what is happening in these present-day philosophical revisions of CBT.

Heidegger's (1927/1962) *Being and Time* is the existential approach most integral to IRT. At any given moment, the focus in IRT is on experience in the present as it is affected by past (Family in the Head) and by the patient's vision of the future (Birthright Self). Changing the primitive brain's maladaptive vision of the future to a vision involving Secure Base patterns is essential to good outcome in IRT. That, basically, is Heidegger's recommended way of being in time. With realized Secure Base, one can be fully in the moment, aware of historical forces and projected states in the future, and therefore can make informed existential choices.

Psychodynamic Therapy: Two Examples

An Internet search of meanings of *psychodynamics* yields an array of definitions. Merriam-Webster (n.d.) provides one that includes IRT: This dictionary defines *psychodynamics* as "the psychology of mental or emotional forces or processes developing especially in early childhood and their effects on behavior and mental states." Two examples of psychodynamic therapy for depression that are closely related to IRT are sketched here: L. S. Greenberg's emotion-focused therapy and Blatt's (2004) recommended treatment for anaclitic and introjective forms of depression.

Emotion-focused therapy (EFT) is a well-validated psychodynamic psychotherapy. Cunha et al. (2012) treated depression with EFT and focused on mechanisms of change in relation to three good-outcome and three poor-outcome cases. New experiences (innovative moments in therapy) were associated with good outcomes, and exploring "insight skills" preceded the constructive tasks of reconceptualization and change at the end of treatment.

Blatt's (2004) treatment for depression recommended different treatment for anaclitic (attachment loss) and introjective subtypes. Treatment needs to be more directive for the anaclitic type, whereas introjective patients are more likely to respond to interventions that lead to insight. In all psychodynamic therapies, a stronger therapy alliance is helpful (Crits-Christoph, Gibbons, Hamilton, Ring-Kurtz, & Gallop, 2011).

Exercise

In 1979, Greist et al. reported that running was an effective treatment for depression. The effect of exercise on mental health, including depression, was replicated by others. For example, Bernstein and McNally (2017) subjected 80 people to negative and positive mood inductions and then randomly assigned them to stretch or jog for 30 minutes. The impact of the negative mood induction was attenuated, as predicted, by the aerobic exercise condition. Ten Have, de Graaf, and Monshouwer (2011) assessed 7,076 Dutch adults for mental disorder and number of hours per week spent in exercise. They found that physical exercise was negatively associated with presence and first onset of mood and anxiety disorders after adjustment for confounders. Neviani et al. (2017) enhanced antidepressant treatment of patients with late-life depression without severe cognitive impairment by adding aerobic exercise to their treatment. Dunn and colleagues (2005) used a randomized 2 × 2 factorial design (frequency by intensity measures by energy expenditure) plus placebo control for 12 weeks to assess the impact of exercise on 80 adults with mild to moderate major depressive disorder ages 20 to 45 years. Depression was measured by the Hamilton Rating Scale for Depression (Hamilton, 1967). Energy expenditures significantly reduced depression ratings at 12 weeks. There was no effect of frequency. These and other studies confirm that exercise can help relieve mood disorders, and there is evidence that intensity of exercise (elevating cardiac activity) contributes more to the effect than frequency.

IRT CASE FORMULATION FOCUSED ON DEPRESSION

This section describes the case formulation that was a prerequisite for planning treatment of a chronically anxious and depressed older woman. The IRT clinician starts with symptoms and identifies related C1AB links and the copy processes that shaped them. In this way, each case is individualized, and the treatment plan is to focus as soon as possible on the "regulators," the Family in the Head.

Grace began therapy with dangerous episodes that could have resulted in impulsive overdosing. These episodes subsided in the early months of treatment, but anxiety, depression, and somatization continued relentlessly. For decades, Grace had been a splendid mother, and she was a beloved member of her community, widely recognized for her generosity and helpfulness. Her mother, however, had clearly communicated that Grace was not to attend to her own needs and wishes. In fact, she actively had to hide her accomplishments, lest she hurt her sister's feelings.

Grace had been virtually 100% devoted to serving others. But as she aged, she began to be sad about never realizing her dreams, which included travel, writing, and "having fun." Her despair was not altogether realistic because her husband seemed quite supportive of her wishes if only she would speak of them and take related action. Sometimes, she would say, "I want to have fun, but I just can't go ahead and travel and write. The thought of it makes me too anxious, and then I get sad because I don't see how I can ever change." When she decided this process was endless and there was nothing left for her even in her final years, she became sad, demobilized, discouraged, and ready to give up completely. As others tried to facilitate meeting her wishes, something always happened to interfere, and the plans would disintegrate. She remained loyal to her mother's rules, and in so doing, she was her own worst enemy.

Treatment began with understanding the case formulation so that she could see that the rules for her were not writ large by the universe; they only represented preferences of her parents at a critical time during her development. She needed to convince herself that self-care was not "selfish" and that she no longer would be vulnerable to attack for thinking about and acting on her own interests. Her case formulation was described this way:

> You get really anxious when you are not serving others because that is what your primitive brain has learned that you need to do to be safe. You have been unusually generous as you have taken care of your family, neighbors, and community. Even though you understand that it is more than reasonable and fair for you to have enjoyment now, the old injunction remains as powerful as ever: The spunky and talented young woman that you once were, with hopes of traveling and writing, remains locked up in a psychological cage. But if you are willing, we can work on setting her free.

STEPS IN IRT TREATMENT FOR DEPRESSION

Collaborate

Such an explanation of the case formulation, followed by a review of the treatment plan, enhances collaboration. For Grace, the emphasis on treatment might begin with the following:

> If you can see that the attacks on you were unfair and that you have every right to be good to yourself, you could start to have good fun in the years that are left for you now. Let's start with small steps as you "defy" the old

rules and resist criticism from Family in the Head. We could work on those exercises until you become stronger than Family in the Head. After you get free of their old instructions and realize you still are a good person, you can work hard on reprogramming your primitive brain in ways that allow you the freedom, the right to travel and see things you love to see and write about and do whatever else you please. Your husband has reassured you that he thinks that would be good.

In IRT, the main work is with Family in the Head, the source of the dysregulation, more than symptom containment. For Grace, fear of punishment from Family in the Head for alleged selfishness is the targeted mechanism for her symptoms of depression and anxiety.

As an example that shows what a difference that can make, a few years ago I saw a video of a therapy session during which a depressed patient described helplessness and despair in relationships. The therapist focused on assertiveness, and the method was to encourage or empower the patient to go ahead and speak her mind. She needed to learn to say no if she preferred and ask directly for what she wanted. Those were reasonable, evidence-based, proven effective interventions. But the patient was completely unresponsive. The process was frustratingly deadlocked, so much so that the audience laughed. The demonstration showed that despite good intentions and good interventions, some patients just won't respond. And that is accurate some of the time.

However, before reaching that conclusion, an IRT therapist would try to help the patient recognize and consider the reasons for her inability to assert. In the video example, as for Grace, it was clear that the self-negation (and depression) were derivatives of rules and values for threat and safety set by attachment figures. Earlier in the demonstration interview, this patient had mentioned that in her family, she (like Grace) had been "criticized and rejected" for any signs of "selfishness." This meant that both Grace and the demonstration patient needed to contemplate the "reasons" for their self-suppression and open up to the possibility that they had the right to have their own views and needs. Until that was addressed, it would feel too dangerous for them to follow the therapist's suggestions, no matter how well validated and effective the "techniques" have proven in large-sample statistics. Absent commitment to try to overthrow the old rules for threat and safety, collaboration in working toward the therapy goal of Secure Base (Tables 2.1, 2.2) would be unlikely for both of them. But if the higher brain were "on board" with the case formulation and the treatment plan, success would not be certain, but it would be possible.

Learn About Patterns

In general, if depressive affect is present, there likely are behaviors of withdrawal and/or defeat. This usually is accompanied by feelings of helplessness and hopelessness that nature selected to facilitate those defenses of last resort. The following is an illustrative list of quotes from patients describing rules copied from attachment figures that inspired lasting depression: "Love is about suffering and death." "I am always the victim." "Obedience is love." "Emotional slavery is love." "Friends always submit." "Everything is over before it starts." "I always react, never decide." "Doing well hurts others." "Life is a zero-sum game: You have to have conspicuous failure to counteract success." "If I meet my own needs, I exploit another person." "I can only take responsibility for negative events." "I am bad if I do not let the other person control." "If I fall apart, then they will love me." "If I do well, I put Mother to shame." "I must speak in final draft or be silent; I get approval by proving my rejectability." "I want to be a child forever." "Independence means aloneness."

Messages that supported deactivation and submission were accompanied by deprivations and other punishments if the patient asserted, took initiative, or refused to comply. Alternatively, the patient may have been told that she was not very smart or that she was helpless, and so she has not tried very hard to master anything. The point is that behind every such self-concept, there is a related message from a loved one or ones. It is true that "children will listen" (Sondheim, 1987).

In IRT, as in most other psychotherapies, patients are asked to agree to work on change in themselves more than in others. Some find this to be very difficult. I have called that pattern "the wrong patient syndrome." If people persist in complaining about others and implying that if others would change, all would be well, the therapist is reduced to: "So our best treatment plan is to get your significant other person in here and change him/her. Right?"

With that fantasy revised so that the patient is willing to work on himself or herself, a review of complementarity theory (Chapter 3) sometimes can help. For example, submission draws or pulls for dominance. So if the depressed patient complains that her partner is too bossy, one possible change is for her to stop being so submissive and instead practice nonaggressive assertiveness (described in Table 3.2, intransitive focus, and in Alberti & Emmons, 2017). A few couples sessions help might consolidate the new pattern for the depressed patient.

Family in the Head and, in fact, family in reality are not always pleased with genuine therapy progress. Change may be met by attack and dismissal. A newly assertive patient might be greeted with, "Well, if you think you are so smart, then go ahead and take care of *this*." For example, Laura, who had a job that paid much less than her husband's, asserted that she would like to have a way to buy some things on her own. After conversations about that, her husband agreed she could have her own credit card and checkbook and a small allowance to deposit in the account.

Not long afterward, they visited Laura's family of origin and invited everyone out to dinner at a favorite restaurant. A good time was had by all, with lots of alcohol and multiple desserts for some. When it was time to pay the bill, her husband announced: "Laura has her own credit card now, and she is paying for dinner tonight; let's all go outside and look around." Laura, left alone at the large table and unsure of how to use the card, received instruction from the waiter and was surprised and terrified by the bottom line, which basically drained her account. Her husband's "affirmation" of her freedom carried more than a suggestion of sadism. What she needed, if not a new husband, was to have asserted further with him and asked him what he had in mind when he did that. Her own view was that she wanted moderate autonomy, not abandonment.

Copy Process: Identification

Copy process is not willful. In fact, people are not often aware of it. Alice, a depressed woman in her late 40s, loved but was irritable with her husband.

> It feels instinctive to treat my husband the ways Mother treated me. I am nasty. I try to stop it, but sometimes I blame him for things I should take responsibility for. Sometimes I make him feel bad about what he has done or has not done, just like Mother did to me. Luckily, I succeeded in not having children [sobbing].... And I met my mother with plenty of nastiness of my own. I did not know how to be better toward her than she was toward me.... This depression is just an extension of that big, long sorrow that I never had a better relationship with a mother of my own. That will never be fixed either.

With that, she described exactly what usually supports lasting depression: an unrelenting wish for what for her never was, never could be, and never would be until a time machine was invented that also ensured that her parents would offer Secure Base conditions. Letting go of that fantasy in relation to Family in the Head and committing to reprogram with Secure Base patterns is the key to recovery.

Copy Process: Recapitulation

Jason (Chapter 1) knew that his trouble completing projects at work recapitulated his response to his father's cruel supervision of homework. He tried to free himself to do his work by saying to the father in his head, "I will not let you control me." His insight was not the cure, but it did contribute to the process of change:

> Awareness has helped me not stress so much about my work blockage. I think that maybe with time, I will be more in charge of myself. I still have not fully appreciated that when I think of me, it is actually a response to him.

Jason was observing that higher brain recognition of the case formulation can focus one on the primitive brain's dominance. That realization can encourage efforts to change the primitive brain—which is exactly what Jason did in several subsequent years as he managed reprogramming his primitive brain on his own.

Recapitulation often is the primary copy process in people who suffer from long-term depression. Possibly that is because it represents continuation of a passive, deactivated position that could be enabled by a shy, withdrawn temperament. Betsy had prolonged episodes of severe depression that were preceded by her childhood with a demanding mother who would make her repeat household tasks many times if not done "perfectly." As an adult, Betsy worked very hard at a low-paying job and did well in that she had offers to be promoted. She refused advancement, saying "I am debilitated by perfectionism.... I am afraid to fail. I don't attempt things because of that fear." Betsy and her therapist had the following therapy dialogue:

Therapist: What if you fail?

Betsy: People will think less of me.

Therapist: Who?

Betsy: Mom. She is perfection. [pause] But she is not perfect.

Therapist: Then you can't love her.

Betsy: [laughs]

Therapist: So the most perfect person you know and love is not perfect and therefore is unworthy of love?

Betsy: I guess. But if I can't do something perfectly, then I wake up wanting to do nothing, and I go on antidepressants again.

This "interpretation" did not bring immediate change, but the discussion of whether her mother's rules should continue to prevail dislodged Betsy's crippling devotion to perfection. Much of the subsequent change came through working on assertion with her kind husband, who, not surprisingly, had his own ideas about how a household should be run. But he was willing to discuss and negotiate when there was disagreement. She became increasingly able to defy her internal mother's demands and to assert with her husband and with her boss at work. Her depression diminished.

Copy Process: Introjection

Theresa had been severely depressed for a year and a half. She had the role of "the difficult child" in a large family. This was based, apparently, on her temper tantrums from a very early age. She had been labeled a bad child for that, but the concept persisted. Here is a brief conversation about the impact of that family myth:

Therapist: Let's work on feeling you are worth working on.

Theresa: That is hard. It is hard to like myself.

Therapist [interpreting]: They don't, so you don't.

Theresa: I know. I hear all these voices telling me I am not OK. So, should I tell them I am a good person?

Therapist: Yes.

Theresa: I understand. It is hard, but I will try.

Theresa read about nonaggressive assertiveness (Alberti & Emmons, 2017) and began to practice it as often as possible. Several months later, she also decided to go to school and train for a good job. With the help of government loans, she managed to do that and subsequently did quite well.

Gifts of Love

Serena, a respected internist, had severe, unremitting major depression for many years. Still, she was an expert caregiver: Patients, family, neighbors, coworkers, and acquaintances were often beneficiaries of her generosity and competence. Despite her high level of function, especially when caregiving, she sobbed uncontrollably much of the time. She had taken multiple antidepressants and anxiolytics, without much relief. She had taken care of her ailing mother since childhood, and her mother was on her deathbed at the time of this session:

Serena [sobbing]: I love her so much. I will miss her when she dies. [long silence]

Therapist: This is so sad. And yet, she has suffered a lot for such a long time. Perhaps, as you have said so many times, she may be relieved to go. Is crying often something she wants from you?

Serena: Well, I have always cried around her. I have always cried so much anywhere. Mother says, "Tears are the windows of the soul. When you cry, you are being cleansed."

Therapist: Mother approves, and knows how to take care of you when you sob?

Serena: She would put her hand on my cheek.

Therapist: I notice you are putting your own hand on your cheek.

Serena: She would say: "Oh, my tender-hearted one."

Therapist: So when you cry, you are assured she is with you?

Serena: Yes. [long silence]

Therapist: Is there another way you could be close to her?

Serena: Wow. Wow. Enough suffering without having to respond in a way that increases the suffering. That opens a whole new way of perceiving being with her.

Therapist: So, you cry when you miss her. When you cry, she is with you. If you can comfortably let her go, you may not need to sob all the time.

Serena: But how? This place *hurts*. I see I do have to let her go. But I worry I have stuffed things.

Therapist: "Stuffed things"?

Serena: This is the way I can feel close to her. I will miss that closeness.

Therapist: Is there any other way to be with her?

Serena: There is not a lot of her left. She still has humor. We can laugh.

Block Problem Patterns

A common blocker to therapy progress is patient insistence that there be restitution from family of origin for unfairness. The demand requires a time machine and a courtroom. The time machine would bring back offending family members; the court would make judgments, mete out punishments, and issue mandates for restitution. Such requirements are, of course, completely unrealistic, even psychotic if not recognized as impossible. Even if there were there a time machine and a friendly court, the courtroom result would be win or lose. The courtroom, psychological or actual, is not a place for healing unless one is obsessed about dominance, justice, and punishment. But that does not code as Secure Base, nor is it symptom free.

Love for one's children can effectively block marital fighting. A couple can cease and desist and practice more adaptive ways of relating when they are reminded that their children will copy what they see. The wish for one's child to have a better life sometimes can overpower one's immersion in his/her own destructive copy processes.

An effort to enlist collaboration in preventing suicidal action is vital. By contrast, in a continuing education workshop led by a suicide expert not long ago, I heard the speaker say, "I tell my adolescent patients that I will call their mother if they leave the session in a suicidal condition." That would not be IRT adherent. Patients in IRT would not be "threatened" with referral to their support system. However, family sometimes are enlisted to help develop a safe suicidal plan, but the tone of the exchanges and the goal are to maximize collaboration toward reaching the goal of ensuring the safety of the patient.

Extensive discussion of and recommendations for addressing suicidal crises in IRT appeared in Chapter 7 of Benjamin (2003b [paperback ed., 2006]). Basically, the strategy is to be aware of the danger, take any immediately needed steps to keep the patient safe, work with Family in the Head to do whatever might help disrupt the messages that support self-sabotage, and then redirect the patient toward his/her chosen healing image. If the problem of short-term safety has been addressed, and the patient is willing, then the forces behind the suicidal wishes can be addressed. Destructive components of the relationships with Family in the Head likely are somehow suggesting that suicide is a good idea. Jacob, for example, was convinced that others would be relieved of the burden he posed. Sometimes the suicidal person is furious with everyone, including himself or herself. Socratic conversations can help:

> You want to escape the trap you are in now, but killing yourself rules out all other possible options to cope with this issue. There is no choice after suicide. How about waiting longer to explore more ways for change? Is it OK to try to save some options?

If yes, the clinician and patient develop an immediate safety plan and make an appointment to work with Family in the Head in the next session.

It is always important to share one's understanding of and empathy for the patient's suffering, whether the issue is suicide or other self-sabotaging behavior. The IRT clinician tries hard to share the patient's perspective and communicate that he/she "gets it" even while maintaining a realistic perspective. Sometimes, primitive brain language can help jolt the patient back to reality: "Can you consider telling the sister in your head to shut up and your demanding dependent internal parents to grow up?" These words, of course, must match the patient's thought processes. A different patient might require self-talk like this: "Go ahead and play holier-than-thou. I have my feet on the ground and am no longer a subject in your kingdom. I choose to live in kinder, gentler, better ways."

After making such an intervention, which is sure to anger Family in the Head, the therapist should monitor the patient's psychological temperature by asking the patient how he or she feels about the exchange and repairing any identified breach in the therapy relationship by reviewing intent, trying to correct any misperceptions, or offering any apologies due.

Sometimes desperately depressed people have unrealistic fantasies about what hospitalization would be like. If so, perhaps the fantasy could be realized by better means. If a person is burned out and angry and disgusted with self and others, a vacation with a trusted person could better meet the need. Such a recommendation should be accompanied by detailed instructions designed to ensure safety and direction on what to do to get safe if those plans fail. For example, the traveling companion would control the medications. Specific behaviors would be identified that would disrupt the vacation and require return home or local hospitalization. If exploring this approach, one must distinguish between genuine relief about such a plan and a deadly calm before a suicidal storm. The latter would mean that the person has decided to act on the suicidal plan, which has pleased the internal critics and brings faux relief. If there is palpable doubt about any evolved alternative plan, it is best simply to use the hospital for safety.

The topics of harm to self and others are addressed in greater detail in Benjamin (2003b [paperback ed., 2006], pp. 226–261). Flow diagrams and examples explain how to use standard interventions (medications, affect management techniques, hospitalization) as needed to address immediate danger and how to address motivation for harm to self or others by using the IRT case formulation and treatment models to shift from maladaptive GOLs of the Yearning Self to Secure Base rules supported by friendlier, better adjusted attachment figures that encourage development of the Secure Base Birthright Self.

Engage the Will to Change

As shown in Figure 5.1, this therapy step is so critical to change that this discussion is organized according to the Prochaska, DiClemente, and Norcross (1992) stages of change. As noted before, the action stage of change in the stages of change model is the most critical and least understood. To focus on action, the action stage is subdivided into phases in IRT (Figure 6.2), which are reviewed here as they appear when treating depression. These phases, like other stages and steps, are approximately sequential, but there is a lot of moving back and forth.

Work on realizing a secure self requires breaking old rules for defining threat and achieving safety, and that is terrifying. Shifting from self-criticism to self-affirmation, for example, can elicit mockery and renewed attack from Family in the Head. Changing those old recordings is like changing any other addiction. Melissa (Chapter 5) described the challenge as she was puzzling over why it was so hard to let go of her "marital" relationship with her father: "Last night, as I was watching one of my favorite distracting TV shows, an answer popped into my head: 'If he can't have me, no one else can.'" The father in her head was demanding fealty. Melissa reflected on her discovery: "Jeez. No wonder it is hard to differentiate! But ever so much more *important* to do so!"

Another example underscores the need to identify maladaptive copy processes and GOLs in order to activate mechanisms of change in psychotherapy.

Dorothy, a certified genius, had grown up in abject poverty with a critical mother and an incestual father. She performed very well in her job as a nuclear engineer but explained that if she let herself feel good about herself in her work,

> Somebody will put up a stop to that. Someone will feel it is necessary to put me in my place. . . . People here have been very positive about having me around. And I am horrified. It makes me really nervous. They definitely are just playing me for a fool.

After some exchanges about that, she explained her suspiciousness:

> I expect my father to show up and make me pay for being good at anything. For having enthusiasm for anything. I can get away with doing things as long as I don't look like I enjoy it. If somebody gives me an award, he will be pissed off.

She described the common need to appease hostile Family in the Head via self-sabotage; that is the primary blocker to change, and it is the primary treatment target. The sections that follow review the phases of the action stage while engaging the will to change when treating depression.

Resist Red Voices, Defy With Green Action

The first step in changing the will to fight for recovery is to begin to talk back to Family in the Head who support maladaptive patterns. Completing behavioral homework that directly challenges the old rules for safety is important, too. This will feel strange, not right, even dangerous. Patient and therapist need to be creative in discovering primitive brain images that describe this situation in imagined consequences of change. For example, Dolores created a metaphor to diagnose her problem and its solution:

> Mother was master puppeteer. I was the puppet. She controlled me my whole life. One day I cut the strings. I looked her [mother in the head] in the eye and cut the strings. "Bye, bye. I am free." I kept repeating this all day. When the puppet has no strings, it collapses. Yet I am still standing. She is not in control of me anymore.

Her metaphor resisted the old rules. The purpose of talking back is to enhance a sense of separation, which is a vital first step toward the development of a healthy, normal (Green) self. It need not be hostile, but it must clearly tag *separation*, otherwise known as *differentiation*. When depression is the primary symptom, the primitive brain images and metaphors created in this phase usually convey overwhelm, helplessness, compromised initiative, being checkmated, and disenfranchisement.

Individuals with passive–aggressive personality disorder almost always have comorbid depression. Because they are uncommonly difficult to treat, it can be helpful to clinician readers to have a review here of the IRT approach to Angela, a depressed and angry middle-aged woman with passive–aggressive personality disorder. This diagnosis is no longer included in the diagnostic nomenclature, but the pattern has remained in the clinic. It likely was banished from the lexicon because of unreliability, but speaking in tongues and opposites and freely contradicting oneself are distinctive markers for this disorder. These individuals have good reasons for their behavior but are quite difficult to treat because they are preoccupied with fixing blame for failed caregiving and receiving restitution. Caregivers easily end up on their list of defaulters. The prototypical case formulation for passive–aggressive personality disorder is described in Benjamin (1996a [2nd ed., 2003a], Chapter 11, "Therapy Is Not Helping" section).

Angela had a will to stay ill as it served her agenda of indicting her mother. The excerpts below are from a session that began with her anger at the therapist because she had not progressed at all despite about 3 weekly sessions. The therapist asked if she wanted to hear a theory of why she was stuck. Her answer was yes.

Therapist: You said if you get feeling happy in marriage and successful in work, your parents are off the hook.

Angela: [cries] They are off the hook no matter what. [sobs]

Therapist: That tells me your agenda is to get them on the hook.

Angela: [silence]

Therapist: To realize they were wrong?

Angela: I can see that is not going to happen . . .

Therapist: Remember when I said you either have to get a lawyer and nail them or give it up?

Angela: Probably true.

Therapist: I need help with the lawyer plan.

Angela: No . . . she would just come into court looking sweet and pitiful. Other kids would stand around saying what a great mom she is. I would sound bitter and crazy. There's no way to prove it . . .

Therapist: Why must Mother admit what she did and did not do?

Angela: She would be tormented.

Therapist: What would that be like?

Angela: [tears] It would be like I am.

Therapist: She would hurt like you do.

Angela: [sobs] There would be nothing she could feel good about. She would be tortured. No way to get out of it. She could not even believe in heaven and eternal peace. She could not fix anything. She would see it is all a big mess. She should be ashamed. She is guilty.

Therapist: Then what?

Angela: [sobs; long silence] She would stay that way.

Therapist: Where would you be?

Angela: I would not have to think about it anymore.

Therapist: If she suffers, you are released?

Angela: Probably. Everybody would know I don't owe her anything, and she would know it, too. . . . If she really understood what kind of mother she was, she would not want to show her face. . . . Somebody has to be in charge of the truth and care what happens. How can I say, "Oh, well, it does not matter. It is in the past. Forget about it"?

Therapist: Without this confrontation, what happens?

Angela: I don't matter. Anybody can do anything to me, and it does not matter.

Clearly, Angela will not change one bit, no matter what the procedure, until she can let go of this agenda. Early IRT treatments begin with a description of the case formulation, the treatment model illustrated with the patient's own examples, and a sketch of the treatment goal of Secure Base. For Angela, that disclosure would include detail about her perceptions of unfairness and experiences of defaulting caregiving and about the origins of the belief that relief follows revenge in the form of eternal punishment for the offending caregiver. Therapist responses to all that are included, too, as in:

> I see that you are gravely injured and am sorry you have suffered and continue to suffer so much. I think we can revisit that trauma and sort it out together so that you would become less trapped in it all. It really is important that you become stronger as your own self and less tangled up in what your mother is or is not. The ultimate goal of this treatment is that you become more secure and peaceful in relation to yourself and others.

Angela declined to work toward that goal and terminated IRT. She might have found a therapist who would ignore her goal of convicting her mother and receiving restitution and listen to her anger, giving her time to "work this through." Advocates of that approach have suggested that at some point, a patient like Angela will "get sick of it and just let it go." That could be, but my experience has been that individuals with passive–aggressive personality disorder, who predictably are depressed, are passionate about winning by losing (Benjamin, 1996a [2nd ed., 2003a], Chapter 11). That is true in therapy as well as in their other relationships. If the strategy ("my pain is worse, thanks to you") is so firmly entrenched that it cannot even be named as a problem, change is highly unlikely. In IRT, transparency and integrity are vital, and so it is not acceptable for the therapist knowingly to work toward a goal (i.e., Secure Base) while the patient has another (i.e., that mother will be brought down in public, possibly even by the therapist).

Face and Relinquish Yearning, Envision Birthright

Facing the need to stop yearning for caregivers to have been different is nearly impossible for passive–aggressive persons and very difficult for most others. It usually takes a while even to recognize the wishes, not to mention then having to move on and relinquish them. Nancy, who was chronically depressed, illustrated this process clearly as she discovered her comorbid anger:

> Last week it suddenly occurred to me that what I thought was "Green," that is, a lack of depression, was not Green at all and that the entire meaning of the "Green" metaphor was about growth, not about avoiding being Red. I realized that I had gotten so caught up in the Red/Green metaphor that I had forgotten what the two colors stood for! So, I started thinking about why I wasn't growing, and then . . . I realized that having to live with my stepfather was damaging my psychological health more than I had ever imagined. I also realized that I still want his love and approval, and that is why I am not progressing in my life. I am also very angry at him, and have been since the day he started dating my mother. And that is stopping me from progressing, too! I honestly didn't know that I was this angry, and that I had been angry for so many years.

Nancy was able to take some steps toward autonomy after that, starting with getting her own apartment. She moved to another city and continued her therapy work on her own, like Jason. She ended up, after several more years, doing very well in her work and social life.

Jane had spent several therapy sessions trying to get the therapist to be, in effect, the mother she never had. For reasons she did not understand, her mother always had excluded her from family events and other favors. As Jane came to understand that her transference relationship with the therapist as a better mother was not going to "work," she became more willing to talk about her need to stop yearning for her mother to embrace her psychologically.

Jane: Why do I keep crying all the time?

Therapist: There is lots to be sad about. But it is important that the sadness is about loss and not a form of yearning.

Jane: I understand. I agree logically that yearning won't help me. But I feel so crazy, mad, confused, unfocused. I need to say out loud again how awful my family [mother and siblings] was to me.

Therapist: I agree.

Jane's story was a tale of an openly extruded child, confirmed in family conferences and in the therapy narrative. For example,

Jane: One time my mother found out I had a glass of wine. She said, "Jesus does not love you, and neither do we. You belong with street people. You are not welcome here. You go ahead and self-medicate." . . . They are awful bigots. Yet they can convince me I am an asshole. When I am with them, I want to be rescued, but I think I have to rescue myself. I don't know if I can. There still is so much pain and confusion. I feel hopeless. I want somebody to make it better.

Therapist: It is so, so painful. . . . But I think you need permission from yourself to thrive without them.

Jane: I can see I do get in the way of that.

Jane continued to revisit and reflect on episodes of rejection and exclusion (Freud's algorithm). Quite a while later, Jane reported that when she told her father about a recent traumatic event, he shrugged and said: "I don't care a bit about what happens to you." She understood that she had increased her family's outrage by living with a man to whom she was not married. She kept on keeping on and eventually managed to get scholarships and a degree in nursing followed by a good job.

Every so often she wrote notes reporting that she was doing well. In reflecting on her success despite the shunning, she noted that in the early years, her father had been her friend and advocate. She also had friends at school, where she did well. That amount of support, plus an adult attachment that was meaningful, despite its own (subtle) version of exclusion, was enough to keep her "on track." The overt rejection by her mother, joined much later by her father, actually may have made it easier for her to stop yearning and move on to work on developing her more secure, Birthright Self.

Face Fear, Disorganization, Emptiness

Nature does a good job of ensuring that everyone is afraid to give up the GOL, the implicitly learned path to safety. Those who face the fear and begin to defy the ancient rules often become disoriented and disorganized.

People panic about loss of self and almost universally say, "If I am not who I have been, then who am I?" Many describe a deep black hole of nothingness. Some flounder around dangerously trying to fill the hole. For others, the worry is about the impact on others if they change. Samantha and Charlene provide examples:

Samantha, disabled by depression, worried about her abusive but nurturant father:

> If I am able to be successful, I do not need him anymore. But he needs me, so when I walk away, he collapses. I do not have stamina to separate his idea of who I am, should be, from who I have been.... Being disabled and needy is much safer for both of us.

Charlene's identity was to serve and rescue others. Burned out and depressed, she had sobbed to the point of exhaustion on behalf of family and friends: "I am trying to come to grips with who I will be if I am not a martyr. If I am not that, then I feel guilty." Fortunately, she understood how costly that was to her and could sense that she herself needed some care. Her homework for several sessions was to come back with a report of some form of self-care or, better yet, self-indulgence. She chose healthy activities, such as hiking or reading a book, that had nothing to do with work. Slowly, she chose more and more daring forms of self-care, culminating eventually in larger choices such as a nice vacation trip.

Build the Birthright, Celebrate Success and Happiness

Although it is good to have a vision of a healing image at all stages of therapy, it is critical to have one before trying to build the Birthright Self. In IRT, the healing image needs to be an image that reflects Secure Base patterns. Recovery does not arrive in a package. Rather, it shows up in small ways, with increasing frequency and reliability, until one day it is experienced as there, as "me." For example, Lisa, who had an extraordinarily traumatic history, provided a glimpse of a "good" day. Following a session during which we described Secure Base patterns and what supports them in contrast to what she had experienced, she wrote: "This a very different way of life. I am not talking mean to myself all the time. Everything feels so much lighter. All days should be like this one!"

Ana and her husband each had been raised in competitive environments. Both were intimidated by tyrannical older siblings, and both were steeped in the tradition of "if you are not one up, you are one down." Ana had the one-down position in marriage and predictably was depressed. We discussed the goal of Secure Base patterns with an emphasis on friendly differentiation (including assertion) and had a rehearsal for a conversation with her husband as they planned an upcoming trip. I told her,

Ask him: "Let's work on this plan together, OK?" Describe and invite. Don't corner and nail as required while you were growing up. Remember to practice friendly differentiation. You might say: "I understand, but I don't agree. I would like to do it a different way. Here is what I suggest . . ." Listen to his responses, and try to negotiate a fair and balanced "deal."

The discussion and the trip went well, by all accounts. Ana's structural change and the consequent differences in how she acted helped her husband, too. They grew together and stayed together.

The mechanism of change that enables people to reach the Secure Base goal is, as noted before, to change the relationship with Family in the Head with an emphasis on revising GOLs. Changes in relation to Family in the Head often reflect the therapy relationship and process, followed by changes in relationships with significant others in the patient's life. The idea that therapy change reflects change in internalized representations also was described by Harpaz-Rotem and Blatt (2005):

> Change in treatment-resistant, adolescent and young adult inpatients seems to involve at least two primary dimensions: 1: disengagement from an intense involvement with parents and 2: development in the structural organized of representations of self and a significant new figure, the therapist. . . . Clinical improvement over the course of treatment was significantly correlated with developmental progression of the significant figure each patient selected to describe (from a grandparent to a close friend) as well as with progression in the developmental organized in which this significant other was described. (p. 266)

Bear Grief

Grief is normal when losing a loved one and lasts about a year. Shear and Shair (2005) suggested that symptoms of normal grief "resolve following revision of the internalized representation of the deceased to incorporate the reality of the death" (p. 253). Complicated grief lasts longer and includes lasting symptoms of depression, including inability to enjoy life, trouble carrying out normal activities, withdrawal from social activities, feeling that life has no meaning, irritability or agitation, and lack of trust in others. These symptoms of lasting depression also are common in IRT patients during the time they are grieving loss of GOLs and recognizing all losses that their devotion to self-sabotage has caused. Symptoms unique to complicated grief include extreme focus on the loss, intense longing, problems accepting the death, numbness or detachment, preoccupation with the sorrow, and bitterness about the loss. These are seen during reconstruction, too.

Here is what Melissa (Chapter 5) said about grief after giving up her GOLs that involved symbiosis with her father:

> I know I have to be gentle on myself, but it is so hard. It just feels like I am completely reinventing myself almost overnight. I said to my husband, "I'm not asking for it to stop, or even slow way down; maybe just one change at a time." My brilliant husband says to me, "This should have all happened in your 20s; then you would have had time to take it one at a time. Now, you don't." Which only added to the grief and made me cry more . . . I mean grief about the fact that I have such a lost part of my life. . . . Sadness now derives from what is good about the changes. I don't feel ambivalent and rageful. I have started another identity. I am giving up wanting to be in the family and not wanting. I feel sad, but not *crazy*. I don't feel like hurling myself off the cliff. Just sad. I could cry all day.

As another example of grief during reconstruction, Sadie had problems letting go of fantasies about the therapist–mother:

Sadie: [cries] I am sad about you. More than them [family].

Therapist: Let's separate sadness that leads to letting go from sadness that holds you in depression.

Sadie: Letting go of you?

Therapist: No, letting go of my being what they promised but never delivered.

Sadie: I wish I had not been around when she died. Why only then? Where was she all my life?

Therapist: I am so sorry. . . . The only time you got close to her was when she was unconscious and near dead. Now lying down in despair is like joining her.

Sadie: [silence]

Therapist: Can you resist that call?

Sadie: I hope so.

Therapist: You realized that was an unfortunate experience . . . so sad that was all you had. Perhaps with G [new man she has been dating] you can build a more adaptive form of attachment.

Learn New Patterns

At this step, interventions in IRT are from many modern cognitive–behavioral approaches. The main task is to reprogram the affect regulators so that the primitive brain perception (C1), affects (A), and predisposed behaviors (B)—that is, the C1AB sequences—become adaptive. This section provides examples of interventions that support experiential learning of new patterns.

Treat Depression by Lowering Expectations of Self and Others

Zelda was going to visit her mother, who was terminally ill. We talked about what Zelda expected to do, and that was to prepare meals, entertain guests, and pick up the house. All that Zelda wanted was for her mother to be a little bit nice to her.

Therapist: You mean that she will be different this time? She won't criticize and complain about you?

Zelda: Well, I guess that is not realistic.

Therapist: How about talking about adjusting your expectations for what she will do?

Zelda: OK. How?

Therapist: As you say, you can try to make her more comfortable. Do you think she will change?

Zelda: I can hope so.

Therapist: If she does, that would be a blessing. What if she does not?

Zelda: More likely. Then I will do the best I can and be very upset. Depressed.

Therapist: And the depression comes from realizing that the hope of having her be as you wish she had been is gone. She will never acknowledge all that you have done and are.

Zelda: I have to agree with that.

Therapist: So let's take another approach.

Zelda: What?

Therapist: Can you expect nothing? Can you go as a prop on her stage, playing the service role as she wishes, helping her construct the scenario as she wishes? And tell yourself, internally, that you are choosing to do this? that you are not compelled to do it? She is dying soon, and you simply want to express your love again and help her on her own terms. The knowledge that you did that for her is yours to rest with; it is not dependent on having her acknowledge it. You have your own internal standards about these final days with her.

Zelda: I can try.

The strategy was to help Zelda learn more about internal control from her own point of reference. In the end, Zelda felt good about what she had given her mother and did not fret about the validation that never came.

Learn About Friendly Differentiation

Because differentiation failure represents failure to have a separate self and depression means the self has been compromised, learning to assert and to differentiate is a major intervention for treating depression. Lessons in nonaggressive assertion (Alberti & Emmons, 2017) or in friendly differentiation (Structural Analysis of Social Behavior) are excellent interventions. Consider a highly problematic situation: the relationship between divorced spouses when younger children are involved. Divorce is adversarial, and so there have to be attacks and defenses. But let that be the work for lawyers. The patient can then try to practice friendly differentiation: for example, "I am sorry you feel that way, but this is what I think and ask for," or "These are the reasons. . . ." That, said repeatedly in different ways, keeps the process civil and, if successful, will be easier on alienated spouses and, most especially, the children.

The same strategy is good for adults struggling with overinvolved parents. Patsy reported that her mother complained that she did not call often enough, visit enough, or show enough caring:

Patsy: Recently she complains I should pay them for my college loan. I was tolerant of all this and said I understood how she felt. My husband said that only encourages her and suggested I punish her instead.

Therapist: Yes, it does seem that supporting her in that could encourage more of it. Would you like me to suggest alternative ways of reacting to her when she does that?

Patsy: Yes, please.

Therapist: OK. First of all, what is the situation with the college loan?

Patsy: I make my payments every month. I earn enough now; I could pay more.

Therapist: OK. How about this:

Therapist as Patsy: "Mother, I make my payments on time every month. If that is not acceptable any more, please say so. I am willing to talk about a new agreement if need be. I think I could even get a bank loan now that I have a steady job."

Patsy as Mother:	"Oh, that's all right. Your father and I can handle things as they are."
Therapist as Patsy:	"OK. Thank you."
Patsy as Mother:	"But I would think you could call more often and show some caring, especially since we have helped you out."
Therapist as Patsy:	"Mother, I do love you. But please stop the attacks and hurtful comments. If you would be friendlier, I would love to talk with and be with you more often. I am so tired of hearing your long lists of all that you think I have done wrong. So if you start in with that again, I will leave the room or hang up the phone. I really hope we can change how this goes and work it out."
Patsy:	She won't like that.
Therapist:	Probably not. But we are trying to help her behave in ways that will make the relationship work better. If she does not respond, then I suppose she will have to settle for the current pattern of not seeing you very often.

Patsy tried this pattern on the next visit, and her mother reacted well. In fact, her mother wanted to come to therapy, too, but Patsy preferred to keep the therapy as her own.

IV

EMPIRICAL SUPPORT

10

VALIDITY OF THE INTERPERSONAL RECONSTRUCTIVE THERAPY MODELS AND EFFECTIVENESS OF TREATMENT

Showing that activation of mechanisms of change affects outcome is an excellent alternative, and presently preferred (Insel, 2010), way to test the effectiveness of a treatment model.

REVIEW: MECHANISM OF CHANGE IN INTERPERSONAL RECONSTRUCTIVE THERAPY

The primary mechanism of change in Interpersonal Reconstructive Therapy (IRT) is to modify the relationship with Family in the Head that has been dictating maladaptive rules for threat and safety, to repair current attachments, and to develop new social relationships that offer components of Secure Base. Hopefully these repaired and new Secure Base attachments can become new internalized representations with more adaptive rules for

---

http://dx.doi.org/10.1037/0000090-010
Interpersonal Reconstructive Therapy for Anger, Anxiety, and Depression: It's About Broken Hearts, Not Broken Brains, by L. S. Benjamin
Copyright © 2018 by the American Psychological Association. All rights reserved.

safety and threat. The change process is not easy because compliance with rules and values of old attachment figures has long helped patients feel loved and safe. Disobedience not only deprives one of reassurance from Family in the Head, but it also can lead to internal accusations of betrayal and ingratitude. The example of Janice provides a reminder of how that works.

Janice was a highly functioning professional who presented with generalized anxiety disorder and health problems, many of them skeletal and muscular. Her somatic symptoms mirrored the severe physical abuse from her father when she was a child and a teen. Among other things, he would punch her head. Janice had been in IRT off and on for many years and had reduced her level of anxiety and changed her social environment in adaptive ways: Her marriage was no longer abusive, and she now had good boundaries with her family of origin. She was doing exceptionally well at her very challenging work as an information technology manager in a large corporation.

During a recent lasting crisis, she had a flare-up of somatic symptoms, including severe headaches, along with increased anxiety and depression. She responded to the crisis optimally, but the associated stresses escalated, as did her somatic symptoms. She and I talked about how her body might be speaking about her pain. Her association to that thought was that as a child, she sometimes would beat her head on the wall. When asked what she felt like when she banged her head, she said the sensations were the same as the headaches. Realizing what she had just said, she asked: "How do I let myself off the hook?" Applying copy process theory, I suggested that with psychic repetition of head banging, she was punishing herself as had her father. She countered,

Janice: No. I punish myself for not being perfect to avoid trouble.

Therapist: Well, you are letting his abusive ways force you into the impossible task of being perfect. I think it is simpler to just say that you do to yourself exactly what he did to you.

Janice: What better way is there to show your respect to your father? My religious values demand respect for elders.

Therapist: Religion and biology both demand that we love our parents, period. We just do.

Janice [after thinking a minute]: So I end up [hurting] exactly where my dad said I should.

Therapist: Yes, and think about this: If you stop punishing yourself, you will dishonor your father.

Janice [reluctantly]: Do I have to dishonor him?

Therapist: If that is what taking better care of yourself means, yes.

Janice: Ooooo, you hit me at rock bottom. *Oooaaafff.*

Janice grasped at a gut level what it was going to cost to become pain free. She knew from experience that Family in the Head always became furious about her "betrayals" of their ways and rules as she succeeded in work and marriage. But she resolved to work on whatever she could do to let go of the last threads of hope for love and caring from the early versions of her parents that were stored as Family in the Head. She saw that she needed to let go. Ironically, several years later, she and her mom and dad were best of friends. Resolving differentiation from Family in the Head and adopting a Secure Base stance of friendly autonomy and friendly enmeshment as described by Structural Analysis of Social Behavior (SASB; Chapter 3) necessarily mean that healthy, comfortable relationships can prevail.

To achieve reconstruction, the affect regulators need to be reprogrammed in more adaptive ways. The process, outlined in Figure 6.2, amounts to a personal Olympics training. To succeed, patients need a knowledgeable coach with the ability to provide emotional support and meaningful structure as they discover and consolidate self-understanding that permits better ways of defining what to fear and how to be safe. Chapters 4 to 9 have included models and examples showing therapists how to do that.

For their part, patients need the ability and willingness to learn to identify their interpersonal and intrapsychic patterns and processes as well as their primitive brain perceptions and feelings. They need considerable courage, self-discipline, and grit to endure the work of changing so that the primitive brain rules for safety and threat become more adaptive. That accomplished, patients have access to new social, affective, and cognitive skills, and as Jason (Chapter 1) and others have shown, their learning and growing psychologically can continue long after IRT sessions stop. The discussion of tests of effectiveness of interventions in IRT begins with a review of effectiveness assessed by contemporary methods.

IRT AND THE RANDOMIZED CONTROLLED TRIAL

Presently, the gold standard for measuring effectiveness in psychotherapy is the randomized controlled trial (RCT). The idea of testing effectiveness in psychotherapy using the same method used to test effectiveness of drugs was advanced by Chambless and Ollendick (2001). But recently, physicians have added the requirement that activation of mechanisms of change needs to be related to outcome. Reasons include the fact that mere comparison of groups leaves the fate of many individuals unexplained and does not directly test whether the alleged mechanism of change actually affected outcome.

IRT has not been tested by an RCT because the CORDS population (comorbid, often rehospitalized, dysfunctional, and suicidal) is officially screened out of RCTs. They have more than one disorder, have a record of treatment resistance, are too unlikely to complete the protocol because of need for rehospitalization, are too dangerous to be on protocol, and more. They are forgotten ones when it comes to research funding, but they also are, according to hospital administrators, heavy users of medical resources.

IRT AND THE EVIDENCE BASE IN PSYCHOTHERAPY

In response to many criticisms of randomized control trials (RCT), an American Psychological Association (2006) task force recommended a more flexible standard for evaluating effectiveness, called *evidence-based practice in psychology* (EBPP). It is defined as "the integration of best research evidence with clinical expertise and patient values" (p. 273) and explicitly follows the lead of evidence-based practice in medicine (EVPM). The following paragraphs list the task force's suggestions for alternative research designs (p. 274) plus remarks about applicability to IRT.

Clinical observation (including individual case studies) is a valuable source of innovations and hypotheses. This standard is met by case examples from my private practice and selections from the 283 IRT case formulation consultations on the medical record. Staff viewing the consultations and patients themselves almost always agreed that his/her case formulation relating their copy processes to presenting symptoms was useful. Gifts of Love (GOLs) were not made explicit to earlier patients in this sample, but the later cases, all of whom did hear about their GOLs, thought that part of the case formulation also made sense.

Qualitative research can be used to describe the subjective, lived experiences. The testimony of IRT clinic participants, including observers as well as patients, supports the content validity of the IRT models and methods. There are many examples. In one, a former psychiatry resident who saw early versions of IRT interviewing wrote to ask the following:

> Do you still use the term "deep tracking"? It was terrific watching you help a person who was experiencing perplexed and confused thinking sound so together and clear. Also, remembering the lessons of the family therapy video about "who wanted the bed moved" is still valuable when working with troubled families.

In another example, a patient in the IRT clinic wrote about her experience with an IRT trainee therapist who now is director of a clinic at the University of Utah Medical Center.

> I can't stress enough how important the experience as a whole was. The environment was safe, and the tools/thought process helped me. I wish

> everyone could have a therapist like J. My life is better, happier, and fuller because of our time and work together. I can't think of one negative thing. Steps in the process were introduced at just the right time. I was able to feel like I was making decisions and sorting through my own issues with facilitation. It gave me confidence in every area of my life.

Although there are quite a few people who decline to pursue IRT after one or two sessions, those who participate in the treatment typically feel they have gained a lot. But most "testimonials" are in words that have not been recorded.

Systematic case studies are particularly useful when aggregated. Eells, Lombart, Kendjelic, Turner, and Lucas (2005) asked 65 experts to develop case formulations from a description of a case and found that the formulations of experts were "more comprehensive, elaborated, complex, and systematic" than those of novices and that their treatment plans were more elaborated and linked better to the formulations. There were few differences among therapy orientations. IRT qualifies as one of the more comprehensive case formulations in that study. In addition, in Benjamin (1996a [2nd ed., 2003a]), a case formulation for each personality disorder in the *Diagnostic and Statistical Manual of Mental Disorders (DSM)* was described in interpersonal terms based on SASB codes of *DSM* items. The descriptions have proved useful to many practicing clinicians.

Single case studies are useful for establishing causal relationships. Some SASB IRT articles have included a lengthy case formulation and treatment (e.g., Benjamin & Critchfield, 2010). Hartkamp and Schmitz (1999) used SASB to show changes in the structure of internalized representations during psychotherapy for individual cases. L. S. Greenberg and Foerster (1996) described "the process of resolving unfinished business" in terms of SASB codes of relationship with internalized representations as they were acted out in a "two-chair technique". The idea that changing internalized representations is a mechanism of change and use of the two-chair technique to accomplish that goal are both important in IRT.

Public health and ethnographic research is useful for tracking use of treatments. There have been no large-sample public health studies involving SASB or IRT case formulations. Ethnic and cultural considerations were discussed in Chapter 9. There are no public health studies using IRT treatment.

Process–outcome studies are especially valuable for identifying mechanisms of change. The evidence relating IRT therapist adherence to outcome, discussed later in this chapter, qualifies as a process study directly related to mechanisms of change. There are recent examples of other research that likewise used the standard of relating mechanisms of change to outcome (e.g., Pereira et al., 2017).

Studies of interventions delivered in naturalistic settings (effectiveness research) are well suited for assessing ecological validity. IRT research clearly has occurred in a natural setting. The inpatient population was based on clinical referrals for assessment of personality disorder and/or treatment resistance documented by high rehospitalization rates, suicide attempts, and comorbidity. The result is a polar opposite of the "pure" sampling required by an RCT.

RCTs and their logical equivalents (efficacy research) are the standard for drawing causal inferences. IRT has not met this EBPP standard, unless relating mechanisms to outcome is considered efficacy research.

Meta-analysis is used to synthesize results and estimate the size of effects. There are no published IRT studies whose effects could be combined in a meta-analysis.

Case Formulation and Treatment Models: Inseparable in IRT

Although not required by EBPP or RCT rules, the specificity of connections between the case formulation and treatment models is extreme. The same mechanisms that define pathology (miscuing) prescribe the treatment interventions (recuing). The case of Janice illustrated that her anxiety and headaches reflected copy processes supported by her love for her father, and so her loyalty to her father's rules needed to be modified. By contrast, conventional psychotherapy models assume one mechanism for pathology (i.e., diathesis/stress) and another for treatment (i.e., teaching affect management and coping skills).

Evidence Supporting the IRT Case Formulation and Treatment Models

Well-validated, evidence-based concepts that are integral to the IRT case formulation and treatment models are in italics in the following description of the IRT case formulation and treatment models. *Natural Biology*, the theoretical basis of IRT models, is based on the *theory of evolution*. The *meaning of normal* and *therapy goals* are specifically defined in terms of Bowlby's (1969, 1977) concept of *Secure Base*, one of the best validated concepts in social science (Cassidy & Shaver, 2008). Bowlby's concept of *internal working models* likewise is founded on substantial evidence (cited in Chapter 2).

SASB-based assessments of *patterns of interactions* with attachment figures and of *links between the past and present* are well validated in published studies (e.g., Benjamin, 1996b; Benjamin, Rothweiler, & Critchfield, 2006). The idea that *copy processes* transfer *information about safety and threat* from one generation to the next is copied from universally accepted descriptions of gene transcription and backed by published evidence (Critchfield & Benjamin, 2008, 2010). The reliability, specificity, and sensitivity of the *IRT case formulation method* that encompasses all presenting symptoms have been directly confirmed in highly comorbid, treatment-resistant inpatients (Critchfield, Benjamin, & Levenick, 2015). The validity of *Gifts of Love* was indirectly confirmed in that study by reliable identification of connections between key figures and presenting symptoms. Other evidence for GOLs was cited earlier (e.g., Sohlberg & Birgegård, 2003; Sohlberg, Claesson, & Birgegård, 2003).

The impact of some process skills (Figure 5.1) on outcome is evidence based. These include *accurate empathy* (Crits-Christoph, Cooper, & Luborsky, 1988) and *emphasis on adaptive (Green) patterns* more than on *maladaptive (Red) patterns* (Karpiak & Benjamin, 2004). Four of the five steps in the IRT treatment model have been correlated with good outcome. They include *collaboration*, a feature that is essential to successful *therapy alliance*. At first, collaboration is only discernible at the higher brain level (C2). As therapy progresses, actual behavioral change and earnest commitment to reprogramming the primitive brain are more apparent. The literature that relates therapy alliance to outcome is large and convincing (Muran & Barber, 2010). *Blocking problem patterns* and *learning new patterns* have prima facie relevance to the therapy task of replacing maladaptive patterns with adaptive patterns. That strategy is central in cognitive–behavioral therapy (CBT), presently the predominant evidence-based practice. *Learning about past relationships and linking them to the present* is standard procedure in psychodynamic therapies, some of which have qualified as evidence based (e.g., transference-focused therapy; mentalization therapy; schema therapy). The journal, *Developmental Psychopathology*, offers overwhelming evidence that interactions with caregivers have very large effects on child development, and logic suggests it is a good idea to consider that, as do psychodynamic therapists, when working with affective symptoms.

The make-or-break step in IRT is Step 4, enable the will to change. Central as it is, its mechanisms may be beyond the reach of evidence. Gill and Cerce (2017) offered an interesting review of and comments about the concept of will and evidence related to different versions of what it is. Quite often, discussions of will are embedded in concern about blame or responsibility, as in the distinction between murder and manslaughter. Blaming rarely is an appropriate focus in psychotherapy. The APA database yields articles on "free will" such as willpower, determination, agency, efficacy, and empowerment. They appear to be "think pieces" rather than studies that clearly define will and provide evidence about how to activate it and to what purposes.

The subject of will is at the heart of the question, Are we humans 100% predetermined? Or do we actually have meaningful choices (and responsibilities) that are not determined by measurable variables? Such questions bring psychology closer to religion, an entirely different way of knowing that typically uses private versions of "evidence." Evidence based or not, in IRT, "enabling the will to change" is necessary. The challenge of defining will and its mechanisms seemingly can be circumvented by using the familiar language of multivariate analysis: The therapist is a moderating variable (i.e., can shape the process) for change, but not a mediating variable (i.e., a presumptive cause of change). Moderators can enhance or suppress mediators. The patient is the mediator of change. This language makes the distinction clearer, but still, the basic mechanism seems beyond reach, as elusive as the Higgs boson, identified at best by its energy.

Amenable to scientific methods or not, experienced clinicians have learned that the patient's "will" to change matters a lot. Ignoring it because it cannot be operationalized is not wise. In IRT, that means the patient faces the need to choose between internal fantasy and current reality. Again, the therapist's assignment is to enable the will to resist old ways of feeling safe and to work hard with practices that help patients install more adaptive C1AB links and dare to renounce the Gifts of Love (i.e., self-sabotaging behaviors) to specific members of Family in the Head who have directly or indirectly sponsored maladaptive rules and values for safety and threat. The therapist can guide, try to protect, and cheerlead the patient, but as in Olympic training, the hardest work, the critical work in realizing a Secure Base self is dependent on the patient's will to push on with an often frightening, depressing, and often unpleasant process.

CONTEMPORARY EFFORTS TO IDENTIFY MECHANISMS OF CHANGE

Recently, there has been more interest in identifying and learning more about mechanisms of change. Pereira et al. (2017) studied changes in anxiety in 47 children assessed by questionnaires about "mediator variables" and anxiety during CBT treatment. They reported that perceived control and interpretation bias accounted for variance in symptoms of anxiety. Yeomans, Clarkin, Diamond, and Levy (2008) suggested that reflective functioning and transference interpretation are mechanisms of change in transference-focused therapy. Christie, Atkins, and Donald (2017) studied the role of values-based action in facilitating outcome measured by well-being in acceptance and commitment therapy. They concluded; "Mindfulness interventions may be enhanced with an explicit focus on values clarification and the application of mindfulness to values-based behavior" (p. 368). Suchman, DeCoste, Ordway, and Bers (2013) reported that helping mothers develop the capacity for mentalizing in mentalizing therapy enhances outcome in treatment of substance-abusing mothers.

That language is a step or two above the level of abstraction considered acceptable in IRT. Here is an example that may help explain why. Suppose a researcher decides to create a rating scale for "the degree to which Freud's algorithm was used." Ratings might be reliable. They might well correlate with outcome. But we would not know much about the raters' basis for their ratings, how to use the algorithm during treatment, or how to teach it to others. A manual is the usual response to that challenge, but readers still do not know what actually went into the ratings unless scores on specific components of the scales were included. To illustrate, the elements mentioned by Freud that might be described and rated in such a carefully defined way (Freud & Breuer, 1959, p. 28):

1. bring the exciting event to clear recollection,
2. arouse with it the accompanying affect in as detailed a manner as possible,
3. express feelings in regard to it in words,
4. repeat the original psychical process as vividly as possible in the state in which it was formed, and
5. talk about it.

Note that Freud (a) identified a precipitating event, (b) activated affect about it, (c) required detail, (d) linked words to affect, and (e) underscored the need for repetition "as vividly as possible." Each of those elements should be on the mind of every clinician of every persuasion if their patients are to get free of the impact of symptom-relevant maladaptive primitive brain learning. Nobody has discovered a shortcut or a better way to address affective and behavioral symptoms during more than a century that has passed since Freud offered that description of the essence of change via therapy process.

MEASURING EFFECTIVENESS BY RELATING ADHERENCE TO THE TREATMENT MODEL TO OUTCOME

The idea of assessing whether it matters if a treatment model is used appropriately and relating that to outcome is straightforward. The strategy was explored decades ago. Efforts foundered on controversy about whether effects could be attributed to the model (adherence measure) or to the "competence" of the clinician (and the patient). Unresolved, this issue lost salience as it was overshadowed by emphasis on the RCT that has dominated psychotherapy research since the early 2000s. For drug protocols, the change agent in RCTs was medication and was tested by comparing a group that received the medication in question with a group treated with a placebo. In psychotherapy research, by contrast, RCTs did not even require evidence that the alleged treatment actually was delivered, not to mention provide a comparison group that was offered a placebo (i.e., inert condition). One challenge was and is that the therapy relationship itself turns out to be much more than an inert channel for delivering a change agent, presumably the therapy technique.

Contemporary approaches to this problem are to measure adherence to the treatment model or treatment integrity and relate that to outcome. Perepletchikova, Treat, and Kazdin (2007) reported that measures of treatment integrity in effectiveness studies of psychotherapy for adults were extremely rare. Goense, Boendermaker, van Yperen, Stams, and van Laar (2014) used their survey of treatment integrity and found the same result in therapy for youth. In sum, more evidence is needed that the treatment models are used in effectiveness tests of psychotherapy and that they make a difference in outcome.

As noted already, it is difficult to separate adherence to a therapy model from therapist general competence, some of which comes with experience. If there are to be new efforts to assess whether and how correct use of a treatment model affects outcome, it is important to try harder to stick to the rules of basic science advocated most powerfully by B. F. Skinner (1987), a founder of behaviorism in psychology. Some of the newer psychotherapies that target mental processes and states of mind sound more like philosophy than psychology. That can be interesting and useful, but probably should not fly under the flag of science. For science, assumptions, definitions, logic, predictions, and evidence should be highly explicit and refutable by clearly described and replicable procedures. Abstract, general rating scales are not acceptable unless their components are clearly defined and rated separately.

STRATEGY FOR TESTING EFFECTIVENESS OF THE IRT TREATMENT MODEL

The main strategy for testing outcome in IRT has been to look for statistically significant pre–post changes in a population that has a record of not changing and then to relate changes to adherent uses of the IRT model. One of the most important mechanisms of change in IRT is to alter the relationship with Family in the Head so that key internalized representations consistently support Secure Base. That goal means that the C1AB links—perceptions of threat and safety (C1) and resultant affects (A) and behaviors (B)—will reflect what Bowlby (1969, 1977) described as Secure Base. It is easiest for observers to measure Secure Base by assessing whether patient behavior usually reflects transitive, intransitive, and introjected behaviors that are basically friendly, moderately enmeshed, moderately differentiated, and well balanced between focus on other and on self (Chapter 3). Such change is achieved by using Freud's algorithm to prepare to renounce maladaptive (Red) copy processes and their associated Gifts of Love and then to build new Secure Base patterns. The measure for activation of mechanisms of change considered in this chapter is the best rating for GOL work during one of the three assessments for GOL work made during the first year of treatment. The following sections describe how that is defined.

Measuring Adherence to the IRT Treatment Model

Using the flow diagrams and tables in Benjamin (2003b [paperback ed., 2006]), the components of the IRT model were translated into the IRT adherence scales by Kenneth L. Critchfield and Mathew Davis (Critchfield, Davis, & Benjamin, 2008), who, along with Christie Pugh Karpiak and selected advanced trainees, applied the adherence measures to therapy sessions in the IRT clinic archive. The sample sizes are small ($N = 15$–25),[1] which means effects must be large to yield $p < .05$ or better.

The first three ratings from the IRT adherence scales are shown in Figure 10.1. There are 11 more scales in the complete version, each measuring therapist and/or patient behavior related to a process skill or a therapy step from the IRT treatment model. Each scale is rated between 0 and +10 to reflect the degree to which components of the IRT treatment model are implemented by the therapist and/or by the patient. Active errors are recorded in a range from 0 to –10. One of the advantages of having a highly detailed, very explicit model is that errors more serious than "good feature is not present" (errors of omission) can be identified. Active errors are distinguished from errors of omission by whether or not they support Red (maladaptive) patterns.

The following is an example of an extreme error, rated at –10 on the IRT adherence scales: A therapist failed to show up for a promised emergency meeting with a suicidal patient without communicating a compelling reason to the patient and sending a substitute provider. Therapists of any stripe would agree that is an example of extreme incompetence and/or nonadherence. IRT theory (case formulation and treatment models) explains in detail why such an incident is nonadherent. This incident involves errors in using accurate empathy, collaborating, blocking maladaptive patterns, supporting Green more than Red, engaging the will to change, learning new patterns, and more. Given that there was immediate danger, the therapist's implicit support of the Red Yearning (maladaptive) Self and explicit failure to try to block intent for self-harm was egregious enough to explain why the event was scored as extreme error.

The following is an example of a still serious, but less than catastrophic error: During an IRT consultation, a patient had accepted the invitation to consider whether there was any unwanted pleasure in the destructive incest

---

[1] When testing SASB and IRT, our experience has been that significant effects in small samples are confirmed as sample sizes build.

GOL: PATIENT AWARENESS/CHOICE LEVEL	Red ← 0.0	0.5	1.0	1.5	2.0	2.5	3.0	3.5	4.0	4.5	5.0 → Green
	< Unaware >			<Pre-Contemplation>		<Contemplation >		< Action >		< Maintenance >	
	-10 -9 -8 -7	-6 -5 -4	-3	-2 -1	0	1 2	3 4	5 6	7 8	9 10	

1. BASELINE OF ACCURATE EMPATHY- Reflects understanding that is:

-consistently hostile, dismissive, needlessly confrontative, and/or uncaring -across ABC's -using patient's words in harmful/distorted ways -strongly amplifies Red strength defined in CF	-at times hostile, dismissive, needlessly confrontative and/or uncaring -"misses" some patient communications -across 1 or 2 ABC's only -distorts patient's words/meanings -amplifies generic Red strength		-may or may not seem caring -seems to "miss" patient in basic ways -substantially inaccurate/imprecise -uses patient's words infrequently -may provide support for Red or Green -CF not used to shape what is emphasized		-consistently caring -"misses" some important communications -across 1 or 2 ABC's only -only sometimes using patient's words -amplifies generic Green strength -sometimes joins or enhances Red strength		-consistently caring -across ABC's -using patient's words -strongly amplifies Green strength defined in CF -without facilitating Red

2. SUPPORTS GREEN MORE THAN RED- Provide ratio of support for Green and Red, respectively. Numbers should add to 100 (e.g., 90:10)

3. INTERVENTIONS RELATE TO THE CF

Clearly/consistently using the CF to: -relate symptoms/events to past learning in ways that enhance Red strength -encourage ABC's opposite to CF goals -motivate/encourage: 1-distance from Green wishes/goals; 2-closeness to Red wishes/goals -choose new learning/homework opposite to CF goals	-not clearly /consistently using the CF but when used, use fits areas listed for ratings -7 to -10	Taking generic approach not clearly guided by the CF -This could include: unconditional acceptance, equal attention to all ABC's, review of symptoms/events without regard to past learning, generic motivational statements, new learning/homework unrelated to CF goals	-not clearly/consistently using the CF for areas listed for ratings 7 to 10	Clearly/consistently using the CF to: -prioritize attention -relate symptoms/events to past learning in ways that enhance green strength -choose which ABC's to support/block -motivate/encourage: 1-distance from Red wishes/goals; 2-closeness to Green wishes/goals -choose new learning/homework

Figure 10.1. Three sections from the IRT Adherence Scale (Critchfield, Davis, & Benjamin, 2008). It measures the degree to which therapists and patients adhere to the instructions in flow charts, diagrams, and tables in Benjamin (2003b [paperback ed. 2006]). The term *ABC* has been updated in this book to *C1AB* to distinguish primitive from higher brain cognition and to reflect the sequencing of events. CF = case formulation. From *Manual for Assessing Adherence in IRT* (p. 31), by K. L. Critchfield, M. J. Davis, and L. S. Benjamin, 2008, Unpublished manuscript. Copyright 2008 by University of Utah. Reprinted with permission.

experience that was supporting her intractable eating disorder by the mechanism of a maladaptive GOL. I have noted that Bulimia can share many interpersonal features with incest. Both involve patterns of secret, dreaded, forbidden, brief pleasure followed by destructive self-punishment and more. During the case consultation, the patient and I had noted that recognition of any positive feelings toward her incestual abuser usually was blocked by inappropriate protectiveness of the abuser and shame and guilt within the patient.

The next day, in a follow-up therapy session with an IRT trainee, the patient began with, "I have been thinking about whether 'abuse' is the right word for it." This was a monumental insight for a person who had been working for years with the idea that the experience was 100% horrible and who therefore had no way to talk about all aspects of her chronic traumatic experience. Rather than acknowledge and follow up on that new and important perspective, the trainee pulled up a checklist on a clipboard and asked: "How is your depression this morning?" That was the trainee's interpretation of what she had been told to do in her other training experiences. Falling in line, the patient dutifully gave a symptom report. The newly uncovered aspect of incest that supported her self-sabotaging GOL was not mentioned again.

The trainee's use of a different treatment model in the fragile context of willingness to talk about a quintessentially relevant issue that had been suppressed for over a decade was a major adherence error in IRT. It slammed shut a door that had temporarily given the patient access to a fuller and richer understanding of her long-lasting eating disorder and to effective work on becoming free of her bondage to the secret suffering with her father. Points to be noted on the adherence scale included the following: The therapist lacked empathy, ignored the case formulation, and supported Red (symptom orientation in a context that had failed for many years) rather than Green behaviors (engagement of the will to address underlying motivation reflected in GOLs to her abuser). That would be rated about –6 on the IRT adherence scale (Figure 10.1).

Therapy Relationship and "Technique": Inseparable in IRT

According to IRT theory, the therapist has the task of helping the patient muster up the courage to challenge internal demons (see Figure 6.2, phases of the action stage), bear the pain of emotionally experiencing how things really were/are, resist attacks from Family in the Head as old rules and values are challenged, and become willing and able to participate in mental exercises and social homework that can reprogram the primitive brain (Chapters 5 and 6). Absent active work in reprogramming the affect regulators (Family in the Head), there will be no lasting change.

Secure Base in the therapy relationship contributes a lot to helping the patient gain enough strength and courage to challenge the old ways, endure the resulting emotional uproar, and participate in the drudgery of the reprogramming exercises. The therapy relationship provides a template for building an internal Secure Base, provided that is what the therapist models. One patient referred to that as she observed that her coaching in therapy provided "training wheels" for her Birthright Self. It is important to reiterate: There are severe boundaries regarding time, place, and manner of relating in therapy. The patient's social network is the proper lattice upon which more adaptive versions of affects, behaviors, and primitive brain cognitions (C1ABs) can be practiced, be strengthened, and flourish.

Given the integral role of the therapy relationship in therapy change, there are no "techniques" to be delivered independently of the therapy relationship. IRT adherence measures therefore make no distinction between adherence (technique) and competence (relevance and quality of the therapy relationship when delivering therapy interventions). A given "technique" such as blocking problem patterns for example, cannot receive a high score if the therapy relationship is not collaborative. IRT adherence raters work with the whole gestalt, like judges of an athletic performance for which the final score fuses assessments of accuracy and manner. Choosing ice skating as a metaphor, an IRT therapist may attempt a "triple axel" (e.g., relate copy process or GOL to current symptoms in a treatment-resistant patient) but execute poorly (e.g., fail to elicit collaboration, lack accurate empathy, and fail to use the Green/Red distinction to preclude perceived "attack"). The adherence score in that example is near zero. The intervention does not enable Red, nor does it build Green. It should have little or no impact on the therapy process. Such a patient probably would continue with her Red baseline of outrage at her spouse and/or demand yet another medical procedure to help her become more comfortable.

The impact of adherence in IRT can be studied at macro and micro levels. Macro results reflect what happens on average, across individual therapist–patient pairs in a given research study. Micro results reflect what happens within an individual treatment in relation to an individual's short-term and long-term results. An egregious error, illustrated by the therapist who made an unannounced, poorly explained "no-show" for a suicidal patient, can have an impact visible at the micro level in the form of a suicide attempt, complaint to administrators, escalation of symptoms, or dropping out of therapy, for example. Usually errors are not that extreme. When used at the micro level, the adherence ratings of each specific feature can serve as an excellent tool for self-evaluation and self-directed training. The same patterns might be identified at the group level by high error scores for one group of therapists compared to another; or one population of patients compared to another.

Both macro and micro levels of investigation are informative, but there is nothing that can surpass the effects of constant self-study by therapists. Keep asking: "What happened after I did X?" and: "I wonder why." Find an answer. Checking in at times with colleagues or consultants also is a good idea, no matter what your level of experience.

The Outpatient Sample and the Change Subsample

The IRT clinic at the University of Utah Neuropsychiatric Institute was the source of our research sample. Usually inpatient cases were referred for assessment and possible treatment of suspected personality disorders or other reasons for treatment resistance. After the consultation interview, if a trainee was available, patients were offered follow-up inpatient treatment closely supervised by me and my colleague, Ken Critchfield.[2] As noted before, our research measures of those who participated in follow-up with inpatient IRT with an advanced graduate student suggested that the population be named CORDS: comorbid, often rehospitalized, dysfunctional, and suicidal. The research view was that if the model works with this population, it surely works with "standard outpatients." The research on the CORDS population is promising, and our experience in our private practices is that use of IRT also yields good results for highly functional "standard outpatients."

There were advantages and disadvantages to working with CORDS patients. One disadvantage was stress for trainees related to the difficulty of the work. Some of our graduate students were unable to tolerate the intense responsibility for the care of seriously disturbed individuals. A surprisingly large number felt unable to adhere to the requirement that one's inpatients must be seen every day. Two students were overwhelmed by the patient pathology and responded with externalization. Two others expected "validation" during group supervision, and experienced suggestions to try alternative, more adherent interventions as criticism rather than helpful guidance. But fortunately, most IRT students were open to learning and were hardworking, caring, well informed, smart, curious, and successful in meeting the requirements of the admittedly challenging task of learning to deliver adherent IRT to this very difficult, treatment-resistant population. An unintended benefit of the difficulties was that the wide range of skills in adhering to the model added variance, giving extra leverage to research findings in this small sample. It was clear during supervisions and it is clear in the data that adherence makes a big difference.

As noted, our CORDS patients were ruled out of participation in an RCT because of complexity and difficulty. Moreover, the time needed to train therapists and to treat these patients was uncommonly long, and limited resources meant that the N for this research was very small. Working at the

---

[2]When I write "our," I refer to me and Ken, who, as I approached retirement, increasingly provided supervision of treatments along with maintaining his original responsibility for designing and conducting research studies in the clinic.

level of $N = 1$, we were responsible to account for every outcome, whether the treatment was successful or not.[3]

Advantages of working with CORDS patients included the fact that this population had resisted an array of treatments, and therefore any pre–post changes in important variables such as number of suicide attempts, symptoms, and rehospitalizations are remarkable. It should be noted that we did not, as is the convention, ignore dropouts by removing them from the data base and reporting them as dropouts. We continued to track the hospital and public records for follow-up information such as number of suicide attempts and number of rehospitalizations. And the four individuals who were able to reconstruct by staying on several years as IRT outpatients moved on in their lives on very different, much more adaptive trajectories. While patients were in our care, there has only been one death. By actively searching public records, we have learned of the deaths of two more who were formerly in outpatient treatment with us (one for only five sessions); they did not complete the reconstructive process and their deaths occurred years after our last contact.

When it comes to successful reconstruction, we only went to the moon a few times, but to go at all was important. Work with this population using trainees with relatively little prior experience was a harsh test of IRT theory and practice.

Suicide Attempts

In the total sample of 36 outpatients, the rate of suicide attempts in the year prior to the IRT consultation was an average of .722 attempts per person. During the first year in IRT treatment, it dropped to .139. This assessment included a scan of hospital records for possible readmissions of dropouts. The difference is associated with $p < .002$ according to a matched-pairs t test and confirmed by a nonparametric Wilcoxon test comparing numbers of attempts in the two years ($Z = -3.036, p < .000$). The decrease is remarkable in light of the total sample's average record of 2.1 lifetime suicide attempts before they were seen in the IRT clinic.

Rehospitalizations

When the number of hospitalizations for 29 people during the year before their first outpatient treatment in IRT was compared to the number of hospitalizations for them during their first treatment year, there were no significant differences. In fact, the rate of rehospitalization was quite high, at 31%. The number is elevated by the severity of their conditions and

---

[3] My major professor, Harry Harlow, said, "If I need a large N to detect an effect, it is not large enough to interest me." His famous and lasting work with monkeys (learning to learn; the power of curiosity; the incomparably large effect of soft ventral contact in establishing attachment) was based on very few subjects per cell in the experimental design.

also by the fact that our data on rehospitalization are based on the unusual procedure of including dropouts detected by inspection (with permission) of subsequent hospital records.

However, if the IRT model was used with greater fidelity, rehospitalization rates were greatly reduced. Better adherence ratings were associated with reductions[4] in rehospitalization rates according to a Wilcoxon signed ranks test between adherence scores and change in rehospitalization status from the year before treatment to the year of treatment, $Z = -3.26, p < .001$. A score of 3 on the adherence scale (Figure 10.1) theoretically marked the boundary between common markers of good therapy and interventions more unique to IRT. A chi-square analysis separating therapist–patient dyads rated below 3 in adherence from dyads rated 3 and above predicted rehospitalization (yes or no) during the first year of IRT treatment, $Z(1) = 7.128, p < .008$. These counts also were tested by a Fisher's exact test, which yielded $p < .014$. The counts showed that 51.7% of the sample was classified as adherent and not rehospitalized while 24.1% of the sample was classified as nonadherent and rehospitalized. Together, these results mean that adherence to the IRT treatment model at the level of +3 or above (the marker of interventions more unique to IRT) predicted whether each individual was rehospitalized or not for 75.8% of the patients in the IRT clinic during the first year.

Changes in Symptoms Dependent on Availability of Pre–Post Data for Year 1

Evidence of change in ratings of affective symptoms and personality patterns was dependent on trainee and patient willingness to fill out forms at the beginning of treatment and again at the end of the first year. Cooperation in that was spotty, and so sample sizes for assessing change during the first year of treatment vary quite a bit for the different measures. This information, which required patient participation in providing both pre and post measures, was assessed in a separate change database resulting in a smaller fixed universe of CORDS patients willing to stay in treatment for a year and provide most or all of the pre and post measures.[5] They were selected for the change sample

---

[4]The formula was 1,1 = 0 if there was no change in rehospitalization when comparing the prior year to the first year of treatment. Other possibilities included 1,0 = −1; 0,1 = +1; and 0,0 = 0 change.
[5]The reason for selecting a subsample defined by participants who provided both pre and post change scores even though the total and change samples are comparable overall is that small-N research is very sensitive to small changes in sample size and associated changes in enhancer and suppressor effects. An example might be change in depression and the nature of current interactions with attachment figures. That is an individual effect that is treated as random in statistical analyses, although few would argue it is irrelevant. There are many such knowable and unknowable differences among individuals. Restricting assessment of change to the fixed universe (those willing to provide pre and post measures on a specific important variable) holds constant some of such important between-individual variances. It does have the disadvantage of reducing power. The decision was to err in the direction of losing power over including more unknown between-individual variance, affecting some reports of significance.

if they completed the Wisconsin Personality Disorders Inventory (WISPI; M. H. Klein, Benjamin, & Smith, 1996) at baseline (i.e., Session 1), That yielded 14 cases and they also had completed at least five of the six pre–post (12-month) measures of personality disorder, anger, anxiety, and depression.

Comparability of the change and total samples is suggested by the fact that differences between the means of these two samples were less than 2% of one standard deviation for every patient- or therapist-generated variable. The heterogeneity of pathology in the change database is shown by the hospital discharge diagnoses for the 14 patients that are in it. They were: major depression, 38.5%; major depression + generalized anxiety disorder, 30.7%; bipolar disorder, 15.4%; major depression + posttraumatic stress disorder (PTSD), 7.7%; and major depression + alcohol dependence, 7.7%. As usual, personality disorder rarely appeared in the medical record. According to baseline ratings on the WISPI and the Structured Clinical Interview for *DSM–IV* Axis II personality disorders (First, Gibbon, Spitzer, Williams, & Benjamin, 1997), the highest rank personality diagnosis in the change sample was OCPD. Avoidant and borderline personality disorders were tied for second and third place, followed by passive–aggressive personality disorder. That is very close to results for the total sample and to the interviewer's (my own) diagnoses.

Changes in Anger

Only seven patients completed the State–Trait Anger Expression Inventory—2 (STAXI–2; Spielberger, 1999) at the beginning and again at the end of the first year of treatment.[6] Everyone decreased in baseline anger, and that directional change was significant at the level of .008 by the sign test and .016 by the binomial test. A Wilcoxon signed ranks test of whether work with best GOL in Year 1 had anything to do with this change yielded .754, $p < .06$. From a clinical perspective, these results suggest that the Natural Biological framing of anger in terms of its function and focus on the perceived need for control or distance (usually in relation to a loved one) rather than on anger per se were effective.

It seems subjectively that anger is more amenable to higher brain control (choice) than is depression or anxiety. For example, if patients became aware that their anger toward a child was simple copying of an abusive parent and remembered how it felt to be its target, they were better able to reject the impulse to attack and focus instead on whether control or distance was appropriate and, if so, how better to accomplish that. Unfortunately, such "insight"

---

[6]The initial level of trait anger (19.2) was within range of normal (18.1) and outpatient (20.0) samples, which are surprisingly close and associated with large standard deviations (6.2, 5.4, and 6.0, respectively). It is hard to know what to make of that, especially as a sample of prisoners also scored within normal limits (Etzler, Rohrmann, & Brandt, 2014). Regardless of lack of specificity, the scale has content validity.

is not enough to be able to choose to make such relatively rapid change (within 1 year) in anxiety or depression. Again, perhaps that is because they appear to be more "reflexive," less amenable to choosing, and dependent completely on primitive brain function. One can "talk oneself out of anger" (C2) more easily than anxiety or depression.

Changes in Anxiety

There were no significant changes in anxiety measured by the Beck Anxiety Inventory (Beck & Steer, 1993) during the first year of treatment in IRT. This is a valid result and not surprising because anxiety is a signal that threat is present. Evolution has provided that anxiety is the most unpleasant and unrelenting threat affect, and that helps ensure that the individual will maintain concern about the threat and keep working to figure out what to do about it until the threat is conquered or clearly avoided. There also was no discernible correlation, parametric or nonparametric, between best GOL work in Year 1 and changes in anxiety.

Ultimately, after more than 1 year of treatment, IRT was helpful to some of our anxious patients (e.g., Amy, Chapter 1). Again, maladaptive cuing of what to fear and how to be safe acquired early in life in relation to attachment figures is very difficult to undo. Prolonged exposure therapy clearly can be helpful for PTSD based on adult trauma (Foa, Hembree, & Rothbaum, 2009),[7] but that procedure may not be so effective with adults such as the patients in the IRT clinic who carry threatening internalizations from childhood.

Changes in Depression

Nine of the 13 patients who provided ratings of depression (Beck Depression Inventory [BDI]; Beck, Steer, & Brown, 1996) at the beginning of treatment and again at 1 year improved. Making the conservative assumption that this population was as likely to improve as it was to deteriorate, a binomial test was used, and the result was "not significant." If the sample is divided by severity, with high severity marked at 3 or more previous hospitalizations, results become very clear. The 8 less severe cases (having had only 2 or fewer previous hospitalizations) improved, while the 4 more severe cases

---

[7]This is a vital topic when treating veterans abused by war for love of country. Many are helped by prolonged exposure treatments and by cognitive processing therapy. For those who are not, a treatment described in *Thank You for Your Service* (Finkle, 2013) seems promising from the perspective of IRT theory. The ultimately successful treatment for a veteran featured in this book was to live for nearly a year in a lovely private resort with fellow victims. That makes much sense according to Natural Biology. In that setting, it would seem that residuals of long-term living in extreme danger are countered with experiences of true understanding and bonding in a place that offers safety, generosity, understanding, and credible support. The approach deserves research follow-up.

deteriorated. A Fisher's exact test of the two levels of severity by outcome (improve/deteriorate) was significant at the $p < .002$ level.

Individual (post–pre) scores on depression (BDI) are plotted on the vertical axis of Figure 10.2. The horizontal axis marks the highest GOL scores recorded during the sampling within the first year. The axis representing the Awareness and Choice Scale (Figure 10.1) intersects the vertical axis at 0, the point at which there was no change in depression. All cases above the horizontal axis happened to be in the less severe group and improved in depression, whereas all those below it fell in the more severe group and deteriorated slightly in depression scores. The Awareness and Choice Scale assesses evidence that patients are working on challenging their Gifts of Love (GOLs) to Family in the Head. In IRT, blaming Family in the Head is not the point. Addressing one's own compliance with the ancient rules and values is the issue. Adherence raters score the GOL scale after they have made ratings for every other component of the treatment model, including all process skills and all therapy steps for a given session (Figure 10.1).

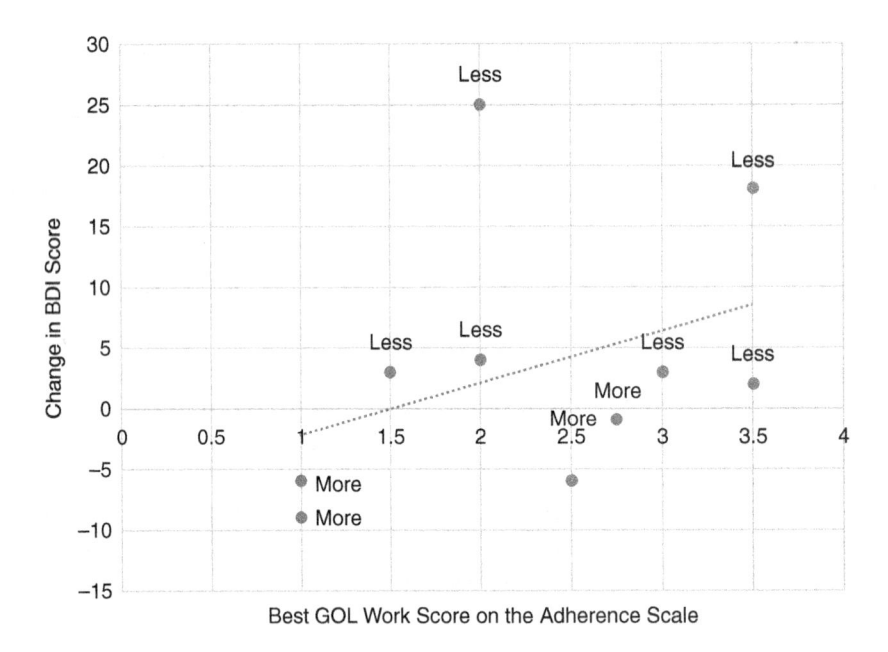

Figure 10.2. Best GOL work and changes in depression in Year 1. Better work with the concept of Gifts of Love is associated with more improvement in depression in the less severe CORDS cases during the first year of treatment. But the four more severe cases, defined by having had three or more previous hospitalizations, became slightly more depressed during the first year of outpatient treatment. They included Amy, who received electroconvulsive therapy for the first 9 months. BDI = Beck Depression Inventory; GOL = Gift of Love.

In Figure 10.2, the line that goes upward from the lower left corner to the upper right corner represents the correlation between depression scores and highest observer ratings of GOL work for each case during the first year of treatment. The product–moment correlation represented by that line and the scatter around it is .598 ($p < .001$); the nonparametric rho is .625 ($p < .05$). With only one possible exception,[8] the correspondence between GOL work and improvement in depression is apparent at the level of $N = 1$. These results, which include everyone in the sample, illustrate the advantages of (a) using the research strategy of connecting mechanisms to outcome and (b) reporting at the level of individuals, as in Figures 9.1 and 10.2.

Changes in Personality Disorders

Personality disorders are notably resistant to treatment. Of all the symptoms in the psychiatric diagnostic lexicons, they are the most likely to be considered to be "willful" and not so amenable to medical (meaning *physical*) interventions. In fact, ever since the diagnostic revolution represented by the third edition of the *DSM* (American Psychiatric Association, 1980), personality disorders had been set apart on a special "axis." Presently, in the *DSM–5*, they have been returned to their earlier place, listed with clinical disorders such as anxiety and depression. As noted in Chapter 9, there is controversy about how to describe them, as well as how to treat them. For the analyses reported here, *personality disorder* was defined by ratings on the WISPI. Items in the WISPI are the *DSM* items translated to interpersonal descriptions by SASB in Benjamin (1996a [2nd ed., 2003a]).

Recall that the most common personality patterns in the change sample were OCPD, avoidant personality disorder, and borderline personality disorder. Wilcoxon matched-pairs nonparametric tests suggested that the obsessive–compulsive and borderline patterns were mitigated, but not enough to establish statistical significance. The changes during Year 1 did correlate with best GOL work. It appears that patients who were beginning to work with GOLs improved in some ways, but the process was incomplete at the end of Year 1. Avoidant patterns showed a strong, nearly significant trend to have gotten worse. That might reflect withdrawal as patients with OCPD tried to hold off their efforts to control others and begin to learn new patterns. This change in avoidant patterns showed no connection to ratings for good work with GOLs.

The fact that SASB introject ratings consistently show powerful correlations with symptoms and symptom change suggests that the self-concept is

---

[8] That is the "less severe" case that had a very high GOL rating but showed relatively little improvement. That result might be attributed to the "things get worse before they get better" concept discussed in relation to progress through the phases of the action stage (Figure 6.2).

the mediator of the cacophony of voices from Family in the Head. Change in introject has long been recognized by others as a consistent measure of improvement during psychotherapy at the individual and small- and large-group levels (Dennhag & Armelius, 2012; Halvorsen & Monsen, 2007; Hartkamp & Schmitz, 1999; Henry, Schacht, & Strupp, 1990; Lindfors, Knekt, Virtala, Laaksonen, & Helsinki Psychotherapy Study Group, 2012; Marble, Høglend, & Ulberg, 2011; Nissen-Lie et al., 2017; Ybrandt, 2008). That is illustrated in the top panel of Figure 10.3, which presents the average profile of introject ratings "as I normally am"[9] before and after outpatient treatment in a sample of more than 13,000 German outpatients (N pre = 14,794; N post = 13,009). For this group, psychotherapy decreased introjected hostility and increased friendliness toward self, ending with a clear peak on self-protection. The middle panel shows pre and post measures of introject "at best" in the tiny IRT sample ($N = 6$) during the first year of IRT treatment. The trends in the large and small samples are similar. Both show circumplex order and have a profile that peaks on self-protection, the normative (Secure Base) position. The bottom panel shows ratings of introjects "at worst" by the CORDS patients in the IRT clinic. The difference between the middle and lower panels documents the clinical observation that the best condition improves first while the threat-based parts of self-concept are more resistant to change. Reference to Natural Biology explains why.

Summary of Outcome Results

Most patients in the IRT clinic had already had a wide range of prior treatments, including medications and psychotherapies. Despite the records of treatment resistance, during the first year in IRT treatment, there were significant decreases in number of suicide attempts compared to the year before. Rehospitalizations were reduced for the cases showing adherence to the IRT model at or above level 3, the marker of the point where some IRT interventions go beyond what is good therapy process. More unique features include explicitly using the case formulation (copy processes, GOLs), speaking of affects embedded in C1AB chains, and being explicit about differences between the primitive and higher brain. In other words, better results with this very difficult population did require some of the unique features of IRT added to ordinary constructive therapy process.

Depression was decreased, too, but only for the less severe cases (i.e., less than three prior hospitalizations). Trait anger improved for every person ($n = 7$) who turned in pre and post rating forms assessing trait hostility. Adherent work with Gifts of Love made a difference in that good work with

---

[9]The German administrators changed the standard instruction from rating self "at best" to "as I normally am," so the ratings for the two samples are not totally comparable.

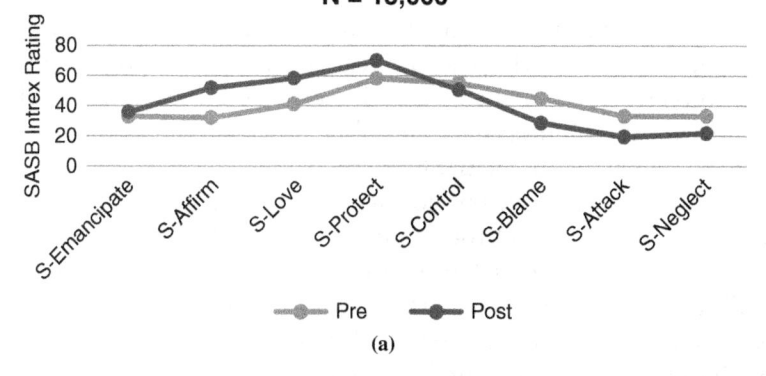

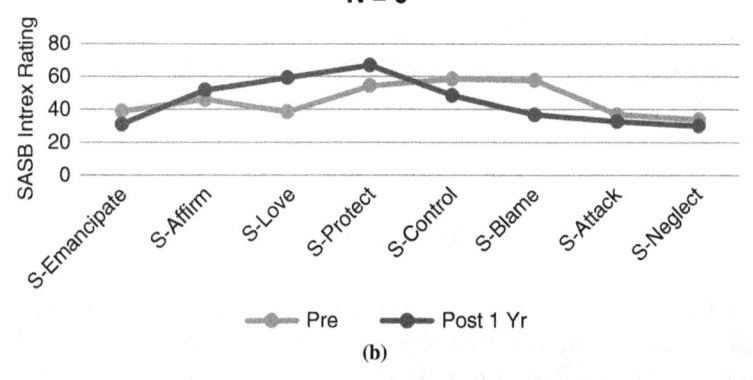

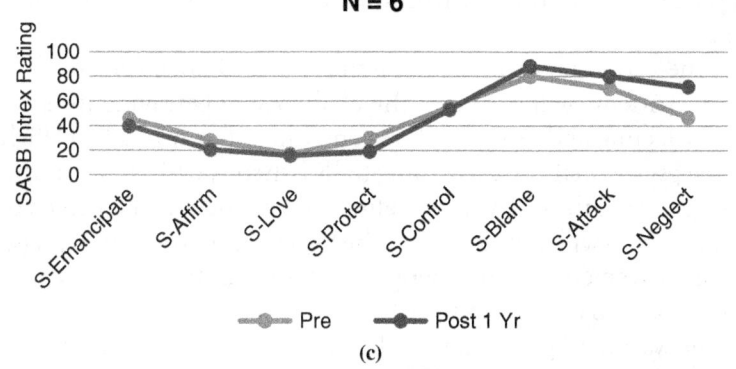

Figure 10.3. Introject changes during treatment in very large and very small samples. Data from a completed outpatient treatment in a large sample (a) reflect circumplex order with decreased introjected hostility and increased friendliness toward self "as I normally am" with a clear peak on self-protection. Trends in pre and post measures of introject "at best" in the tiny IRT sample (*N* = 6) measured at the end of Year 1 (b) are very much like changes found in the very large sample. Ratings by CORDS patients of their introjects "at worst" (c) made no change whatsoever. This reflects the probability that the best condition improves first, whereas the threat-based parts of self-concept are more resistant to change. Reference to Natural Biology explains why.

it was correlated with improvements in depression and trait anger. Anxiety did not improve at all during the first year. That is not surprising, given the expectation (Figure 6.2) that anxiety will increase early in the action phase of change because it is frightening to defy old rules for safety and because Family in the Head will attack the patient for disloyalty.

There was a suggestive but not significant trend ($p < .12$) for improvement in symptoms of OCPD, the dominant personality diagnosis for the sample. There also was a positive but not significant trend for that improvement in OCPD to be correlated with best GOL work. There was a nearly significant increase in features of avoidant personality disorder ($p < .06$), and that was tentatively interpreted as a natural consequence of switching from the salient OCPD feature of trying to take control of everything in service of perfection to backing off or withdrawing instead of bossing people around. Withdrawal is a salient feature of avoidant personality disorder, and these data suggest it also is an adaptive step out of patterns for OCPD on the way to reconstruction. More detail about these and later results from the IRT clinic will appear in peer-reviewed papers written with Critchfield and others.

IRT IS NOT FOR ALL PATIENTS

IRT is for treatment-resistant clients and/or others who want to work toward permanent change that replaces current cuing for safety and threat systems with Secure Base internalizations. Such a reconstruction is lengthy and expensive. It requires grit from therapists as well as patients in sticking with a process that at times is painful, always difficult, and with uncertain outcome.

At the action phase of enabling the will to change (Figure 6.2), more than a few patients will say no to the challenge of betraying internal "protectors" by feeling and doing well. At one time, that was called "flight into health" by psychoanalysts. According to IRT theory, withdrawal at that time would suggest that the old ways of feeling safe override the perceived benefits of change. Others will quit therapy at the beginning of the action phase without any improvement—some angry, some resigned. It is not easy to predict who will choose to change and why.

Some warning signs of impaired progress are substance abuse or mania. Fromm-Reichmann (Bullard, 1959) and others observed that mania can be an antithetical response to perception of profound loss. Procedures in IRT do demand confrontation with and acceptance of profound loss (Figure 6.2). Sometimes these interfering regressions can be stabilized with medications and/or psychodynamic interventions and then the possibility of continuing on through the phases of action to complete reconstruction can go forward.

Again, the will can make a difference; it cannot determine destiny, but it can at least point in one direction or another.

IRT IS NOT FOR ALL THERAPISTS

The microanalytic procedure of assessing therapist–patient interactions during therapy has proven helpful during many IRT consultations with therapists playing their most difficult case. The case formulations are perceived as useful whether the therapist favors CBT, psychodynamic therapy, systemic family therapy, emotion-focused therapy, or something else. The paragraphs that follow describe an IRT consultation with an expert CBT therapist whose patient, Harry, suffered from obsessive–compulsive behaviors, substance abuse, and other behaviors at high risk of undermining his career as a well-respected consultant in wealth management.

Despite his view that his central problem was the OCD, it was not much of a stretch to infer that in his primitive brain, Harry wanted to join his drunken father in ignominy, even if it meant neglecting his son as his father had neglected him. Moreover, he believed that maintaining sobriety would mean submission to his mother and his wife. So Harry was going toward disability with the father in his head while the therapist was assuming Harry meant it when he said he wanted to control his symptoms of OCD. On the IRT adherence scale, their severe discrepancy in goals would be scored about –2 for Section 3 (i.e., fail to consider the case formulation).

To close that gap and begin therapy in a collaborative way, Harry needed to explore his hurt and his love for his father and decide what direction he wanted his life to go. That meant that differentiation from father in the head was essential before Harry would be free to succeed in managing addiction and self-sabotage. Unfortunately, "insight" alone was not likely to make Harry decide to follow the program and go to Alcoholics Anonymous for support in sobriety as he learned to use the CBT skills constructively. That would, in fact, be ideal. But Harry probably would need an intensive trial using Freud's algorithm to revisit his childhood loneliness over his drunken father before he could break free from his identification with his father. After that, the CBT and dialectical behavior therapy skills training would be extremely useful.

CONCLUSIONS

IRT is a method to help the clinician decide on optimal choices of interventions from any approach on a moment-to-moment basis. The case formulation and treatment models provide guidance by accounting for what is supporting symptoms and offering strategies to unlock devotion to self-sabotage so that teaching more effective ways of self-management then has a better chance to succeed. As usual, more research is needed.

Despite cross-referencing to CBT and other approaches, it is true that, on average, an IRT therapist would discuss Family in the Head and focus more on the past than would, for example, a therapist using CBT or interpersonal therapy (Klerman, Weissman, Rounsaville, & Chevron, 1994). Does work with Family in the Head matter? Probably, because Natural Biology provides that loyalty to and love for them sustain the maladaptive patterns in relation to safety and threat that account for affective symptoms. Differentiation from Family in the Head is required for patients to become free enough to practice and incorporate Secure Base behaviors and relationships. Further study with less pathological and larger samples could answer the question of whether structural reorganization that comes with revising Family in the Head yields better and longer lasting change in symptoms.

RECOMMENDATIONS FOR YOUNGER THERAPISTS

If readers are stunned by learning in 2018 that modern psychotherapies have not gone beyond what Freud described in 1892 as the essence of the therapy change process, perhaps they would be interested also to know that psychoanalysts have developed many interesting, probably effective ways of enhancing Freud's algorithm. Although I do not believe in the validity of Freud's primary drive theory that pits the id (aggression, sexuality) against the superego (a representative of society), I have found the rest of the psychoanalytic paradigm, especially as described by many object relations theorists, to be profound and extremely useful in many ways. Those who are curious might consider reading about psychotherapy from some of the early "Great Ones." Examples include the following:

- The original papers by Sigmund Freud (1959b) are recommended. An engaging introduction, *Mourning and Melancholia*, provides an informative discussion of depression as he saw it in 1917 (Freud, 1917/1959a).
- For a rich summary of major psychoanalytic therapies, it is hard to beat Jay R. Greenberg and Stephen A. Mitchell's (1984) *Object Relations in Psychoanalytic Theory*.
- *Psychoanalytic Practice* is a highly readable, authentic book, even a "manual" about how to deliver psychoanalysis by two German psychoanalysts, Helmut Thoma and Horst Kachele (1991).

- John Bowlby's (1977, 2005) *The Making and Breaking of Affectional Bonds* are classics. This should be read and reread by everyone who believes attachment matters.
- Frieda Fromm-Reichmann (Bullard, 1959) and Wilhelm Reich (1933/1990) offered especially rich and sometimes daring examples of effective psychoanalytic clinical interventions in difficult cases, although the reader may need to bracket Reich's version of a hyperbaric chamber.
- Margaret S. Mahler's (1968) work on individuation is critically important because differentiation usually is the main issue in severe disorders.
- Worthy departures from psychoanalysis were described by Carl Rogers (1951) on client-centered therapy, by B. F. Skinner (1953) on operant conditioning, and by Rollo May (1969) on the existential self. Samples of May's wisdom include the following:
  - "The opposite of courage in our society is not cowardice, it is conformity" (as cited in Kimbro & Hill, 1991, p. 104).
  - "It is an old and ironic habit of human beings to run faster when we have lost our way" (May, 1969, p. 15).
  - "Depression is the inability to construct a future" (May, 1969, p. 243).

This is a short reading list and does not include all available gems. Hopefully it is a useful way to get started. Here's to happy reading and improved practice and research in psychotherapy by, as Isaac Newton said, "standing on the shoulders of giants."

GLOSSARY

antithesis: Predictive principle based on the SASB model. It happens when two people have opposite positions on all three dimensions: interpersonal focus, affiliation, and interdependence. For example, a depressed mother withdraws much of the time (Detach, weep alone: −6, +3 on the full model) for years. When her daughter becomes a mother, she is overly dedicated to the antithesis in relation to her own child (Protect: +6, −3).

autoimmunity: Medical process during which the immune system mounts "protective" attacks on its own (self) cells. Self-sabotaging Gifts of Love are a psychiatric equivalent, in that attempts to adapt backfire.

Birthright Self: Constellation of C1ABs that are Green (adaptive). The Birthright Self evolves when a child is offered Secure Base conditions described by Bowlby (1969, 1977). SASB codes of Secure Base mother–child interactions show that the Birthright Self is friendly, moderately enmeshed, moderately differentiated, and delivered with a developmentally appropriate focus on self and other. A secure person has the courage to pursue optimal, well-socialized self-realization.

complementarity: Predictive principle based on the SASB model. It happens when two people have reciprocal focus at identical positions on the horizontal and vertical axes in interpersonal space defined by SASB. For example, one person Trusts (focus on self) and the other Protects (focus on other). Both people are focused on the same object, and each is moderately friendly, moderately enmeshed (+6, −3 on the full model).

C1AB: Sequence of events consisting of the following:

C1 = Primitive brain perception of conditions related to threat and safety,
A = Affect that is triggered by C1, and
B = Behavior that is predisposed by A.

The general meaning is this: C1 = perceive a threat, A = fear it, and B = avoid or master it. C1AB sequences remind the clinician to address affective symptoms (A) by finding out what is threatening the patient before trying to quash them.

copy processes: Nature's method for transmitting, from one generation to the next, information about what to fear and how to be safe. There are three copy processes: (a) be like him/her (identification), (b) act as you did with him/her (recapitulation), and (c) treat yourself as you were treated (introjection).

CORDS: Comorbid, Often Rehospitalized, Dysfunctional, and Suicidal. The IRT clinic at the University of Utah Neuropsychiatric Institute served patients referred for assessment of personality disorder and/or treatment resistance, and the clinic used the term CORDS to describe these patients.

differentiation: Psychoanalytic concept that describes the critical and stormy developmental task of separating oneself psychologically from the parent. The optimal version is described by SASB as friendly autonomy. Differentiation is the opposite of enmeshment.

enmeshment: Psychoanalytic concept that describes failure to differentiate, a relationship without boundaries. Enmeshment is the opposite of differentiation.

evidence based: Effective according to a randomized controlled trial (RCT). CORDS patients would be screened out of any RCT because of their complexity, dangerousness, and record of treatment resistance. IRT meets the alternative standards for evidence-based practice in psychology. More importantly, IRT meets the most recently recommended test of effectiveness: to show that activation of mechanisms of change improves outcome.

Family in the Head: Term for what Bowlby called *internal working models of attachment figures* and what other object relations psychoanalysts call *internalized representations*. Mirror neurons (Chapter 2) implement copied information about objects, and this copied information is stored within complex circuits that include the cortex and midbrain affect regulators, such as the hypothalamic–pituitary–adrenal axis.

Freud's algorithm: Repetitive process in most psychotherapies wherein the patient identifies specific stresses, calls them to mind as vividly as possible. Patients must find words to describe the event in great detail and reexperience the associated affects with full intensity. Patients must repeat this process many, many times. The most direct parallel in modern therapies is Prolonged Exposure (Foa et al., 2005). I have named this process *Freud's algorithm* because it was first described by Freud in 1892.

functional analysis of negative affects: Analysis of how affective symptoms serve adaptive functions. IRT theory holds that affective symptoms evolved to facilitate adaptation. The adaptive functions of anger are to create distance from or control of a threat. Anxiety keeps the person active until a solution to a perceived threat is found. Depression predisposes withdrawal, hiding, and negation of self, all of which reduce threat value and serve as a defense of last resort against threat.

Gift of Love (GOL): Term for copy process. The statement "Every psychopathology is a Gift of Love" (Benjamin, 1994) summarizes the idea that implementing a copy process elicits positive (parasympathetic) affects signaling security and well-being, even if that which is copied is self-sabotaging and maladaptive. Compliance with expectations of attachment figures is the critical requirement for parasympathetic release. GOLs function as an addiction, and relinquishing maladaptive versions of GOL is a primary treatment goal.

Green: Adaptive C1ABs. The goal of therapy is to transform Reds (maladaptive C1ABs) to Greens (adaptive C1ABs). In clinical practice, the terms *Green* and *Red* often are reified. Patients often say something like "My Red got me yesterday, but today I am Green."

higher brain: Part of the brain that is based in the cortex and that sponsors (among other things) reason, logic, and abstract ability. The higher brain is vulnerable to being overruled by the primitive brain whenever threat is perceived or loss of safety looms.

identification: Copy process that involves perceiving, feeling, and doing (C1AB) whatever the attachment figure did in a particular situation. For example, "I identify with my mother whenever my husband is critical." Identification, recapitulation, and introjection (the three copy processes) have been validated in inpatient and outpatient databases (Critchfield & Benjamin, 2008, 2010).

intransitive action: *Transitive* and *intransitive* are grammatical terms that describe verbs. A transitive verb refers to action that focuses on (acts upon) another person (direct object), as in "he *hit* her." An intransitive verb describes a state of being, as in "She *had* a headache." The SASB model points basically are verbs with the first surface (focus on other) representing transitive actions and the second (focus on self) representing intransitive states or conditions.

introjection: Copy process that involves treating oneself as one has been treated by the attachment figure. For example, "My mother told me I was worthless, and I believe I am worthless." Introjection has been well validated in many samples, including one with over 13,000 German patients (Mestel, 2012).

IRT: Interpersonal Reconstructive Therapy, a psychotherapy that seeks to reconstruct personality and affective patterns as distinct from symptom containment or control. The IRT manual is by Benjamin (2003b, 2006), and this current book enriches the approach by anchoring the procedures in Natural Biology and featuring unusual detail about how to negotiate the elusive action stage of change.

Natural Biology: Set of psychological principles based primarily on functional analyses of the sympathetic and parasympathetic nervous systems, that respectively sponsor attempts to adapt to perceived threat and to find safety. The following is an illustrative list of some of the implications: Sympathetic nervous system release of cortisone and epinephrine supports copied C1AB patterns in response to threat. Parasympathetic system release of dopamine, serotonin, and opioids inspires rest and relaxation C1AB patterns appropriate to safe conditions. One can benefit from this chemistry by medication prescription and/or by revising one's relationship with Family in the Head (affect regulators) to become better able to practice modern behavioral methods to improve affect regulation. Natural Biology is consistent with genetic research, which has established that genes are affected by interactions with attachment figures via gene expression or silencing or by epigenetic processes. These thoughts help patients understand that their brain is not "broken" or cast by unchangeable DNA sequences, but rather that their normal brain mechanisms have been programmed by maladaptive circumstances and that it is possible (but not easy) to reprogram them.

normal developmental sequence according to Natural Biology: Life for primates begins with powerful automatic attachment to caregivers based on proximity, frequency, and, as Harlow (1958) showed, "ventral contact." As the peripheral nervous system becomes enervated, the process of differentiation begins. It starts with exploration under the protective watch of caregivers and then differentiation is greatly increased by peer play that facilitates development of social and cognitive skills needed to function adaptively as an adult in "the herd." Humans' cognitive skills also are enhanced by education. By adulthood, pair bonding brings reproduction as well as a variety of other ways one can contribute to the survival of the next generation.

opposition: SASB predictive principle that describes a negative way of identifying with a caregiver. For example, the mother often was blaming, and so the child as an adult is very affirming. SASB codes for opposites are at opposite points in interpersonal space while maintaining the same focus.

primitive brain: The Subcortical part of the brain is vital to adaptation in nature because it constantly monitors conditions of threat and safety, usually outside of awareness. If threat is detected, the primitive brain takes over and complex, creative higher brain activity is unlikely. When survival is at stake, nothing else matters. The rules for survival are not easy to change, in psychotherapy or otherwise.

primitive brain learning: Form of learning (e.g., copying) that occurs under perceived conditions of threat and safety. Primitive brain learning is automatic and lasting and based primarily on proximity and frequency to figures present early in life. The most visible example of it is language learning in a child.

recapitulation: Copy process that predisposes the person to behave with others under a given threat condition as he/she did with an attachment figure. For example, a son submits to his wife when she is angry as he did with his mother.

Red: Maladaptive C1ABs that are experienced as a compelling "state." If, for example, a mother lost her temper with her son yesterday and recognizes she was acting like her own mother, she might say she "was Red yesterday" or that her "Red took over." Patients often agree they feel "possessed" by a specific member of Family in the Head under a given stress.

SASB: Structural Analysis of Social Behavior, a model that dissects interpersonal and intrapsychic patterns in terms of three underlying dimensions: (a) attachment (hate to love), (b) interdependence (enmeshment to differentiation), and (c) attentional focus (transitive action toward another, intransitive response to another, introjection or transitive action turned inward). SASB predictive principles of complementarity, similarity or opposition, and introjection are very important when linking early learning with attachment figures to presenting problems. SASB ratings of relationship with attachment figures provide reliable measures of Family in the Head and patient views of relationships with others that may be experienced as stressful. An objective coding system serves to compare rater and observer views in the same metric. In this book, SASB ratings provide an evidence base in support of many aspects of the IRT models. Research publications by others have used SASB in a variety of ways related to psychopathology, psychotherapy, and other psychosocial activities.

Secure Base: Concept defined by Bowlby (1969, 1977) meaning optimal patterns of attachment. An extensive literature shows that a Secure Base is related to optimal health and functioning. SASB codes for behavioral descriptions of Secure Base show it involves a baseline of friendliness, moderate degrees of enmeshment or differentiation, and an age-appropriate balance of interpersonal focus between self and other. Introjection of Secure Base experiences facilitates internal Secure Base and optimal health.

transitive action: *Transitive* and *intransitive* are grammatical terms that describe verbs. A transitive verb refers to action that focuses on (acts upon) another person (direct object), as in "he *hit* her." An intransitive verb describes a state of being, as in "she *had* a headache." The SASB model points basically are verbs with the first surface (focus on other) representing transitive actions and the second (focus on self) representing intransitive states or conditions.

Yearning Self: Constellation of C1AB patterns that are Red (maladaptive). The Yearning Self is supported by feeling safer when executing GOLs (complying with maladaptive rules and values) of a specific attachment figure. GOL explains statements like this: "Dad beat and raped me, and so does my boyfriend. I know it is bad for me, but it feels right." Recapitulating loyalty to a member of Family in the Head is described by the term *Yearning Self*. The yearning is based on a wish that the receiver of a GOL will relent and affirm, love, and protect the patient after all.

REFERENCES

Ackerknecht, E. H. (1974). The history of the discovery of the vegetative (autonomic) nervous system. *Medical History, 18*, 1–8. http://dx.doi.org/10.1017/S0025727300019189

Ainsworth, M. D. S., Blehar, M. C., Waters, E., & Wall, S. (1978). *Patterns of attachment*. Hillsdale, NJ: Erlbaum.

Alberti, R. E., & Emmons, M. L. (2017). *Your perfect right: Assertiveness and equality in your life and relationships* (10th ed.). Atascadero, CA: Impact.

Allen, J. P., Insabella, G., Porter, M. R., Smith, F. D., Land, D., & Phillips, N. (2006). A social–interactional model of the development of depressive symptoms. *Journal of Consulting and Clinical Psychology, 74*, 55–65. http://dx.doi.org/10.1037/0022-006X.74.1.55

American Psychiatric Association. (1980). *Diagnostic and statistical manual of mental disorders* (3rd ed.). Washington, DC: Author.

American Psychiatric Association. (1994). *Diagnostic and statistical manual of mental disorders* (4th ed.). Washington, DC: Author.

American Psychiatric Association. (2000). *Diagnostic and statistical manual of mental disorders* (4th ed., text rev.). Washington, DC: Author.

American Psychiatric Association. (2013). *Diagnostic and statistical manual of mental disorders* (5th ed.). Washington, DC: Author.

American Psychological Association. (2006). Evidence-based practice in psychology. *American Psychologist, 61*, 271–285. http://dx.doi.org/10.1037/0003-066X.61.4.271

Axelrod, G. (Producer), & Frankenheimer, J. (Producer & Director). (1962). *The Manchurian candidate* [Motion picture]. United States: United Artists.

Barber, J. P., & Crits-Christoph, P. (1993). Advances in measures of psychodynamic formulations. *Journal of Consulting and Clinical Psychology, 61*, 574–585. http://dx.doi.org/10.1037/0022-006X.61.4.574

Bateman, A., & Fonagy, P. (2004). Mentalization-based treatment of BPD. *Journal of Personality Disorders, 18*, 36–51. http://dx.doi.org/10.1521/pedi.18.1.36.32772

Bateson, J., Jackson, D. D., Haley, J., & Weakland, J. (1956). Toward a theory of schizophrenia. *Behavioral Science, 1*, 251–264. http://dx.doi.org/10.1002/bs.3830010402

Baum, C., Chew, S., Goldenring, J., Kurtzman, A., Solomon, M. (Producers), & Lahti, C. (Director). (2001). *My first mister* [Motion picture]. United States: Paramount Classics.

Beck, A. T., Rush, A. J., Shaw, B. E., & Emery, G. (1979). *Cognitive therapy of depression*. New York, NY: Guilford Press.

Beck, A. T., & Steer, R. A. (1993). *Manual for the Beck Anxiety Inventory*. San Antonio, TX: Psychological Corporation.

Beck, A. T., Steer, R. A., & Brown, G. K. (1996). *Manual for the Beck Depression Inventory—II*. San Antonio, TX: Psychological Corporation.

Bedics, J. S., Atkins, D. C., Comtois, K. A., & Linehan, M. M. (2012). Weekly therapist ratings of the therapeutic relationship and patient introject during the course of dialectical behavioral therapy for the treatment of borderline personality disorder. *Psychotherapy, 49*, 231–240. http://dx.doi.org/10.1037/a0028254

Benjamin, L. S. (1968). Harlow's facts on affects. *Voices, 4*, 49–59.

Benjamin, L. S. (1974). Structural Analysis of Social Behavior. *Psychological Review, 81*, 392–425. http://dx.doi.org/10.1037/h0037024

Benjamin, L. S. (1979a). Structural analysis of differentiation failure. *Psychiatry: Interpersonal and Biological Processes, 42*, 1–23. http://dx.doi.org/10.1080/00332747.1979.11024003

Benjamin, L. S. (1979b). Use of Structural Analysis of Social Behavior (SASB) and Markov chains to study dyadic interactions. *Journal of Abnormal Psychology, 88*, 303–319. http://dx.doi.org/10.1037/0021-843X.88.3.303

Benjamin, L. S. (1986). Operational definition and measurement of dynamics shown in the stream of free associations. *Psychiatry: Interpersonal and Biological Processes, 49*, 104–129. http://dx.doi.org/10.1080/00332747.1986.11024313

Benjamin, L. S. (1987). Use of the SASB dimensional model to develop treatment plans for personality disorders, I: Narcissism. *Journal of Personality Disorders, 1*, 43–70. http://dx.doi.org/10.1521/pedi.1987.1.1.43

Benjamin, L. S. (1993). Every psychopathology is a gift of love. *Psychotherapy Research, 3*, 1–24. http://dx.doi.org/10.1080/10503309312331333629

Benjamin, L. S. (1994). SASB: A bridge between personality theory and clinical psychology. *Psychological Inquiry, 5*, 273–316. Critics follow, pp. 317–335. http://dx.doi.org/10.1207/s15327965pli0504_1

Benjamin, L. S. (1995). *Intrex long, medium and short form questionnaires*. Salt Lake City: University of Utah.

Benjamin, L. S. (1996a). *Interpersonal diagnosis and treatment of personality disorders* (2nd ed.). New York, NY: Guilford Press.

Benjamin, L. S. (1996b). Introduction to the special section on Structural Analysis of Social Behavior. *Journal of Consulting and Clinical Psychology, 64*, 1203–1212. http://dx.doi.org/10.1037/0022-006X.64.6.1203

Benjamin, L. S. (2000). *SASB Intrex user's manual*. Salt Lake City: University of Utah.

Benjamin, L. S. (2003a). *Interpersonal diagnosis and treatment of personality disorders* (2nd ed.). New York, NY: Guilford Press.

Benjamin, L. S. (2003b). *Interpersonal reconstructive therapy: Promoting change in nonresponders*. New York, NY: Guilford Press.

Benjamin, L. S. (2006). *Interpersonal reconstructive therapy: An integrative, personality-based treatment for complex cases* [Paperback ed. of 2003b]. New York, NY: Guilford Press.

Benjamin, L. S. (2015a). The arts, crafts, and sciences of psychotherapy. *Journal of Clinical Psychology, 71,* 1070–1082. http://dx.doi.org/10.1002/jclp.22217

Benjamin, L. S. (2015b). Commentary: Every psychopathology is still a gift of love. In B. M. Strauss, J. P. Barber, & L. G. Castonguay (Eds.), *Visions in psychotherapy research and practice: Reflections from presidents of the Society for Psychotherapy Research* (pp. 58–63). New York, NY: Routledge Behavioral Sciences.

Benjamin, L. S., & Critchfield, K. L. (2010). An interpersonal perspective on therapy alliances and techniques. In J. C. Muran & J. P. Barber (Eds.), *The therapeutic alliance: An evidence-based guide to practice* (pp. 123–149). New York, NY: Guilford Press.

Benjamin, L. S., Critchfield, K. L., & Mestel, R. (2017). *Parental threats and increased comorbidity of psychiatric symptoms.* Manuscript in preparation.

Benjamin, L. S., & Cushing, G. (2000). *Reference manual for coding social interactions in terms of Structural Analysis of Social Behavior.* Salt Lake City: University of Utah.

Benjamin, L. S., & Friedrich, F. J. (1991). Contributions of Structural Analysis of Social Behavior (SASB) to the bridge between cognitive science and a science of object relations. In M. J. Horowitz (Ed.), *Person schemas and maladaptive interpersonal patterns* (pp. 379–412). Chicago, IL: University of Chicago Press.

Benjamin, L. S., Rothweiler, J. C., & Critchfield, K. L. (2006). The use of Structural Analysis of Social Behavior (SASB) as an assessment tool. *Annual Review of Clinical Psychology, 2,* 83–109. http://dx.doi.org/10.1146/annurev.clinpsy.2.022305.095337

Benjamin, L. S., Serdahely, W., & Geppert, T. V. (1971). Night training through parents' implicit use of operant conditioning. *Child Development, 42,* 963–966. http://dx.doi.org/10.2307/1127464

Bernier, A., Carlson, S. M., & Whipple, N. (2010). From external regulation to self-regulation: Early parenting precursors of young children's executive functioning. *Child Development, 81,* 326–339. http://dx.doi.org/10.1111/j.1467-8624.2009.01397.x

Bernstein, E. E., & McNally, R. J. (2017). Acute aerobic exercise hastens emotional recovery from a subsequent stressor. *Health Psychology, 36,* 560–567. http://dx.doi.org/10.1037/hea0000482

Bishop, J., & Lane, R. C. (2002). The dynamics and dangers of entitlement. *Psychoanalytic Psychology, 19,* 739–758. http://dx.doi.org/10.1037/0736-9735.19.4.739

Blatt, S. J. (2004). Developmental origins (distal antecedents). In *Experiences of depression: Theoretical, clinical, and research perspectives* (pp. 187–229). Washington, DC: American Psychological Association.

Bond, A. J. (2005). Antidepressant treatments and human aggression. *European Journal of Pharmacology, 526,* 218–225. http://dx.doi.org/10.1016/j.ejphar.2005.09.033

Bornstein, M. H. (2014). Human infancy . . . and the rest of the lifespan. *Annual Review of Psychology, 65,* 121–158. http://dx.doi.org/10.1146/annurev-psych-120710-100359

Bowlby, J. (1969). *Attachment and loss: Vol. 1. Attachment.* London, England: Tavistock.

Bowlby, J. (1977). The making and breaking of affectional bonds. I. Aetiology and psychopathology in the light of attachment theory. An expanded version of the Fiftieth Maudsley Lecture, delivered before the Royal College of Psychiatrists, 19 November 1976. *The British Journal of Psychiatry, 130,* 201–210. http://dx.doi.org/10.1192/bjp.130.3.201

Bowlby, J. (2005). *The making and breaking of affectional bonds.* New York, NY: Routledge Classics.

Bratton, S. C., Ray, D., Rhine, T., & Jones, L. (2005). The efficacy of play therapy with children: A meta analytic review of treatment outcomes. *Professional Psychology: Research and Practice, 36,* 376–390. http://dx.doi.org/10.1037/0735-7028.36.4.376

Brennan, B., & Visty, R. (Writers & Producers). (1999). A conversation with Koko. In *Nature* [Television series]. Arlington, VA: Public Broadcasting Service. Retrieved from https://www.youtube.com/watch?v=SNuZ4OE6vCk

Bretherton, I. (1992). The origins of attachment theory: John Bowlby and Mary Ainsworth. *Developmental Psychology, 28,* 759–775. http://dx.doi.org/10.1037/0012-1649.28.5.759

Brown, M. Z., Comtois, K. A., & Linehan, M. M. (2002). Reasons for suicide attempts and nonsuicidal self-injury in women with borderline personality disorder. *Journal of Abnormal Psychology, 111,* 198–202. http://dx.doi.org/10.1037/0021-843X.111.1.198

Bryan, C. J., Corso, K. A., Neal-Walden, T. A., & Rudd, M. D. (2009). Managing suicide risk in primary care: Practice recommendations for behavioral health consultants. *Professional Psychology: Research and Practice, 40,* 148–155.

Buckley, P. F. (1999). The role of typical and atypical antipsychotic medications in the management of agitation and aggression. *The Journal of Clinical Psychiatry, 60,* 32–60.

Bullard, D. M. (Ed.). (1959). *Psychoanalysis and psychotherapy: Selected papers of Frieda Fromm-Reichmann.* Chicago, IL: University of Chicago Press.

Carlisle, M., Uchino, B. N., Sanbonmatsu, D. M., Smith, T. W., Cribbet, M. R., Birmingham, W., . . . Vaughn, A. A. (2012). Subliminal activation of social ties moderates cardiovascular reactivity during acute stress. *Health Psychology, 31,* 217–225. http://dx.doi.org/10.1037/a0025187

Carpenter, L. L., Tyrka, A. R., Ross, N. S., Khoury, L., Anderson, G. M., & Price, L. H. (2009). Effect of childhood emotional abuse and age on cortisol responsivity in adulthood. *Biological Psychiatry, 66,* 69–75. http://dx.doi.org/10.1016/j.biopsych.2009.02.030

Cassidy, J., & Shaver, P. R. (Eds.). (2008). *Handbook of attachment: Theory, research and clinical applications* (2nd ed.). New York, NY: Guilford Press.

Chambless, D. L., & Ollendick, T. H. (2001). Empirically supported psychological interventions: Controversies and evidence. *Annual Review of Psychology, 52,* 685–716. http://dx.doi.org/10.1146/annurev.psych.52.1.685

Chartrand, T. L., & Lakin, J. L. (2013). The antecedents and consequences of human behavioral mimicry. *Annual Review of Psychology, 64,* 285–308. http://dx.doi.org/10.1146/annurev-psych-113011-143754

Charuvastra, A., & Cloitre, M. (2008). Social bonds and posttraumatic stress disorder. *Annual Review of Psychology, 59,* 301–328. http://dx.doi.org/10.1146/annurev.psych.58.110405.085650

Child Welfare Information Gateway. (2013). *Parent–child interaction therapy with at-risk families.* Washington, DC: U.S. Department of Health and Human Services. Retrieved from https://www.childwelfare.gov/pubPDFs/f_interactbulletin.pdf

Choi, J., Jeong, B., Polcari, A., Rohan, M. L., & Teicher, M. H. (2012). Reduced fractional anisotropy in the visual limbic pathway of young adults witnessing domestic violence in childhood. *NeuroImage, 59,* 1071–1079. http://dx.doi.org/10.1016/j.neuroimage.2011.09.033

Christie, A. M., Atkins, P. W. B., & Donald, J. N. (2017). The meaning and doing of mindfulness: The role of values in the link between mindfulness and well-being. *Mindfulness, 8,* 368–378. http://dx.doi.org/10.1007/s12671-016-0606-9

Cicchetti, D., & Toth, S. L. (2005). Child maltreatment. *Annual Review of Clinical Psychology, 1,* 409–438. http://dx.doi.org/10.1146/annurev.clinpsy.1.102803.144029

Colligan, R. C., Morey, L. C., & Offord, K. P. (1994). The MMPI/MMPI-2 Personality Disorder scales: Contemporary norms for adults and adolescents. *Journal of Clinical Psychology, 50,* 168–200. http://dx.doi.org/10.1002/1097-4679(199403)50:2<168::AID-JCLP2270500207>3.0.CO;2-E

Comer, J. S., Mojtabai, R., & Olfson, M. (2011). National trends in the antipsychotic treatment of psychiatric outpatients with anxiety disorders. *The American Journal of Psychiatry, 168,* 1057–1065. http://dx.doi.org/10.1176/appi.ajp.2011.11010087

Connolly, M. B., Crits-Christoph, P., Demorest, A., Azarian, K., Muenz, L., & Chittams, J. (1996). Varieties of transference patterns in psychotherapy. *Journal of Consulting and Clinical Psychology, 64,* 1213–1221. http://dx.doi.org/10.1037/0022-006X.64.6.1213

Conroy, D., & Benjamin, L. S. (2001). Psychodynamics in sport performance enhancement consultation: Application of an interpersonal theory. *The Sport Psychologist, 15,* 103–117. http://dx.doi.org/10.1123/tsp.15.1.103

Constantino, M. J. (2000). Interpersonal process in psychotherapy through the lens of the Structural Analysis of Social Behavior. *Applied & Preventive Psychology, 9,* 153–172. http://dx.doi.org/10.1016/S0962-1849(05)80002-2

Craske, M. G., & Waters, A. M. (2005). Panic disorder, phobias, and generalized anxiety disorder. *Annual Review of Clinical Psychology, 1*, 197–225. http://dx.doi.org/10.1146/annurev.clinpsy.1.102803.143857

Crespo, D., & Schaefer, S. (Producers & Directors). (2007). *Arranged* [Motion picture]. United States: Cicala Filmworks.

Critchfield, K. L., & Benjamin, L. S. (2008). Internalized representations of early interpersonal experience and adult relationships: A test of copy process theory in clinical and non-clinical settings. *Psychiatry: Interpersonal and Biological Processes, 71*, 71–92. http://dx.doi.org/10.1521/psyc.2008.71.1.71

Critchfield, K. L., & Benjamin, L. S. (2010). Assessment of repeated relational patterns for individual cases using the SASB-based Intrex questionnaire. *Journal of Personality Assessment, 92*, 480–489. http://dx.doi.org/10.1080/00223891.2010.513286

Critchfield, K. L., Benjamin, L. S., & Levenick, K. (2015). Reliability, sensitivity, and specificity of case formulations for comorbid profiles in Interpersonal Reconstructive Therapy: Addressing mechanisms of psychopathology. *Journal of Personality Disorders, 29*, 547–573. http://dx.doi.org/10.1521/pedi.2015.29.4.547

Critchfield, K. L., Davis, M. J., & Benjamin, L. S. (2008). *Manual for assessing adherence in IRT.* Unpublished manuscript, University of Utah, Salt Lake City.

Crits-Christoph, P., Connolly, M. B., & Shaffer, C. (1999). Reliability and base rates of interpersonal themes in narratives from psychotherapy sessions. *Journal of Clinical Psychology, 55*, 1227–1242. http://dx.doi.org/10.1002/(SICI)1097-4679(199910)55:10<1227::AID-JCLP5>3.0.CO;2-S

Crits-Christoph, P., Cooper, A., & Luborsky, L. (1988). The accuracy of therapists' interpretations and the outcome of dynamic psychotherapy. *Journal of Consulting and Clinical Psychology, 56*, 490–495. http://dx.doi.org/10.1037/0022-006X.56.4.490

Crits-Christoph, P., Gibbons, M. B., Hamilton, J., Ring-Kurtz, S., & Gallop, R. (2011). The dependability of alliance assessments: The alliance–outcome correlation is larger than you might think. *Journal of Consulting and Clinical Psychology, 79*, 267–278. http://dx.doi.org/10.1037/a0023668

Cunha, C., Gonçalves, M. M., Hill, C. E., Mendes, I., Ribeiro, A. P., Sousa, I., . . . Greenberg, L. S. (2012). Therapist interventions and client innovative moments in emotion-focused therapy for depression. *Psychotherapy, 49*, 536–548. http://dx.doi.org/10.1037/a0028259

Cushing, G. (2003). Interpersonal origins of parenting among addicted and non-addicted mothers. *Dissertation Abstracts International: Section B. Sciences and Engineering, 64*(3), 1485.

Davis, M. J. (2012). A comparison of low and high structure practice for learning interactional analysis skills. *Dissertation Abstracts International: Section B. Sciences and Engineering, 73*(2), 124.

Dennhag, I., & Armelius, B.-Å. (2012). Baseline training in cognitive and psychodynamic psychotherapy during a psychologist training program: Exploring client outcomes in therapies of one or two semesters. *Psychotherapy Research*, 22, 515–526. http://dx.doi.org/10.1080/10503307.2012.677332

Depping, M. S., Nolte, H. M., Hirjak, D., Palm, E., Hofer, S., Stieltjes, B., . . . Thomann, P. A. (2017). Cerebellar volume change in response to electroconvulsive therapy in patients with major depression. *Progress in Neuro-Psychopharmacology & Biological Psychiatry*, 73, 31–35. http://dx.doi.org/10.1016/j.pnpbp.2016.09.007

Derogatis, L. (1994). *Symptom Checklist—90—Revised (SCL–90–R): Administration, scoring and procedures, Manual II.* Baltimore, MD: Clinical Psychiatric Research.

DeWahl, D. (2009). *The age of empathy: Nature's lessons for a kinder society*. New York, NY: Harmony Books.

DiGiuseppe, R., & Tafrate, R. C. (2003). Anger treatment for adults: A meta-analytic review. *Clinical Psychology: Science and Practice*, 10, 70–84. http://dx.doi.org/10.1093/clipsy.10.1.70

DiGiuseppe, R., & Tafrate, R. C. (2007). *Understanding anger disorders*. New York, NY: Oxford University Press.

Douglas, K. S., & Skeem, J. L. (2005). Violence risk assessment: Getting specific about being dynamic. *Psychology, Public Policy, and Law*, 11, 347–383. http://dx.doi.org/10.1037/1076-8971.11.3.347

Downey, S., Gambino, D., Dobkin, D. (Producers), & Dobkin, D. (Director). (2014). *The judge* [Motion picture]. United States: Warner Bros.

Drabman, R. S., & Thomas, M. H. (1977). Children's imitation of aggressive and prosocial behavior when viewing alone and in pairs. *Journal of Communication*, 27, 199–205. http://dx.doi.org/10.1111/j.1460-2466.1977.tb02148.x

Dunn, A. L., Trivedi, M. H., Kampert, J. B., Clark, C. G., & Chambliss, H. O. (2005). Exercise treatment for depression: Efficacy and dose response. *American Journal of Preventive Medicine*, 28, 1–8. http://dx.doi.org/10.1016/j.amepre.2004.09.003

Eaton, A. (Producer), & Winterbottom, M. (Director). (1996). *Jude* [Motion picture]. United States: Gramercy Pictures.

Eells, T. D., Lombart, K. G., Kendjelic, E. M., Turner, L. C., & Lucas, C. P. (2005). The quality of psychotherapy case formulations: A comparison of expert, experienced, and novice cognitive–behavioral and psychodynamic psychotherapists. *Journal of Consulting and Clinical Psychology*, 73, 579–589. http://dx.doi.org/10.1037/0022-006X.73.4.579

Ehrenberg, M., Kleinbaum, R., Levy, J., Saxon, E., Veinberg, N. (Producers), & Radford, M. (Director). (2014). *Elsa & Fred* [Motion picture]. United States: Millennium Entertainment.

Elkin, E., Gibbons, R. D., Shea, M. T., & Shaw, B. F. (1996). Science is not a trial (but it can sometimes be a tribulation). *Journal of Consulting and Clinical Psychology*, 64, 92–103. http://dx.doi.org/10.1037/0022-006X.64.1.92

Elliott, R. (2013). Person-centered/experiential psychotherapy for anxiety difficulties: Theory, research and practice. *Person-Centered & Experiential Psychotherapies*, 12, 16–32. http://dx.doi.org/10.1080/14779757.2013.767750

Ellis, A. (1973). *Humanistic psychotherapy: The rational emotive approach.* New York, NY: Julian Press.

Erikson, E. H. (1959). *Identity and the life cycle: Selected papers.* New York, NY: International Universities Press.

Etzler, S. L., Rohrmann, S., & Brandt, H. (2014). Validation of the STAXI–2: A study with prison inmates. *Psychological Test and Assessment Modeling, 56,* 178–194.

Eyberg, S. M., & Pincus, D. (1999). *Eyberg Child Behavior Inventory and Sutter-Eyberg Student Behavior Inventory: Professional manual.* Odessa, FL: Psychological Assessment Resources.

Eyberg, S. M., & Robinson, E. A. (1982). Parent–child interaction training: Effects on family functioning. *Journal of Clinical Psychology, 11,* 130–137. http://dx.doi.org/10.1080/15374418209533076

Fairbairn, W. R. D. (1952). *An object-relations theory of the personality.* New York, NY: Basic Books.

Finkle, D. (2013). *Thank you for your service.* New York, NY: Farrar, Straus & Giroux.

First, M. B., Gibbon, M., Spitzer, R. L., Williams, J. B. W., & Benjamin, L. S. (1997). Structured Clinical Interview for *DSM–IV* Axis II personality disorders (SCID–II). Washington, DC: American Psychiatric Press.

Fiske, A., Wetherell, J. L., & Gatz, M. (2009). Depression in older adults. *Annual Review of Clinical Psychology, 5,* 363–389. http://dx.doi.org/10.1146/annurev.clinpsy.032408.153621

Florsheim, P., Tolan, P. H., & Gorman-Smith, D. (1996). Family processes and risk for externalizing behavior problems among African American and Hispanic boys. *Journal of Consulting and Clinical Psychology, 64,* 1222–1230. http://dx.doi.org/10.1037/0022-006X.64.6.1222

Foa, E. B., Hembree, E. A., Cahill, S. P., Rauch, S. A., Riggs, D. S., Feeny, N. C., & Yadin, E. (2005). Randomized trial of prolonged exposure for posttraumatic stress disorder with and without cognitive restructuring: Outcome at academic and community clinics. *Journal of Consulting and Clinical Psychology, 73,* 953–964. http://dx.doi.org/10.1037/0022-006X.73.5.953

Foa, E. B., Hembree, E. A., & Rothbaum, B. O. (2009). *Prolonged exposure for PTSD: Emotional processing of traumatic experiences—A therapist guide.* New York, NY: Oxford University Press.

Fournier, J. C., DeRubeis, R. J., Shelton, R. C., Hollon, S. D., Amsterdam, J. D., & Gallop, R. (2009). Prediction of response to medication and cognitive therapy in the treatment of moderate to severe depression. *Journal of Consulting and Clinical Psychology, 77,* 775–787. http://dx.doi.org/10.1037/a0015401

Fouts, R., & Mills, S. (1998). *Next of kin: What my conversations with chimpanzees have taught me about intelligence, compassion and being human.* New York, NY: Penguin Books.

Franklin, M. E., & Foa, E. B. (2011). Treatment of obsessive compulsive disorder. *Annual Review of Clinical Psychology, 7,* 229–243. http://dx.doi.org/10.1146/annurev-clinpsy-032210-104533

Freud, S. (1959a). Mourning and melancholia. In E. Jones (Ed.), *Sigmund Freud: Collected papers* (Vol. 4, pp. 152–170). New York, NY: Basic Books. (Original work published 1917)

Freud, S. (1959b). *Sigmund Freud: Collected papers* (E. Jones, Ed.; Vols. 1–5). New York, NY: Basic Books.

Freud, S., & Breuer, J. (1959). On the psychical mechanism of hysterical phenomena. In E. Jones (Ed.), *Sigmund Freud: Collected papers* (Vol. 1, pp. 24–41). New York, NY: Basic Books. (Original work published 1893)

Gale Encyclopedia of Medicine. (2008). *Stockholm syndrome.* Retrieved from http://medical-dictionary.thefreedictionary.com/Stockholm+syndrome

Gendlin, E. (1999). Implicit entry and focusing. *The Humanistic Psychologist, 27,* 80–88. http://dx.doi.org/10.1080/08873267.1999.9986899

Gill, M. J., & Cerce, S. C. (2017). He never willed to have the will he has: Historicist narratives, "civilized" blame, and the need to distinguish two notions of free will. *Journal of Personality and Social Psychology, 112,* 361–382. http://dx.doi.org/10.1037/pspa0000073

Goense, P., Boendermaker, L., van Yperen, T., Stams, G.-J., & van Laar, J. (2014). Implementation of treatment integrity procedures: An analysis of outcome studies of youth interventions targeting externalizing behavioral problems. *Zeitschrift für Psychologie, 222,* 12–21. http://dx.doi.org/10.1027/2151-2604/a000161

Grace, W. J., & Graham, D. T. (1952). Relationship of specific attitudes and emotions to certain bodily diseases. *Psychosomatic Medicine, 14,* 243–251.

Graham, D. T., Lundy, R. M., Benjamin, L. S., Kabler, J. D., Lewis, W. C., Kunish, N. W., & Graham, F. K. (1962). Specific attitudes in initial interviews with patients having different "psychosomatic" diseases. *Psychosomatic Medicine, 25,* 260–266.

Green, H. (1964). *I never promised you a rose garden.* New York, NY: Holt, Rinehart & Winston.

Greenberg, J. R., & Mitchell, S. A. (1984). *Object relations in psychoanalytic theory.* Cambridge, MA: Harvard University Press.

Greenberg, L. S. (1983). Toward a task analysis of conflict resolution in Gestalt therapy. *Psychotherapy: Theory, Research & Practice, 20,* 190–201. http://dx.doi.org/10.1037/h0088490

Greenberg, L. S. (2004). Emotion-focused therapy. *Clinical Psychology & Psychotherapy, 11,* 3–16. http://dx.doi.org/10.1002/cpp.388

Greenberg, L. S., & Foerster, F. S. (1996). Task analysis exemplified: The process of resolving unfinished business. *Journal of Consulting and Clinical Psychology, 64,* 439–446. http://dx.doi.org/10.1037/0022-006X.64.3.439

Greenberg, L. S., Ford, C. L., Alden, L. S., & Johnson, S. M. (1993). In-session change in emotionally focused therapy. *Journal of Consulting and Clinical Psychology, 61,* 78–84. http://dx.doi.org/10.1037/0022-006X.61.1.78

Greist, J. H., Klein, M. H., Eischens, R. R., Faris, J., Gurman, A. S., & Morgan, W. P. (1979). Running as treatment for depression. *Comprehensive Psychiatry, 20,* 41–54. http://dx.doi.org/10.1016/0010-440X(79)90058-0

Gunnar, M., & Quevedo, K. (2007). The neurobiology of stress and development. *Annual Review of Psychology, 58,* 145–173. http://dx.doi.org/10.1146/annurev.psych.58.110405.085605

Guttman, L. (1966). Order analysis of correlation matrixes. In R. B. Cattell (Ed.), *Handbook of multivariate experimental psychology* (438–458). Chicago, IL: Rand McNally.

Halvorsen, M. S., & Monsen, J. T. (2007). Self-image as a moderator of change in psychotherapy. *Psychotherapy Research, 17,* 205–217. http://dx.doi.org/10.1080/10503300600608363

Hamilton, M. (1967). Development of a rating scale for primary depressive illness. *British Journal of Social and Clinical Psychology, 6,* 278–296. http://dx.doi.org/10.1111/j.2044-8260.1967.tb00530.x

Harlow, H. (1958). The nature of love. *American Psychologist, 13,* 673–685. http://dx.doi.org/10.1037/h0047884

Harpaz-Rotem, I., & Blatt, S. J. (2005). Changes in representations of a self-designated significant other in long-term intensive inpatient treatment of seriously disturbed adolescents and young adults. *Psychiatry: Interpersonal and Biological Processes, 68,* 266–282. http://dx.doi.org/10.1521/psyc.2005.68.3.266

Hartkamp, N., & Schmitz, N. (1999). Structures of introject and therapist patient interaction in a single case study of inpatient psychotherapy. *Psychotherapy Research, 9,* 199–215. http://dx.doi.org/10.1080/10503309912331332691

Hayes, S. C., Villatte, M., Levin, M., & Hildebrandt, M. (2011). Open, aware, and active: Contextual approaches as an emerging trend in the behavioral and cognitive therapies. *Annual Review of Clinical Psychology, 7,* 141–168. http://dx.doi.org/10.1146/annurev-clinpsy-032210-104449

Health Insurance Portability and Accountability Act, Pub. L. No. 104-191, § 264, 110 Stat. 1936 (2004).

Heidegger, M. (1962). *Being and time* (J. Macquarrie & E. Robinson, Trans.). Oxford, England: Blackwell. (Original work published 1927)

Henry, W. P., Schacht, T. E., & Strupp, H. H. (1990). Patient and therapist introject, interpersonal process, and differential psychotherapy outcome. *Journal of Consulting and Clinical Psychology, 58,* 768–774. http://dx.doi.org/10.1037/0022-006X.58.6.768

Hettema, J., Steele, J., & Miller, W. R. (2005). Motivational interviewing. *Annual Review of Clinical Psychology, 1,* 91–111. http://dx.doi.org/10.1146/annurev.clinpsy.1.102803.143833

Hettema, J. M., Neale, M. C., & Kendler, K. S. (2001). A review and meta-analysis of the genetic epidemiology of anxiety disorders. *The American Journal of Psychiatry, 158*, 1568–1578. http://dx.doi.org/10.1176/appi.ajp.158.10.1568

Holsboer, F., & Ising, M. (2010). Stress hormone regulation: Biological role and translation into therapy. *Annual Review of Psychology, 61*, 81–109, C1–C11. http://dx.doi.org/10.1146/annurev.psych.093008.100321

Hornblow, A., Jr. (Producer), & Cukor, G. (Director). (1944). *Gaslight* [Motion picture]. United States: Metro-Goldwyn-Mayer.

Humes, D. L., & Humphrey, L. L. (1994). A multimethod analysis of families with a polydrug-dependent or normal adolescent daughter. *Journal of Abnormal Psychology, 103*, 676–685. http://dx.doi.org/10.1037/0021-843X.103.4.676

Humphrey, L. L., & Benjamin, L. S. (1986). Using Structural Analysis of Social Behavior to assess critical but elusive family processes: A new solution to an old problem. *American Psychologist, 41*, 979–989. http://dx.doi.org/10.1037/0003-066X.41.9.979

Iacoboni, M. (2009). Imitation, empathy, and mirror neurons. *Annual Review of Psychology, 60*, 653–670. http://dx.doi.org/10.1146/annurev.psych.60.110707.163604

Ichise, M., Vines, D. C., Gura, T., Anderson, G. M., Suomi, S. J., Higley, J. D., & Innis, R. B. (2006). Effects of early life stress on [^{11}C]DASB positron emission tomography imaging of serotonin transporters in adolescent peer- and mother-reared rhesus monkeys. *The Journal of Neuroscience, 26*, 4638–4643. http://dx.doi.org/10.1523/JNEUROSCI.5199-05.2006

Insel, T. R. (2010). Faulty circuits. *Scientific American, 302*(4), 44–51. http://dx.doi.org/10.1038/scientificamerican0410-44

James, W. (1947). Philosophy and its critics. In D. J. Bronstein, Y. H. Krikorian, & P. P. Wiener (Eds.), *Basic problems of philosophy* (pp. 687–699). New York, NY: Prentice-Hall. (Original work published 1911)

Johnston, A., DeLuca, D., Murtaugh, K., & Diener, E. (1977). Validation of a laboratory play measure of child aggression. *Child Development, 48*, 324–327. http://dx.doi.org/10.2307/1128922

Jones, A. (2005). An examination of three sets of MMPI–2 personality disorder scales. *Journal of Personality Disorders, 19*, 370–385. http://dx.doi.org/10.1521/pedi.2005.19.4.370

Joyce, P. R., McHugh, P. C., Light, K. J., Rowe, S., Miller, A. L., & Kennedy, M. A. (2009). Relationships between angry–impulsive personality traits and genetic polymorphisms of the dopamine transporter. *Biological Psychiatry, 66*, 717–721. http://dx.doi.org/10.1016/j.biopsych.2009.03.005

Junkert-Tress, B., Schnierda, U., Hartkamp, N., Schmitz, N., & Tress, W. (2001). Effects of short-term dynamic psychotherapy for neurotic, somatoform, and personality disorders: A prospective 1-year follow-up study. *Psychotherapy Research, 11*, 187–200. http://dx.doi.org/10.1080/713663890

Kagan, J. (1994). *Galen's prophecy: Temperament in human nature.* New York, NY: Basic Books.

Kagan, J., & Snidman, N. (2004). *The long shadow of temperament.* Cambridge, MA: Belknap Press/Harvard University Press.

Karlssen, H. (2011). How psychotherapy changes the brain. *Psychiatric Times, 28*(8), 1–3.

Karpiak, C. P., & Benjamin, L. S. (2004). Therapist affirmation and the process and outcome of psychotherapy: Two sequential analytic studies. *Journal of Clinical Psychology, 60,* 659–676. http://dx.doi.org/10.1002/jclp.10248

Karpiak, C. P., Critchfield, K. L., & Benjamin, L. S. (2011, July). *Empathy, adherence, and outcome in Interpersonal Reconstructive Psychotherapy with treatment-resistant patients.* Paper presented at the meeting of the Society for Psychotherapy Research, Berne, Switzerland.

Kernberg, O. F., Selzer, M. A., Koeningsberg, H. W., Carr, A. C., & Applebaum, A. H. (1989). *Psychodynamic psychotherapy of borderline patients.* New York, NY: Basic Books.

Kessler, R. C., Coccaro, E. F., Fava, M., Jaeger, M., Jin, R., & Walters, E. (2006). The prevalence and correlates of DSM–IV intermittent explosive disorder in the National Comorbidity Study Replication. *Archives of General Psychiatry, 63,* 669–678. http://dx.doi.org/10.1001/archpsyc.63.6.669

Kimbro, D., & Hill, N. (1991). *Think and grow rich: A Black choice.* New York, NY: Random House.

Kleim, J. A., & Jones, T. A. (2008). Principles of experience-dependent neural plasticity: Implications for rehabilitation after brain damage. *Journal of Speech, Language, and Hearing Research, 51,* S225–S239. http://dx.doi.org/10.1044/1092-4388(2008/018)

Klein, D. N., Kotov, R., & Bufferd, S. J. (2011). Personality and depression: Explanatory models and review of the evidence. *Annual Review of Clinical Psychology, 7,* 269–295. http://dx.doi.org/10.1146/annurev-clinpsy-032210-104540

Klein, M. H., Benjamin, L. S., & Smith, T. L. (1996). *The Wisconsin Personality Inventory: WISPI–IV.* Madison: University of Wisconsin.

Klein, M. H., Mathieu-Coughlan, P., & Kiesler, D. J. (1986). The Experiencing Scales. In L. S. Greenberg & W. M. Pinsof (Eds.), *The psychotherapeutic process: A research handbook* (pp. 21–71). New York, NY: Guilford Press.

Klerman, G. L., Weissman, M. M., Rounsaville, B. J., & Chevron, E. S. (1994). *Interpersonal psychotherapy of depression: A brief, focused, specific strategy.* Northvale, NJ: Jason Aronson.

Krahé, B., Busching, R., & Moller, I. (2012). Media violence use and aggression among German adolescents: Associations and trajectories of change in a three-wave longitudinal study. *Psychology of Popular Media Culture, 1,* 152–166. http://dx.doi.org/10.1037/a0028663

Krampen, G. (2009). Psychotherapeutic processes and outcomes in outpatient treatment of antisocial behavior: An integrative psychotherapy approach. *Journal of Psychotherapy Integration, 19*, 213–230. http://dx.doi.org/10.1037/a0017069

Kreibig, S. D. (2010). Autonomic nervous system activity in emotion: A review. *Biological Psychology, 84*, 394–421. http://dx.doi.org/10.1016/j.biopsycho.2010.03.010

Kübler-Ross, E. (1969). *On death and dying.* New York, NY: Collier Books/Macmillan.

LeDoux, J. E. (2002). *Synaptic self: How our brains become who we are.* New York, NY: Penguin Books.

LeDoux, J. E. (2013, April 7). For the anxious, avoidance can have an upside. *New York Times.* Retrieved from https://opinionator.blogs.nytimes.com/2013/04/07/for-the-anxious-avoidance-can-have-an-upside/

Leonardo, E. D., & Hen, R. (2006). Genetics of affective and anxiety disorders. *Annual Review of Psychology, 57*, 117–137. http://dx.doi.org/10.1146/annurev.psych.57.102904.190118

Lindfors, O., Knekt, P., Heinonen, E., Härkänen, T., Virtala, E., & Helsinki Psychotherapy Study Group. (2015). The effectiveness of short- and long-term psychotherapy on personality functioning during a 5-year follow-up. *Journal of Affective Disorders, 173*, 31–38. http://dx.doi.org/10.1016/j.jad.2014.10.039

Lindfors, O., Knekt, P., Virtala, E., Laaksonen, M. A., & Helsinki Psychotherapy Study Group. (2012). The effectiveness of solution-focused therapy and short- and long-term psychodynamic psychotherapy on self-concept during a 3-year follow-up. *Journal of Nervous and Mental Disease, 200*, 946–953. http://dx.doi.org/10.1097/NMD.0b013e3182718c6b

Linehan, M. (1993). *Cognitive–behavioral treatment of borderline personality disorder.* New York, NY: Guilford Press.

Losada, A., Márquez-González, M., Romero-Moreno, R., Mausbach, B. T., López, J., Fernández-Fernández, V., & Nogales-González, C. (2015). Cognitive–behavioral therapy (CBT) versus acceptance and commitment therapy (ACT) for dementia family caregivers with significant depressive symptoms: Results of a randomized clinical trial. *Journal of Consulting Clinical and Psychology, 83*, 760–772. http://dx.doi.org/10.1037/ccp0000028

Low, P. (2017). Overview of the autonomic nervous system. *Merck Manual, professional edition.* Retrieved from http://www.merckmanuals.com/professional/neurologic-disorders/autonomic-nervous-system/overview-of-the-autonomic-nervous-system

Lowyck, B., Vermote, R., Verhaest, Y., Vandeneede, B., Wampers, M., & Luyten, P. (2015). Hospitalization-based psychodynamic treatment for personality disorders: A five-year follow-up. *Psychoanalytic Psychology, 32*, 381–402. http://dx.doi.org/10.1037/a0038959

Luborsky, L. (1984). *Principles of psychoanalytic psychotherapy: A manual for supportive–expressive treatment*. New York, NY: Basic Books.

MacLeod, C., & Mathews, A. (2012). Cognitive bias modification approaches to anxiety. *Annual Review of Clinical Psychology, 8*, 189–217. http://dx.doi.org/10.1146/annurev-clinpsy-032511-143052

Mahler, M. S. (1968). *On human symbiosis and the vicissitudes of individuation*. New York, NY: International Universities Press.

Mann, M., Climan, S., King, G., Evans, C., Jr. (Producers), & Scorsese, M. (Director). (2004). *The aviator* [Motion picture]. United States: Warner Bros. & Miramax.

Marble, A., Høglend, P., & Ulberg, R. (2011). Change in self-protection and symptoms after dynamic psychotherapy: The influence of pretreatment motivation. *Journal of Clinical Psychology, 67*, 355–367. http://dx.doi.org/10.1002/jclp.20771

Martin, A. (2007). The representation of object concepts in the brain. *Annual Review of Psychology, 58*, 25–45. http://dx.doi.org/10.1146/annurev.psych.57.102904.190143

Massad, P. M., & Hulsey, T. L. (2006). Causal attributions in posttraumatic stress disorder: Implications for clinical research and practice. *Psychotherapy: Theory, Research, Practice, Training, 43*, 201–215. http://dx.doi.org/10.1037/0033-3204.43.2.201

Masten, A. S., & Narayan, A. J. (2012). Child development in the context of disaster, war, and terrorism: Pathways of risk and resilience. *Annual Review of Psychology, 63*, 227–257. http://dx.doi.org/10.1146/annurev-psych-120710-100356

May, R. (1969). *Love and will*. New York, NY: W. W. Norton.

Mayberg, H. S., Lozano, A. M., Voon, V., McNeely, H. E., Seminowicz, D., Hamani, C., . . . Kennedy, S. H. (2005). Deep brain stimulation for treatment-resistant depression. *Neuron, 45*, 651–660. http://dx.doi.org/10.1016/j.neuron.2005.02.014

McCarty, S. K. (1997). A structural analysis of marital conflict resolution. *Dissertation Abstracts International: Section B. Sciences and Engineering, 58*(6), 3369.

McCullough, J. P., Jr., Klein, D. N., Borian, F. E., Howland, R. H., Riso, L. P., Keller, M. B., & Banks, P. L. C. (2003). Group comparisons of DSM–IV subtypes of chronic depression: Validity of the distinctions, Part 2. *Journal of Abnormal Psychology, 112*, 614–622. http://dx.doi.org/10.1037/0021-843X.112.4.614

McEwen, B. S. (2005). Stressed or stressed out: What is the difference? *Journal of Psychiatry & Neuroscience, 30*, 315–318.

McEwen, B. S. (n.d.). Bruce S. McEwen, Ph.D. [Web page]. Retrieved from https://www.rockefeller.edu/our-scientists/heads-of-laboratories/863-bruce-s-mcewen/

McEwen, B. S., & Gianaros, P. J. (2011). Stress- and allostasis-induced brain plasticity. *Annual Review of Medicine, 62*, 431–445. http://dx.doi.org/10.1146/annurev-med-052209-100430

McGilloway, S., Mhaille, G. N., Bywater, T., Furlong, M., Leckey, Y., Kelly, P., . . . Donnelly, M. (2012). A parenting intervention for childhood behavioral problems: A randomized controlled trial in disadvantaged community-based settings. *Journal of Consulting and Clinical Psychology, 80*, 116–127. http://dx.doi.org/10.1037/a0026304

McGonigle, M. A. (1994). A structural analysis of hostility in the marital context. *Dissertation Abstracts International: Section B. Sciences and Engineering, 54*(8), 4398.

Meaney, M. J. (2010). Epigenetics and the biological definition of Gene × Environment interactions. *Child Development, 81*, 41–79. http://dx.doi.org/10.1111/j.1467-8624.2009.01381.x

Meehan, J., Kaur, N., Hunt, I. M., Turnbull, P., Robinson, J., Bickley, H., . . . Appleby, L. (2006). Suicide in mental health in-patients and within 3 months of discharge: National clinical survey. *British Journal of Psychiatry, 188*, 129–134. http://dx.doi.org/10.1192/bjp.188.2.129

Merriam-Webster. (n.d.). *Psychodynamics*. Retrieved from https://www.merriam-webster.com/dictionary/psychodynamics

Mestel, R. (2012). *SASB database on lease from Robert Mestel, research director*. Bad Groeningen, Germany: HELIOS Klinik.

Methikalam, B., Wang, K. T., Slaney, R. B., & Yeung, J. C. (2015). Asian values, personal and family perfectionism, and mental health among Asian Indians in the United States. *Asian American Journal of Psychology, 6*, 223–232. http://dx.doi.org/10.1037/aap0000023

Mikulincer, M. (1998). Adult attachment style and individual differences in functional versus dysfunctional experiences of anger. *Journal of Personality and Social Psychology, 74*, 513–524. http://dx.doi.org/10.1037/0022-3514.74.2.513

Milius, S. (2010). Life: Will groom for snuggles: Market forces govern infant's value within monkey groups. *Science News, 178*(12), 9. http://dx.doi.org/10.1002/scin.5591781207

Millon, T. (1987). *Manual for the Millon Clinical Multiaxial Inventory II*. Minneapolis, MN: National Computer Systems.

Moore, A. M. (1998). Why people drink: Alcohol dependence from an interpersonal perspective. *Dissertation Abstracts International: Section B. Sciences and Engineering, 59*(5), 2426.

Moran, M. (2008). *The fallen world*. Monterey, KY: Larkspur Press.

Muran, J. C., & Barber, J. P. (Eds.). (2010). *The therapeutic alliance: An evidence-based guide to practice*. New York, NY: Guilford Press.

National Institute of Mental Health. (2016). *Anxiety disorders*. Retrieved from https://www.nimh.nih.gov/health/topics/anxiety-disorders/index.shtml

National Institute of Mental Health. (n.d.). *Suicide*. Retrieved from https://www.nimh.nih.gov/health/statistics/suicide/index.shtml

Neufeld, M. (Producer), & West, S. (Director). (1999). *The general's daughter* [Motion picture]. United States: Paramount Pictures.

Neviani, F., Belvederi Murri, M., Mussi, C., Triolo, F., Toni, G., Simoncini, E., . . . Neri, M. (2017). Physical exercise for late life depression: Effects on cognition and disability. *International Psychogeriatrics, 29*, 1105–1112. http://dx.doi.org/10.1017/S1041610217000576

Newman, M. G., Castonguay, L. G., Borkovec, T. D., Fisher, A. J., Boswell, J. F., Szkodny, L. E., & Nordberg, S. S. (2011). A randomized controlled trial of cognitive–behavioral therapy for generalized anxiety disorder with integrated techniques from emotion-focused and interpersonal therapies. *Journal of Consulting and Clinical Psychology, 79*, 171–181. http://dx.doi.org/10.1037/a0022489

Nissen-Lie, H. A., Rønnestad, M. H., Høglend, P. A., Havik, O. E., Solbakken, O. A., Stiles, T. C., & Monsen, J. T. (2017). Love yourself as a person, doubt yourself as a therapist? *Clinical Psychology & Psychotherapy, 24*, 48–60. http://dx.doi.org/10.1002/cpp.1977

Oliver, M. (1986). *Dream work*. New York, NY: Atlantic Monthly Press.

OPD Working Group. (2001). *Operationalized psychodynamic diagnostics: Foundations and manual*. Seattle, WA: Hogrefe & Huber.

Park, J. H. (2005). A validation study of the Structural Analysis of Affective Behavior: Further development and empirical analysis. *Dissertation Abstracts International: Section B. Sciences and Engineering, 65*(10), 5418.

Pereira, A. I., Muris, P. R., Magda, S., Marques, T., Goes, R., & Barros, L. (2017). Examining the mechanisms of therapeutic change in a cognitive–behavioral intervention for anxious children: The role of interpretation bias, perceived control, and coping strategies. *Child Psychiatry and Human Development*. Advance online publication. http://dx.doi.org/10.1007/s10578-017-0731-2

Perepletchikova, F., Treat, T. A., & Kazdin, A. E. (2007). Treatment integrity in psychotherapy research: Analysis of the studies and examination of the associated factors. *Journal of Consulting and Clinical Psychology, 75*, 829–841. http://dx.doi.org/10.1037/0022-006X.75.6.829

Pincus, A. L., Dickinson, K. A., Schut, A. J., Castonguay, L. G., & Bedics, J. (1999). Integrating interpersonal assessment and adult attachment using SASB. *European Journal of Psychological Assessment, 15*, 206–220. http://dx.doi.org/10.1027//1015-5759.15.3.206

Pizzagalli, D. A. (2014). Depression, stress, and anhedonia: Toward a synthesis and integrated model. *Annual Review of Clinical Psychology, 10*, 393–423. http://dx.doi.org/10.1146/annurev-clinpsy-050212-185606

Plomin, R., Foch, T. T., & Rowe, D. C. (1981). Bobo clown aggression in childhood: Environment, not genes. *Journal of Research in Personality, 15*, 331–342. http://dx.doi.org/10.1016/0092-6566(81)90031-3

Porges, S. W. (1995). Orienting in a defensive world: Mammalian modifications of our evolutionary heritage: A polyvagal theory. *Psychophysiology, 32*, 301–318. http://dx.doi.org/10.1111/j.1469-8986.1995.tb01213.x

Primitive brain is "smarter" than we think, MIT study shows. (2005, February 23). *MIT News*. Retrieved from http://news.mit.edu/2005/basalganglia

Prochaska, J. O., DiClemente, C. C., & Norcross, J. C. (1992). In search of how people change: Applications to addictive behaviors. *American Psychologist, 47*, 1102–1114. http://dx.doi.org/10.1037/0003-066X.47.9.1102

Qin, P., & Nordentoft, M. (2005). Suicide risk in relation to psychiatric hospitalization: Evidence based on longitudinal registers. *Archives of General Psychiatry, 62*, 427–432. http://dx.doi.org/10.1001/archpsyc.62.4.427

Reber, A. S. (1989). Implicit learning and tacit knowledge. *Journal of Experimental Psychology: General, 118*, 219–235. http://dx.doi.org/10.1037/0096-3445.118.3.219

Reich, W. (1990). *Character analysis* (3rd ed., enlarged). New York, NY: Farrar Straus & Giroux. (Original work published 1933)

Reik, T. (1983). *Listening with the third ear: The inner experience of a psychoanalyst.* New York, NY: Farrar Straus & Giroux.

Resick, P. A., Monson, C. M., & Chard, K. M. (2014). *Cognitive processing therapy: Veteran/military version: Therapist and patient materials manual.* Washington, DC: Department of Veterans Affairs. Retrieved from https://www.div12.org/wp-content/uploads/2015/07/CPT-Materials-Manual.pdf

Rogers, C. R. (1951). *Client-centered therapy.* Cambridge, MA: Riverside Press.

Rosenblum, L. A., & Harlow, H. F. (1963). Approach–avoidance conflict in the mother-surrogate situation. *Psychological Reports, 12*, 83–85. http://dx.doi.org/10.2466/pr0.1963.12.1.83

Rothweiler, J. C. (2004). An evaluation of the internal and external validity of the Intrex and Interpersonal Adjective Scales. *Dissertation Abstracts International: Section B. Sciences and Engineering, 65*(2), 1038.

Russell, J. A. (1980). A circumplex model of affect. *Journal of Personality and Social Psychology, 39*, 1161–1178. http://dx.doi.org/10.1037/h0077714

Saaty, T. L., & Vargas, L. G. (1993). A model of neural impulse firing and synthesis. *Journal of Mathematical Psychology, 37*, 200–219. http://dx.doi.org/10.1006/jmps.1993.1013

Sanders, L. (2013, January 16). Depression gene search disappoints: Comprehensive effort to find DNA links to low mood comes up empty. *Science News*. Retrieved from https://www.sciencenews.org/article/depression-gene-search-disappoints

Sandor, C. (1996). An interpersonal approach to substance abuse. *Dissertation Abstracts International: Section A. Humanities and Social Sciences, 57*(2), 0879.

Schloredt, K. A. (1997). Child maltreatment: An application of interpersonal theory. *Dissertation Abstracts International: Section B. Sciences and Engineering, 57*(7), 4724.

Science News. (2009, January 31). *Darwin turns 200* [Special section]. *Science News, 175*(3), 1–36.

Seligman, M. (1975). *Helplessness: On depression, development and death*. San Francisco, CA: W. H. Freeman.

Selye, H. (1946). The general adaptation syndrome and the diseases of adaptation. *The Journal of Clinical Endocrinology and Metabolism, 6*, 117–230. http://dx.doi.org/10.1210/jcem-6-2-117

Selye, H. (1950). Stress and the general adaptation syndrome. *British Medical Journal, 1*, pp. 1383–1392.

Shakespeare, W. (1988). The taming of the shrew. In *William Shakespeare: The complete works* (pp. 329–358). New York, NY: Dorset Press.

Shapiro, F. (2001). *Eye movement desensitization and reprocessing: Basic principles, protocols, and procedures* (2nd ed.). New York, NY: Guilford Press.

Sharma, S., Powers, A., Bradley, B., & Ressler, K. J. (2016). Gene × Environment determinants of stress- and anxiety-related disorders. *Annual Review of Psychology, 67*, 239–261. http://dx.doi.org/10.1146/annurev-psych-122414-033408

Shear, K., & Shair, H. (2005). Attachment, loss, and complicated grief. *Developmental Psychobiology, 47*, 253–267. http://dx.doi.org/10.1002/dev.20091

Singer, W., & Rauschecker, J. P. (1982). Central core control of developmental plasticity in the kitten visual cortex: II. Electrical activation of mesencephalic and diencephalic projections. *Experimental Brain Research, 47*, 223–233.

Skinner, B. F. (1953). *Science and human behavior*. New York, NY: Free Press.

Skinner, B. F. (1987). Whatever happened to psychology as the science of behavior? *American Psychologist, 42*, 780–786. http://dx.doi.org/10.1037/0003-066X.42.8.780

Skowron, E. A., Cipriano-Essel, E. A., Benjamin, L. S., Pincus, A. L., & Van Ryzin, M. (2013). Cardiac vagal tone and quality of parenting show concurrent and time-ordered associations that diverge in abusive, neglectful, and nonmaltreating mothers. *Couple & Family Psychology: Research and Practice, 2*, 95–115. http://dx.doi.org/10.1037/cfp0000005

Skowron, E. A., Stanley, K. L., & Shapiro, M. D. (2009). A longitudinal perspective on differentiation of self, interpersonal and psychological well-being in young adulthood. *Contemporary Family Therapy, 31*, 3–18. http://dx.doi.org/10.1007/s10591-008-9075-1

Smith, T. L. (2002). Specific psychosocial perceptions and specific symptoms of personality and other psychiatric disorders. *Dissertation Abstracts International: Section B. Sciences and Engineering, 63*(6), 3026.

Smith, T. W., & Brown, P. C. (1991). Cynical hostility, attempts to exert social control, and cardiovascular reactivity in married couples. *Journal of Behavioral Medicine, 14*, 581–592. http://dx.doi.org/10.1007/BF00867172

Smith, T. W., McGonigle, M. A., & Benjamin, L. S. (1998). Sibling interactions, self-regulation, and cynical hostility in adult male twins. *Journal of Behavioral Medicine, 21*, 337–349. http://dx.doi.org/10.1023/A:1018774629400

Smith, T. W., Uchino, B. N., Berg, C. A., & Florsheim, P. (2012). Marital discord and coronary artery disease: A comparison of behaviorally defined discrete groups. *Journal of Consulting and Clinical Psychology, 80,* 87–92. http://dx.doi.org/10.1037/a0026561

Sohlberg, S., & Birgegård, A. (2003). Persistent complex subliminal activation effects: First experimental observations. *Journal of Personality and Social Psychology, 85,* 302–316. http://dx.doi.org/10.1037/0022-3514.85.2.302

Sohlberg, S., Claesson, K., & Birgegård, A. (2003). Memories of mother, complementarity and shame: Predicting response to subliminal stimulation with "Mommy and I are one." *Scandinavian Journal of Psychology, 44,* 339–346. http://dx.doi.org/10.1111/1467-9450.00353

Sondheim, S. (1987). Children will listen [song]. In *Into the woods* [Musical].

Spielberger, C. D. (1999). *The State–Trait Anger Expression Inventory—2 (STAXI–2): Professional manual.* Odessa, FL: Psychological Assessment Resources.

Spinelli, S., Chefer, S., Carson, R. E., Jagoda, E., Lang, L., Heilig, M., . . . Stein, E. A. (2010). Effects of early-life stress on serotonin$_{1A}$ receptors in juvenile rhesus monkeys measured by positron emission tomography. *Biological Psychiatry, 67,* 1146–1153. http://dx.doi.org/10.1016/j.biopsych.2009.12.030

Strand, J. G. (1996). The interpersonal construals of pedophiles: Structural Analysis of Social Behavior observer coding. *Dissertation Abstracts International: Section B. Sciences and Engineering, 56*(9), 5186.

Substance Abuse and Mental Health Services Administration. (n.d.). *Motivational interviewing.* Retrieved from https://www.integration.samhsa.gov/clinical-practice/motivational-interviewing

Suchman, N. E., DeCoste, C., Ordway, M. R., & Bers, S. (2013). Mothering from the inside out: A mentalization-based individual therapy for mothers with substance use disorders. In N. E. Suchman, M. Pajulo, & L. C. Mayes (Eds.), *Parenting and substance abuse: Developmental approaches to intervention* (pp. 407–433). New York, NY: Oxford University Press. http://dx.doi.org/10.1093/med:psych/9780199743100.003.0020

Suddendorf, T., & Whiten, A. (2001). Mental evolution and development: Evidence for secondary representation in children, great apes, and other animals. *Psychological Bulletin, 127,* 629–650. http://dx.doi.org/10.1037/0033-2909.127.5.629

Sullivan, H. S. (1953). *The interpersonal theory of psychiatry.* New York, NY: Norton.

Teicher, M. H., & Samson, J. A. (2016). Annual research review: Enduring neurobiological effects of childhood abuse and neglect. *Journal of Child Psychology and Psychiatry, 57,* 241–266. http://dx.doi.org/10.1111/jcpp.12507

ten Have, M., de Graaf, R., & Monshouwer, K. (2011). Physical exercise in adults and mental health status: Findings from the Netherlands Mental Health Survey and Incidence Study (NEMESIS). *Journal of Psychosomatic Research, 71,* 342–348. http://dx.doi.org/10.1016/j.jpsychores.2011.04.001

Teti, D. M., Heaton, N., Benjamin, L. S., & Gelfand, D. M. (1995, May). *Quality of attachment and caregiving among depressed mother–child dyads: Strange situation classifications and the SASB coding system.* Paper presented at the meeting of the Society for Applied Behavioral Analysis, Washington, DC.

Thoma, H., & Kachele, H. (1991). *Psychoanalytic practice* (Vol. 1, English ed.). New York, NY: Springer-Verlag.

Tinbergen, N. (1951). *The study of instinct.* Oxford, England: Clarendon Press.

Toth, S. L., Rogosch, F. A., Sturge-Apple, M., & Cicchetti, D. (2009). Maternal depression, children's attachment security, and representational development: An organizational perspective. *Child Development, 80,* 192–208. http://dx.doi.org/10.1111/j.1467-8624.2008.01254.x

Ulberg, R., Høglend, P., Marble, A., & Sørbye, Ø. (2009). From submission to autonomy: Approaching independent decision making: A single-case study in a randomized, controlled study of long-term effects of dynamic psychotherapy. *American Journal of Psychotherapy, 63,* 227–243.

Utiger, R. D. (2017). Hypothalamus. In *Encyclopedia Brittanica.* Retrieved from https://www.britannica.com/science/hypothalamus

van der Horst, F. C. P., Leroy, H. A., & van der Veer, R. (2008). "When strangers meet": John Bowlby and Harry Harlow on attachment behavior. *Integrative Psychological & Behavioral Science, 42,* 370–388. http://dx.doi.org/10.1007/s12124-008-9079-2

Van Velsor, P., & Cox, D. L. (2001). Anger as a vehicle in the treatment of women who are sexual abuse survivors: Reattributing responsibility and accessing personal power. *Professional Psychology: Research and Practice, 32,* 618–625. http://dx.doi.org/10.1037/0735-7028.32.6.618

Walters, R. H., & Brown, M. (1963). Studies of reinforcement of aggression: III. Transfer of responses to an interpersonal situation. *Child Development, 34,* 563–571. http://dx.doi.org/10.2307/1126752

Watson, D., & Tellegen, A. (1985). Toward a consensual structure of mood. *Psychological Bulletin, 98,* 219–235. http://dx.doi.org/10.1037/0033-2909.98.2.219

Whooley, M. A., & Wong, J. M. (2013). Depression and cardiovascular disorders. *Annual Review of Clinical Psychology, 9,* 327–354. http://dx.doi.org/10.1146/annurev-clinpsy-050212-185526

Widiger, T. A., & Canyon, C. C. S. (1994). LSB on the SASB, the FFM, and IPC. *Psychological Inquiry, 5,* 329–332. http://dx.doi.org/10.1207/s15327965pli0504_7

Wong, D. L., Tai, T. C., Wong-Faull, D. C., Claycomb, R., & Kvetňanský, R. (2008). Adrenergic responses to stress: Transcriptional and post-transcriptional changes. *Annals of the New York Academy of Sciences, 1148,* 249–256. http://dx.doi.org/10.1196/annals.1410.048

World Health Organization. (2017). Welcome to ICD10Data.com. Retrieved from http://www.icd10data.com/

Ybrandt, H. (2008). The relation between self-concept and social functioning in adolescence. *Journal of Adolescence, 31,* 1–16. http://dx.doi.org/10.1016/j.adolescence.2007.03.004

Yeomans, F. E., Clarkin, J. F., Diamond, D., & Levy, K. N. (2008). An object relations treatment of borderline patients with reflective functioning as the mechanism of change. In F. N. Busch (Ed.), *Mentalization: Theoretical considerations, research findings, and clinical implications* (pp. 159–181). Mahwah, NJ: Analytic Press.

Yeomans, F. E., Clarkin, J. F., & Kernberg, O. F. (2015). *Transference-focused psychotherapy for borderline personality disorder: A clinical guide.* Arlington, VA: American Psychiatric Publishing.

Young, J. E., Klosko, J. S., & Weishaar, M. E. (2003). *Schema therapy: A practitioner's guide.* New York, NY: Guilford Press.

INDEX

Abreaction, 104
Acceptance and commitment therapy (ACT), 219–220
Accurate empathy (process skill), 112–115
Action stage of change, 127, 133–149
    anxiety and stress in, 192
    and family therapy, 149
    higher brain motivation, 134
    impaired progress of, 268–269
    and loop of psychopathology, 136–140
    and maintenance of gains, 148–149
    phases of, 140–148
    primitive brain motivation, 135–136
Adaptive behaviors, 38–39
Adaptive statements (process skill), 115–116
Add-ons, 192–193
Adherence
    to IRT, importance of, 148–149
    and rehospitalization, 261
    and therapy relationship, 258
Adherence ratings, 258
Adherence scales, 255–257
Affective disorders
    symptoms of, 22
    in women, 35
Affective responses, 79
Affective symptoms, 16, 39
    and depression, 41
    and Gifts of Love, 124
    and introjection, 65
Affect regulators
    internalized representations as, 79
    reprogramming of, 247
Affiliation, 38
Affirmation, parental, 172
Aggression, 167–168
    and Gifts of Love, 123–124
    and sexuality, 124
Agoraphobia, 183–184
Alarm stage, of stress, 177
Alberti, R. E., 120
Alcohol, and anxiety, 201

Allen, J. P., 207
Ambivalence, about change, 167–168
American Psychological Association, 248
Amy case example, 3–6, 128
    action phase of change in, 141
    Gifts of Love in, 135
    will to change in, 140
Anankastic personality disorder, 66–67
Angela case example, 232–234
Anger, 153–173
    adaptive purpose of, 37, 86
    blocking problem patterns (step), 160–164
    changes in, 262–263
    collaboration (step), 157–158
    and depression, 206–207, 209
    diagnoses and explanations for, 153–155
    engaging the will to change (step), 164–171
    functional analysis of, 17
    learning about patterns (step), 159–160
    learning new patterns (step), 171–173
    Natural Biology of, 36–38
    punishment for expressions of, 78
    SASB and function of, 73–74
    and threat, 25
    understanding and treating, 156–157
Anger management training, 156
Angry–impulsive personality traits, 155
Anhedonia, 205
ANS (autonomic nervous system), 22–24
Antidepressants, as treatments for anger, 156
Antipsychotics
    as treatments for anger, 156
    as treatments for anxiety disorders, 180
Antithesis, 68–70

Anxiety, 175–201
    abuse of drug treatments for, 200–201
    in action stage of change, 192
    adaptive purpose of, 37, 86
    blocking problem patterns (step),
        190–191
    changes in, 263
    collaboration (step), 184–186
    and depression, 206–207, 209
    engaging the will to change (step),
        191–199
    functional analysis of, 177–178
    and genetics, 176–177
    as "in-between" activating affect, 40
    learning about patterns (step), 186–190
    learning new patterns (step), 199–200
    medications for treatment of,
        179–180
    Natural Biology of, 36–38
    SASB and function of, 73–74
    and stress, 177–179
    subtypes of, 183–184
    treating anger with, 164
Arranged (film), 129
Artzybasheff, Boris, 201
Assessment
    medical, in treatment of
        depression, 204
    risk of suicide, 208–209
    of Secure Base, 254
    Standard Series (SASB
        assessment), 59
    of symptoms, in case formulation
        model, 90
Associative learning, 42
Atkins, P. W. B., 252
Attachment, 29–32
    and affiliation axis, 72
    and complementarity, 68
    disrupted, 35
    as goal of therapy, 73
    insecure, 34, 155
    reflexes, 25
    secure, 25–33
Attachment figures. *See also* Family in
    the Head
    abuse by, 189, 194
    as cause of anxiety, 182
    and copy processes, 79
    discussed in interviews, 96

and Family in the Head, 87
    qualifications for, 32
    as threats, 74–76
    trauma inflicted by, 135–136
Attribution-based treatments,
    for anger, 156
Autoimmune disorders, 101–102
Autonomic nervous system (ANS),
    22–24
Autonomy
    in anxiety case example, 185
    and conflict, 60
    and enmeshment, 60–63
    friendly, 119–120
    supporting, 119
The Aviator (film), 99

Baby rhesus monkey experiment,
    29–31
Bateson, J., 73
Beck Depression Inventory (BDI),
    263–264
Behavioral changes, 11
Behavioral coaching, 171–172
Behavioral responses, 79
Behavioral techniques, 10
Behavioral technologies, 127
Behaviors. *See also* C1AB links
    adaptive, 38–39
    angry, 165
    blaming and angry, 160–161
    copied, 5–6
    Secure Base, 27–28
    self-sabotaging, 6, 42, 124,
        189–190
Being and Time (Heidegger), 220
Benjamin, L. S., 31, 38n, 58–59, 71,
    154, 165, 249, 255
Benzodiazepines, 201
Berg, C. A., 154
Bernier, A., 119
Bernstein, E. E., 221
Bers, S., 252
Betsy case example, 161–162
Biological Psychiatry, 205
Birgegård, A., 80, 193, 207
Birthright Self, 20, 113, 118–119, 125,
    235–237
    in action stage of change, 141–147
    and anger, 158, 169

breaking loop of psychopathology
with, 138
in treatment of anxiety, 194–196,
198–199
Bishop, J., 155
Blaming
and angry behavior, 160–161
and case formulation model, 98
ineffective for psychotherapy, 34
Blatt, S. J., 207, 220, 237
Blocking problem patterns (step)
evidence supporting, 251
treatment model for, 125–126
for treatment of anger, 160–164
for treatment of anxiety, 190–191
for treatment of depression, 228–230
Bobo the Clown studies, 155n1
Boendermaker, L., 254
Borderline personality disorder (BPD),
10, 216
mini-crisis in, 108
treating anger with, 159
treatment model for, 107–112
Bornstein, M. H., 205
Bowlby, J., 26, 34, 59, 105, 250
BPD. See Borderline personality disorder
Bradley, B., 176
Brain damage, from childhood stress,
34–35
Brain plasticity, 48–49, 132
Brainwashing, 73
Bratton, S. C., 156
Breuer, J., 104, 253
Bryan, C. J., 209
Bullard, D. M., 268
Busching, R., 155

C1AB (primitive brain perception–
affect–behavior) links, 36–37
and anger, 156, 159
in case formulation model, 86–87
evidence supporting, 38–41
functions of anger, anxiety, and
depression in, 73–74
in interviews, 95–96
Natural Biology of, 24–25
primitive brain motivation to
change, 135
reprogramming, 113
Cancer patients, 49

Canyon, C. C. S., 70
Cardiovascular disease, 209
Caregivers, of dementia patients, 219
Carlisle, M., 154
Carlson, S. M., 119
Carpenter, L. L., 35
Case examples, rapidly reconstructed,
131
Case formulation, 9–10, 85–102
for anxiety, 183–184
assessment of symptoms in, 90
and blame, 98
case example, 88–89, 97–98
connecting, to treatment, 134
and copy processes, 93–94, 123
current stresses linked to symptoms in,
90, 93
evidence supporting, 99–101,
250–252
explaining, to patients, 18–21,
94–95
and Family in the Head, 93
and fictional depictions of copy
processes, 98–99
and Gifts of Love, 114
interviewing style for, 95–97
and medical views of psychopathology, 101
Natural Biology in, 86–88
Red GOLs and autoimmune
disorders, 101–102
in research designs, 249
for suicidal patients, 125
and suitability of IRT, 269
and treatment models, 250
Case formulation (process skill), 116
CBM (cognitive bias modification), 181
CBT (cognitive–behavioral therapy),
180, 218–219
Cerce, S. C., 251
Chambless, D. L., 247
Change
active engagement in, 129–130
after psychotherapy, 48–49
ambivalence about, 168
facilitating, 21
fear related to, 235–236
reaction to, 224
Chartrand, T. L., 42
Child development, 205

Choi, J., 34
Christie, A. M., 252
Chronic abuse, victims of, 115
Cicchetti, D., 34
Cipriano-Essel, E. A., 59
CircumSteps (computer program), 70–72
Claesson, K., 80
Clarkin, J. F., 252
Claycomb, R., 33, 178–179
Clinical observation, 248
Coding. *See* SASB coding
Cognitive–behavioral therapy (CBT), 180, 218–219
Cognitive bias modification (CBM), 181
Cognitive restructuring, 156
Collaboration
  in preventing suicide, 228–230
  with therapists, 95
  as vital component in IRT, 148
Collaboration (step)
  evidence supporting, 251
  treatment model of, 119–121
  for treatment of anger, 157–158
  for treatment of anxiety, 184–186
  for treatment of depression, 222–223
Commitment
  lack of, to therapy, 131–132
  to therapy, 120–121
Comorbidity
  inpatient sample with, 214–215
  in outpatient sample, 262
  patients with, 10
  variations in, 210–215
Complementarity
  and depression, 224
  evidence-based tests of, 68, 69
  in SASB, 64
  testing for, in real data sets, 70–71
Complementary matches, 28
Complexity, of SASB, 72–73
Confidentiality, 130n
Conflict
  Gifts of Love in, 80–81
  marital, 228
  SASB coding of, 59–60
Confrontation
  with angry patients, 167–168
  of passivity in patients, 145

Connections, exploring, 95–96
Connolly, M. B., 122
Contact comfort, 25–26
Contemplation stage of change, 127, 191
Control
  and anger, 74
  in parent–child relationship, 200
  of threats, and anxiety, 181–182
Cooper, A., 112
Copied behaviors, 5–6
Coping, 73–74
Copy processes, 9–10, 19–20
  and attachment figures, 79
  C1AB links, 41–42
  and case formulation, 123
  and case formulation model, 93–94
  evidence base for, 250
  fictional depictions of, 98–99
  and Gift of Love, 162–163
  identifying maladaptive, 230–231
  involving therapists, 122
  and Natural Biology, 41–43
  in parenting methods, 128
  testing for, in real data sets, 71–72
  theory of, 246–247
  types of, 87
CORDS patients (comorbid, often rehospitalized, dysfunctional, and suicidal), 247–248, 259–260
Core algorithm, 112n
Coronary heart disease, 210
Corso, K. A., 209
Cortical brain, 47
Craske, M. G., 176
Critchfield, K. L., 71, 255
Crits-Cristoph, P., 112
Cues, maladaptive, 36
Culture
  and depression, 207–208
  and symptoms, 76–78
Cunha, C., 220

Davis, M. J., 117, 255
DBT. *See* Dialectical behavior therapy
DBT skills-training exercises, 110
Deciders, 139
DeCoste, C., 252
Deep tracking, 116
De Graaf, R., 221

Dementia, 219
Dependency, 128
Depression, 203–241
    adaptive purpose of, 86
    and affective symptoms, 41
    assessing suicide, 208–209
    blocking problem patterns (step), 228–230
    changes in, 263–265
    collaboration (step), 222–223
    comorbid with, 206–207, 209–216
    as defense, 37
    definitions of, 204
    engaging the will to change (step), 230–238
    and Family in the Head, 207
    functional analysis of, 177–178
    and genetics, 204–206
    and helplessness, 40
    impact of, on significant others, 216–217
    impact of culture on, 207–208
    IRT case formulation for, 221–222
    learning about patterns (step), 223–228
    learning new patterns (step), 238–241
    Natural Biology of, 36–38
    and perfectionism, 18–19
    SASB and function of, 73–74
    and stress, 178
    treatments for, 218–221
Despair, facing, 168–169
Developmental processes, 120
Developmental Psychopathology, 251
Developmental stages, 32–33
"Diagnosis Using Structural Analysis of Social Behavior," 38n
Diagnostic and Statistical Manual of Mental Disorders (DSM), 249
Diagnostic and Statistical Manual of Mental Disorders, fifth ed. *(DSM–5)*
    depression in, 206
    intermittent explosive disorder in, 153
    personality disorders in, 216
Dialectical behavior therapy (DBT), 106, 110, 127, 139
Diamond, D., 252

DiClemente, C. C., 127, 191, 230
Differentiation, 26–29, 231
    in case formulation, 97
    from Family in the Head, 126
    friendly, 28, 173, 240–241
    inhibition of, 40
    in treatment of anger, 156
    in treatment of anxiety, 195
DiGiuseppe, R., 155, 156
Disclose, 40
Disorganization
    in change process, 144
    in treatment of anger, 168–169
    in treatment of anxiety, 196–198
Disrupted attachment, 35
Domestic violence
    anger treatments with abusers, 156
    exposure to, 34–35
    preventing, 172
    preventing, in families, 172
Donald, J. N., 252
Dopaminergic neurobiological model of angry–impulsive personality traits, 155
Douglas, K. S., 154
DSM *(Diagnostic and Statistical Manual of Mental Disorders)*, 249
DSM–5. See *Diagnostic and Statistical Manual of Mental Disorders*, fifth ed.
Dunn, A. L., 221

EBPP (evidence-based practice in psychology), 248
Eells, T. D., 249
EF (executive functioning), 119
Effectiveness research, 249–250
Efficacy research, 250
EFT. See Emotion-focused therapy
Elliott, R., 180
Elsa & Fred (film), 129
EMDR (eye movement desensitization and reprocessing), 106, 127
Emily case example, 158
Emmons, M. L., 120
Emotional abuse, 35–36
Emotional deprivation in childhood, 155
Emotion-focused therapy (EFT), 106, 127, 139, 145–146, 220

Empathy
  in action stage of change, 145
  effectiveness of, 115–116
  peripatetic, 96
  as process skill, 112–115
  as vital component in IRT, 148
Emptiness
  in change process, 144
  in treatment of anger, 168–169
  in treatment of anxiety, 196–198
Enablers, 106–107
Engaging the will to change (step)
  and action stage of change, 139
  research on, 251–252
  treatment model of, 126–127
  for treatment of anger, 164–171
  for treatment of anxiety, 191–199
  for treatment of depression, 230–238
Enmeshment, 30
  and autonomy, 60–63
  friendly, 27
Entitlement, 164–165
Envelope of potential, 45, 176, 205
Envisioning birthright, 234–235
Epigenetic mechanisms, 46–47
Epinephrine, 33, 178–179
Erikson, E. H., 32
Errors, on adherence scales, 255, 257
Ethics, in research methods, 178n1
Ethnographic research, 249
Evidence base, for case formulation model, 99–101
Evidence-based practice in psychology (EBPP), 248
Evidence-based treatments, for anger, 154
Evolutionary theory, 33–34
Executive functioning (EF), 119
Exhaustion, stage of stress, 177–178
Expectations
  adjusting, 239–240
  of hospitalization, 229–230
  of parents, 200
Experiencing Scales, 220
Exploratory questions, in interviews, 95
Eye movement desensitization and reprocessing (EMDR), 106, 127

Families, preventing violence in, 172
Family in the Head, 9, 20–21, 116n
  and analyzing resistance, 116
  and anger, 158, 163, 171
  and attachment figures, 87
  breaking loop of psychopathology with, 138
  and case formulation model, 93
  challenging, in treatment of anger, 166–168
  and depression, 206–207, 222–223
  as echoed C1AB sequences, 42
  fear of challenging, 120
  and Gifts of Love, 80
  grief when losing, 147
  importance of, 270
  as internalized representations, 79
  and mechanisms of change, 245–247
  and Natural Biology, 43–44
  as reflection of natural process, 122
  resisting, in action stage of change, 141
  and suicide, 229
Family therapy
  and action stage of change, 149
  in case example, 184–185
Fantasies, expressing anger via, 154–155
Fear
  in action stage of change, 144–146
  in treatment of anger, 168–169
  in treatment of anxiety, 196–198
Finkle, D., 263n
Fiske, A., 218
Five Rs, 129
Florsheim, P., 76, 154
fMRI studies, 43
Foa, E. B., 181
Foerster, F. S., 249
Fournier, J. C., 218
Franklin, M. E., 181
Free association, in interviews, 96
Freud, Sigmund, 26n, 104, 253, 270
Freud's algorithm, 104–107, 253
Friendly autonomy, 119–120
Friendly differentiation, 28, 173, 240–241
Friendly enmeshment, 27
Fromm-Reichmann, Frieda, 268
Frustration, anger due to, 155
Full model, of SASB, 54, 56–58

GAD (generalized anxiety disorder), 176, 184–200
GAS (general adaptation syndrome), 177
Gaslight (film), 129
Gatz, M., 218
Gene expression
    and anxiety, 177
    and maternal care, 46
General adaptation syndrome (GAS), 177
Generalized anxiety disorder (GAD), 176, 184–200
The General's Daughter (film), 99
Genetics
    and anxiety, 176–177
    and depression, 204–206
    and Natural Biology, 45–47
    and temperament, 45–47
Genomes, 45
Genotype–phenotype relations, 46
Geonese, P., 254
"Getting anger out," 154
Gianaros, P. J., 132
Gifts of Love (GOLs), 9–10, 20, 87
    and affective symptoms, 124
    and aggression, 123–124
    in Amy case example, 6
    and anger, 157, 160, 162–164
    and case formulation, 114
    in case formulation, 93–94
    as core of IRT, 148–149
    and depression, 227–228, 264–265
    and Natural Biology, 44–45
    normative, for interdependence, 30n
    and personality disorders, 265
    primitive brain motivation to work with, 135
    rating of work on, 254–255
    in research designs, 248
    in SASB, 79–81
    and sense of self, 235–236
    stages of grief in giving up, 169–171
    and treatment of anxiety, 187–190
    validity of, 250–251
Gill, M. J., 251
GOLs. *See* Gifts of Love
Gorman-Smith, D., 76
Grace case example, 221–223
Graham, D. T., 109, 199n2

Green actions, 141
    in action stage of change, 166–168
    taking, in treatment of anxiety, 193–194
    in treatment of depression, 231–234
Green affects, 87
Greenberg, Joanne (H. Green), 5
Greenberg, L. S., 106, 127–128, 139, 145–146, 220, 249
Green statements (process skill), 115–116
Greist, J. H., 221
Grief
    in action stage of change, 147–148
    in Melissa case example, 238
    in treatment of anger, 169–171
    in treatment of anxiety, 199
    in treatment of depression, 237–238
Group therapy, 110
Growth Collaborator, 113
Gunnar, M., 15, 35, 48

Haley, J., 73
Happiness, treatment of anger and, 173
Härkänen, T., 49
Harlow, H. F., 25, 29, 44–45, 260
Harpaz-Rotem, I., 237
Hartkamp, N., 249
Hayes, S. C., 218, 219
"Healing image," 121–122
Heidegger, M., 220
Heinonen, E., 49
Hembree, E. A., 181
Hen, R., 183
Hettema, J. M., 176
Higher brain control (choice), 262
Higher brain motivation, 134, 191
Higher brain perception, 47
Hildebrandt, M., 218
Høglend, P., 119
Holsboer, F., 179
Homework, in IRT, 128–129
Hormones, and stress, 179
Hospitalization
    expectations of, 229–230
    and suicide, 208–209
Hostility, 31
    of caregivers, and anxiety, 189
    cultural differences in, 78
    and introjection, 100–101

HPA (hypothalamic–pituitary–adrenal) axis, 24
Hughes, Howard, 99
Hulsey, T. L., 156
Humanistic play therapy, 156
Humes, D. L., 58, 79
Humphrey, L. L., 58, 79
Hydraulic model, of anger, 17
Hypothalamic–pituitary–adrenal (HPA) axis, 24
Hypothalamus, 24n–25n
Hypothesizing, 16–17

Identification (copy process), 41, 186–187, 225
IED (intermittent explosive disorder), 153–154
Imagery, as effective therapy intervention, 125
Important person and his or her internalized representation (IPIR), 116n
Incredible Years Basic Parent Training Program, 182–183
I Never Promised You a Rose Garden (Greenberg), 5
Informal uses of SASB coding, 59–60
Inpatients
    comorbidity in, 214–215
    explaining case formulations with, 96–97
Insecure attachments, 34, 155
Interactions, SASB analysis of, 54–55, 57
Interactive perspective (process skill), 116–118
Interdependence, 38
Intermittent explosive disorder (IED), 153–154
Internal control, 239–240
Internalized relationships, 106, 207
Internalized representations. *See also* Family in the Head
    as affect regulators, 79
    grief when losing, 147
    neurology of, 43–44
Interpersonal coaching, 146
Interpersonal Reconstructive Therapy (IRT), 245–271
    evidence base for, 248–252
    measuring effectiveness of treatment model, 253–268

mechanisms of change in, 245–247, 252–253
    randomized controlled trial, 247–248
    real-life application of, 8
    suitability of, 268–269
    and younger therapists, 270–271
Interpersonal relationships, 38
Interventions
    delivered in naturalistic settings, 249–250
    imagery as effective, 125
Interviewing
    in case formulation model, 95–97
    motivational, 134
Intimacy–distance struggles, 108
Intransitive, 63
Introjection
    and anger, 159–160
    and anxiety, 187–188
    in case formation, 99–101
    as copy process, 41, 226–227
    and personality disorders, 265–267
    in SASB, 65
IPIR (important person and his or her internalized representation), 116n
IRT. *See* Interpersonal Reconstructive Therapy
Ising, M., 179

Jackson, D. D., 73
James, William, 16
Jane case example, 164–165
Janice case example, 246–247
Jasmine case example, 123
Jason case example, 6–8, 102, 126, 128, 135, 140, 225–226
Jeong, B., 34
Jill case example, 157
John case example, 136–140
Jones, L., 156
Jones, T. A., 132
Jordan case example, 170–171
Joseph case example, 18–21, 36, 42, 76, 182
Josephine case example, 167–168
"The Journey" (Oliver), 125
Joyce case example, 163–164
Joyce, P. R., 155
Jude (film), 99
The Judge (film), 129

Karlssen, H., 132
Karpiak, C. P., 66, 255
Kazdin, A. E., 254
Kendjelic, E. M., 249
Kendler, K. S., 176
Kessler, R. C., 154
Kiesler, D. J., 220
Kleim, J. A., 132
Klein, M. H., 220
Klosko, J. S., 111
Klute syndrome, 124, 160
Knekt, P., 49
Koko (gorilla), 32–33
Krahé, B., 155
Krampen, G., 156
Kreibig, S. D., 24
Kübler-Ross, E., 169
Kvetňanský, R., 33, 178–179

Lakin, J. L., 42
Lane, R. C., 155
Laura case example, 224–225
Learning about patterns (step)
   evidence supporting, 251
   treatment model of, 121–125
   for treatment of anger, 159–160
   for treatment of anxiety, 186–190
   for treatment of depression, 223–228
Learning new patterns (step), 122
   evidence supporting, 251
   treatment model of, 127–130
   for treatment of anger, 171–173
   for treatment of anxiety, 199–200
   for treatment of depression, 238–241
LeDoux, J. E., 127, 181
Legitimate anger, 168
Leonardo, E. D., 183
Levin, M., 218
Levy, K. N., 252
Lindfors, O., 49
Linehan, M., 110
Linking C1AB sequences (process skill), 118
Lombart, K. G., 249
Losada, A., 219
Lower brain motivation, 191
Lowyck, B., 49
Luborsky, L., 112
Lucas, C. P., 249

Macro levels, of adherence ratings, 258
Maintenance (stage of change), 127, 148–149
Maladaptive cues, 36
Maladaptive messages, 121
Maladaptive statements, 115–116
Maltreated children, 34, 44, 48
The Manchurian Candidate (film), 129
Mania, 268
Marble, A., 119
Marital conflict, 228
Markov program, 58–59
Martha case example, 160–161
Martin, A., 43–44
Mary case example, 141–144
Massad, P. M., 156
Maternal care, 46
Maternal sensitivity, 119
Mathieu-Coughlan, P., 220
McCarty, S. K., 80
McEwen, B. S., 34, 132, 177
McEwen, Bruce, 34
McGilloway, S., 182–183
McNally, R. J., 221
Meaney, M. J., 45–46
Mechanisms of change
   and Family in the Head, 245–247
   in IRT, 245–247, 252–253
   and Secure Base, 245–247
Medical assessment, in treatment of depression, 204
Medical views of, psychopathology, 101
Medications
   and Natural Biology, 47–48
   for treatment of anxiety, 179–180, 200–201
   as treatment of choice, 105–106
   for treatment of comorbid patients, 210
   for treatment of depression, 204, 218
Meehan, J., 208
Melissa case example, 107–112, 117, 128, 130, 230, 238
Mental disorders, and anger, 154
Mentalization therapy, 110–111
Meta-analysis, 250
Methikalam, B., 207, 208
Micro levels, of adherence ratings, 258
Mindfulness, 127
Mind-mindedness, 119

Mission creep, 186
Mobilization
    anxiety as, 193–194
    in depression, 206–207
Moller, I, 155
Monshouwer, K., 221
Moran, Michael, 50–51
Motivation
    higher brain, 134, 191
    lower brain, 191
    primitive brain, 135–136
Motivational interviewing, 134
Mountain West culture, 76–78
My First Mister (film), 172

Narcissistic personality disorder, 165
National Institute of Mental Health
    (NIMH), 180, 208
Natural Biology, 8–9, 15–51
    of anger, anxiety, and depression,
        36–38
    anxiety in, 180, 190
    as basis of IRT models, 250
    in case formulation model, 86–88
    and copy processes, 41–43
    and depression, 205–206
    explaining, to patients, 18–21
    and Family in the Head, 43–44
    and genetics, 45–47
    and Gifts of Love, 44–45
    grief explained by, 147
    and medications, 47–48
    normal development through secure
        attachment, 25–33
    pathological development, 33–36
    positive adaptations in, 148
    primitive brain and C1AB links, 24–25
    and psychotherapy, 47–49
    and SASB model, 38–41
    stress and anxiety in, 177
    sympathetic and parasympathetic
        nervous systems, 22–24
    theory of, 16–18
    threat detection by primitive brain, 153
    in treatment model, 111
Naturalistic settings, interventions
    delivered in, 249–250
Neale, M. C., 176
Neal-Walden, T. A., 209
Negative affects, 39

Nervous systems, 86–87
Neuroception, 25
Neviani, F., 221
Newman, M. G., 180
Newton's inverse square law, 28n
Nonaggressive assertiveness, 120, 158,
    240–241
Norcross, J. C., 127, 191, 230
Normal development
    discussing, with patients, 97
    Natural Biology of, 25–33
Northern Midwest culture, 76–78

Object relations psychoanalysis, 105
Observer coding system, 58–59
Obsessive–compulsive personality
    disorder (OCPD), 187
Oliver, Mary, 125
Ollendick, T. H., 247
One-word model, of SASB, 56–58
Operationalized Psychodynamic
    Diagnosis (OPD), 75
Opioids, 201
Opposition
    evidence-based tests of, 69
    in SASB, 65
Oppositionalism, 165
Ordway, M. R., 252
Outcome results, of outpatient sample,
    266, 268
Outpatients
    explaining case formulations with,
        96–97
    sample of, 259–268

Panic disorder, 176
Paranoia, 191
Parasympathetic nervous system
    (PNS), 22–24
Parent–child interaction therapy
    (PCIT), 128–129, 172
Parenting training, 182–183
Parents
    adaptive interpretations of actions
        by, 136
    as attachment figures, 128–129
    expectations of, 200
Park, J. H., 78
Passive–aggressive personality disorder,
    165, 231–232

Pathological development, 33–36
Patients
   cancer, 49
   caregivers of dementia, 219
   CORDS, 247–248, 259–260
   explaining case formulation model to, 94–95
   inpatient. *See* Inpatients
   outpatient. *See* Outpatients
   regression by, 170
   treatment-resistant, 232–234
Pattern recognition
   and anxiety, 176–177
   by therapists, 60–63
Patterson, Penny, 32–33
Paula case example, 166
Pauline case example, 88–98, 192–193
PCE (person-centered experiential) therapies, 180
PCIT (parent–child interaction therapy), 128–129, 172
Perceptions, responses driven by, 79
Pereira, A. I., 252
Perepletchikova, F., 254
Perfectionism, and depression, 18–19, 207–208, 226
Peripatetic empathy, 96
Personality disorders
   changes in, 265–266
   and depression, 209, 216
   and threat affects, 209–210
   threat affects in, 211–213
   with trait anger, 155
Person-centered experiential (PCE) therapies, 180
Phenotypes, 45
Phobias, 183
Physical exercise, 221
Physical health, and anger, 154
Pincus, A. L., 59, 73
Pizzagalli, D. A., 205
PNS (parasympathetic nervous system), 22–24
Poetry, 125
Polcari, A., 34
Porges, S. W., 24, 25
Positive affects, 37–38
Posttraumatic stress disorder (PTSD), 156
Powers, A., 176

Precontemplation stage of change, 127, 191
Predictive principles, of SASB, 66–70
Preparation stage of change, 127, 191–192
Primary drive theory, 154
Primitive brain, 129
   awareness, 25
   and cortical brain, 47
   free association in, 114
   motivation in action stage of change, 135–136
   Natural Biology of, 24–25
   perception, 25
   reprogramming, 223, 225–226
   threat detection by, 153
Primitive brain perception–affect–behavior links. *See* C1AB links
Processing, 104
Process–outcome studies, 249
Process skills, 251. *See also specific skills*
Prochaska, J. O., 127, 191, 230
Projective identification, 115, 217
Prolonged exposure therapy, 106, 181
Psychiatric affective symptoms, 36
Psychoanalysis, history of, 105
Psychodynamic therapy, 220–221
Psychological testing, subjectivity in, 4n
Psychopathology
   and case formulation model, 101
   loop of, 136–140
   medical views of, 101
Psychotherapy
   and Natural Biology, 47–49
   for treatment of anxiety, 180–183
   for treatment of depression, 218
PTSD (posttraumatic stress disorder), 156
Public health research, 249

Qualitative research, 248–249
Quevedo, K., 15, 35, 48

Randomized controlled trials (RCTs)
   for cognitive–behavioral therapy, 180
   designs, 108
   Interpersonal Reconstructive Therapy, 247–248
   measuring effectiveness with, 253
   and their logical equivalents, 250

Rating scale, 252–253
Ray, D., 156
RCTs. *See* Randomized controlled trials
RE (relationship episodes), 122
Recapitulation (copy process), 41, 187, 225–226
Red affects, 87
Red Gifts of Love, 101–102
Redirection, in treatment of anxiety, 181
Red messages, 121
Red statements, 115–116
Red voices, 141
    learning to silence, 146
    resisting, 166–168
    in treatment of anxiety, 193–194
    in treatment of depression, 231–234
Reframing
    to block problem patterns, 190
    in treatment of anxiety, 196
Regression, by patients, 170
Regressive Loyalist, 113
Rehospitalization, 260–261
Reik, T., 96
Relationship episodes (RE), 122
Relationships
    building, in treatment of anger, 172
    control in parent–child, 200
    measuring, with SASB models, 58–59
Reprogramming, 104
    of affect regulators, 247
    C1AB links, 113
    primitive brain, 223, 225–226
    in therapy, 139
    in treatment of anxiety, 181
Resilience, 182–183
Response prevention procedures, 181
Ressler, K. J., 176
Rhine, T., 156
Robert case example, 159
Rogers, C. R., 112, 220
Rohan, M. L., 34
Rosenblum, L. A., 44–45
Rothbaum, B. O., 181
Rudd, M. D., 209

"The Sacrifice" (Moran), 50–51
Sadism, 160
Sadness, about loss of GOLs, 170–171

Safety plan, for suicidal patients, 125
Safety systems
    and nervous systems, 22–24
    recuing, 119
Samson, J. A., 35
Sanders, L., 205
Sandor, C., 201
SASB. *See* Structural Analysis of Social Behavior
SASB coding, 54–55, 57–58
    brainwashing explained by, 73
    informal uses of, 59–60
    observer coding system, 58–59
Schadenfreude, 155, 160
Schema treatment, 111
Schmitz, N., 249
Secure attachment, 25–33
Secure Base, 119–121
    and anger, 158
    and anxiety, 182–183
    assessment of, 254
    behaviors, 27–28
    and Birthright Self, 236–237
    and copy processes, 79
    as goal of therapy, 148
    in humans, 26–29
    and mechanisms of change, 245–247
    patients' view of therapist as, 197–198
    and potential clash with culture, 208
    and SASB, 73
    in therapy relationship, 257–258
    in treatment of anger, 172
Secure Base parenting, 128–129
Secure Base (Green) patterns, 118
Self-care, 128
Self-loathing, 169
Self-negation, 223
Self-sabotaging behaviors, 6, 42, 124, 189–190
Self-talk
    to block problem patterns, 190
    in treatment of anxiety, 193
Selye, H., 177–178, 206
Sense of self
    and Gifts of Love, 235–236
    in gorillas, 32–33
Sensory–Motor Imagery, 125
Separate, 40
Separation, 231
Serotonin, 38, 40

Severe psychopathology, 124
Sexual abuse, exposure to, 34–35
Sexuality, and aggression, 124
Shair, H., 237
Shapiro, M. D., 26
Sharma, S., 176
Shear, K., 237
Similarity
    evidence-based tests of, 69
    in SASB, 64–65
Single case studies, 249
Skeem, J. L., 154
Skinner, B. F., 220, 254
Skowron, E. A., 26, 59
Slaney, R. B., 207, 208
Sleep problems, 193–194
Smith, T.W., 154
SNS (sympathetic nervous system), 22–24
Social homework, in IRT, 10
Socialization, 26
Sohlberg, S., 80, 193, 207
Somatic symptoms, 246
Sørbye, Ø., 119
Spinelli, S., 35
Stages of change, 127
Stages of change model, 10–11
Stams, G.-J., 254
Standard Series (SASB assessment), 59
Stanley, K. L., 26
Stockholm syndrome, 73
Stress
    in action stage of change, 192
    and anxiety, 177–179
    and depression, 206–207
    impact of, on the brain, 34–35
    linked to symptoms, 90, 93
    and symptoms of mental disorder, 33
Structural Analysis of Affective Behavior, 78
Structural Analysis of Social Behavior (SASB), 9, 53–81
    anger and, 159
    antithesis, 65
    complementarity, 64
    criticisms of, predictive principles, 70–73
    evidence-based tests of predictive principles of, 66–70
    and function of anger, anxiety, and depression, 73–74
    and Gifts of Love, 79–81
    and impact of culture, 76–78
    internalized representations in, 79
    introjection, 65
    in IRT, 111
    models of, 54–63
    and Natural Biology, 38–41
    opposition, 65
    and Secure Base, 73
    similarity, 64–65
    and Structural Analysis of Affective Behavior, 78
    and threats, 74–76
The Study of Instinct (Tinbergen), 16
Substance abuse
    and depression, 106–107
    of medications that treat anxiety, 180, 200–201
Suchman, N. E., 252
Suddendorf, T., 43
Suicide, 124, 228–230
    as angry behavior, 161–162
    assessing risk of, in depressed patients, 208–209
    attempts of, 260
    and hospitalization, 208–209
Sullivan, H. S., 96
Sympathetic nervous system (SNS), 22–24
Symptoms
    changes in, 261–262
    stress linked to, 90, 93
Symptom substitution, 108
Systematic case studies, 249

Tachistoscopic flashes, 80
Tafrate, R. C., 155, 156
Tai, T. C., 33, 178–179
Teicher, M. H., 34, 35
Temperament
    and anxiety, 176–177
    and genetics, 45–47
Ten Have, M., 221
TFP (transference-focused therapy), 106, 110
Thank You for Your Service (Finkle), 263n

Therapists
  competence of, 254
  as moderators vs. mediators, 251–252
  pattern recognition by, 60–63
  self-evaluation of, 258–259
  suitability of IRT for, 269
  viewed as Secure Base, by patients, 197–198
  younger, 270–271
Therapy goals, 73, 148
Therapy relationship, 197–198, 257–259
Therapy steps, 118–130
Threat affects
  and adaptive behaviors, 38–39
  in case formulation model, 86
  perceived impact of patients', 217
  and personality disorders, 209–213
Threats
  and comorbidity, 215
  and nervous systems, 22–24
  and SASB, 74–76
Threat systems, recuing, 119
Tinbergen, N., 16
Tolan, P. H., 76
Toth, S. L., 34
Tough love, 106–107
Trait theory, 117–118
Transference analysis, 122
Transference distortion, 167
Transference-focused therapy (TFP), 106, 110
Transference problems, 197–198
Transitive, 63
Transparency, of therapists, 95
Trauma, inflicted by attachment figures, 135–136
Treat, T. A., 254
Treatment model, 10, 103–132
  blocking problem patterns (step), 125–126
  for borderline personality disorder, 107–112
  and brain plasticity, 132
  case examples, 130–132
  and case formulation, 250
  collaboration (step), 119–121
  connecting case formulation to, 134
  engaging the will to change (step), 126–127
  evidence supporting, 250–252
  and Freud's algorithm, 104–107
  goal of, 112
  learning about patterns (step), 121–125
  learning new patterns (step), 127–130
  measuring adherence to, 255–257
  process skills in, 112–118
  therapy steps of, 113
Treatment-resistant patients, 232–234
Turner, L. C., 249
Two-chair technique, 128

Uchino, B. N., 154
Ulberg, R., 119
Uncovering the unconscious, 116

Van Laar, J., 254
Van Ryzin, M., 59
Van Yperen, T., 254
Verbal abuse, 35–36
Veterans, 263n
Villatte, M., 218
Virtala, E., 49

Wang, K. T., 207, 208
Waters, A. M., 176
Weakland, J., 73
Weishaar, M. E., 111
Wetherell, J. L., 218
Whipple, N, 119
Whiten, A., 43
Whooley, M. A., 209–210
Widiger, T. A., 70
William case example, 171–172
Within normal limits (WNL), 112
Wong, D. L., 33, 178–179
Wong, J. M., 209–210
Wong-Faull, D. C., 33, 178–179
Working through phase, 104, 139
"Wrong patient syndrome," 224

Yearning Self, 113, 118, 127, 141–145, 194–196
Yeomans, F. E., 252
Yeung, J. C., 207, 208
Young, J. E., 111
Your Perfect Right (Alberti & Emmons), 120

ABOUT THE AUTHOR

Lorna Smith Benjamin, PhD, is a psychotherapist; creator of Structural Analysis of Social Behavior (SASB), a model for describing interactions with self and others; and creator of Interpersonal Reconstructive Therapy (IRT), which was developed for "treatment-resistant" psychiatric patients on the basis of what she learned after decades of using SASB in research and clinical practice.

Dr. Benjamin received her undergraduate degree from Oberlin College and her graduate degree from the University of Wisconsin. During her graduate studies, she got firsthand experience with the continuity between infrahuman primates and humans as a graduate student of Harry Harlow in his laboratory at the University of Wisconsin. Her specializations there also included learning theory, neurophysiology, and mathematical psychology. That was followed in the department of psychiatry at the University of Wisconsin, Madison, by internship, more clinical training, and then academic appointments that progressed from research associate to full professor.

A skiing addict, Dr. Benjamin moved to Utah in 1987, where she sponsored a dozen graduate students in the University of Utah department of psychology and concurrently held an appointment as adjunct professor in the department of psychiatry. Her assignment there was to consult for personality disordered cases at the University of Utah Neuropsychiatric Institute (UNI). Her psychopathology practicum at UNI eventually became the IRT clinic in 2002. Since then, she has collaborated extensively with Dr. Ken Critchfield, who joined her in the clinic first as a postdoctoral fellow, then as director of research, and later as director of the clinic until Dr. Benjamin retired in 2012. Dr. Critchfield moved to James Madison University, where, as associate professor, he continues to harvest information from the IRT database and teach clinical skills related to IRT. Dr. Benjamin resumed work at UNI on a part-time contract and presently is active offering consultations and in-house mini-workshops about psychotherapy, analyzing data, and writing. She also provides day-long or multiday workshops for professionals on IRT and SASB, usually emphasizing personality disorders.